lonely planet

Belize

Carolyn Miller Carlstroem

Debra Miller

LONELY PLANET PUBLICATIONS
Melbourne • Oakland • London • Paris

BELIZE

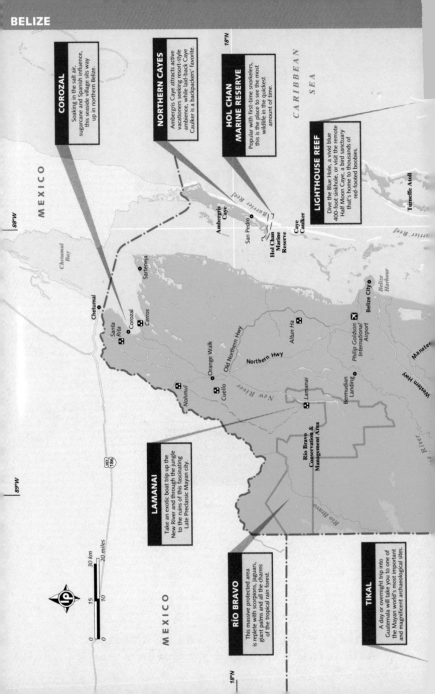

COROZAL
Soaking in the salt air, sugarcane and Spanish influence, this seaside village sits way up in northern Belize.

NORTHERN CAYES
Ambergris Caye attracts active vacationers seeking resort-style ambience, while laid-back Caye Caulker is a backpackers' favorite.

HOL CHAN MARINE RESERVE
Popular with first-time snorkelers, this is the place to see the most wildlife in the quickest amount of time.

LIGHTHOUSE REEF
Dive the Blue Hole, a vivid blue 400-foot sinkhole, or visit the remote Half Moon Caye, a bird sanctuary that's home to thousands of red-footed boobies.

LAMANAI
Take an exotic boat trip up the New River and through the jungle to the ruins of this fascinating Late Preclassic Mayan city.

RÍO BRAVO
This massive protected area is replete with scorpions, jaguars, giant palms and all the charms of the tropical rain forest.

TIKAL
A day or overnight trip into Guatemala will take you to one of the Mayan world's most important and magnificent archaeological sites.

MEXICO

CARIBBEAN SEA

Turneffe Atoll

Barrier Reef

Ambergris Caye

San Pedro

Caye Caulker

Hol Chan Marine Reserve

Chetumal Bay

Chetumal

Corozal

Sarteneja

Cerros

Santa Rita

Nohmul

Cuello

Orange Walk

Old Northern Hwy

Altun Ha

Northern Hwy

New River

Lamanai

Bermudian Landing

Philip Goldson International Airport

Belize City

Belize Harbour

Río Bravo Conservation & Management Area

Río Bravo

Western Hwy

Manatee

MEXICO

88°W

89°W

18°N

Mex 186

30 km
20 miles
15
10
0
0

N

Contents

INTRODUCTION   11

FACTS ABOUT BELIZE   13

History 13
Geography 16
Geology 17
Climate 17
Ecology & Environment . . 18
Flora 19

Fauna 20
National Parks
& Reserves 24
Government & Politics . . 26
Economy 27
Population & People 27

Education 28
Arts 28
Society & Conduct 29
Religion 29
Language 29

THE MAYAN WORLD   30

FACTS FOR THE VISITOR   34

Highlights 34
Planning 35
Responsible Tourism 37
Tourist Offices 37
Visas & Documents 37
Embassies & Consulates . . 38
Customs 39
Money 40
Post & Communications . . 41
Digital Resources 42
Books 43
Films 44
Newspapers & Magazines 45

Radio & TV 45
Photography 45
Time 45
Electricity 45
Weights & Measures 45
Laundry 45
Toilets 45
Health 45
Women Travelers 51
Gay & Lesbian Travelers . . 52
Disabled Travelers 52
Senior Travelers 52
Travel with Children 52

Dangers & Annoyances . . 53
Emergencies 53
Business Hours 53
Public Holidays
& Special Events 53
Activities 54
Work 54
Accommodations 55
Food 55
Drinks 57
Entertainment 57
Spectator Sports 57
Shopping 57

GETTING THERE & AWAY   59

Air 59
Land 63
Sea 63

GETTING AROUND   64

Air 64
Bus 64

Car 67
Hitchhiking 68

Boat 69
Organized Tours 69

BELIZE CITY   70

History 70
Orientation 71
Information 71
Walking Tours 74
Organized Tours 78

Swimming 79
Places to Stay 79
Places to Eat 82
Entertainment 84
Spectator Sports 84

Shopping 84
Getting There
& Away 85
Getting Around 86

AROUND BELIZE CITY   87

**Heading up the
Northern Highway** 87
Community
Baboon Sanctuary 87

Altun Ha 90
Crooked Tree 91
**Heading out the
Western Highway** 93

Belize Zoo 93
Monkey Bay
Wildlife Sanctuary 94

2   Contents

NORTHERN CAYES   96

Ambergris Caye   Caye Chapel 127   Lighthouse Reef Atoll . . . 128
& San Pedro 99   St George's Caye 127
Caye Caulker 116   Turneffe Atoll 127

NORTHERN BELIZE   130

Orange Walk 131   Río Bravo Conservation &   Corozal & Around 142
Lamanai 136   Management Area 139   Consejo Shores 147
                            Chan Chich Lodge 141   Sarteneja & Around . . . 147

CAYO DISTRICT (WESTERN BELIZE)   150

Belmopan 152   San Ignacio (Cayo) 157   Mountain Pine Ridge
Guanacaste   Around San   Area 171
National Park 155   Ignacio (Cayo) 162   Benque Viejo
West Toward San Ignacio 156   del Carmen 179

SOUTHERN BELIZE   181

Manatee Highway   Tobacco Caye,   Placencia 201
to Gales Point 182   South Water Caye   Punta Gorda 209
Gales Point 182   & Glover's Reef 192   Around Punta Gorda –
Along the   Hopkins Area 194   Out to Sea 213
Hummingbird Highway . . 184   Cockscomb Basin   Around Punta Gorda –
Dangriga 186   Wildlife Sanctuary 197   On Land 214

EXCURSION TO TIKAL (GUATEMALA)   219

Tikal 219   Flores & Santa Elena . . . 225   El Remate & Biotopo
Uaxactún 225   Cerro Cahuí 228

INDEX   234

BELIZE MAP INDEX

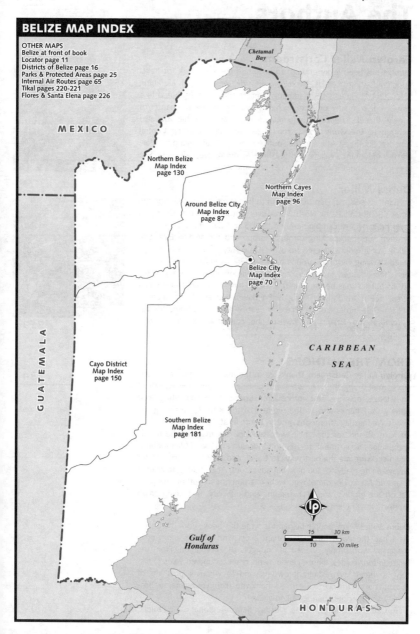

OTHER MAPS
Belize at front of book
Locator page 11
Districts of Belize page 16
Parks & Protected Areas page 25
Internal Air Routes page 65
Tikal pages 220-221
Flores & Santa Elena page 226

Chetumal Bay

MEXICO

Northern Belize
Map Index
page 130

Northern Cayes
Map Index
page 96

Around Belize City
Map Index
page 87

Belize City
Map Index
page 70

GUATEMALA

CARIBBEAN
SEA

Cayo District
Map Index
page 150

Southern Belize
Map Index
page 181

| 0 | 15 | 30 km |
| 0 | 10 | 20 miles |

*Gulf of
Honduras*

HONDURAS

The Authors

Carolyn Miller Carlstroem

Carolyn has been lucky enough to both and live and work for travel since graduating from UC Berkeley with a degree in English literature. She is Lonely Planet's US marketing director and has contributed to a number of company projects, including writing the Belize chapter of Lonely Planet's *Belize, Guatemala & Yucatán.* She has traveled throughout the world's best tropical destinations, including Central America, Southeast Asia and the South Pacific, but is also happy exploring the mountains, valleys and seashore of her native California. She lives in Oakland, California, with her husband Paul.

Debra Miller

Born in Nova Scotia, Deb (no relation to her coauthor) grew up on the other side of Canada, in North Vancouver, British Columbia. The travel fever hit early, first camping around the US and Canada with her family, then later backpacking through Europe and the Middle East. She finally got a writing degree from the University of Victoria and peppered studying with trips around North America and Mexico. After college she worked as a reporter, covering environmental issues for a variety of publications before joining Lonely Planet's Oakland office as a senior editor for Pisces Diving & Snorkeling guides. In addition to *Belize,* Deb wrote Lonely Planet's *Seattle* and coauthored *British Columbia* and *Pacific Northwest.* She currently lives in Atlanta, Georgia.

FROM THE AUTHORS

Carolyn Miller Carlstroem Thanks go to the many Belizeans and travelers I met along the way who were willing to share their wealth of knowledge, opinions and enthusiasm, especially Adelina Jeffries and Katie Valk. Thanks also to the women of the Kitty for teaching me about Wednesday afternoons, and to the folks at Tipple Tree Beya and Hamansi Resort for their help with the Hopkins map. In the travel-companions department, thanks go to Richard and Joan Miller for once again showing me the best ways to travel, and to Paul Carlstroem for always being ready for the next big adventure. At LP thanks to Mariah Bear and Maria Donohoe, who were instrumental in getting this project off the ground, and LP marketing and publicity for holding down the fort while I went out exploring.

Debra Miller Many people helped me write this book, from the travelers I had the good fortune to share beers with, to the anonymous passersby who simply handed me nuggets of information. From the Belizean tour guides, whose gentle manners tell a hundred years of history, to hotel and restaurant owners, and to whoever puts lots of coconut milk in the rice 'n' beans – I thank you all for your generous hospitality and gracious sharing of knowledge.

To Cameron Griffith, of the Western Belize Regional Cave Project, the best hitchhiker I ever picked up: Thanks for sharing your visions, both inside and outside of caves. To all the folks involved in BVAR and the Belize Department of Archaeology: Your work is so immediate and inspiring. Special thanks to Drs Jaime Awe and Allan Moore and Peter Zubrzycki for taking me to Caracol and welcoming me into the fold.

Thanks also to Emilio Awe and Rafael, for illuminating the wonders of Tunichil Muknal; to the Novelo brothers in Orange Walk for showing me the secrets of Lamanai; and to the invigorating folks – Ramone, Charlene and Guadalupe – at La Milpa field station at Río Bravo. You are amazing.

More gratitude to Golda Tillett at the Belize Tourism Board and Omar Ayuso at the Belize Tourism Industry Association. Thanks also to Bob Jones and Katie Valk for bestowing invaluable local information that's just impossible to find elsewhere. Thanks to Rosita Arvigo for the interview and update on her remarkable work.

My appreciation also goes to the folks at LP: Maria Donohoe (for asking in the first place); Rebecca Northen for her editing wizardry and for keeping it fun; and cartographers Sean Brandt and Buck Cantwell for creating excellent maps.

Thanks also to Rob for keeping home as adventurous and unique as any foreign country, and to my family for always enthusiastically supporting my wanderlust. Finally, a big bear hug and a cool Belikin toast to my co-author and soul sister Carolyn Miller Carlstroem – thanks for sharing Belize.

This Book

This is the first edition of *Belize*. Carolyn Miller Carlstroem served as the coordinating author, writing the introductory chapters, as well as Belize City, Northern Cayes and Southern Belize. Debra Miller wrote the Getting There & Away and Getting Around chapters, as well as Around Belize City, Northern Belize and the Cayo District (Western Belize). Carolyn Hubbard updated the Excursion to Tikal (Guatemala) chapter. Portions of this book were based on the 4th edition of *Belize, Guatemala & Yucatán*, which was written by Ben Greensfelder, Conner Gorry, Carolyn Miller Carlstroem and Sandra Bao.

FROM THE PUBLISHER

This guide was produced in Lonely Planet's Oakland office by a fun crew made up of the following people: Rebecca Northen edited the book, with Maria Donohoe providing expert guidance as senior editor. Kevin Anglin proofed the book and edited the Tikal chapter, which was proofed by Emily K Wolman. Suki Gear lent her eyes as a 'second senior,' and Ken DellaPenta indexed the book.

Buck Cantwell served as lead cartographer. He and Narrinder Bansal drew the maps, with senior cartographer Sean Brandt at the helm. Cartographic data specialist Molly Green helped Buck with research and gathering references, and cartographers Dion Good, Patrick Huerta, Brad Lodge, Carole Nuttall, Herman So, Patrick Phelan and Rudie Watzig helped edit the maps. All heeded the final word of US cartography manager Alex Guilbert.

Beca Lafore designed the color pages and laid out the book, with the help of senior designer Tracey Croom. Emily Douglas and Tracey designed the cover. Justin Marler created most of the illustrations, with others drawn by Hugh D'Andrade and Hayden Foell. US design manager Susan Rimerman oversaw all their efforts.

Special thanks to the authors for helping to make it such an enjoyable process.

ACKNOWLEDGMENTS

Grateful acknowledgment is made to the Belize Department of Archaeology for reproduction permission regarding the following maps: Altun Ha, Caracol and Xunantunich.

Foreword

ABOUT LONELY PLANET GUIDEBOOKS

The story begins with a classic travel adventure: Tony and Maureen Wheeler's 1972 journey across Europe and Asia to Australia. Useful information about the overland trail did not exist at that time, so Tony and Maureen published the first Lonely Planet guidebook to meet a growing need.

From a kitchen table, then from a tiny office in Melbourne (Australia), Lonely Planet has become the largest independent travel publisher in the world, an international company with offices in Melbourne, Oakland (USA), London (UK) and Paris (France).

Today Lonely Planet guidebooks cover the globe. There is an ever-growing list of books, and there's information in a variety of forms and media. Some things haven't changed. The main aim is still to help make it possible for adventurous travelers to get out there – to explore and better understand the world.

At Lonely Planet we believe travelers can make a positive contribution to the countries they visit – if they respect their host communities and spend their money wisely. Since 1986 a percentage of the income from each book has been donated to aid projects and human-rights campaigns.

Updates Lonely Planet thoroughly updates each guidebook as often as possible. This usually means there are around two years between editions, although for more unusual or more stable destinations the gap can be longer. Check the imprint page (usually following the color map at the beginning of the book) for publication dates.

Between editions up-to-date information is available in two free newsletters – the paper *Planet Talk* and email *Comet* (to subscribe, contact any Lonely Planet office) – and on our Web site www.lonelyplanet.com. The *Upgrades* section of the Web site covers a number of important and volatile destinations and is regularly updated by Lonely Planet authors. *Scoop* covers news and current affairs relevant to travelers. And, lastly, the *Thorn Tree* bulletin board and *Postcards* section of the site carry unverified, but fascinating, reports from travelers.

Correspondence The process of creating new editions begins with the letters, postcards and emails received from travelers. This correspondence often includes suggestions, criticisms and comments about the current editions. Interesting excerpts are immediately passed on via newsletters and the Web site, and everything goes to our authors to be verified when they're researching on the road. We're keen to get more feedback from organizations or individuals who represent communities visited by travelers.

Lonely Planet gathers information for everyone who's curious about the planet – and especially for those who explore it firsthand. Through guidebooks, phrasebooks, activity guides, maps, literature, newsletters, image library, TV series and Web site we act as an information exchange for a worldwide community of travelers.

Research Authors aim to gather sufficient practical information to enable travelers to make informed choices and to make the mechanics of a journey run smoothly. They also research historical and cultural background to help enrich the travel experience and allow travelers to understand and respond appropriately to cultural and environmental issues.

Authors don't stay in every hotel because that would mean spending a couple of months in each medium-size city and, no, they don't eat at every restaurant because that would mean stretching belts beyond capacity. They do visit hotels and restaurants to check standards and prices, but feedback based on readers' direct experiences can be very helpful.

Many of our authors work undercover; others aren't so secretive. None of them accept freebies in exchange for positive write-ups. And none of our guidebooks contain any advertising.

Production Authors submit their manuscripts and maps to offices in Australia, the USA, UK or France. Editors and cartographers – all experienced travelers themselves – then begin the process of assembling the pieces. When the book finally hits the shops, some things are already out of date, we start getting feedback from readers and the process begins again...

WARNING & REQUEST

Things change – prices go up, schedules change, good places go bad and bad places go bankrupt – nothing stays the same. So, if you find things better or worse, recently opened or long since closed, please tell us and help make the next edition even more accurate and useful. We genuinely value all the feedback we receive. A well-traveled team reads and acknowledges every letter, postcard and email and ensures that every morsel of information finds its way to the appropriate authors, editors and cartographers for verification.

Everyone who writes to us will find their name listed in the next edition of the appropriate guidebook. They will also receive the latest issue of *Planet Talk*, our quarterly printed newsletter, or *Comet*, our monthly email newsletter. Subscriptions to both newsletters are free. The very best contributions will be rewarded with a free guidebook.

We may edit, reproduce and incorporate your comments in all Lonely Planet products, such as guidebooks, Web sites and digital products, so let us know if you don't want your comments reproduced or your name acknowledged.

Send all correspondence to the Lonely Planet office closest to you:

Australia: Locked Bag 1, Footscray, Victoria 3011
USA: 150 Linden St, Oakland, CA 94607
UK: 10a Spring Place, London NW5 3BH
France: 1 rue du Dahomey, 75011 Paris

Or email us at: talk2us@lonelyplanet.com.au

For news, views and updates, see our Web site: www.lonelyplanet.com

HOW TO USE A LONELY PLANET GUIDEBOOK

The best way to use a Lonely Planet guidebook is any way you choose. At Lonely Planet, we believe the most memorable travel experiences are often those that are unexpected, and the finest discoveries are those you make yourself. Guidebooks are not intended to be used as if they provided a detailed set of infallible instructions!

Contents All Lonely Planet guidebooks follow roughly the same format. The Facts about the Destination chapters or sections give background information ranging from history to weather. Facts for the Visitor gives practical information on issues like visas and health. Getting There & Away gives a brief starting point for researching travel to and from the destination. Getting Around gives an overview of the transport options when you arrive.

The peculiar demands of each destination determine how subsequent chapters are broken up, but some things remain constant. We always start with background, then proceed to sights, places to stay, places to eat, entertainment, getting there and away, and getting around information – in that order.

Heading Hierarchy Lonely Planet headings are used in a strict hierarchical structure that can be visualized as a set of Russian dolls. Each heading (and its following text) is encompassed by any preceding heading that is higher on the hierarchical ladder.

Although inclusion in a guidebook usually implies a recommendation, we cannot list every good place. Exclusion does not necessarily imply criticism. In fact there are a number of reasons why we might exclude a place – sometimes it is simply inappropriate to encourage an influx of travelers.

Entry Points We do not assume guidebooks will be read from beginning to end, but that people will dip into them. The traditional entry points are the list of contents and the index. In addition, however, some books have a complete list of maps and an index map illustrating map coverage.

There may also be a color map that shows highlights. These highlights are dealt with in greater detail in the Facts for the Visitor chapter, along with planning questions and suggested itineraries. Each chapter covering a geographical region usually begins with a locator map and another list of highlights. Once you find something of interest in a list of highlights, turn to the index.

Maps Maps play a crucial role in Lonely Planet guidebooks and include a huge amount of information. A legend is printed on the back page. We seek to have complete consistency between maps and text and to have every important place in the text captured on a map. Map key numbers usually start in the top left corner.

Introduction

Belize embraces a beguiling mixture of Caribbean and Latin cultures, infused with a colonial history brought to its shores by early British settlers. The fact that English is the official language makes it all the easier for most travelers to get to know the country and absorb its cultures. The people are friendly, open and relaxed – everyone here seems to know how to have a good time – and though tourism is big business, travelers rarely feel commodified: Belizeans readily offer visitors help and advice, and they're committed to avoiding the pitfalls of mass-market tourism. The preservation of the country's many natural wonders is a high priority; some pioneers of the ecotravel movement started their work in Belize, and the local tourism industry boasts many earth-friendly innovations.

Both in population and landmass, Belize is a tiny country, and to this it owes much of its charms. The entire population numbers only about 256,000 (the size of a small city in Mexico, Europe or the USA), making it Central America's least populous country. Its 8866-sq-mile (23,300-sq-km) area – 174 miles (280km) long and 68 miles (109.5km) at its widest – makes it only slightly larger than Wales or Massachusetts. Yet despite its diminutive size, the country offers a variety of terrain and plenty of opportunity for adventure. You can go snorkeling and diving in the cayes (pronounced 'keys'); hiking and caving inland; bird- and wildlife-viewing in the country's robust network of unspoiled national parks and wildlife preserves; or exploring at any of several Mayan ruins,

which you're likely to have to yourself outside peak tourism hours.

Belize is a very young country. Formerly known as British Honduras, it gained independence in 1981 and has been through only five governmental administrations since this changeover. As a result of being settled and populated by various waves of migration since the 1500s, the country collectively possesses an open, accepting and tolerant attitude. It seems to be that everyone here knows or is somehow related to everyone else. With this comes a feeling that you're always looked after – that although you may never have met, it's reasonable to assume that you have some sort of connection. The respect and courtesy that comes from this dynamic is extended to travelers, even in the most visited parts of the country.

Many visitors opt for a 'surf and turf' vacation, dividing their time between the cayes in the Caribbean Sea and the mountainous region of western Belize. Travelers who wish to get off the beaten track – to get to know Belize and its people beyond the lodges and tours – need only travel a couple of hours from Belize City, heading north to, say, Corozal or south to Punta Gorda. The country is an independent traveler's dream – an efficient network of buses making frequent runs in all directions, as well as a web of internal air routes,

means that it's easy to get from point to point without much waiting around or advance planning.

While good values, comfortable lodges and wholesome cheap meals are available here, travelers will not be working on the same budget scale as they would be in neighboring Guatemala or Mexico. The Belize tourist industry has invested heavily in bringing travelers, mainly US travelers, to the country and in pointing out the value one gets for the price here. For the most part, they've been successful, and while prices are high compared to its neighbors, the rush of tourists to the country, and those who return again and again, indicate that it's worth paying Caribbean prices over Latin American ones. Budget travelers should not despair: There are bargains to be had and areas of Belize often figure prominently on the itineraries of backpackers – especially stops in San Ignacio (Cayo), Caye Caulker and Placencia.

Those looking for relaxation, adventure and wildlife in a small, easy-to-get-around package will be enamored by Belize, and indeed, many travelers return year after year. You'll get the best of both world's here – there's a well-trodden tourist trail and all the amenities that come with it, but step off the trail and you'll find that you're in a Central American country with unlimited opportunities for adventure.

Facts about Belize

HISTORY
The Maya

Belize's most important ancient culture is that of the Maya, a people whose descendants live on in the country today. The earliest evidence of the Maya can be found at the ruins of Cuello in the Orange Walk District, thought to be in existence from 1000 BC. The heyday of Mayan civilization, known as the Classic period, was from AD 250 to AD 900 – sometimes further broken down into Early Classic (AD 250 to AD 600) and Late Classic (AD 600 to AD 900). During the Classic period there were Mayan centers in Altun Ha, Lubaantun, El Pilar, Xunantunich and Caracol.

The Maya could be loosely grouped into three classes: the rulers, who inherited their positions; traders, who plied wares such as cocoa, cotton, honey and precious stones by land and sea; and farmers, the majority group, who grew corn, beans, rice and squash and kept turkey as game meat.

The Belize shoreline was a major trading center and widely inhabited by the Maya during the Classic period. Mayas dug the channel at Bacalar Chico (between present-day Ambergris Caye and Mexico) 1500 years ago. Creating this shortcut to the mainland, effectively opening up a lucrative trade route, was one of the first acts that separated Belize from Mexico's Yucatán Peninsula.

Overall, the Mayan culture mysteriously declined after AD 900. Most historians attribute the decline to food shortages, probably brought on by climate changes.

While the population certainly declined, there were still Mayan settlements existing when the Spanish first came to Belize in the 1600s. In Lamanai, for example, there are ruins of a Catholic church, evidence that there were plenty of Maya to convert. Many Maya accepted early conversion in Lamanai, but rejected it in the 1640s.

As the Spanish forayed into Belize, many Maya in the coastal regions retreated inland. They remained entrenched in the jungles of western Belize and often skirmished with Spanish and British settlers as the Europeans tried to gain more control of the region.

European Settlement

The region probably had its first contact with Europe in the early 1500s, when the Spanish began to inhabit the Central American region. The Spanish were interested in Belize for its large quantity of logwood – a wood valuable as a dye in Europe. But because of its fierce Maya and inhospitable terrain, Belize was never a priority for the Spaniards, who were more interested in the gold and silver that could be more easily taken from neighboring Honduras and Mexico.

The Baymen Shipments of such treasures piqued the interest of British pirates, known as Baymen because they spent most of their time in the Bay of Honduras. They found the convoluted coastline of Belize an ideal place to play hide-and-seek with Spanish transport ships.

The pirating business began to dry up around 1670 when Spain asked the British to crack down on their marauding citizens through the Treaty of Madrid. The Baymen looked west and realized that there was a fortune to be made inland by pulling valuable logwood from the forests. In 1673, through the Treaty of Paris, the Spanish allowed the Baymen to log in a prescribed portion of Belize, in hopes of containing them to a specific area, keeping the rest of Central America for Spain. Such logging became the primary economic base for the British in Belize, and remained so for nearly a century.

Slavery Logwood also brought slavery to Belize as the Baymen began to discover that mining logwood was much more labor-intensive than pirating. The first record of slaves in Belize (brought from Africa via the Caribbean) was in 1725, and by 1790 slaves made up 75% of Belize's registered population (the Maya weren't included in the census), while 10% were European and the rest were freed slaves or free settlers of mixed ancestry. The British abolished slavery throughout the British Empire in 1833, mainly because the industrial revolution created a need for a wage-earning labor force to purchase goods. In Belize, however, the former slaves were required to remain indentured to their former owners until 1838. Beyond this point former slaves were not allowed to own land, perpetuating a system in which freed slaves remained dependent on land owners. No compensation was offered to the former slaves, although former slave owners were compensated for their loss of 'property.'

British Colonization

Although Spain still considered Belize to be its territory, it gave the Baymen, and thereby the British, more and more control of the land by way of successive treaties throughout the 18th century.

As British economic interests in the Caribbean increased, so too did British involvement in Belize. In the 1780s the British actively protected the former pirates' logging interests, at the same time assuring Spain that Belize was indeed a Spanish possession. This was a fiction. By this time, Belize was already British by tradition and sympathy.

The Battle of St George's Caye, on September 10, 1798, was the last attempt by Spain to protect its interests in Belize. From that point on Belize was under British rule, although it didn't formally become a Crown colony until 1871.

The Baymen were an independent, unruly bunch and were slow to cooperate with either Spain or the British government. In the early days of the settlement, Britain didn't provide much governmental structure, and the Baymen brought it upon themselves to create a democratic system by which their settlement was run. Burnaby's Code was enacted in 1765 and continued to be the primary structure until 1840, when Britain put an executive council in place. The code was a practical one with 12 articles and regulations. Most involved rules against stealing servants and property, but within the code, systems for levying and collecting taxes, settling disputes and determining punishments (usually fines) were also established. The Baymen's first code demonstrated a move toward gentility that is somewhat unexpected for this time and place: 'Whoever shall be found guilty of profane cursing and swearing in disobedience of God's Commands [shall] forfeit and pay for every such Offence the sum of Two shillings and six pence….'

The Mahogany Trade

Logwood continued to be the primary economic force in Belize until the late 1700s. At that point, synthetic dyes and suppliers of logwood from other parts of the world lessened demand, and the economy took a

The Battle of St George's Caye

Belize celebrates September 10th as the day the British defended the country from Spain for the last time. One point that is universally agreed upon by historians is that the Baymen were able to defend their land because they had shallow draft boats that allowed them to successfully maneuver around the shallows of the reef, while the larger Spanish boats were limited in where they could attack. The myth of the Battle of St George's Caye is that slaves and free men fought side by side in the battle. This has caused much tension and derision in the country. Many believe the tale to be an apology for slavery, a claim that the slaves were content enough to fight beside their masters to defend 'their' territory. Today, while September 10th is still celebrated in Belize, as National Day, the battle itself is no longer publicly glorified.

tumble. The Baymen quickly turned their attention from one forest product to another as the demand for mahogany matched the region's ample supply. The mahogany industry flourished until the mid-1800s, but it collapsed as well when African sources of the wood brought fierce price competition.

War of the Castes

Though it happened north in the Yucatán Peninsula, the War of the Castes (1847–1901), between the Maya of the Yucatán Peninsula and the Spanish and Mestizos who controlled the area, was important in the development and settlement of Belize. For Belizeans, the war presented a trade boom in arms, ammunition and other supplies sold to the Maya rebels in the Yucatán.

More profoundly, the war also brought a flood of refugees to Belize, especially in the northern areas – what are now the Corozal and Orange Walk Districts – and in the northern cayes of Ambergris and Caulker. First came the Spanish and Mestizo lieutenants, driven out by the wrath of the Maya; then came the Maya themselves when the Spanish regained control of the Yucatán. The Mayan refugees brought new farming skills that were of great value in expanding the horizons and economic viability of Belizean society.

The 20th Century

The first half of the 20th century was a difficult time in Belize, and misrule by the British led to the country's agitation for independence. Belize sent troops to fight for the British in WWI, but because of their race, they were relegated to labor camps. This humiliation brought on rioting and unrest and contributed to the sentiment that Britain did not have the best interests of Belize's citizenry at heart. The economy worsened during the Great Depression and WWII, leading popular sentiment toward independence. This feeling was fueled in 1947 when India gained independence.

Independence Democratic institutions and political parties were established over the following years, and self-government eventually became a reality in 1962. Coincidentally and symbolically, in the early 1960s Belizeans switched to the Central American standard of driving on the right. This was brought about partially because Hurricane Hattie had wiped out the lefty cars that remained on the road. In 1973 the

The Guatemala Claim

The ownership dispute between Spain and Britain over Belize continues its legacy in the country even today.

When Guatemala gained independence from Spain in 1821, it claimed Belize as its own, since Spain still had unofficial sovereignty over the region. Britain dismissed the claim, since Guatemala had never occupied Belize, and since the Spanish hadn't challenged British control of the country since the Battle of St George's Caye. Britain negotiated a deal with Guatemala in 1863 whereby the larger inland country would be allowed access to the Caribbean Sea from Guatemala City via a road built at British expense. Because Guatemala was involved in a war with El Salvador at the time, the government never signed the agreement, and the British allowed the agreement to lapse.

To this day, Guatemala continues to hold on to its claim of Belize, usually asserting its belief during times of domestic strife as a distraction from interior problems. Until 1991 the Guatemalan constitution claimed Belize as its 23rd state. Various agreements and negotiations have been proposed throughout the years, but none have been to the satisfaction of either country. Recent negotiations have the governments on either side hoping for a resolution in 2002. The latest negotiations are favorable to Belize, offering Guatemala access to Belize's coastline, but not requiring that Belize surrender any land.

name of the country was officially changed from British Honduras to Belize. On September 21, 1981, Belize officially became an independent nation, but it remains a member of the British Commonwealth.

Belizean independence was not celebrated by neighboring Guatemala, which had long claimed Belize as part of its national territory (see the boxed text). The Guatemalans threatened war, but British troops stationed in Belize kept the territorial dispute to a diplomatic squabble. In 1992, a new Guatemalan government signed a treaty recognizing Belize's independence but not relinquishing claim to some 7500 sq miles of land. Intermittent border flare-ups continued. In July 2000, the two countries began formal talks to resolve the longstanding territorial dispute. So far, Belize refuses to let any land go, but has stated that it is willing to explore options for allowing Guatemala expanded access to the sea.

Culture of Colonization

Most Belizeans believe that British colonization has had its ups and downs. The up side includes a better system for social welfare including socialized medicine, mandatory education, a fairly clean record on human rights and a system that acknowledges laborers rights, at least for native Belizeans. Many Belizeans will admit that at least on these counts they are far better off than neighboring countries that were colonized by the Spanish. On the down side, Belizean activists feel they are fighting a system of institutionalized complacency – citizens feel powerless to affect change, even in their immediate communities.

Over the past 20 years Belizeans have been struggling to reintegrate their native culture. As with many colonized areas, diminished emphasis is placed on preexisting traditions, arts and culture. Instead, imported ideas and products are seen to be of more value than what is produced domestically. Foods coming from Britain and the US are considered delicacies, while in

Belize's art scene, local goods are not revered as they are in neighboring Mexico and Guatemala. Indeed many Belizeans have had to leave their country to make their fortunes, sending money home to support a family. Luckily these attitudes seem to be changing, especially as Belize welcomes the 21st century.

GEOGRAPHY

Belize is mainly tropical lowland. The country's Caribbean coastline and northern coastal plain are largely covered in mangrove swamp, which indistinctly defines the line between land and sea. Savannah surrounds the region around Belize City. The south is thick with low-elevation sub-tropical forest. There are higher elevations in western Belize and in the Maya Mountains of the south. Offshore, the limestone bedrock extends eastward into the Caribbean for several

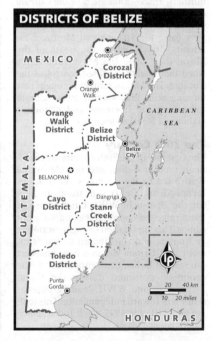

DISTRICTS OF BELIZE

kilometers at a depth of about 15 feet (4.5m). At the eastern extent of this shelf is the longest barrier reef in the Western Hemisphere, second longest in the world (behind Australia's).

North of Belize is Mexico's Yucatán Peninsula and the state of Quintana Roo. The border is defined by the Hondo River. Belize shares both its southern and western borders with Guatemala, defined by the Sarstoon River in the south and an arbitrary line in the west.

GEOLOGY

Belize's 180-mile-long barrier reef, the longest in the Western Hemisphere, is the eastern edge of the limestone shelf that underlies most of Belize and Mexico's Yucatán Peninsula. To the west of the barrier reef the sea is very shallow – usually not much more than 15 feet (4.5m) deep – allowing the numerous islands called cayes (pronounced 'keys') to bask in warm waters.

Inland the soil is a combination of limestone, dolomite and clay. The differences in soil can be seen through the changes of color along the dirt roads that network through the country.

Victoria Peak, in Cockscomb Basin Wildlife Sanctuary, and Doyle's Delight, in Toledo near Belize's southern border, vie for highest peak status – both are around 3680 feet (1104m). Doyle's Delight is said to be about 13 feet (3.9m) taller than Victoria Peak, but Victoria Peak is more visible, and the popular favorite for tallest mountain status.

CLIMATE

Belize is typically hot and humid day and night for most of the year. Rainfall is lightest in the north, heaviest in the south. The southern rain forests receive over 160 inches (4m) of rainfall annually, helping to make the south the country's most humid region.

An exception to Belize's low-lying topography and hot, sticky climate can be found in the Maya Mountains, which traverse western and southern Belize at elevations

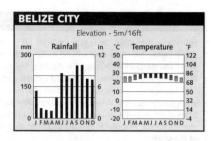

approaching 3300 feet (around 1000m). The mountains enjoy a more pleasant climate than the lowlands – comfortably warm during the day, cooling off a bit at night. But even here the forests are lush, well watered and humid year-round.

Hurricanes

While hurricane season officially lasts from June to November, Belize has traditionally been struck by its most damaging hurricanes in September and November. Spookily, the most extreme hurricanes happened in years ending with '1': the Hurricane of 1931 (before they were named), Hurricane Hattie in 1961, and, most recently, Hurricane Iris in 2001.

Hurricane Iris struck southern Belize in October 2001, bringing profound damage to Placencia, Monkey River and the Mayan villages around Toledo, with winds in excess of 150mph (242km/h). Luckily there was plenty of warning, and with the tragic exception of unfortunates on a live-aboard boat that wasn't evacuated, there was very little loss of life.

Damage to heavily touristed areas tends to get priority. In fact, after Hurricane Keith hit the northern cayes in late October 2000, the islands were open for tourism again by November.

If you are in Belize when a hurricane threatens, the best advice is to head inland. If this isn't possible, you should shelter in the sturdiest concrete building you can find, as far as possible from the coast and away from windows. Hurricanes usually take a while to reach the Central American shore and are well-reported as they make their way across

High-Velocity Winds

Hurricanes that strike the region originate off the coast of Africa, forming as winds rush toward a low-pressure area and swirl around it due to the rotational forces of the Earth's spin. The storms move counterclockwise across the Atlantic, fed by warm winds and moisture, building up force in their 1900-mile (3000km) run toward Central and North America.

A hurricane builds in stages, the first of which is called a tropical disturbance. The next stage is a tropical depression. When winds exceed 39mph (63km/h), the weather system is upgraded to a tropical storm and is usually accompanied by heavy rains. The system is called a hurricane if wind speed exceeds 74mph (119km/h) and intensifies around a low-pressure center, the so-called eye of the storm.

Hurricane systems can range from 50 miles (80km) in diameter to devastating giants hundreds of miles across. Their energy is prodigious – far more than the mightiest thermonuclear explosions ever unleashed on earth. The area affected by winds of great destructive force may exceed 150 miles (240km) in diameter.

The strength of a hurricane is rated from one to five. The mildest, a category 1 hurricane, has winds of at least 74mph (119km/h). The strongest and rarest hurricane, the category 5 monster, packs winds that exceed 155mph (249km/h): Hurricane Mitch, which killed more than 10,000 people in Central America and southeastern Mexico in late 1998, was a rare category 5 hurricane. Hurricanes travel at varying speeds, from as little as 6mph (9.5km/h) to more than 30mph (48km/h).

For current tropical-storm information, go to the *Miami Herald* Web site, w www.herald .com, and scan the menu for hurricane and storm information. Another excellent source is the Web site maintained by the US National Oceanic and Atmospheric Administration, w www.esdim.noaa.gov/weather_page.html.

the Caribbean – it's likely that there will be plenty of time to seek shelter should you have the misfortune of being involved in one.

ECOLOGY & ENVIRONMENT

While the Baymen weren't by any stretch of the imagination conservationists, their methods of selectively pulling logwood and mahogany from forests meant that clear-cutting practices never caught on in the country, and vegetation that was less of a commodity was allowed to survive. Because they relied on waterways to transport their logs, a road system never cleared the way for further settlement of the 'bush,' as the forest jungle is known, protecting the land. Of course the land does have its threats

today, but Belize's challenge is to protect and sustain its existing resources, rather than repair damage.

Today nearly 40% of the country is protected, either by national organizations or private trusts. In Cockscomb Basin Wildlife Sanctuary, Belize has one of the only jaguar reserves in the world. Ecotourism was practically born here, and in the jungle lodges throughout the region you'll meet some of the pioneers of the sustainable tourism movement.

Of the few pressing challenges facing Belize at the moment, one is the Challilo Dam project, proposed for the Macal River. It's widely supported by the government of Belize, and widely despised by environmentalists. Its supporters claim that hydro-electric power is the future for the country's energy needs. Its detractors believe that valuable land and animals, including the scarlet macaw, will be endangered by the project, which is being funded by Fortis, a Canadian power company. At press time the dispute was still going.

A second challenge is that Belize's treasured Mountain Pine Ridge area has lately been decimated by the southern pine beetle, which has destroyed 90% of the pine forest. Plans are in place to replant the pines that have been destroyed, but it is projected that this will take at least 25 years (see the Cayo District (Western Belize) chapter for more information).

Another challenge is lethal yellowing, a fatal disease of coconut palms that has destroyed millions of trees in the Caribbean region over the past 40 years. It reached Belize from the Yucatán in 1992 and rapidly spread down the coast. Only some of the more remote cayes have remained unaffected by the infestation. The disease, caused by an organism called phytoplasma, is spread by insects known as plant-hoppers. Coconut palms die within three to six months of infection. There is no cure for the disease, but healthy trees can be injected with a vaccine every three to four months to keep the bacteria at bay. Unfortunately, the vaccine is prohibitively expensive, so treatment isn't possible in all parts of the country. Another solution is the planting of resistant varieties of coconut, namely Mayalan Dwarfs, which take 40 years to reach maturity, and the Mapan Hybrid, faster growing but not always true breeding.

FLORA

With its hot, moist climate and variety of topsoil, Belize presents an abundance of plant life: over 700 tree species, 250 species of orchid and 4000 species of flowering plants. To the non-botanical eye, the forests of Belize can be roughly broken down into three designations: coastal forest; tropical broadleaf forest (often referred to as rain forest, although technically only the southern-most part of Belize receives enough rain to

World Heritage Sites

In 1996 UNESCO designated and protected Belize's barrier reef as a World Heritage Site. The following seven sites were recognized for demonstrating unique reef development and ecology, providing spectacular scenery and providing habitat for threatened species, including marine turtles, the Western manatee and the American crocodile.

• Bacalar Chico National Park
  and Marine Reserve
• Blue Hole
• Half Moon Caye
• Glover's Reef
• South Water Caye
• Laughing Bird Caye
• Sapadillo Cayes

be officially called rain forest); and pine forest. These differences are caused by amount of rainfall and type of soil in each area. Growing amid these distinctions are numerous varieties of palm, fruit and nut trees.

Coastal Forest

Within coastal forest you'll find coconut, sea grape, provision tree, buttonwood and Norfolk Island pine.

Mangrove stands are most common in coastal Belize and defined as forest growing in or around saltwater. There are four common species: red mangrove, buttonwood, white mangrove and black mangrove. Mangroves are credited with creating the cayes: When coral grows close enough to the surface of the sea, mangrove spores carried by the wind take root on the coral. As they continue to spread and grow, their debris creates solid ground cover, inviting other plants to take root and eventually attracting animal life.

Tropical Broadleaf Forest

One of the fascinating elements of a visit to Belize's tropical forests (also called jungle, bush or rain forest) is the natural layering

Mangroves are common coastal vegetation.

that occurs. Most tropical forests have ground cover (a ground or herb layer); a canopy layer formed from the crowns of the forest's tallest trees; and, in between, shorter sub-canopy or understory trees. Those trees that shoot high above the canopy are known as emergent trees. Growing throughout the layers are hanging vines and epiphytes, or air plants, such as orchids, moss and ferns, which live on other trees but aren't parasites. Among the species living in this realm are cohune palm, ceiba, yemeri, rosewood, strangler fig, gumbo limbo (give-and-take tree) and mahogany. Buttressed roots are a common phenomenon here.

Pine Forest
In the drier lowland areas surrounding Belize City and the sandy areas of the north grow Honduran and Caribbean pine, along with savannah grasses, giant stands of bamboo, some oak and calabash.

The tropical pine forest of western Belize's Mountain Pine Ridge is a fascinating phenomenon. Here, the vegetation of the forest changes abruptly from jungle to pine forest, brought on by differences in soil. Mountain pine grows in this higher elevation, related to the Caribbean pines of the lowland. In this instance 'ridge' does not refer to a topographical feature, rather it is used to identify a type of forest,

signified by its predominant tree. For greater detail on the Mountain Pine Ridge, see the Cayo District (Western Belize) chapter.

FAUNA
Land Animals
Wildcats Prevalent in Belize's forests, jaguars are stealthy creatures that you probably won't see outside of the zoo, although if you're near their habitats you'll see tracks and the remains of their meals. Jaguars were highly endangered – due to game hunting and deforestation – up until the 1980s, when they became protected. While efforts to revive their population have been successful at Cockscomb, the healthiest jaguar population lives in the forests around Río Bravo. They're coming back in such numbers that there have been some whispers lately about allowing them to be hunted again. The spotted and ringed jaguar can grow to over 6 feet (2m) and weigh up to 250lbs (120kg).

Smaller wildcats – ocelot, puma, mountain lion, jaguarundi and margay – are also present in the Belize bush. The spaniel-sized ocelot and the house-cat-sized margay most closely resemble the jaguar. The puma (just smaller than a jaguar) and its midsized cousin the jaguarundi are tan or grayish cats.

Monkeys The black howler monkey is usually an elusive primate, but they're easy to see in Belize. Loud, healthy and stinky troupes live in the treetops at the Community Baboon Sanctuary in Bermudian Landing, the Lamanai ruins, at Cockscomb Basin Wildlife Sanctuary and other forests throughout the country. Their distinctive roars issued late in the afternoon and in the predawn hours seem to echo for miles and can be quite frightening for newcomers. Sometimes howler monkeys will 'greet' visitors by flinging fruit, or, less charmingly, relieving themselves upon the crowd below.

More rare are spider monkeys, which inhabit remote forested areas. You're most likely to see one of these expert tree-swingers kept as a pet. They look something like a smaller, long-tailed version of the gibbon, an ape native to southwest Asia.

Other Mammals Resembling a large guinea pig and weighing up to 22lbs (10kg), the nocturnal paca often live in pairs. Agoutis have similar habits, but more resemble rabbits, with strong back legs that give them speed. They're about half the size of pacas. Both small rodents figure prominently in the diet of the smaller wildcats, and they make frequent appearances on human dinner plates as well.

Tyras, skunks and neotropical otters are small carnivores, in the same family as the mink or weasel. Neotropical otters have four legs that carry them wobbly around coastland where they burrow; however, they do their best work in the water and enjoy fish and shellfish. Tyras and skunks hunt on the ground, foraging for eggs, small rodents and insects.

The coati or quash (sometimes called coatimundi) is a raccoon-like creature, with rusty brown fur and striped tail. They tend to travel in packs and are likely to be seen during daylight hours on the sides of roads or trails. They're very cute, but can cause problems for pets and other small creatures, the same as raccoons. Also in the raccoon family is the nocturnal kinkajou. They live mostly in trees and can be seen on nighttime walks with a flashlight.

Short of leg and tail, stout of build, small of eye, ear and intelligence, the Baird's tapir eats plants, bathes daily and runs like mad when approached. Although it's the official animal of Belize, it's shy and seldom seen in the forest.

You are likely to see a peccary, a sort of wild pig that can weigh 65lbs (30kg) or more, that tends of travel in groups. There are two types, and the names – white-lipped peccary and collared peccary – define their differing characteristics. Like domesticated pigs they're quite smelly. Collared peccaries live in forests throughout Belize, the white-lipped only in the rain forests in the south.

Anteaters and armadillos are also present in the jungle, as well as white-tailed and red brocket deer and a variety of squirrel.

If you spend any time in ruins or caves, you're going to encounter some bats, usually the greater white bats, fruit bats or hairy legged bats. They're harmless to humans, although they can be startling when they fly toward you, using their sonar to turn away in the knick of time.

Insects & Spiders
Belize has plenty of insects and spiders to spy, but fear not, their bites and stings are mostly more of a nuisance than a danger. Fun ones to be on the lookout for include the following: Termites have large nests that are sometimes used by locals for fish bait and to patch holes in boats. Tarantulas (large black wooly spiders that can grow up to 6 inches/15cm) will bite if provoked, but their venom isn't fatal. You'll see leaf cutter ants walking in a line through the forest carrying bits of leaf many times their size over their heads. The scorpion, commonly spotted in the bush, is a nocturnal creature with a tail that can deliver a painful sting – if you're staying in the jungle always shake out your shoes and inspect your clothes before dressing.

The country has an array of butterflies, from the famous blue morpho to the monarch to the malachite. There are a number of butterfly farms in Belize, which are interesting in themselves and a good place to learn about butterflies before identifying them in the wild. Such sanctuaries covered in this guide include Fallen Stones Butterfly Ranch (see the Around Punta Gorda section in the Southern Belize chapter); the Cayo District's Tropical Wings Nature Center, Green Hills Butterfly House and the butterfly farm at Chaa Creek Resort & Spa; and Shipstern Nature Reserve in northern Belize.

Reptiles
Snakes There are up to 60 species of snake living in the forests and waters of Belize and of these only a handful are dangerous. Most harmless snakes are known as colubrids, garden-variety snakes, if you will, with rows of teeth lining their jaws (not that you'll get that close), in contrast to poisonous snakes

or vipers, which have fangs. Colubrids of Belize include the mussurana, blunt-headed tree snake and indigo snake.

It's highly unlikely that you'll run into any dangerous snakes while you're in the country unless they're dead and in a jar, but present here are the wildly poisonous fer-de-lance (commonly known as the tommygoff), earth toned and a particular threat to farmers when they're clearing areas of vegetation; the coral snake, banded with bright red, yellow and black stripes; the tropical rattlesnake; and the boa constrictor, which kills by constriction but can also give you a mean (but venomless) bite.

Iguanas The iguana is a harmless lizard of fearsome appearance. There are three commonly viewed Belizean iguanas: the green iguana, which can grow to 6 feet (2m) and is often spotted in trees along riverbanks; the smaller – 3 feet (1m) – and grayer spiny-tailed iguana, which enjoys climbing trees, but is also happy crawling under rocks and burrowing in dirt; and the similar-sized basilisk, found on shorelines and often called the Jesus lizard for its seeming ability to walk upright on water (they're actually skipping). Iguanas love to bask in the sun on the warm rocks or in the tops of trees. They're considered a delicacy in southern Belize and often referred to as 'bamboo chicken.'

Crocodiles Belize is home to two types of crocodiles: the American crocodile, which can live in both saltwater and freshwater, and the smaller Morelet's croc, which lives only in freshwater. Both are on the endangered species list. The American crocodile usually grows to 13 feet (4m), and the Morelet's to 8 feet (2.4m). They have similar coloring and can be difficult to tell apart if you should see them together in a river or freshwater lagoon – the Morelet's has a wider snout. They're best spied at night, when shining a flashlight causes their eyes to glow red. In daylight, be on the lookout for fast-moving logs – sometimes they're crocs. These crocs don't have the ferocious reputation of their Australian cousins. Belizean crocs tend to stick to prey that's smaller than the average adult human. Still, it's best to keep your distance.

Sea Creatures

Hawksbill, loggerhead, leatherback and green sea turtles can be spotted in the waters of Belize. These turtles live full-time at sea; the females come ashore only to lay

Spotting Wildlife

Nature viewing with a guide can be thrilling, but it's even more exciting when you start to develop the skills to spot animals on your own. There are a couple of tricks that will aid you on your way to seeing creatures.

Most animals are effectively camouflaged, so they're not going to stand out against their natural background. The best way to find them is to look for unusual movement in trees, on the ground or on the surface of water. Whether you're using binoculars or not, a good trick is to scan the horizon rather than peer at one spot. Birds and other animals will ignore you if you stay fairly still and don't make too much noise: Move slowly, make no sudden movements and keep your voice low.

Listen carefully; noises in the forest can be very telling. Keep your binoculars around your neck; they're useful only if you can get to them quickly and with little movement. Your best chance at spotting shy animals is early in the morning when the creatures are having their early meal. Don't overlook the little things like bugs, small reptiles or small birds and crabs; they can be some of the most interesting and accessible wildlife on any excursion. Also, bring someone else along: Pointing out your finds to another is almost as satisfying as spotting them yourself.

their eggs. While all sea turtles are endangered, the hawksbill, which was hunted for its shell, is the only one currently protected in Belize. (See the Gales Point section, in the Southern Belize chapter, for details on turtle conservation.) Coastal development has also taken a huge toll on the turtle population by destroying the beaches where they lay their eggs, although most of the casualties come as the result of poaching and of egg-hunting – sea turtle eggs are believed by the uninformed to be an aphrodisiac. You may see turtle or turtle eggs on a menu, and there's a chance they may have been taken legally, but they're best avoided.

The West Indian manatee can be seen at the mouths of rivers, in coastal lagoons and around the cayes. They're the only non-meat-eating sea mammal in existence, and are said to have more in common with elephants than whales, seals or dolphins. Also known as the sea cow, these gentle, slow-moving creatures are threatened by increased boat traffic (you'll see some with scars from propellers) and erosion that threatens their sea grass feeding areas. They can grow to 11 feet (3.5m) and can weigh over a ton (2000lbs or 900kg). See the Northern Cayes chapter for the boxed text about manatee conservation.

The two most commonly sighted species of dolphin are the Atlantic spotted dolphin and the bottle-nosed dolphin. They look similar – sleek, tubular, tapering at the snout and tail. The former is gray and usually from 4 to 10 feet long (1.2m to 3m). The latter is gray to dark blue, 6 to 12 feet (1.9m to 3.6m) long, and has a rounded forehead. Your chances of spotting them offshore in Belize are good; sometimes you can see them from the shore, and they love to run with the bows of ships.

Whale sharks can be seen off the coast of Belize between March and June, most commonly during the week after the full moon, when these filter-feeding behemoths come in close to the reef to dine on spawn. These fish are the world's largest breed of shark (yes, they're sharks not whales), growing to a whopping 46 feet (14m) and weighing up to 15 tons, although the average size is 25 feet (7.6m). They can live up to 150 years (in

people years!). They're gray with random light-yellow spots and stripes and are quite harmless to humans.

Other sharks – nurse, reef, lemontip and hammerhead – and a variety of rays often make appearances. They tend to leave divers and snorkelers alone. (See the Northern Cayes chapter for more information on sharks and rays.)

Sharing the coral with the larger animals is a myriad of reef fish from larger barracuda and groupers to parrotfish, angelfish and clown fish (they're the ones who like to nestle into the anemones). If you stay still in large patches of coral, you'll be able to hear the fish crunching. Sea horses can sometimes be seen in grassy shallow areas.

Look also for spiny lobster (also called langouste), which don't have claws like their cousins in the north, giant conch shells, stone crabs and box fish. Most dive and snorkel boats have laminated fish-identifier cards on board; they're helpful to study before you look in the sea.

There are over 40 species of coral on view in these waters, from hard elkhorn and staghorn coral (named because they branch like antlers) to gorgonian fans and other soft formations that sway with the current.

Birds

As you might imagine, birds are numerous and varied throughout the region. In fact, bird-watching in itself is enough reason to plan an extended stay here. In addition to the species listed below, you'll have the potential of seeing hummingbirds, kingfishers, motmots, parrots, woodpeckers, tinamous, tanagers and trogans.

The best time for bird-watching is early morning. March and early April reveal the best variety: Trees are losing their leaves, water is getting scarce, forcing the birds out of their hiding-places, and migrating birds are heading north for the summer. Following are some of the most commonly sited or commonly sought-after birds.

Seabirds Magnificent frigate birds are constantly soaring over the sea and coastline on pointed prehistoric-looking wings that can span up to 6 feet (2m). They have difficulties taking off from the ground, so their method of hunting is to swoop down and catch fish as they jump from the sea. They often hang out around fisherfolk and other birds so that they can swoop in on discarded or dropped catch. Males have red throats that are displayed during courtship.

Notable is the colony of red-footed boobies living out at Half Moon Caye, sharing a habitat with the magnificent frigate birds. They're plunging birds, diving from great heights deep into the sea to catch fish. The frigate birds often try to snatch their catch away as they resurface.

Brown pelicans, gulls and terns are also in evidence along the seashore.

Vultures & Raptors Inland along the sides of the road and flying overhead you'll see large turkey, black and king vultures. Their job is to feast on dead animals. The turkey vultures have a red head; king vultures have a black-and-white color scheme with a red beak; and the black vulture appears in black and shades of gray.

Raptors, or birds of prey, usually hunt rodents and small birds. Commonly seen in Belize are the osprey (look for their huge nests atop houses and telephone posts), the peregrine falcon, roadside hawk and the American kestrel. Most raptors are territorial and solitary, making it all the more spooky when you see one watching you from a road sign or an overhead wire.

Herons & Egrets Herons and egrets can be found in marshes and along rivers and lake and ocean shorelines. They search for prey – water bugs, grubs and small fish – by swishing their feet around in the water, then spearing with their beaks whatever gets stirred up. Egrets are usually white, herons are brown. White cattle egrets can be found in pastures, usually one to a cow or horse.

Other Well-Known Species Recently hunted for food in Belize and a hot item on the pet black market, the scarlet macaw, a member of the parrot family, is highly endangered. It is believed that there are less

than 200 left in the country. They're on view only a few months of the year in the village of Red Bank or deep in the Cockscomb Basin Wildlife Sanctuary. Your best chance of seeing this rare and splendid bird is mid-January through March.

The jabiru stork is the largest flying bird in the Americas, standing up to 5 feet (1.5m) tall, with a wingspan of 10 to 12 feet (3m to 3.6m). Jabirus can commonly be seen in the Crooked Tree Wildlife Sanctuary. Like herons and egrets they feed by wading in shallows, enjoying fish and reptiles.

The keel-billed toucan is the national bird of Belize. Its best-known feature is its huge bill, which is very light because it is almost hollow. The purpose of these over-sized beaks is unknown. Toucans like to stay at treetop level and nest in holes in trees.

The Montezuma oropendola weaves a sack-like nest, sometimes nearly a yard in length. Colonies can be seen hanging from the branches of tall trees in lowland areas. The bird has a chestnut-colored body, black head and neck and golden yellow outer tail feathers. Their calls are varied, loud and at times mechanical sounding.

The 'pheasant' of Mayan lore is actually the ocellated turkey, a beautiful bird that looks something like a peacock.

Endangered Species

Belize is a conservation-conscious country and much is done to protect the endangered species that live within its borders. Among Belize's endangered or threatened species are the hawksbill, green and leatherback sea turtles, the Morelet's and American crocodiles, the scarlet macaw, the jabiru stork and the manatee. Deforestation and hunting are primary causes of endangerment in the country, although the manatees are threatened by increased boat traffic in the cayes.

NATIONAL PARKS & RESERVES

The country's first national park was established in 1981, and at this point over 40% of Belize is protected in some way or another. The largest national park is Chiquibul, encompassing the Mountain Pine Ridge area.

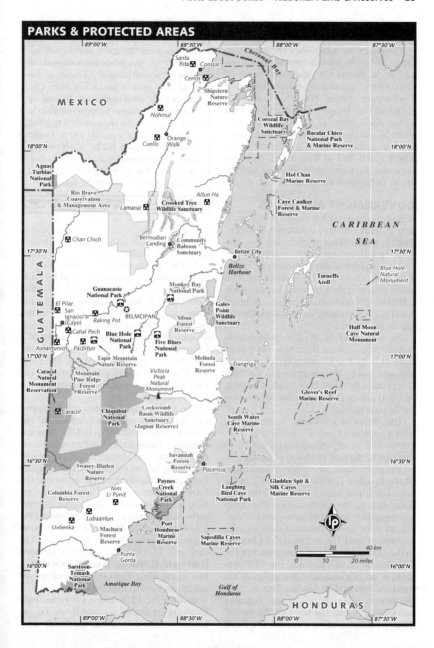

PARKS & PROTECTED AREAS

MEXICO

Santa Rita
Corozal
Cerros
Shipstern Nature Reserve
Nohmul
Cuello
Orange Walk
Corozal Bay Wildlife Sanctuary
Bacalar Chico National Park & Marine Reserve

Aguas Turbias National Park
Rio Bravo Conservation & Management Area
Lamanai
Altun Ha
Crooked Tree Wildlife Sanctuary
Hol Chan Marine Reserve
Caye Caulker Forest & Marine Reserve

Chan Chich
Bermudian Landing
Community Baboon Sanctuary
Belize City
Belize Harbour

CARIBBEAN SEA

Blue Hole Natural Monument

Monkey Bay National Park
Guanacaste National Park
El Pilar
San Ignacio (Cayo)
Baking Pot
BELMOPAN
Cahal Pech
Blue Hole National Park
Xunantunich
Pacbitun
Five Blues National Park
Sibun Forest Reserve
Gales Point Wildlife Sanctuary
Turneffe Atoll
Half Moon Caye Natural Monument

Tapir Mountain Nature Reserve
Melinda Forest Reserve
Dangriga

GUATEMALA

Caracol Natural Monument Reservation
Mountain Pine Ridge Forest Reserve
Victoria Peak Natural Monument
Caracol
Chiquibul National Park
Cockscomb Basin Wildlife Sanctuary (Jaguar Reserve)
Glover's Reef Marine Reserve
South Water Caye Marine Reserve

Swasey-Bladen Nature Reserve
Savannah Forest Reserve
Placencia
Columbia Forest Reserve
Nim Li Punit
Paynes Creek National Park
Laughing Bird Caye National Park
Gladden Spit & Silk Cayes Marine Reserve
Lubaantun
Uxbenka
Machaca Forest Reserve
Port Honduras Marine Reserve
Sapodilla Cayes Marine Reserve
Punta Gorda

Sarstoon-Temash National Park
Amatique Bay
Gulf of Honduras
HONDURAS

0   20   40 km
0   10   20 miles

The largest protected area is Río Bravo, a private reserve in northern Belize.

The Belize Audubon Society (☎ 2-35004, fax 2-34985, w www.belizeaudubon.org), 12 Fort St, Belize City, maintains many of the country's parks and reserves, including Cockscomb Basin Wildlife Sanctuary, Crooked Tree Wildlife Sanctuary and Half Moon Caye Natural Monument. Lately there has been a movement toward community management of protected areas, which you'll find at Five Blues National Park and the Community Baboon Sanctuary at Bermudian Landing.

GOVERNMENT & POLITICS

British colonial rule left Belize with a tradition of representative democracy that continued after independence. Luckily, the country did not succumb to the general pattern of political development in Central America, where bullets often have had more influence than ballots. Despite its establishment by pirates, Belize has a political scene that's surprisingly nonviolent, though hardly incorrupt.

As a member of the Commonwealth, Belize recognizes the British monarch as its head of state. The Crown is represented on Belizean soil by the governor-general, who is appointed by the monarch with the advice of the Belizean prime minister. This role is largely ceremonial.

The Belizean legislature is bicameral, with a popularly elected house of representatives and an appointed senate similar in function to the British House of Lords.

The prime minister, currently Said Musa of the People's United Party (PUP), is the actual political head of Belize. The PUP was born in the 1950s during the early movement for independence. George Price, the nation's first prime minister, was the founder of the PUP and one of the leaders in the charge toward independence. For the first decade of its existence, the PUP was seen as anti-British, and the colonial authorities harassed its leaders. But by 1961 the British government saw that Belizean independence was the wave of the future. Price went from being considered a thorn

Wallix, Ballix

Scotsman Peter Wallace is credited with establishing the first British land-settlement in Belize in the mid-1600s at the mouth of the Belize River, north of what is now Belize City. Wallace is also often credited with the naming of Belize. Some believe the name was given to the area because the waters around that first settlement were very muddy and in Mayan language the word *belixe* means muddy water. Others believe that the name developed from a corruption of the name Wallace to Wallix, Ballix and, eventually, Belize.

in the British side to being the prospective leader of a fledgling nation.

In 1964 Belize got a new constitution for self-government, and the PUP, led by Price, won the elections of 1965, 1969, 1974 and 1979. The PUP was the leading force for full independence, achieved in 1981. Despite this success, the party did not fulfill Belizeans' dreams of a more prosperous economy, a failure due in part to world market conditions beyond the party's control. The party was also seen as having been in power too long and was widely accused of complacency and corruption.

The PUP's main opposition, a conservative, multiparty coalition later named the United Democratic Party (UDP), won the elections of 1984 under the slogan 'It's time for a change,' and Manuel Esquivel replaced George Price as prime minister. Priding itself on its handling of the economy, the UDP gained more ground in municipal elections held at the end of the decade. But the early national election of September 1989 held a surprise: The PUP took 15 seats in the house of representatives while the UDP took only 13. The venerable Price changed places with Esquivel, taking the prime minister's seat while Esquivel resumed his old seat at the head of the opposition.

In 1993 the PUP called early elections, secure in its popularity and intent on extending its mandate for an additional three years. To most Belizeans, a PUP victory was a foregone conclusion. Many of the PUP adherents didn't bother to vote, but UDP supporters did, and the UDP squeaked to victory by the slimmest of margins – a single vote in some districts. Esquivel became prime minister again, while PUP supporters looked on in disbelief.

In 1996 Price announced his retirement as head of the PUP, opening the way to a noisy power struggle among his lieutenants. Said Musa won the struggle and in the 1998 election led the PUP to victory and unseated Esquivel. Currently the PUP has control of the central and local governments.

General elections are held at intervals of not longer than five years, so there will be another election by August 2003.

Dean Barrow, who was Esquivel's right-hand man for many years, is now the leader of the opposition UDP party, and would likely become prime minister if the PUP is defeated.

ECONOMY

Though the logwood and mahogany trades brought some small measure of prosperity in the late 18th and early 19th centuries, Belize has never been a rich country. Its economic history in the past hundred years has been one of getting by, benefiting from economic aid granted by the UK and the USA, from money sent home by Belizeans living and working abroad and from the foreign currency generated by its small agricultural sector. The banana industry is the largest employer in the country. The US is Belize's primary trading partner, and in addition to sugar, citrus (mainly for fruit juices) and bananas, fish (mainly lobster) and timber are also key export items. Dairy farming, especially among the Mennonite population, is growing in importance as is the livestock industry.

Increasingly, Belize is relying on tourism to improve the standard of living. The government has invested heavily in foreign public-relations campaigns while working to improve the travel infrastructure on the home front. Because of these efforts, the country has seen record increases in visitors and tourist dollars.

The cayes depend on tourism and fishing for their income, but these two pursuits are sometimes in conflict. The spiny lobster and some types of fish have been seriously over-exploited, and lobster trapping is now seasonally restricted.

Lobster trappers employ some of the same methods today as they have for the past century. If you're around before or after lobster season you'll see stacks of lobster traps piled up in seaside villages. When lobster season approaches, these will disappear, as the trappers take them and place them out at sea. When it's time to check their traps, the trappers dive down to the sea bottom to retrieve their catch or pull them up with long-handled sticks. It used to be that the lobster trappers used landmarks and memory to keep track of their traps; these days it's all done using handheld GPS (Global Positioning Satellite) systems.

In the 1980s and 1990s Belize developed something of a reputation as a transshipment point for the illicit drug trade, especially around Belize City. This industry seems to have died down, reducing the dangers associated with high-volume drug transportation. Recreational drug use is still prevalent, but it happens discreetly.

POPULATION & PEOPLE

For such a tiny country (population around 256,000), Belize enjoys a fabulous, improbable ethnic diversity. Creoles – descendants of the British pirates who first settled here to exploit the country's forest resources and African slaves – now represent only 31% of Belize's population, but theirs continues on as the prevalent culture. Racially mixed and proud of it, Creoles speak a fascinating, unique dialect of English that, though it sounds familiar at first, is not easily intelligible to a speaker of standard English. Most of the people you will meet and interact with in Belize City and Belmopan will be Creole.

Over the last 10 years, Mestizos (or Latins, people of mixed Central American Indian and Spanish heritage) have become the largest ethnic group in the country, now at 44%. The first migration of Mestizos happened during the War of the Castes of the mid-1800s, when refugees from the Yucatán flooded into northern Belize, the Cayo District and the northern Cayes. Continuing this pattern over the last few years, thousands of political refugees have moved into Belize from troubled neighboring Central American countries. While English remains the official language of the country, Spanish is the predominant first language. This has caused some tension among the Creole population, who for the most part are fiercely proud of their country's Anglo roots.

The Maya of Belize make up just under 10% of the population and are divided into three linguistic groups. The Yucatec live in the north, near the border of Mexico's Yucatán Peninsula. The Mopan live in western Belize around the border town of Benque Viejo del Carmen and in southern Belize in and around Punta Gorda. The Kekchi Maya also live in the Punta Gorda area. In recent years, political refugees from Guatemala and El Salvador have contributed to Belize's Kekchi Maya population. Use of the Mayan language is decreasing, and both Spanish and English are becoming more widespread among the Maya.

Southern Belize is the home of the Garifunas (or Garinagus, also called Black Caribs), who account for just less than 7% of the population. The Garifunas are of South American Indian and African descent. They look more African than Indian, but they speak a language that's much more Indian than African, and their unique culture combines aspects of both peoples.

Mennonites represent a small, but influential group in Belize – see the Northern Belize chapter for more details. While they keep to themselves in settlements in western Belize, and a handful in the southern and northern regions, they provide most of the dairy products consumed in the country. Nearly all of the chicken that is consumed in Belize is grown, cleaned and packaged by Mennonites. It's popular because it means a pluck-free meal, but old-timers will tell you

it's not as good as the 'local' chicken that used to live and die underfoot.

Other ethnic groups in Belize include small populations of Europeans, North Americans, Chinese, Lebanese and East Indians.

EDUCATION

Education is free and compulsory in Belize to age 14. After that, instruction is free, but students are required to buy their own books, which is a hardship and a deterrent to higher education. Most schools are state-subsidized church schools, mainly run by Catholics, Methodists and Anglicans, although recently evangelical religions such as the Seventh Day Adventists have opened schools. It's estimated that 70% to 75% of Belizeans over the age of 15 can read and write.

ARTS

Belize's music is strongly tied to the Caribbean, and throughout the country you'll hear a happy mix of marimba, calypso, soca, steel drumming and, of course, reggae. Here, as in most island destinations and college towns, Bob Marley is king.

Punta rock is the official musical style of Belize. Its origins are from the music of the Garifuna – drum heavy with plenty of call and response. It features a multiplicity of musical overlays from Latin, Caribbean and Mayan cultures. This frenetic music is designed to get your hips moving. Aziatic has blended punta with R&B, jazz and pop to create what some are now calling punta pop. Probably the most well-known Punta stylists are the Punta Rebels. Andy Palacio, one of the founding members of the band, has done some interesting solo work as well. Titiman Flores also has his share of followers.

Punta is also a verb, and it's considered the traditional dance of the region.

Brukdown, another Belizean style of music, was developed by Creoles working in logging camps during the 18th and 19th centuries. It involves an accordion, banjo, harmonica and a percussion instrument – traditionally the jawbone of a pig is used, the teeth rattled with a stick. Wilfred Peters'

Boom and Chime Band is perhaps the best known of the brukdown artists; you should see them if you get the chance.

Santino's Messengers is the most ubiquitous band in all of Belize. They travel to fairs and festivals throughout the country and often give live performances in Belize City when they're not out on the road in their big yellow truck. Theirs is a combination of punta, calypso and traditional Caribbean standards.

Although he hasn't lived in Belize since he was a child, Jamal Shyne Barrow is perhaps the best-known Belizean musician. Barrow was a promising rap artist, a protégé of Sean 'P Diddy' Combs, until his participation in a 1999 New York nightclub shooting involving Combs and his then-girlfriend Jennifer Lopez. Barrow is currently serving out a 10-year sentence for opening fire in the nightclub. He is also the son of Dean Barrow, the head of Belize's UDP party.

If you happen to be on Ambergris Caye in January, be on the lookout for Jerry Jeff Walker. The hard-living, left-leaning Texan (by way of upstate New York) is most famous for having written 'Mr Bojangles,' but his legions of loyal fans credit him with helping define the Austin sound. He has a home south of San Pedro and hosts a 'fan-appreciation' week in town every January. Jerry Jeff performs live and often conducts benefit concerts for Belizean concerns. If you can't see him live, you'll undoubtedly hear his album, 'Cowboy Boots and Bathing Suits,' played in bars around the village.

SOCIETY & CONDUCT

Because of the mix of ethnicities and cultures in Belize, the people of the country are extremely tolerant and accepting of the differences in others. For travelers this means that you will feel welcomed and comfortable in most situations. You're expected to reciprocate by treating your hosts with courtesy, respect and patience.

Care should be taken in traditional Mayan areas – don't take photos without first asking for permission. In Dangriga and other Garifuna towns, you'll find that people can be brusque or at least reserved when they first meet you, but tend to warm up after they see you around a bit.

Belizeans aren't shy about identifying themselves and others by race and pointing out the differences in cultures – this may be a bit surprising if you come from a world where acknowledging racial differences is less commonplace.

RELIGION

Belize's mixture of religions generally trails after its ethnic composition. Roman Catholics and Protestants (mainly Anglicans and Methodists, but also Mennonites, Seventh Day Adventists and Jehovah's Witnesses) prevail, but Belize's tradition of tolerance has welcomed Buddhists, Hindus and Muslims. Mayan communities continue to practice traditional Mayan rites, usually blended with Catholicism.

LANGUAGE

Belize is officially English-speaking, and most of its citizens, with the exception of new arrivals from Guatemala, Honduras and Mexico, read and speak English fluently. Creole people speak their own colorful dialect (arguably a language) as well as standard English, flavored with the Caribbean's musical lilt. You'll hear Garifuna spoken in the south. Spanish is the first language in the north and in some towns in the west. Other languages in the mix are Mayan, Chinese, Mennonite German and Hindi.

THE MAYAN WORLD
Religion

WORLD-TREE & XIBALBÁ

For the Maya, the world, the heavens and the mysterious 'unseen world' or underworld called Xibalbá (shi-bahl-**bah**) were all one great, unified structure that operated according to the laws of astrology and ancestor worship. The towering ceiba tree was considered sacred. It symbolized the Whack Chan, or world-tree, which united the 13 heavens, the surface of the earth and the nine levels of the underworld of Xibalbá. The world-tree had a sort of cruciform shape and was associated with the color blue-green. In the 16th century, the Franciscan friars arrived and required the Indians to venerate the cross; this Christian symbolism meshed easily with established Mayan beliefs.

POINTS OF THE COMPASS

In Mayan cosmology, each point of the compass had special religious significance. East was most important, as it is where the sun is reborn each day; its color was red. West was black because it is where the sun disappears. North was white and is the direction from which the all-important rains come, beginning in May. South was yellow because it is the 'sunniest' point of the compass.

Everything in the Mayan world was seen in relation to these cardinal points, with the world-tree at the center. But the cardinal points were only the starting point for the all-important astronomical and astrological observations that determined fate. (See Calendar System, later in this section.)

BLOODLETTING

Humans had certain roles to play within this great system. Just as the great cosmic dragon shed its blood, which fell to the earth as rain, so humans had to shed blood to link themselves with Xibalbá.

Bloodletting ceremonies were the most important religious ceremonies, and the blood of kings was seen as the most acceptable for these rituals. Thus when the friars said that the blood of Jesus, the King of the Jews, had been spilled for the common people, the Maya could easily understand the symbolism.

SACRED PLACES

Mayan ceremonies were performed in natural sacred places as well as in their human-made equivalents. Mountains, caves, lakes, cenotes, rivers and fields were all sacred and had special importance in the scheme of things. Pyramids and temples

TOM BOYDEN

Left: Caves were sometimes used for rituals and sacrifices.

were thought of as stylized mountains; sometimes they had secret chambers within them, like the caves in a mountain. A cave was the mouth of the creature that represented Xibalbá, and to enter it was to enter the spirit of the secret world. This is why some Mayan temples have doorways surrounded by huge masks: As you enter the door of this 'cave,' you are entering the mouth of Xibalbá.

The plazas around which the pyramids were placed symbolized the open fields or the flat land of the tropical forest. What we call stelae were to the Maya 'tree-stones'; that is, sacred tree-effigies echoing the sacredness of the world-tree. These tree-stones were often carved with the figures of great Maya kings, for the king was the world-tree of Mayan society.

As these places were sacred, it made sense for succeeding Maya kings to build new and ever grander temples directly over older temples, as this enhanced the sacred character of the spot. The temple being covered over was not seen as mere rubble to be exploited as building material, but as a sacred artifact to be preserved. Certain features of these older temples, such as the large masks on the façades, were carefully padded and protected before the new construction was placed over them.

Ancestor worship and genealogy were very important to the Maya, and when they buried a king beneath a pyramid, or a commoner beneath the floor or courtyard of his or her *na,* the sacredness of the location was increased.

SHAMANISM & CATHOLICISM

The ceiba tree's cruciform shape was not the only correspondence the Maya found between their animist beliefs and Christianity. Both traditional Mayan animism and Catholicism have rites of baptism and confession, days of fasting and other forms of abstinence, religious partaking of alcoholic beverages, burning of incense and the use of altars.

Today, the Mayan practice of Catholicism is a fascinating fusion of shamanist-animist and Christian ritual. The traditional religious ways are so important that often a Maya person will try to recover from a malady by seeking the advice of a shaman-healer rather than a medical doctor. Use of folk remedies linked with animist tradition is widespread in Mayan areas.

Calendar System

In some ways, the ancient Mayan calendar – still used in certain parts of the region – is more accurate than the Gregorian calendar we use today. Without sophisticated technology, Mayan astronomers were able to ascertain the length of the solar year, the lunar month and the Venus year. Their calculations enabled them to pinpoint eclipses with uncanny accuracy. Their lunar cycle was a mere seven minutes off today's sophisticated technological calculations, and their Venus cycle errs by only two hours for periods covering 500 years.

Time and the calendar, in fact, were the basis of the Mayan religion, which resembled modern astrology in some respects. Astronomical observations played such a pivotal role in Mayan life that astronomy and religion were linked and the sun and moon were worshiped. Most Mayan cities were constructed in strict accordance with celestial movements (see Architecture & Archaeology, later in this section).

Counting System

The Mayan counting system was elegantly simple: Dots were used to count from one to four; a horizontal bar signified five; a bar with one dot above it was six, with two dots was seven etc. Two bars signified 10, three bars 15. Nineteen, the highest common number, was three bars stacked up and topped by four dots.

To signify larger numbers the Maya used positional numbers – a fairly sophisticated system similar to the one we use today and much more advanced than the crude additive numbers used in the Roman Empire.

In positional numbers, the position of a sign as well as the sign's value determine the number. For example, in our decimal system the number 23 is made up of two signs: a 2 in the 'tens' position and a 3 in the 'ones' position; two tens plus three ones equals 23.

The Maya used not a decimal system (base 10) but a vigesimal system, that is, a system with base 20; positions of increasing value went not right to left (as ours do) but from bottom to top. The bottom position showed values from one to 19; the next position up showed values from 20 to 380. The bottom and upper positions together could show up to nineteen 20s plus nineteen 1s (ie, 399). The third position up showed values from 400 up to nineteen 400s (ie, 7600). The three positions

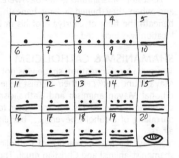

together could signify numbers up to 7999. By adding more positions one could count as high as needed.

Such positional numbers depend upon the concept of zero, a concept that the Romans never developed but the Maya did. The zero in Mayan numbering was represented by a stylized picture of a shell or some other object – anything except a bar or a dot.

The Mayan counting system was used by merchants and others who had to add up many things, but its most important use – and the one you will encounter during your travels – was in writing calendar dates.

Language

During the Classic period, the Mayan lands were divided into two linguistic areas. In the Yucatán Peninsula and Belize people spoke Yucatec, and in the highlands and Motagua Valley of Guatemala they spoke a related language called Chol. People in El Petén were likely to speak both languages, as this was where the linguistic regions overlapped.

Left: Bars and dots formed the basis of the Mayan counting system.

Yucatec and Chol were similar – about as similar as Spanish and Italian – a fact that facilitated trade and cultural exchange.

In addition, both Yucatec and Chol were written using the same hieroglyphic system, so a written document or inscription could be understood by literate members of either language group.

The written language of the Classic Maya was complex. Glyphs could signify a whole word or just a syllable, and the same glyph could be drawn in a variety of ways. Sometimes extra symbols were appended to a glyph to help indicate pronunciation. Reading ancient Mayan inscriptions and texts accurately takes a great deal of training and experience. In fact, many aspects of the written language are still not fully understood, even by the experts.

Architecture & Archaeology

Mayan architecture is amazing for its achievements, but perhaps even more amazing for what it did not achieve. Mayan architects never seem to have used the true arch (a rounded arch with a keystone), and they never thought to put wheels on boxes and use them as wagons to move the thousands of tons of construction materials needed in their tasks. They had no metal tools – they were technically a Stone Age culture – yet they could build breathtaking temple complexes and align them so precisely that windows and doors were used as celestial observatories of great accuracy.

The arch used in most Mayan buildings is the corbeled arch (or, when used for an entire room rather than a doorway, corbeled vault). In this technique, large flat stones on either side of the opening are set progressively inward as they rise. The two sides nearly meet at the top, and this 'arch' is then topped by capstones. Though they served the purpose, the corbeled arches limited severely the amount of open space that was beneath them. In effect, Mayan architects were limited to long, narrow vaulted rooms.

The Maya also lacked draft animals (horses, donkeys, mules, oxen). All the work had to be done by humans, on their feet, with their arms and with their backs, without wagons or even wheelbarrows.

THE CELESTIAL PLAN

Every major work of Mayan architecture had a celestial plan. Temples were aligned in such a manner as to enhance celestial observation, whether of the sun, moon or certain stars and planets, especially Venus. The alignment might not be apparent except at certain conjunctions of the celestial bodies (eg, an eclipse), but the Maya knew each building was properly 'placed' and that this enhanced its sacred character.

Temples usually had other features that linked them to the stars. The doors and windows, for example, might be aligned in order to frame a celestial body at a certain exact point in its course on a certain day of a certain year.

Facts for the Visitor

HIGHLIGHTS

Belize has a little something for everyone, and following are compilations of the bests for each category.

Ruins

Caracol is the most remote, therefore potentially the most rewarding for adventurous travelers. **Lamanai** has the best tour – you travel to the ruins by riverboat, spotting birds, turtles and crocodiles along the way. **Altun Ha** is small, pretty and accessible; it can be reached on a short day trip from the cayes. The view from El Castillo at **Xunantunich** is hard to beat, and the carvings on the side of the temple are beautifully preserved.

Diving & Snorkeling

Hol Chan and **Shark Ray Alley**, off San Pedro on Ambergris Caye, are at the top of the list for snorkelers and novice divers. You'll see a huge variety of sea life at the former, and get a chance to swim with sharks (of the fairly harmless nurse variety) and stingrays at the latter.

The **Lighthouse Reef** dives, including the **Blue Hole**, are at the top of the list for 'been there, done that' set. **Glover's Reef** is harder to get to from the northern Cayes, therefore it gets less traffic, the coral is more pristine and the sea life is plentiful. If you're around March through June after a full moon you'll have a good chance of seeing whale sharks off **Gladden Split**, best accessed from Placencia or Hopkins.

Wildlife-Viewing & Birding

There are miles of protected and easily accessed wilderness in Belize, and much of it is teeming with wildlife. You'll need a good guide to see the rarest of animals. Top spots include the **Río Bravo Conservation & Management Area** (also an off-the-beaten-track highlight), **Cockscomb Basin Wildlife Sanctuary**, **Mountain Pine Ridge** and the **Community Baboon Sanctuary** at Bermudian Landing.

Good birding spots include **Crooked Tree Wildlife Sanctuary**, **Chan Chich Lodge**, **Cockscomb Basin** and **Guanacaste National Park**. Seasonally, birders make the pilgrimage to **Red Bank** in southern Belize to see scarlet macaws.

Caves

Barton Creek Cave is the most popular of the Belize cave tours, although it's a fairly mass-market experience, and crowded. In the Cayo District, **Actun Tunichil Muknal** gets high marks for adventure, as does **Che Chem Ha Cave**. In southern Belize, **Ian Anderson's Caves Branch Adventure Company** runs tours of various intensities – from tube floats to multi-day jungle treks – on a private estate.

Islands

Belize has plenty of offshore islands, referred to as cayes (pronounced 'keys'), to visit. The northern cayes are the most visited, and in these waters there are two speeds: Ambergris and Caulker. You'll soon figure out where you fit into the mix.

For the cushy traveler, top-end **Ambergris Caye** is the ticket. It's the most Americanized, offering all the requisite comforts (maybe more), and attracts an active, family-oriented crowd. With the exception of a few in-town hotels, you'll be hard-pressed to find a room under US$100 here.

Caye Caulker has long been a mecca for budget travelers, and it's fighting (and beating) the pressures to cater to higher-end travelers. It's got everything a hot-and-tired budget traveler could want; of course you'll still pay more for beachfront here, but you'll be happy with your investment.

Farther south, **Tobacco Caye** is also popular with the budget set. There's good snorkeling right off the shore, and for the truly indolent, this could be as close to paradise as you get.

South Water Caye attracts high-end travelers interested in quick-and-easy access to

Glover's Reef, which has some of the best diving in the Caribbean.

Placencia isn't a caye, but it gets lumped in here because it's sometimes referred to as the 'caye you can drive to.' It's often compared to Caulker because it attracts backpackers. Lately it's been getting crowded, but it's a great scene – definitely the partyingest stretch of shoreline in Belize.

Jungle Lodges
The most and best jungle lodges are in western Belize's Cayo District. They include **Blancaneaux Lodge**, **Chaa Creek Resort & Spa** and **duPlooy's Jungle Lodge**. In the north the ultra-remote **Chan Chich Lodge** is popular with bird-watchers, and **Lamanai Outpost Lodge**, near the ruins at Lamanai, is great for river and jungle explorers.

Culture
Belize City is widely despised by people who don't live there for being dirty, crowded, dangerous and unwelcoming. But this is the heart of Belize, and it's difficult to truly appreciate the amalgam of cultures in Belize without seeing them in action here. It's easily navigated by using the same street smarts you employ in any major American or European city.

Dangriga is the heart of Belize's Garifuna culture, with not much in the way of obvious attractions for visitors, but worth a spin through for the culturally curious.

Corozal, in the north, and **San Ignacio**, in the west, possess a stronger Latin influence than the rest of Belize.

Surrounding Punta Gorda are the **Mayan villages of Toledo**, presenting a fascinating juxtaposition of ancient traditions and modern-day Mayan practices. A tour combining the villages of San Antonio or Santa Cruz with the nearby ancient ruins of Lubaantun, Nim Li Punit or Uxbenka will leave you with a profound understanding of the strength of the ancient Mayan culture and how it endures today.

Off the Beaten Track
In the north, **Sarteneja** is a sleepy fishing village that's very difficult to reach and great to hide out in for a few days. **Río Bravo Conservation & Management Area** is deep in the jungle, and here's where you'll have the best chance of seeing a jaguar. **Hopkins** is a small Garifuna village in southern Belize, where the beach is wide and the living is easy.

PLANNING
When to Go
Belize's high season is between November and April; low season is May through October, although there is a spike in traffic during the North American summer, June through August. Christmas, New Year's and Easter week are ultra-peak times, where some of the more mercenary resorts hike their rates up. June to October is considered the wet season, and though it definitely rains more frequently during these months, the showers usually don't last long enough to spoil an entire day. While hurricane season is considered to be summer and early fall, historically Belize's major hurricanes have hit in late September or October.

What Kind of Trip
Keep in mind that Belize is a tiny place and it's relatively easy to get anywhere within half a day, especially if you're willing to fly. Most travelers opt for what's called a surf-and-turf vacation: a bit of time at the sea, a bit of time inland. You can easily catch three prime pursuits – sea, jungle, ruins – in a week. The best beaten track is between the northern Cayes – Ambergris and Caulker – and Cayo in western Belize. Here you'll get the crowds, but also the tourist infrastructure that will allow you to cover a lot of ground.

If you want to stay put, it's easy to base yourself in the northern Cayes and take some day trips to close-by mainland attractions like Altun Ha, the Community Baboon Sanctuary, Lamanai or Caves Branch.

More adventurous folks may want to consider working on the north-south axis as well: up to Corozal or the Orange Walk District, or south to the seaside village of Hopkins or Placencia. Those interested in more solitude with their beach might consider Glover's Reef or Tobacco Caye instead of the northern Cayes.

Two to three weeks will allow you to choose from the above options and go deeper into the Mountain Pine Ridge in the Cayo District, perhaps to the ruins of Carocol, or on a day trip to Tikal. With this amount of time, you could also base yourself in Placencia or Hopkins and explore some of the inland areas of southern Belize.

Maps

If you're driving, pick up a copy of Emory King's annual *Driver's Guide to Beautiful Belize*, sold in bookstores and gift shops in Belize City. The guide has basic maps and detailed route descriptions, which are helpful since road markers in Belize are few and far between.

International Travel Maps publishes a helpful folding map of Belize. Order it direct from ITMB (☎ 604-879-3621, fax 604-879-4521, ⓦ www.itmb.com), 530 W Broadway, Vancouver BC, V5Z 1E9, or from Map Link (☎ 805-692-6777, fax 805-692-6787), 30 S La Patera Lane, Unit 5, Santa Barbara, CA 93117.

What to Bring

Following is a list of recommended items for a trip to Belize. The best advice is to travel lightly, but check and double-check that you don't leave essentials behind.

Be aware that restrictions have tightened profoundly about what you can pack in your carry-on luggage. Sharp objects like scissors, tweezers, clippers and pocketknives must be checked. Consult your carrier for current packing restrictions before you fly.

Clothes Belize is hot and humid and you will rarely find yourself in need of a sweater. For the most part you'll live in shorts, T-shirts, sandals and festive tropical wear for nighttime. Women traveling alone should consider bringing a long skirt or pants for public transportation or solo explorations, in order to deflect unwanted attention.

Waterproof sandals, such as Tevas, are great when you're around water and boats, but pull on some socks or consider closed-toed shoes if you're spending time in the bush or planning any jungle walks; it's much better to avoid sharp vegetation and stinging insects. You may also want to consider lightweight, moisture-wicking long pants and long-sleeved shirts as protection from

---

Tips on Tours

Most of the tours you'll take in Belize will be fun, interesting and much more fulfilling than if you visited a place by yourself. Following are some tips to help you choose the best tour operators and get the best value from your tour.

• Make sure that your tour guide and tour operator are licensed by the Belize Tourism Board (BTB).

• Find out what's included in the cost of your tour; often entry fees and lunch are not included in the quoted price. If lunch is not included, it's perfectly reasonable to bring your own lunch.

• Restaurants pay tour guides commissions to bring them patrons, and the commission is often built into the price of your meal. Do not feel obligated to eat at the place recommended by your tour operator. Also, do not feel obligated to buy your tour operator lunch; his or her lunch will be provided. If you want to reward your guide for a job well done, a tip is fine compensation.

• Ask how many others will be on the tour. An overcrowded vehicle can be misery. Also, the larger the group, the more waiting around you'll do.

• Ask to see the boat or the vehicle you will be spending the day in. Make sure it meets your comfort and safety standards.

• Tipping is not mandatory, but if you feel compelled to do so, 10% is a fair amount.

bugs and sun. If that seems like too much attire to bear, be prepared to douse yourself in sunscreen and bug repellent.

Even the shortest walk in this climate may turn your trusty daypack into a soggy millstone strapped to your back. Consider a small shoulder bag or fanny pack instead.

Don't forget your swimsuit, and consider bringing an old T-shirt to wear when snorkeling to prevent sunburn. A light-color canvas or straw hat will prove indispensable.

Incidentals Consider bringing a flashlight or head lamp. (For some reason, the hotels in Belize rarely have bedside reading lamps, so if you like to read before you doze off this will be particularly handy.)

- citronella candle – romantic and repellent
- extra batteries
- Walkman and portable speakers
- duct tape – good for repairs
- first-aid kit (see the Health section, later in this chapter)
- binoculars
- extra film and camera batteries
- waterproof sunscreen
- lip balm
- sun hat
- water bottle with shoulder strap
- pocketknife
- alarm clock
- sewing kit
- clothesline
- sunglasses
- plastic bags
- shampoo, soap, shaving gear
- spare eyeglasses and contact lenses
- ear plugs
- small padlock for luggage
- notepad and pen
- tampons
- contraceptives

RESPONSIBLE TOURISM

Don't remove coral or shells from the sea. Mind your fins when diving or snorkeling; the coral is fragile and endangered (see Considerations for Responsible Diving in

the Northern Cayes chapter). Avoid purchasing any items made from turtle shell or coral. Don't swim with the manatees or attempt to piggyback a sea turtle. You may like it, but they find it very stressful.

Do not take or buy any Mayan artifacts – it's illegal, and some say you'll be hexed!

Use air-con judiciously. It's expensive and an enormous strain on local energy reserves. Instead, move more slowly than normal and use fans; you'll find that you adjust to the heat in a couple of days.

When in the jungle, stay on trails to avoid trampling fragile plants. Appreciate wildlife from a distance. Never feed wild animals, including those in the sea.

Do not order lobster or crab off-season. Do not fish in protected areas.

Dispose of trash properly, even if it means carrying it with you until you find a trash bin.

Interact with local people. Appreciate and learn as much as possible about the different cultural traditions of the areas you visit. Ask questions.

TOURIST OFFICES

The Belize Tourism Board (☎ 2-31910, 2-31913, fax 2-31943, ☎ 800-624-0686 in North America, e btbb@btl.net, w www.travel belize.org) is headquartered in the Central Bank Building on Gabourel Lane in Belize City. It also maintains a branch in Germany: (☎ 711-233 947), Bopserwaldstrasse 40-G, D-70184, Stuttgart.

Belize Tourism Industry Association (☎ 2-75717, 2-71144, fax 2-78710, e btia@btl.net), 10 N Park St, Belize City, is Belize's private-sector tourism organization. This association publishes *Destination Belize,* a helpful visitor's guide available from information kiosks and hotels throughout the country.

VISAS & DOCUMENTS
Passport & Visas

Passports are required to enter Belize.

Visas are not required for citizens of the EU, the British Commonwealth (except India), Mexico, the USA, Costa Rica or Austria – providing they have a valid passport and an onward or roundtrip airplane ticket. A visitor's permit valid for 30 days will be stamped in your passport at a border crossing or at the airport. If you're planning to stay more than 30 days you must extend your permit by paying US$25 at an immigration office.

Citizens of other countries can obtain a visa for US$25 from the nearest Belizean embassy or consulate, or, if there isn't a Belizean consulate in your country, you can apply at a British embassy. It is possible to obtain a visa from the immigration office at Philip Goldson International Aiport if you're unable to obtain one at home. Contact the Immigration & Nationality Department (☎ 8-22611, 8-22423), in Belmopan, for more information.

Travel Insurance

A travel insurance policy to cover theft, loss and medical problems is a good idea. Some policies offer varying medical-expense options; the higher ones are chiefly for countries such as the USA, which has extremely high medical costs. There is a wide variety of policies available, so read the small print.

Some policies specifically exclude 'dangerous activities,' which can include scuba diving, motorcycling and even trekking. A locally acquired motorcycle license is not valid under some policies. Check that the policy you're considering covers ambulances or an emergency flight home.

You may prefer a policy that pays doctors or hospitals directly rather than requiring you to pay on the spot and claim later. If you have to claim later, make sure you keep all documentation. Some policies ask you to call back (collect) to a center in your home country, where an immediate assessment of your problem is made.

Driver's License & Permits

If you plan to drive in Belize, you'll need to bring a valid driver's license from your home country. See also Insurance under Car in the Getting Around chapter.

Copies

All important documents (passport data page, credit cards, travel insurance policy, tickets, driver's license etc) should be photo-copied. Leave one copy with someone at home and keep another with you, separate from the originals.

You can also store details in Lonely Planet's free online Travel Vault in case you lose the copies or can't be bothered with them. Your password-protected Travel Vault can be accessed online from anywhere in the world. To create it, log on to Ⓦ www.ekno .lonelyplanet.com.

EMBASSIES & CONSULATES
Belizean Embassies & Consulates

Because Belize is a small country and far from rich, its diplomatic affairs overseas are usually handled by the British embassies and consulates.

Some consulates mentioned below are actually honorary consulates or consular agencies. These posts can usually issue visas, but they refer more complicated matters to the nearest full consulate or the Belizean embassy's consular section.

Canada

Honorary Consul: (☎ 514-871-4741, fax 514-397-0816) 1080 Beaver Hall Hill, Suite 1720, Montreal, QC H2Z 1S8
Honorary Consul: (☎ 416-865-7000, fax 416-865-7048) Suite 3800, South Tower, Royal Bank Plaza, Toronto, ON M5J 2J7

Germany

Honorary Consul: (☎ 71-423 925, fax 71-423 225) Lindenstrasse 46-48, 74321 Beitigheim, Bissingen

Guatemala

Embassy: (☎ 334-5531, 331-1137, fax 334-5536) Avenida La Reforma 1-50, Zona 9, Edificio El Reformador, Suite 803, Guatemala City

Honduras

Consulate: (☎ 504-551-6191, fax 504-551-6460) 2 Avenida 7 Calle No 102, Colonia Bella Vista, San Pedro Sula

Mexico

Embassy: (☎ 5-520-12-74, fax 5-520-60-89) Calle Bernardo de Gálvez 215, Colonia Lomas de Chapultepec, Mexico, DF 11000
Consulate: (☎ 9-832-77-28) Avenida Obregón 226, Chetumal
c/o British Consulate: (☎ 928-39-62) Calle 58 No 450, at Calle 53, Fraccionamiento del Norte, Mérida

UK

Belize High Commission to London: (☎ 020-7499 9728, fax 020-7491 4139) 22 Harcourt House, 19 Cavendish Square, London W1M 9AD

USA

Embassy: (☎ 202-332-9636, fax 202-332-6888) 2535 Massachusetts Ave NW, Washington, DC 20008

Consulate General: (☎ 323-469-7343, fax 323-469-7346) 5825 Sunset Blvd, Suite 206, Hollywood, CA 90028

Embassies & Consulates in Belize

A few countries have ambassadors stationed in Belize. Many others appoint nonresident ambassadors who handle Belizean affairs from their home countries. Embassies and consulates tend to be open from about 9am to noon Monday to Friday. Unless otherwise mentioned, all the offices listed below are in Belize City.

Canada

Consulate: (☎ 2-31060, fax 2-30060) 85 N Front St

Denmark

Consulate: (☎ 2-72172, fax 2-77280) 13 Southern Foreshore

Europe

Commission of the European Union: (☎ 2-72785, 2-32070) on Eyre St at Hutson St

France

Honorary Consul: (☎ 2-32708, fax 2-32416) 109 New Rd

Germany

Honorary Consul: (☎ 2-24371, fax 2-24375) 3½ miles, Western Hwy

Guatemala

Embassy: (☎ 93-2531, fax 93-2532), Church St, Benque Viejo del Carmen

Israel

Honorary Consul: (☎ 2-73991, fax 2-30463) 4 Albert St

Italy

Honorary Consul: (☎ 2-78449, fax 2-73056) 18 Albert St

Mexico

Embassy: (☎ 2-30194, 2-31388, fax 2-78742) 20 N Park St; also an office in Belmopan

Netherlands

Honorary Consul: (☎ 2-73612, fax 2-75936) 14 Central American Blvd

Norway

Honorary Consul: (☎ 2-77031, fax 2-77062) 1 King St

Panama

Consulate: (☎ 2-34282, fax 2-30653) 5481 Princess Margaret Dr

Sweden

Honorary Consul: (☎ 2-30623) 11 Princess Margaret Dr

Switzerland

Consulate: 41 Albert St

UK

British High Commission: (☎ 8-22146, fax 8-22761) Embassy Square, Belmopan

USA

Embassy: (☎ 2-77161, fax 2-30802) 29 Gabourel Lane

Your Own Embassy

It's important to realize what your own embassy – the embassy of the country of which you are a citizen – can and can't do to help you if you get into trouble. Generally speaking, it won't be much help in emergencies if the trouble you're in is remotely your own fault. Remember that you are bound by the laws of the country you are in. Your embassy will not be sympathetic if you end up in jail after committing a crime locally, even if such actions are legal in your own country.

In genuine emergencies, you might get some assistance, but only if other channels have been exhausted. For example, if you need to get home urgently, a free ticket home is exceedingly unlikely – the embassy would expect you to have insurance. If you have all your money and documents stolen, it might assist with getting a new passport, but a loan for onward travel is out of the question.

Some embassies used to keep letters for travelers or have a small reading room with home newspapers, but these days, the mail-holding service has usually been stopped.

CUSTOMS

Customs officers only get angry and excited about a few things: drugs, weapons, large amounts of currency and automobiles. They can also be sensitive to any goods that might be sold while you're in the country, so if you're bring in packaged items, or items that don't appear to be immediately useful in your travels, you may be taxed. As is common at many borders these days, you may also be relieved of plant or animal products if you attempt to bring them into the country.

Normally the customs officer will not look seriously in your luggage and may not look at all. Be formal and polite and you shouldn't have any trouble.

Note: Do not attempt to take illegal drugs or any sort of firearms or ammunition into the country.

MONEY
Currency
The Belizean dollar (BZ$) bears the portrait of Queen Elizabeth II and is divided into 100 cents. Coins come in denominations of one, five, 10, 25 and 50 cents and one dollar (although you'll rarely see one- or five-cent coins since most prices are rounded up to at least 10); bills (notes) are all of the same size but differ in color and come in denominations of two, five, 10, 20, 50 and 100 dollars.

The Belizean dollar's value has been fixed for many years at US$0.50. Prices are generally quoted in Belizean dollars, written as '$30 BZE,' though you will also occasionally see '$15 US.' To avoid surprises, be sure to confirm with service providers whether they are quoting prices in US or Belizean dollars. Often people will quote prices as '20 dollars Belize, 10 dollars US' just to be clear.

The smaller the town you're in, the more difficult it is to exchange large bills, so be sure to have small denominations if you're heading off the tourist trail.

Exchange Rates
Currency exchange rates at press time were as follows:

country	unit		Belizean dollar
Australia	A$1	=	BZ$1.02
Canada	C$1	=	BZ$1.23
euro	€1	=	BZ$1.77
Guatemala	Q1	=	BZ$0.25

country	unit		Belizean dollar
Japan	¥100	=	BZ$1.50
Mexico	N$1	=	BZ$0.22
New Zealand	NZ$1	=	BZ$0.84
United Kingdom	UK£1	=	BZ$2.84
United States	US$1	=	BZ$1.97

Exchanging Money
Cash & Traveler's Checks Most businesses accept US currency in cash without question, though US coins aren't accepted. They usually give change in Belizean dollars, though they may return US change if you ask for it and they have it.

US traveler's checks are widely accepted. It's best to keep smaller denominations if you're going to be in less traveled spots, where there may not be much change in the till.

Canadian dollars and UK pounds sterling are exchangeable at any bank, although traveler's checks in currencies other than US dollars are not consistently accepted by Belizean businesses. It's very difficult to exchange currencies of foreign countries other than these three in Belize.

Moneychangers around border-crossing points will change your US cash for Belizean dollars legally at the standard rate of US$1=BZ$2. If you change money or traveler's checks at a bank, you may get only US$1=BZ$1.97; they may also charge a fee of BZ$5 (US$2.50) to change a traveler's check.

ATMs & Credit Cards ATMs for Belizean banks are becoming common, but they don't yet accept foreign ATM cards. If you depend upon your ATM card for money, stock up on cash in Mexico or Guatemala before entering Belize.

Major credit cards such as Visa and MasterCard are accepted at all airline and car-rental companies and at the larger hotels and restaurants everywhere; American Express is often accepted at higher-end places and is becoming more common among the smaller establishments.

A common method of procuring cash in Belize is to get cash advanced on credit cards, easily done in any bank. Ask first what the fee for the cash advance is; it varies from bank to bank and town to town. Often the banks charge a flat fee, so draw as large an amount as you're comfortable with to make the most of the charge. Note that your banking institution at home is likely to charge a small exchange fee on this as well.

International Transfers There are Western Union locations in all of the major towns covered in this book.

Security
Petty crime is a problem in Belize, so it's best to keep a handle on your money. High-end resorts have safes. Don't be flashy with your money, jewelry or equipment. Be careful about leaving valuables in your room.

Costs
Though a poor country, Belize is more expensive than you might anticipate. A small domestic economy, socialized welfare system and large proportion of imports keep prices high. A fried-chicken dinner that costs US$3 in Guatemala goes for US$6 in Belize. Budget travelers will find it difficult to spend less than US$20 per day for a room and three meals – this may mean sharing a bunk room, which will range from US$7 to US$12. A more realistic bottom-end figure is US$25, and US$30 makes life a lot easier. Mid-range travelers will be fine on between US$50 and US$75 a day. Deluxe accommodations average around US$150. Note that this book lists high-season rates throughout; figure 10% less for low season.

Tipping & Bargaining
In highly touristed areas, tipping tour leaders, dive operators and waitstaff is becoming more common, but this should be done only if you feel the service warrants it. Tips need go no higher than 10%.

Bargaining is not a huge part of the culture in Belize: Shops generally have set prices on goods. Hotels and guest houses are required to list their rates with the BTB and expected to stick to them. However, it's not a bad idea to ask for any special offers, cor-porate rates or multi-day rates when you're making arrangements; you may be able to get the price down a bit if business is slow.

Taxes & Refunds
Belize levies an 8% value-added tax (VAT) on retail sales, as well as a 7% tax on hotel rooms, meals and drinks. The rates listed in this book for accommodations in Belize do not include the 7% room tax. If you stay in a small hotel or guest house for just one night and don't insist on a receipt, you may not be charged the hotel tax. Foreign visitors do not get a refund of the VAT.

POST & COMMUNICATIONS
Post
By airmail to Canada or the USA, a postcard costs BZ$0.30, a letter BZ$0.60. To Europe it's BZ$0.40 for a postcard or BZ$0.75 for a letter.

It is possible to receive incoming mail through the post offices of the major towns mentioned in the books. Mail should be addressed to: your name, c/o General Delivery, town, district, Belize, Central America. It will be held for up to two months and must be claimed with a picture ID. If you have an American Express card you can receive incoming mail at the American Express office in Belize City (☎ 2-77363), 41 Albert St.

Telephone
See the boxed text on the following page regarding Belize's phone number change.

The telephone system is operated by Belize Telecommunications Ltd (BTL), with offices in major towns (open 8am to noon and 1pm to 4pm Monday to Friday and 8am to noon Saturday).

Local calls from coin-operated pay phones cost the flat rate of BZ$0.25. Coin-operated phones are increasingly rare, however, and most people use prepaid debit cards, which can be purchased in denominations of BZ$10, BZ$20 and BZ$50 at BTL offices and most grocery stores. With these, local calls are usually a flat rate of BZ$0.15. Long-distance calls within Belize (using prepaid phone cards) will cost between

Belize's Number Change

At press time, Belize Telecommunications Ltd (BTL) was scheduled to change all Belizean phone numbers to seven digits as of May 2002. The change means that callers will be required to dial all digits whether calling from outside an area or city or within it.

For an initial period following the number changes, callers will be immediately forwarded to the new number. After that, a recording should provide you with information. The new numbers will also be reflected in BTL's April 2002 phone directory.

For number conversions, go to the BTL Web site, **w** www.btl.net. You can also check the Lonely Planet Web site (**w** www.lonelyplanet.com/upgrades; see *Belize, Guatemala & Yucatán*), where we will post new information as it becomes available.

BZ$0.05 and BZ$0.55 a minute. The large American long-distance companies provide international service as well, but their rates may not be much different than BTL's.

The country code is 501. At press time the system worked as follows: To call one part of Belize from another, dial ☎ 0 (zero), then the one- or two-digit area code, then the four- or five-digit local phone number. You must also dial ☎ 0 and the area code when you're making a local call with a phone card. You do not need to dial the zero when calling from outside the country.

Here are some useful numbers: directory assistance ☎ 113; local & regional operator ☎ 114; long-distance (trunk) operator ☎ 110; international operator ☎ 115; fire & ambulance ☎ 90; police ☎ 911.

Cell Phones Renting a cell phone can be arranged at rental-car agencies throughout Belize, and in some hotels. The price is around US$5 a day, not including the price of calls. In order to make calls you must purchase a BTL phone card and program the call credit into your phone.

At press time, BTL's monopoly on the Belize phone system made it difficult for travelers to use their own cell phone service in the country. To use your own cell phone, you must bring it to a BTL office and have it programmed to their system; this will cost around US$40. After that, rates will be the same as regular long-distance service within the country, purchased via prepaid phone card.

BTL's monopoly is scheduled to end in 2003, which should create competitive rates for phone and Internet access.

Fax, Email & Internet Access

Fax service is available at many hotels and businesses. BTL provides Internet access to local residents with accounts, charging by the hour. Most hotels will send email messages for guests. Internet cafés are starting to crop up in Belize's tourist centers; rates average around US$3 for 15 minutes. BTL's service is crashy – the joke in the country is that BTL stands for 'Betta Try Later' – but it only goes down for short periods of time, and cafés are fairly generous about refunding your money if there are problems with the service. CompuServe and America Online do not have nodes in Belize at the time of this writing, so if you are planning to carry a laptop, it's not going to be cost-effective to log on from your personal computer since you'll have to make an international call for access.

As mentioned above, BTL's monopoly in the country is scheduled to end in 2003, which should change the climate for Internet access.

DIGITAL RESOURCES

The World Wide Web is a rich resource for travelers. You can research your trip, hunt down bargain airfares, book hotels, check on weather conditions or chat with locals and other travelers about the best places to visit (or avoid!).

There's no better place to start your Web explorations than the Lonely Planet Web site (**w** www.lonelyplanet.com). Here, you'll find succinct summaries on traveling to most places on earth; postcards from other travelers; and the Thorn

Tree bulletin board, where you can ask questions before you go or dispense advice when you get back. You will also find travel news and updates to many of our most popular guidebooks, and the subWWWay section links you to the most useful travel resources elsewhere on the Web.

Several helpful Web sites offer information for travelers to Belize. The best starting points are **w** www.belizetravel.org, the Belize Tourism Board's official Web site, and **w** www.belizenet.com, which provides excellent travel and accommodations information and links to regional Web sites. The country's best travelers' message board is found at **w** www.belizeforum.com (not to be confused with **w** www.belizeforums.com, which is just an OK message board). Ambergris Caye's Web site, **w** www.ambergriscaye.com, contains good background information for all of Belize and a helpful message board about travel to San Pedro and environs.

For news and current events check out the news digests on **w** www.turq.com/belizefirst and the weekly **w** www.reporterbelize.com.

The entertaining **w** www.belizeans.com offers a quirky look at Belizean lifestyle and culture, with content provided by both resident and expat Belizeans.

BOOKS

Most books are published in different editions by different publishers in different countries. As a result, a book might be a hardcover rarity in one country while it's readily available in paperback in another. Fortunately, bookstores and libraries can do a search by title or author, so your local bookstore or library is the best place to go for advice on the availability of the following recommendations.

Nature & Wildlife

The best all-in-one nature guide is *Belize & Northern Guatemala: The Ecotravellers' Wildlife Guide* (A volume in the The Ecotravellers' Wildlife Guides Series), by Les Beletsky, offering helpful descriptions along with full-color drawings and photographs.

If you're planning on doing some birdwatching, pick up *Birds of Mexico and Northern Central America,* by Steve NG Howell and Sophie Webb, or *A Field Guide to Mexican Birds: Mexico, Guatemala, Belize, El Salvador,* from Peterson Field Guides.

Lonely Planet's *Diving & Snorkeling Belize,* by Franz O Meyer, provides detailed descriptions of dive sites and extensive photos of underwater wildlife.

Jaguar: One Man's Struggle to Establish the World's First Jaguar Preserve, by Alan Rabinowitz, covers the founding of the Jaguar Reserve in Cockscomb Basin.

History & Politics

Emory King publishes the four-volume *Great Story of Belize,* recounting the country's history up to 1950. It's widely available in bookstores and gift shops throughout the country. King's history is quite detailed, but has come under criticism for glamorizing the swashbuckling ways of the early British settlers. A contrasting point of view is put forth in Belize historian Assad Shoman's *13 Chapters in the History of Belize.* Taught in Belize high schools, this book emphasizes the downside of colonialism.

Garifuna History, Language & Culture of Belize, Central America & the Caribbean, by Sebastian Cayetano (available in Belize), gives a thorough overview of the Garifuna people and their culture.

Though it was published in 1995, *Inside Belize,* by Tom Barry, still offers a reasonable description of Belize's social, political and economic climate.

Our Man in Belize (out of print, but worth looking for), by Richard Timothy Conroy, is a fun and engaging tale of Conroy's stint at the US consulate in Belize City in the early 1960s. It accurately describes the flavor of the country, and presents a vivid picture of the devastation wrought on Belize City by Hurricane Hattie.

Mayan History Joyce Kelly's *An Archaeological Guide to Northern Central America* offers the best descriptions of the Mayan sites of Belize, along with those in Guatemala and Mexico.

Locally published by Cubola Productions, *Warlords and Maize Men – A guide to the Maya Sites of Belize,* by Byron Foster, is recommended for its descriptions of the lives of the Maya.

Ronald Wright's *Time Among the Maya: Travels in Belize, Guatemala, and Mexico* relates his many travels along La Ruta Maya in the 1980s. The book provides a good juxtaposition of ancient Mayan history and the present-day Mayas who remain in the region.

Fiction

On Heroes Lizards And Passion, by Zoila Ellis (available in Belize), and *Snapshots of Belize: An Anthology of Short Fiction* (published in Belize by Cubola Productions) feature short stories of past and present Belize.

Emory King

Emory King is one of the best-known personalities of Belize. An American, he settled in Belize in 1953 after having been shipwrecked off the northern cayes. He has become one of the chief chroniclers of Belize life and culture, writing from the perspective of an American expatriate. He's credited with many of the most quotable lines about the country, including, 'If you want to make a small fortune in Belize, start with a big one,' and his books are recommended for anyone who is considering moving down. His books are commonly featured in bookstores and gift shops throughout the country, and can be ordered from **w** www.emoryking.com. They include *I Spent It All in Belize* and *Hey Dad, This is Belize!* (both tales of his personal experience here), and four volumes of *The Great Story of Belize.* His annual *Driving Guide to Beautiful Belize* is a must-have for anyone planning to get behind the wheel.

Recently, Emory has been the national film commissioner of Belize, and was instrumental is bringing film crews here to film *Temptation Island* and the Benjamin Bratt vehicle *After the Storm.*

Belize, by Carlos Ledson Miller, is the closest you'll get to a Belizean bodice-ripper. The story begins in 1961 as Hurricane Hattie approaches, and tells the story of a Belizean-American man and his two sons. It provides details on what Belize City and Ambergris Caye were like 30 years ago and is a fun read when you're able to walk through the neighborhoods mentioned in the book. It offers a realistic portrayal of Belize's recent history covering such subjects as the mahogany industry, drug smuggling, hurricanes, the move to independence and the development of ecotourism.

Cookbooks

Belizious Cuisine, published by the Los Angeles Belizean Educations Network (**w** www.lafn.org/community/laben), features 200 dishes from Belize and instructions for preparing them with easy-to-find spices and ingredients.

General

Rosita Arvigo's *Sastun: My Apprenticeship With a Maya Healer* and *Rainforest Remedies: One Hundred Healing Herbs of Belize,* written with Dr Michael Balick, explore Belize's natural healing movement.

Adapter Kit: Belize: A Traveler's Tools for Living Like a Local, by Lan Sluder, is recommended for those considering settling in Belize, as is Emory King's *How to Invest or Retire in Belize.*

FILMS

There have been a handful of movies filmed in Belize over the years. They're nothing to notify the Academy about, but worth renting for some flavor. The most recent is *After the Storm* (2001), starring Benjamin Bratt and Armand Assante, based on an Ernest Hemingway novel. Best-known is *Mosquito Coast* (1986), starring Harrison Ford and River Phoenix, based on the Paul Theroux novel about a family who moves to the tropics in search of utopia. Belize served as a stand-in for Africa in *Heart of Darkness* (1984), based on the novel by Joseph Conrad, starring John Malkovich, and *Dogs of War* (1980), starring Christopher Walken.

NEWSPAPERS & MAGAZINES

Belizean newspapers are small in size, circulation and interest and present news by party line. *Amandala* (**w** www.belizemall.com/amandala) has the largest circulation. *Belize Times* (**w** www.belizetimes.com) represents the PUP perspective, while the *Guardian* is the voice of the opposition UDP. The *Reporter* (**w** www.reporterbelize.com) appears to present the most neutral coverage, and offers a weekly email version.

Foreign newspapers are difficult to find in the country, so if you need your daily dose of news from home, be prepared to log on in Internet cafés.

RADIO & TV

Love-FM is the most widely broadcast radio station in Belize, with spots at 95.1 and 98.1 on the dial. It's a charming mix of local news, public-service announcements and the world's best love songs. KREM, at 96.5, plays a more modern selection of music.

Channel 5 is the country's primary TV station. Programming consists mainly of re-broadcast US satellite feeds and a few hours of local content, such as local news, ceremonies and special sporting events. Channel 7 also carries some domestic programming, but mainly serves as an events and job board for Belize businesses and the government. There are live news broadcasts on both channels at 6pm weekdays. Most hotels with TVs in their guest rooms provide cable service with several dozen channels, including CNN, BBC, Discovery, HBO, MTV and the major US networks (ABC, NBC, CBS and Fox).

PHOTOGRAPHY

Print film can be purchased in camera stores and gift shops, but slide film is difficult to come by. Be sure to check the freshness date before purchasing.

Always ask permission before photographing people; they'll usually consent, but it's the polite thing to do, especially when you're in the traditional Mayan areas.

Check out Lonely Planet's *Travel Photography,* by Richard I'Anson, for tips on making the most of your vacation snaps.

TIME

North American central standard time (GMT/UTC minus six hours) is the basis of time throughout Belize, although daylight saving time is not observed.

ELECTRICITY

Electrical current and plugs are the same as those used in the USA and Canada – two flat prongs, sometimes with a third, round grounder prong.

WEIGHTS & MEASURES

Both metric and imperial systems are used, so the chart inside the back cover of this book will be helpful to you no matter where you are. Roads are measured in miles, but it's likely that your rental car will measure mileage in kilometers. When you see quarts and gallons, they are the smaller American measure, not the larger British imperial measure.

LAUNDRY

Locations of laundries are listed throughout this book. You can generally get your laundry done in a day if you bring it in early enough. Cost is usually US$5 a load. Self-service Laundromats are rare.

TOILETS

Except in the most remote areas, your toilet will flush. You'll find that most accommodations offer nice, modern, tiled bathrooms, and even many low-end hotels and guest houses offer private baths.

HEALTH

According to the US Centers for Disease Control and Prevention, stomach sicknesses are the most common problems plaguing travelers in Belize, followed by traffic accidents. Your health while traveling depends on your predeparture preparations, your daily health care while traveling and how you handle any medical problem that does develop. While the potential dangers can seem quite frightening, in reality, few travelers will experience anything more than a stomachache. This information is provided for reference in case of need, although for

Medical Kit Checklist

The following is a list of items you should consider including in your medical kit – consult your pharmacist for brands available in your country.

❏ **Aspirin or paracetamol (acetaminophen in the USA)** – for pain or fever

❏ **Antihistamine** – for allergies (eg, hay fever); to ease the itch from insect bites or stings and to prevent motion sickness

❏ **Cold and flu tablets, throat lozenges and nasal decongestant**

❏ **Multivitamins** – for long trips when dietary vitamin intake may be inadequate

❏ **Antibiotics** – for traveling well off the beaten track. See your doctor, as they must be prescribed, and carry the prescription with you.

❏ **Lomotil or immodium** – 'blockers' for diarrhea

❏ **Prochlorperazine or metaclopramide** – for nausea and vomiting

❏ **Rehydration mixture** – to prevent dehydration, which may occur, for example, during bouts of diarrhea – particularly important when traveling with children.

❏ **Insect repellent, waterproof sunscreen, lip balm with sunscreen and eye drops**

❏ **Calamine lotion, hydrocortisone or other sting-relief spray**

❏ **Aloe vera** – to ease irritation from sunburn, bites or stings

❏ **Antifungal cream or powder**

❏ **Antiseptic** – for cuts and grazes

❏ **Bandages, Band-Aids (plasters) and other wound dressings**

❏ **Water-purification tablets or iodine**

❏ **Scissors, tweezers and a thermometer** – note that mercury thermometers are prohibited by airlines and you may no longer pack sharp objects in your carry-on luggage.

Be aware that antibiotics should not be taken indiscriminately, but if you begin a course of antibiotics, finish it. Taking antibiotics can lead to breakouts, stomach discomfort and yeast and urinary tract infections and should be taken only if you feel that there is no alternative.

most visitors it will constitute only entertaining reading.

Mainland Belize is a three-hour flight from Houston and Miami, and it's common for both Belizeans and travelers to head to the states for treatment of major ailments or injuries. Belize has a national system of health care, so any treatment in a public hospital is available at no cost. However, it is recommended that you make a donation to the hospital if you do make a visit. There are private hospitals in Belize City and in Santa Elena in the Cayo District.

Predeparture Planning

Immunizations Discuss vaccination requirements with your doctor. If you're only visiting the cayes, it's likely that you won't need to bother, but it's good common sense to be up-to-date on your vaccinations – diphtheria and tetanus, hepatitis, polio, cholera, rabies and typhoid – before leaving home. There are currently no vaccinations required for entry into Belize, but proof of immunization against yellow fever may be required for entry if you are traveling from an infected country in Africa or Central or South America.

Plan ahead for getting your vaccinations: Some of them require more than one injection, while others should not be given together. Note that some vaccinations should not be given during pregnancy or to people with allergies – discuss this with your doctor. It is recommended that you seek medical advice at least six weeks before traveling. Be aware that there is often a greater risk of disease for children and pregnant women.

Health Insurance Make sure that you have adequate health insurance. See Travel Insurance, under Visas & Documents earlier in this chapter, for details.

Other Preparations Make sure you are healthy before you start traveling. If you are going on a long trip, be sure to see a dentist before you go. If you wear glasses, take a spare pair and your prescription.

If you require a particular medication, take an adequate supply, as it may not be available locally. Take part of the packaging showing the generic name rather than the brand, which will make getting replacements easier. To avoid any problems, it's a good idea to have a legible prescription or letter from your doctor to show that you legally use the medication.

Basic Rules

Food Generally, food is safely prepared in Belize, although when you're in areas that are not widely traveled you may want to avoid unpeeled fruits and vegetables.

Busy restaurants tend to be safest, since the food is cooked and eaten quickly, while empty restaurants are questionable, since ingredients may sit for a while and dishes may need to be reheated. If a place looks clean and well run, then the food is probably fine. When in doubt, inspect the kitchen to see if surfaces and utensils look clean, perishables are in a cool spot and animals and bugs are not in sight.

Water The quality of water varies from place to place in Belize, but most of the tap water here comes from rainwater. Ask if the water is safe before drinking it and, when in doubt, stick to bottled water. Ice is mostly made from purified water and restaurants know better than to serve you anything else. Again, when in doubt, ask, but it's more likely to be for your peace of mind than your stomach's comfort.

Environmental Hazards

Heat Exhaustion Dehydration and salt deficiency can cause heat exhaustion. Take time to acclimatize to high temperatures, drink sufficient liquids and do not do anything too physically demanding until you're used to the heat.

Salt deficiency is characterized by fatigue, lethargy, headaches, giddiness and muscle cramps; salt tablets may help, but adding extra salt to your food is better.

Motion Sickness Eating lightly before and during a trip will reduce the chances of motion sickness. Try to find a place that minimizes movement – near the wing on aircraft,

and in the center of boats and buses. Fresh air usually helps; reading and cigarette smoke hurt. Keeping an eye on the road, while you're on the road, and keeping an eye on the horizon when you're out to sea can help you maintain your equilibrium, and your breakfast. Commercial motion-sickness medications can cause drowsiness but are often effective. You'll need to take it before a trip commences, sometimes the night before. Ginger (available in capsule form) and peppermint (including mint-flavored sweets and gums) are natural preventatives.

Prickly Heat Prickly heat is an itchy rash caused by excessive perspiration trapped under the skin. It usually strikes people who have just arrived in a hot climate. Keeping cool, bathing often, drying the skin and using a mild talcum or prickly-heat powder may help.

Sunburn In the tropics, in the desert or at sea you can get sunburned surprisingly quickly, even through cloud cover. Use a sunscreen, a hat, and a barrier cream for your nose and lips. Calamine lotion, aloe or a commercial after-sun preparation are good for mild sunburn. Protect your eyes with good-quality sunglasses, particularly if you will be near water.

Infectious Diseases

Diarrhea Simple things – such as a change of water, food or climate – can cause a mild bout of diarrhea, but a few rushed toilet trips with no other symptoms is not indicative of a major problem.

Dehydration is the main danger with any diarrhea – children and the elderly dehydrate particularly quickly. Fluid replacement remains the mainstay of managing dehydration. Soda water, weak black tea with a little sugar, or soft drinks allowed to go flat and diluted 50% with clean water are all good.

Gut-paralyzing drugs like Lomotil or immodium can be used to bring relief from the symptoms, although they do not actually cure the problem. Use these drugs only when absolutely necessary – that is, if you must travel.

Note that these drugs are not recommended for children under the age of 12.

Antibiotics may be required in certain situations: diarrhea with blood or mucus (dysentery), diarrhea with fever, profuse watery diarrhea, persistent diarrhea not improving after 48 hours and severe diarrhea. These suggest a more serious cause of diarrhea, and in these situations, the gut-paralyzing drugs should be avoided, as should alcohol.

Hepatitis Hepatitis is a general term for inflammation of the liver. It is a common disease worldwide. There are several different viruses that cause hepatitis, and they differ in the way that they are transmitted. The symptoms are similar in all forms of the illness and include fever, chills, headache, fatigue, feelings of weakness, and aches and pains; these are followed by loss of appetite, nausea, vomiting, abdominal pain, dark urine, light-colored feces, jaundiced (yellow) skin and yellowing of the whites of the eyes. People who have had hepatitis should avoid alcohol for some time after the illness, as the liver needs time to recover.

Hepatitis A is transmitted by contaminated food and drinking water. You should seek medical advice, but there is not much you can do apart from resting, drinking lots of fluids, eating lightly and avoiding fatty foods. Hepatitis E is transmitted in the same way as hepatitis A; it can be particularly serious in pregnant women.

There are almost 300 million chronic carriers of **hepatitis B** in the world. It is spread through contact with infected blood, blood products or bodily fluids – for example, through sexual contact, unsterilized needles and blood transfusions – or through contact with blood via small breaks in the skin. Other risk situations include shaving or having a tattoo or body piercing done with contaminated equipment. The symptoms of hepatitis B may be more severe than type A, and the disease can lead to long-term problems, such as chronic liver damage, liver cancer or a long-term carrier state.

Hepatitis C and D are spread in the same way as hepatitis B and can also lead to long-term complications.

There are vaccines against hepatitis A and B, but there are currently no vaccines against the other types of hepatitis. Following the basic rules about food and water (hepatitis A and E) and avoiding risky situations (hepatitis B, C and D) are important preventative measures.

HIV & AIDS Infection with the human immunodeficiency virus (HIV) may lead to acquired immune deficiency syndrome (AIDS), which is a fatal disease. Exposure to contaminated blood, blood products or bodily fluids may put you at risk, so it goes without saying that you should not have unprotected sex, nor should you share needles. However, if you still need convincing, be aware that Belize has one of the highest reported HIV infection rates in Central America. Vaccinations, acupuncture, tattooing and body piercing can be potentially as dangerous as intravenous drug use.

If you do need an injection, ask to see the syringe unwrapped in front of you, or take a needle and syringe pack with you. HIV/AIDS can also be spread through infected-blood transfusions. While fear of HIV infection should never preclude treatment for serious medical conditions, you may want to avoid bloodwork if possible. Belizeans often travel to Houston, Miami or Guatemala for serious ailments. In the recent past, a tragic mistake was made at Karl Heusner Memorial Hospital and untested, HIV-tainted blood was used in a series of blood transfusions. Everything indicates that safeguards are now in place to assure that this doesn't happen again.

Sexually Transmitted Diseases STDs are spread through sexual contact with an infected partner. Abstinence is the only 100% preventative measure, however, using condoms is also effective. See the HIV/AIDS and Hepatitis sections, above. Other STDs include gonorrhea, herpes and syphilis: sores, blisters or rashes around the genitals and discharges or pain when urinating are common symptoms. In some STDs, such as wart virus or chlamydia, symptoms may be less marked or not observed at all, especially in women. Syphilis symptoms eventually disappear completely, but the disease continues and can cause severe problems in later years. If you do have unprotected sex, get tested when you return home. The treatment of gonorrhea and syphilis is done with antibiotics. Each sexually transmitted disease requires specific antibiotics. There is no cure for herpes, which causes blisters, or for HIV.

Typhoid A dangerous gut infection, typhoid fever is caused by contaminated water and food. Medical help must be sought.

In its early stages, sufferers may feel they have a bad cold or flu on the way, as early symptoms are a headache, body aches and a fever that rises a little each day until it is around 104°F (40°C) or more. The victim's pulse is often slow relative to the degree of fever present – unlike a normal fever, during which the pulse increases. There may also be vomiting, abdominal pain, diarrhea or constipation.

In the second week, the high fever and slow pulse continue, and a few pink spots may appear on the body; trembling, delirium, weakness, weight loss and dehydration may occur. Complications such as pneumonia, perforated bowel or meningitis may occur.

Insect-Borne Diseases

Malaria This disease is present in some rural areas of Belize, but cases are rare and antimalarial treatments are advisable only if you're to be spending an extended period of time in the jungle. This serious and potentially fatal disease is spread by mosquito bites. Symptoms range from fever, chills and sweating, headache, diarrhea and abdominal pains to a vague feeling of ill health. Seek medical help immediately if malaria is suspected. Without treatment, malaria can rapidly become more serious and can be fatal.

Travelers are advised to prevent mosquito bites at all times. The following are some preventative measures:

- Wear light-colored clothing.
- Wear long pants and long-sleeved shirts.
- Use mosquito repellents containing the compound DEET on exposed areas (prolonged overuse of DEET may be harmful, especially to children, but its use is considered preferable to being bitten by disease-transmitting mosquitoes). Use only the recommended quantity of DEET; overapplying doesn't increase effectiveness.
- Avoid perfumes or aftershave.
- Use a mosquito net – it may be worth carrying your own.
- Apply repellent to clothes to deter mosquitoes and other insects.

Dengue Fever This viral disease is transmitted by mosquitoes and is fast becoming one of the top public-health problems in the tropical world. Unlike the malaria mosquito, the *Aedes aegypti* mosquito, which transmits the dengue virus, is most active during the day and is found mainly in urban areas, in and around human dwellings.

Signs and symptoms of dengue fever include a sudden onset of high fever, headache, joint and muscle pains (hence its old name, 'breakbone fever'), and nausea and vomiting. A rash of small red spots sometimes appears three to four days after the onset of fever. In the early phase of illness, dengue may be mistaken for other infectious diseases, including malaria and influenza.

You should seek medical attention as soon as possible if you think you may be infected. A blood test can exclude malaria and indicate the possibility of dengue fever. There is no specific treatment for dengue. Recovery may be prolonged, with fatigue lasting for several weeks. Aspirin should be avoided, as it increases the risk of hemorrhaging. There is no vaccine against dengue fever. The best prevention is to avoid mosquito bites at all times by covering up and by using insect repellents containing the compound DEET and mosquito nets – see the Malaria section, earlier, for more advice on avoiding mosquito bites.

Cuts, Bites & Stings

Cuts & Scratches Wash any cut well and treat it with an antiseptic. Where possible, avoid bandages and Band-Aids, which can keep wounds wet. Coral cuts are notoriously slow to heal, and if they are not adequately cleaned, small pieces of coral can become embedded in the wound.

Bites & Stings Bee and wasp stings are usually more painful than dangerous, however, in people who are allergic to them, severe breathing difficulties may occur, requiring urgent medical care. Calamine lotion or a sting-relief spray will give relief, and ice packs will reduce the pain and swelling. There are some spiders with dan-

The Botfly – Myth or Mayhem?

You will undoubtedly hear tales of botfly larvae infestations while you're in Belize. Rarely will you actually meet someone who's had the displeasure of personal botfly acquaintance – it always seems to have happened to a 'friend of a friend' or writers of other guidebooks. But real scientists concur that botflies come into being in a compellingly disgusting manner.

Here's what happens: The mother botfly lays her egg on the rostrum of a mosquito. When the mosquito bites, the botfly egg is deposited under the skin of its unsuspecting victim. The botfly hatches into a larva and begins to grow. Unsuspecting victim goes on with life, maybe goes home after vacation, and one day notices that one mosquito bite isn't healing, in fact, it's getting larger. Sometimes the victim goes to the doctor, but the doctor, not realizing that the patient has been to the land of the botfly, sends him/her home with some unhelpful antibiotic cream. The 'mosquito bite' continues to grow, and at some point the victim notices – horrors! – that the bite is moving. Squirming, really, as if there is a worm growing under the skin. And there is!

Maybe then victim goes back to doctor, thinks to tell him/her of his/her trip to Belize, the doctor puts two and two together. Other stories have quick-thinking well-informed moms, mates or jungle healers reaching this conclusion and then exorcising the botfly themselves. How, you ask? The answer is as gross as the botfly itself. In order to breathe, the botfly larva runs a tube from its body to the surface of its carrier's skin. One treatment is to cover the bump with Vaseline – the botfly will have to work its way out of your skin to breath, and then you must kill it. Another option: Place a tobacco leaf over your carbuncle. The nicotine kills the larva, but then you or a loved one must tweeze it out. Method number three is much more humane: Place a small piece of hamburger or steak on the surface of the skin over the botfly airhole. The larva will worm out of your flesh and into the meat. To the botfly, cow is tastier than human, it seems. Then you can squish it and discard.

Botflies are found in deep jungle, so you're not likely to get one by hanging out on Caye Caulker. If you're spending time in the bush, avoiding mosquito bites and washing thoroughly daily will help keep the larvae away. And always let your doctor know if you've been someplace unusual.

gerous bites, but antivenins are usually available.

Scorpions aren't uncommon in the jungles of Belize. Stings are notoriously painful, and in some rare cases they can be fatal. Scorpions often hide in shoes or clothing. When you're camping, or in a rustic setting, be sure to inspect your clothing carefully before dressing and shake your shoes before inserting your toes.

Sandflies are present on beach areas near mangrove swamps along the coast of Belize. Their bites are relatively harmless, although they can be uncomfortable and unsightly. Unfortunately, insect repellant with DEET isn't always effective against them. Some recommend keeping them away by covering your legs and ankles with baby oil (be careful to avoid sunburn); citronella is also a popular remedy although it seems that these repellents don't work for everyone. For long-term travelers there's good news – most develop a tolerance to their bites after a few weeks.

Jellyfish Avoid contact with these sea creatures, which have stinging tentacles. At certain times of the year, jellyfish larvae, known in Belize as 'pica pica,' are present in the sea. Your dive master will warn you if the pica pica is about. Even at this early stage they can sting, and care should be taken to avoid contact – wear a full wet suit and apply oil or Vaseline to exposed skin. Dousing in vinegar will deactivate any stingers that have not 'fired.' Calamine lotion, antihistamines and analgesics may reduce the reaction and relieve the pain.

Snakes To minimize your chances of being bitten, always wear boots, socks and long pants when walking through undergrowth where snakes may be present. Don't put your hands into holes and crevices, and be careful when collecting firewood.

Snakebites do not cause instantaneous death, and antivenins are usually available. Immediately wrap the bitten limb tightly, as you would for a sprained ankle, and then attach a splint to immobilize it. Keep the victim still and seek medical help, bringing the dead snake, if possible, for identification.

Don't attempt to catch the snake if there is a possibility of being bitten again. Tourniquets and sucking out the poison are now comprehensively discredited.

Women's Health

Gynecological Problems Poor diet and lowered resistance due to the use of antibiotics for stomach upsets can lead to vaginal infections when traveling in hot climates. Wearing loose-fitting clothes and cotton underwear may help prevent these infections. Yeast infections, characterized by a rash, itch and discharge, can be treated with Nystatin suppositories, now available over the counter in the US. If you're susceptible to yeast infections, it's not a bad idea to bring treatment with you. Alternatively, douches of vinegar, lemon juice or yogurt can be used for treatment. Trichomoniasis is a more serious infection; symptoms are a discharge and a burning sensation when urinating. Male sexual partners must also be treated, and if a vinegar-water douche is not effective, medical attention should be sought. Metronidazole (Flagyl) is the prescribed drug.

Pregnancy Pregnant women should avoid all unnecessary medication, although vaccinations and malarial prophylactics should still be taken where needed. Some vaccinations that are normally used to prevent serious diseases (eg, yellow fever) are not advisable during pregnancy. In addition, some diseases are much more serious in pregnant women (and may increase the risk of problems with the pregnancy). Additional care should be taken to prevent illness, and particular attention should be paid to diet and nutrition.

Most miscarriages occur during the first three months of pregnancy, so this is the most risky time to travel. The last three months of pregnancy should be spent within reasonable distance of good medical care, as serious problems can develop at this time.

WOMEN TRAVELERS

In Belize, especially on the cayes, it's commonly believed that unescorted women are on the lookout for male companionship, and the men in Belize, especially in the heavily touristed areas, can be quite forward with their advances. In most cases, this is done light-heartedly, but it can be disconcerting if you're from a culture where men are less overt in their attentions. Do like your mother told you, be direct, say no, then ignore them – they're likely to go away. If you're feeling particularly hassled, seek out the company of a local woman or a family; this tends to give you an extra layer of respectability, which will cause your harasser to back away. Avoid situations in which you might find yourself alone with one or more men unknown to you at remote archaeological sites, on empty city streets or on secluded stretches of beach.

GAY & LESBIAN TRAVELERS

There isn't much of a gay scene in Belize, although we wouldn't go so far as to say that people are secretive or closeted, just lowkey. While it's an incredibly tolerant society, the underlying Central American machismo and traditional religious beliefs make Belize a place where same-sex couples might want to exercise caution when it comes to displaying affection in public.

A growing number of gay- and lesbianoriented tour operators offer package tours and cruises to destinations throughout Central America. Visit the Out & About Web site (**W** www.outandabout.com) for a comprehensive list of gay and lesbian tour operators and links to their individual sites; you can also find links to other gay travel sites and a list of recommended travel agencies.

Further information on gay and lesbian travel in Latin America can be obtained through the US or Australian offices of the International Gay & Lesbian Travel Association (IGLTA; ☎ 800-448-8550 in the USA, iglta@iglta.org, **W** www.iglta.com); in Australia, contact IGLTA Australia/NZ/Asia/Pacific (☎ 2-9818 6669, fax 2-9878 6660, Rhopkins@iglta.org).

DISABLED TRAVELERS

In the US, Mobility International (☎ 541-343-1284, fax 541-343-6812, **W** www.miusa.org), PO Box 10767, Eugene, OR 97440, advises disabled travelers on mobility issues. In Australia and New Zealand, try the National Information Communication Awareness Network (Nican; ☎ 02-6285 3713, **W** www.nican.com.au), PO Box 407, Curtin, ACT 2605. In the UK, there's the Royal Association for Disability and Rehabilitation (Radar; ☎ 020-7250 3222, **W** www.radar.org.uk), 12 City Forum, 250 City Rd, London EC1V 8AF.

Some other sources on the Internet include **W** www.access-able.com, which provides good general travel advice, and the Emerging Horizons site (**W** www.emerging horizons.com), which has well-written articles and regular columns chock full of handy advice. For a list of services available to disabled passengers by airline, go to **W** www.everybody.co.uk/airindex.htm.

SENIOR TRAVELERS

Belize is quite popular with active senior citizens, and the travel industry is skilled at meeting the comfort levels of a variety of age groups. You'll find that you're treated with friendly, casual respect wherever you go. Let your hosts know in advance if you have mobility problems or special needs – tour operators will do their best to match you up with the right groups and activities. Be sure to allow yourself time to adjust to the heat when you first arrive, and drink plenty of water.

The American Association of Retired Persons (AARP; ☎ 800-424-3410, **W** www.aarp.org) is an advocacy group for Americans 50 years and older and a good resource for travel bargains. Non-US residents can get one-year memberships for US$10.

Grand Circle Travel (☎ 617-350-7500, 800-350-7500) offers escorted tours and travel information in a variety of formats, and distributes a useful free booklet, 'Going Abroad: 101 Tips for Mature Travelers.'

TRAVEL WITH CHILDREN

Children are highly regarded in Belize and can often break down barriers and open doors to local hospitality. Most of the major attractions in the region – sea life, exploring caves and ruins, watching for birds, wildlife and bugs – are as delightful for kids as they are for grown-ups, and most activities are set up to accommodate children. You'll find plenty of traveling families all over the country, especially during North American school breaks. For a wealth of good ideas, pick up a copy of Lonely Planet's *Travel with Children,* by Cathy Lanigan.

DANGERS & ANNOYANCES

Petty theft is the greatest danger (and annoyance) to travelers in Belize. Take care not to show obvious displays of wealth. Keep a close eye on camera or computer equipment. Don't leave valuables in your car, especially in plain view. Keep an eye on your bags when you're traveling by bus.

One of the leading causes of death in Belize is the automobile. The country is a network of two-lane roads and the quality of vehicles ranges from speedy SUVs to lumbering sugarcane freighters. Passing happens frequently and often not safely. Wear your seatbelt, take care driving after dark (not every vehicle has functioning lights) and keep an eye on what's going on behind you and in front of you.

EMERGENCIES

Belize's emergency line is ☎ 90, which works for police, medical, fire or marine emergencies. There is a force of tourist police operating in Belize City, San Pedro and Caye Caulker (see each section for local numbers). If you run into problems let both the regular police and tourist police know, as well as your hotelier. It's a small country, everyone seems to know each other and word travels fast, so if you report your problems you're likely to help others avoid them.

BUSINESS HOURS

Banking hours vary from bank to bank, but most are open 8am to 1:30pm Monday to Thursday and 8am to 4:30pm Friday. Shops and businesses often close for lunch during the noon hour. Most businesses, offices and city restaurants close on Sunday. Note that in smaller towns, the popular Belizean restaurants usually close before 6pm.

PUBLIC HOLIDAYS & SPECIAL EVENTS

In the following list, dates are specified where applicable, and national holidays are denoted with an asterisk.

January 1 – New Year's Day*

February (dates vary) – Fiesta de Carnival – celebrated in northern Belize, Sunday to Tuesday before the beginning of Lent

March 9 – Baron Bliss Day* – honors the memory of one of the great benefactors of Belize

April (dates vary) – Holy Week – various services and processions are held in the week leading up to Easter Sunday.

May 1 – Labor Day*

First weekend in May – Cashew Festival – Crooked Tree Village, Belize

May 25 – Commonwealth Day*

June (date varies) – Feast of San Pedro – San Pedro, Ambergris Caye

June (dates vary) – Lobster Season opens – Placencia, Caye Caulker and San Pedro have lobster festivals on successive weekends in June and early July, after the season officially opens, usually the first or second weekend of the month.

July (dates vary) – Benque Viejo Festival – Benque Viejo del Carmen, Cayo

August (dates vary) – Feast of St Luis – San Antonio, Toledo

August (date varies) – Costa Maya Festival – San Pedro, Ambergris Caye – a celebration of Mayan coastal culture with participants from Belize and the Yucatán

September 10 – National Day* (St George's Caye Day)

September 21 – Independence Day*

October 12 – Pan American Day* (Columbus Day)

November 19 – Garifuna Settlement Day – Dangriga and Hopkins

December 25 – Christmas*

December 26 – Boxing Day*

ACTIVITIES
Diving & Snorkeling
Boasting the longest barrier reef in the Western Hemisphere and three out of the four fringing coral atolls in the Caribbean, Belize is a year-round magnet for divers and snorkelers.

Caving
Cave-exploration is big business in western and southern Belize. Check those sections for details. Be aware that some cave tours are more strenuous than others, and let your tour operator know about your physical limitations before setting out.

Bicycling
Mountain-biking has become a common way to explore the hills in western Belize. It's been slower to catch on in other parts of the country, because the less-traveled tourist routes have difficulty keeping and maintaining bikes that will be good enough for the rough terrain of rural Belize. Bicycling is a common and pleasant mode of transportation in the towns and villages of the country, and, outside of Belize City, it's easy to arrange rentals.

Kayaking & Rafting
The Mopan and Macal Rivers in western Belize offer great opportunities for kayaking, as do the rivers of southern Belize. There's not much rough water to worry about, mainly it's a leisurely activity. Sea kayaking is popular out in the cayes.

Hiking
Most of the hiking that you'll do in Belize is going to be with a guide and for the purposes of nature viewing, not endurance testing. There is an extensive network of trails through the region, but they are not clearly marked for first-time visitors. An exception is Cockscomb Basin Wildlife Sanctuary, which has a well-maintained 12-mile trail network. Cockscomb and Mountain Pine Ridge are the most challenging areas for hikers, since most of Belize's terrain elsewhere is flat.

It gets hot and humid and buggy out in the bush, so always start early, bring plenty of water and protect yourself from mosquitoes.

Sailing & Windsurfing
Boating is the name of the game in all of the coastal destinations. Because the reef protects the shoreline from surge, it's possible to sail right from the shore. One word of caution – there's plenty of powerboat traffic off the coasts, so it's important to keep to less congested areas, especially as a novice.

Fishing
Anglers are attracted to this part of the world for the chance to achieve a Grand Slam: catching bonefish, permit and tarpon all in one day. In addition, wahoo, sailfish, snook, snapper, barracuda and grouper also bite, mostly on a catch-and-release basis.

WORK
It's pretty tough for foreigners to get work in Belize; the government has very strict labor laws in the interests of employing a local workforce. To obtain legal work, you must first apply for residency, which is possible after having lived in Belize continuously for six months. The fee for legal residence is US$100 and depending on your nationality you may be required to pay a deposit as well, which is refundable after three years. Your prospective employer must then petition the labor department to hire you, proving that every effort was made to hire a Belizean national. For more information, contact the Department of Immigration & Nationality Services (☎ 8-22611, 8-22423) or the Labour Department (☎ 8-22204), both in Belmopan.

Volunteer Work
Teachers for a Better Belize (☎ 314-822-1569, ⓦ www.twc.org/belize/credits.html), 13606 Peacock Farms Rd, St Louis, MO 63131-1232, is a US-based organization that sends volunteers to schools in the Toledo District to train local teachers.

There are several organizations that run volunteer expeditions in Belize. Among them are Raleigh International (☎ 020-7371 8585, W www.raleighinternational.org), 27 Parsons Green Lane, London SW6 4HZ UK, and Trekforce Expeditions (☎ 020-7828 2275, W www.trekforce.org.uk/about.htm), 34 Buckingham Palace Rd, London, SW1W. Contact the International Volunteer Programs Association (W www.volunteerinternational.org) for more recommendations.

ACCOMMODATIONS

Accommodations here range from quaint grass shacks to luxury lodges. Belize is more costly than other Central American destinations, so the budget options listed in this book will tend to be quite basic.

The Belize Tourism Board requires that all businesses offering travelers accommodations be licensed and publish a rate schedule. Bargaining is not the norm here, but in slower times it's fine to ask about corporate rates or discounts for multi-day stays. Rates depend on where you are. You'll always pay more for coastal access and views, but rates will be lower in southern or northern Belize than in the northern cayes or in Cayo.

You may want to book ahead on festival weekends, or if you're staying in a place that is particularly popular (these are usually noted in the text).

The Belize Tourism Board has encouraged budget hotels to upscale to include tiled bathrooms in most rooms, so you'll find private baths available in most of the country's accommodations. There isn't a formal network of hostels in the country, but each town has at least one bargain-basement accommodation, where you can arrange for a bunk in a cheap room. If you're traveling on a narrow shoestring, consider bringing your own bedding and mosquito net.

Camping is done fairly casually in Belize; some of the lower-priced guest houses have campsites, but they'll be fairly primitive. If you're camping, ask around, it's likely that you'll be able to make informal arrangements. You will need to bring your own equipment, and a strong mosquito net is recommended.

FOOD

Being a young, small, somewhat isolated and relatively poor country, Belize never developed an elaborate native cuisine. Recipes in Belize are mostly borrowed – from the UK, the Caribbean, Mexico and the USA. Even so, there is some good food to be had, especially the fresh-fish options available in seaside locales. Each community has its own local favorites. In the north and west you'll find more Central American dishes on menus.

Beans and rice prevail on Belizean menus and plates. They come in two varieties: 'rice and beans,' wherein the rice and beans are cooked together, and 'stew beans with rice,' where beans in a soupy stew are served in a bowl, and rice is served separately on a plate. Each variation is usually served with chicken, beef, pork or fish. For garnish, sometimes you'll get coleslaw, potato or fried plantain. Both varieties of rice and beans are flavored with coconut milk.

Meals are not usually very spicy, but the popular Marie Sharp's hot sauces are at virtually every table to liven things up if you need it (see the boxed text 'Marie Sharp' in the Southern Belize chapter).

Some restaurants serve wild game such as armadillo, venison and the guinea-pig-like gibnut (also called 'paca'). Conservationists frown on this practice.

Garifuna dishes sometimes appear on restaurant menus, but there are few Garifuna restaurants in the country. If you have a chance to try a Garifuna meal you shouldn't pass it up. The dish you'll see most commonly on menus is 'boil-up,' a stew made of root vegetables and beef or chicken. Less common is *alabundiga,* a dish of grated green bananas, coconut cream, spices, boiled potato and peppers served with fried fish fillet (often snapper) and rice. Similar to alabundiga but without the vegetables, *tapu* is shredded green banana, cooked in coconut milk and spices, served with fish.

Rice & Beans

Following is a basic recipe for rice and beans. Everyone has their variations on this recipe, but the common denominator to this Belizean classic (beyond the rice and beans) is that it's always flavored with coconut milk and cooked uncovered, which helps give the rice its thick chewy consistency.

(Serves 4-6)

1 cup dried navy, pinto or black beans (or 2 cups canned beans if you're in a hurry)
2 cloves garlic, chopped
1 small onion, chopped
$^1/_2$ tsp ground cumin
1 tsp each oregano, thyme, paprika, ginger and cilantro
1 tsp recado paste (optional; a smokey-flavored spice found in specialty markets)
1 bay leaf
2 cups uncooked rice
up to 1 cup of coconut milk
salt & pepper to taste

If using dried beans, wash, rinse, soak overnight and drain beans. In a large pot or Dutch oven, add beans, garlic, onion, spices, bay leaf and enough water to cover the mixture by 1 inch. Cook slowly for two to three hours, or until tender, adding water to keep beans covered. If using canned beans, drain, rinse and add enough fresh water to cover the beans by 1 inch. Add garlic, onion, spices and bay leaf and simmer on low heat for about 20 minutes to flavor the beans.

Add rice and coconut milk (it has a strong flavor and is high in calories, so you may not want to add an entire cup) and enough water to cover mixture by 1 inch; bring to a boil, then turn down heat and simmer uncovered until liquid is absorbed and rice is soft (it may be necessary to add more water). This should take around 25 minutes. Salt and pepper to taste.

Serve with chicken, beef or fish, or on its own.

Mayan meals are hard to come by unless you're in the villages of southern Belize. *Caldo* – a stew usually made with chicken (sometimes beef or pork), corn and root vegetables – is the most common Mayan dish served in the villages.

Mexican snacks, such as tacos, *salabutes* and tostadas – all a variation on the fried tortilla, meat and cheese theme – are often available as midday snacks from food carts or small cafés. Mexican soups, such as *chirmole* (chicken with a chile-chocolate sauce) and *escabeche* (chicken with lime and onions), commonly appear on menus.

In the beach towns of San Pedro, Caye Caulker and Placencia, you'll have no problems lining up a variety of meals – from banana pancakes to cheese quesadillas to burgers and, of course, the best and freshest

seafood around. Reef fish are always on the menu. Lobster is available from mid-June to mid-February (to discourage poaching, don't order it the rest of the year), and it's always the most expensive item on the menu. Conch season begins when lobster season ends. This large snail-like sea creature has a chewy consistency, much like calamari, and is often prepared in ceviche or conch fritters. Seafood is barbecued, steamed or stewed. A common preparation is 'Creole-style,' where seafood, peppers, onions and tomatoes are stewed together.

Vegetarian items are not hard to come by in most of Belize, but if you're camping, visiting rural areas or taking part in a beach barbecue you should make your requirements known well before setting off. Be prepared for rice, beans and tortillas. Stew beans are often prepared with ham or bacon, so you might want to double-check on base ingredients before ordering.

DRINKS
Nonalcoholic Drinks
Delicious and refreshing fruit juices are available throughout Belize. Most commonly served are orange, papaya and mango, but you'll also see watermelon, soursop and grapefruit juices on the menu.

Brewed coffee or espresso drinks are a rarity here, so when you find them, be sure to enjoy. Coffee is often of the instant variety. Tea and milo are readily available.

Because of refrigeration issues, fresh milk is not always available in restaurants; instead, canned condensed milk or reconstituted powdered milk will be served.

Alcoholic Drinks
Belikin is the native beer of Belize (the main temple of Altun Ha is pictured on each bottle) and you'll be hard-pressed to find any other beer on the menu, except in the resorts. Fear not, the Belikin is always cold and refreshing. Most commonly served is Belikin Regular, a lager, but Belikin recently began brewing a lower calorie, lower alcohol beer, called Lighthouse Lager. It's lighter mostly because it comes in a smaller bottle, but it's quickly become popular all over the country. Belikin Stout is also available in the same bottles as Belikin Regular; the only way to identify which is which is to check the bottle tops: Stout are blue, regular are green. Cost is usually around US$2 a bottle, although this can vary from place to place.

Rum is prevalent in Belize. One Barrel, a thick, spicy concoction, recently was judged the best rum in the Caribbean. Coconut rum is also enjoyed throughout the country. Special rum punches made with delicious fresh fruit juices are usually on the menu at upscale bars. Although probably not indigenous to Belize, the national drink, according to Belize bartenders, is a coconut rum–pineapple juice concoction known as the 'panty-ripper' or 'brief-ripper,' depending on your gender.

Middle-class Belizeans have recently begun discovering wine. Red wines imported from Australia are usually the best-priced wines on the menu, although it's possible to get reasonably priced Californian and Chilean wines as well.

ENTERTAINMENT
Concerts featuring local musicians or traveling bands are held intermittently throughout the country. When big acts (such as Santino's Messengers, Titiman Flores or Punta Rebels) do play, the shows are promoted nationally on radio programs, and locally by means of postering. Live music usually brings in crowds of all ages, and Belizeans will travel from all corners of the country to enjoy. Concerts tend to last well into the early morning hours.

Check local newspapers for information on traditional performances. The Bliss Institute in Belize City often stages music and dance. There's usually a musical component to every festival in the country – large tents are erected and bands and dance troupes come to perform all night long. Maya and Punta performances are often staged at high-end resorts throughout Belize; these often seem canned, but sometimes it's the best you're going to get, since cultural performances don't happen regularly. Again, notices of performances will be hung all over town.

SPECTATOR SPORTS
It's fairly easy to find out when and where sporting events are happening. Just ask around. Formal and informal league soccer and basketball are played throughout the country, and games usually draw a big, high-spirited crowd. Bicycle and horse races are sometimes held on major national holidays. The Marion Jones Sports Complex in Belize City frequently hosts sporting events. Call the National Sports Council (☎ 2-72051, 2-72092, 2-75335) for a schedule of sporting events in Belize City and beyond.

SHOPPING
Belizeans do not trade in handicrafts at the level that Mexicans and Guatemalans do; instead, most gift shops in the country

do a booming business in T-shirts, imported sarongs and Belikin beer paraphernalia. Popular handicrafts from the region include folding mahogany deck chairs, *zirecote* (ironwood) carvings of various sizes, baskets woven by Mayan women in southern Belize and carved rosewood bowls. These make nice souvenirs, but they tend to be expensive when compared with similar items purchased in Guatemala or Mexico.

Some Belizean-made consumables are popular as souvenirs and useful when you're traveling. Among these are Rainforest Remedies, a line of all-natural health products – digestive aids, insect repellents, salves etc – produced by the Ix Chel Farm near San Ignacio (W www.rainforestremedies.com) – see the Around San Ignacio (Cayo) section in the Cayo District (Western Belize) chapter for more information; Marie Sharp's hot sauce; and Rasta Pasta spice packets, for creating traditional Belizean dishes at home. Books and recordings by Belizean artists can be purchased from Cubola Productions (W www.belizebusiness.com/cubola).

Getting There & Away

AIR
Airports & Airlines

Philip Goldson International Airport (BZE), at Ladyville, 9 miles (16km) northwest of the Belize City center, handles all international flights. The smaller Municipal Airport (TZA), closer to town, handles the bulk of small-plane travel within Belize (see the Getting Around chapter for information).

Three carriers serve Belize from international destinations: American (direct from Miami and Dallas), Continental and Grupo TACA (direct from Houston). Most international air routes to Belize City go through these gateways. American and Continental travel from cities throughout the US, while Grupo TACA serves Belize indirectly from New Orleans, Los Angeles, New York and Toronto, with connections in San Salvador (El Salvador) or Guatemala City (Guatemala).

Grupo TACA also offers direct flights between Belize City and San Salvador, and Roatan and San Pedro Sula (Honduras), as well as connecting flights from Guatemala, Panama, Nicaragua and Costa Rica.

The above-mentioned airlines all have offices in Belize City:

American Airlines (☎ 2-32522, fax 2-31730, ☎ 800-433-7300 in the US & Canada, ⓦ www.aa.com), on New Rd at Queen St

Continental Airlines (☎ 2-78309, 2-78223, fax 2-78114, ☎ 800-231-0856 in the US & Canada, ⓦ www.continental.com), 80 Regent St

Grupo TACA (☎ 2-72332, 2-77257, fax 2-75213, ☎ 800-535-8780 in the US & Canada, ⓦ www.taca.com), 41 Albert St

Buying Tickets

On any trip, the airplane ticket usually takes the biggest bite out of your wallet, but you can greatly reduce the cost by doing a little research. Long-term travelers will find a host of discount tickets valid for 12 months, permitting multiple stopovers with open dates. It gets a little trickier for short-

---

Warning

The information in this chapter is particularly vulnerable to change: Prices for international travel are volatile, routes are introduced and canceled, schedules change, special deals come and go, and rules and visa requirements are amended. Airlines and governments seem to take a perverse pleasure in making price structures and regulations as complicated as possible. You should check directly with the airline or a travel agent to make sure you understand how a ticket (and any ticket you may buy) works. In addition, the travel industry is highly competitive, and there are many lurks and perks.

The upshot of this is that you should get opinions, quotes and advice from as many airlines and travel agents as possible before you part with your hard-earned cash. The details given in this chapter should be regarded as pointers and are not a substitute for your own careful, up-to-date research.

---

term travel, but cheaper fares are available by traveling midweek, staying over a Saturday night or taking advantage of quickie promotional offers, often available on the Internet.

American, Continental and TACA all offer last-minute 'Web specials,' on their Internet sites. These are often great deals, but in order to take advantage of them your dates need to be flexible, and the tickets are usually non-refundable or levy high change fees.

Travel agents offer good deals as well; they regularly buy blocks of seats at a discount and pass the savings on to travelers. As such, travel agents often offer better deals than the airlines themselves. Plus, travel agents usually have a cancellation or ticket-change policy that lets you alter your ticket for a small fee, whereas Web specials typically do not. If possible, track down an agent that specializes in booking flights to

Air Travel Glossary

Cancellation Penalties If you have to cancel or change a discounted ticket, there are often heavy penalties involved; insurance can sometimes be taken out against these penalties. Some airlines impose penalties on regular tickets as well, particularly against 'no-show' passengers.

Courier Fares Businesses often need to send urgent documents or freight securely and quickly. Courier companies hire people to accompany the package through customs and, in return, offer a discount ticket which is sometimes a phenomenal bargain. However, you may have to surrender all your baggage allowance and take only carry-on luggage.

Full Fares Airlines traditionally offer 1st class (coded F), business class (coded J) and economy class (coded Y) tickets. These days, so many promotional and discounted fares are available that few passengers pay full economy fare.

Lost Tickets If you lose your airline ticket, an airline will usually treat it like a traveler's check and, after inquiries, issue you with another one. Legally, however, an airline is entitled to treat it like cash: if you lose it, it's gone forever. Take good care of your tickets.

Onward Tickets An entry requirement for many countries is a ticket out of the country. If you're unsure of your next move, the easiest solution is to buy the cheapest onward ticket to a neighboring country or a ticket from a reliable airline that can later be refunded if you do not use it.

Open-Jaw Tickets These are return tickets that permit you to fly into one place but return from another. If available, these tickets can save you backtracking to your arrival point.

Overbooking Because almost every flight has some passengers that fail to show up, airlines often book more passengers than they have seats. Usually excess passengers make up for the no-shows, but occasionally somebody gets 'bumped' onto the next available flight. Guess who it is most likely to be? The passengers who check in late.

Promotional Fares These are officially discounted fares, available from travel agencies or direct from the airline.

Reconfirmation If you don't reconfirm your flight at least 72 hours prior to departure, the airline may delete your name from the passenger list. Call to find out if your airline requires reconfirmation.

Restrictions Discounted tickets often have various restrictions – for example, they may need to be paid for in advance, or altering them may incur a penalty. Other restrictions include minimum and maximum periods you must be away.

Round-the-World Tickets RTW tickets give you a limited period (usually a year) in which to circumnavigate the globe. You can go anywhere the carrying airlines go as long as you don't backtrack. The number of stopovers or total number of separate flights is decided before you set off, and these tickets usually cost a bit more than a basic return flight.

Transferred Tickets Airline tickets cannot be transferred from one person to another. Travelers sometimes try to sell the return half of a ticket, but officials can ask you to prove that you are the person named on the ticket. On an international flight, tickets are compared with passports.

Travel Periods Ticket prices vary with the time of year. There is a low (off-peak) season and a high (peak) season, and often a low-shoulder season and a high-shoulder season as well. Usually the fare depends on your outward flight – if you depart in the high season and return in the low season, you pay the high-season fare.

Latin America or Caribbean destinations, and you're bound to find a deal.

Firms such as STA Travel, which has offices worldwide, Council Travel in the USA, Travel CUTS in Canada and Usit Campus in the UK are not going to disappear overnight and they offer good prices to most destinations.

Remember, 'high season' in Belize is November to February, when ticket prices are usually higher. If you travel in the off season, your chance of finding cheaper flights increases.

Travelers with Special Needs
If you have special dietary needs, excessive baggage (eg, full dive gear), a disability, a fear of flying, or you're if traveling with small children, contact the airline well in advance (a month is a good benchmark) to discuss special arrangements. As your departure date approaches, confirm any special arrangements; try to call about 48 hours before your flight.

Departure Tax
Departure taxes and airport-use fees of BZ$30 (US$15) are levied on non-Belizean travelers departing Goldson International Airport for foreign destinations. You'll also have to pay a security screening fee of US$1.25 and a conservation fee of US$3.75, bringing your departure total to US$20. Be sure to have the US$ or BZ$ cash on hand, as there are no ATMs at the airport and their money exchange charges exorbitant rates for credit-card cash advances.

To/From Cancún (Mexico)
Mexicana's regional affiliate, Aerocaribe (☎ 52-98-84-20-00 in Cancún, ☎ 800-531-7921 in the USA, w www.aerocaribe.com), used to offer direct flights between Cancún and Belize City. Service is currently suspended but may resume in the future, so it's worth checking into if you're wanting to fly this route. If you are still intent on flying, Aerocaribe does offer daily flights from Cancún to Chetumal, where you can catch a Northern Transport bus across the border to Corozal. From there, you can fly on one of

the local airlines to San Pedro, on Ambergris Caye, (US$35 one way, 20 minutes) or continue on the bus to Belize City.

To/From Guatemala City
TACA offers four flights weekly between Guatemala City and Belize City via San Salvador. Aerovías (☎ 332-7470 in Guatemala) flies between Belize City and Guatemala City via Flores (Guatemala) on Monday, Wednesday and Friday. The flight between the two cities takes about 90 minutes and costs around US$75.

To/From Tikal (Guatemala)
Maya Island Air (☎ 2-31140 in Belize City, ☎ 25-2219 at Philip Goldson International Airport, ☎ 26-2435 in San Pedro) and Tropic Air (☎ 2-45671 in Belize City, ☎ 25-2302 at Philip Goldson International Airport, ☎ 26-2012 in San Pedro) offer guided tours of Tikal (day or overnight) from San Pedro, on Ambergris Caye, or from Belize City's Goldson International Airport.

Tours leave San Pedro at 7am and 1pm, stopping to pick up passengers at the international airport, and leaving again for Flores (Guatemala) at 8:30am and 2:30pm. Planes leave Flores on the return trip at 9:30am and 3:30pm (Tropic Air) or 9:50am and 3:50pm (Maya Island Air). A tour package including airfare, ground transportation to Tikal, lunch and a guided tour of the archaeological site at Tikal costs US$285 from San Pedro, or US$208 from Belize City; departure taxes and overnight stays are extra. The one-way, 50-minute flight to Flores from Belize City with no tour services costs US$88.

The USA & Canada
San Francisco is the USA's hub for cheap tickets, and Toronto is Canada's, although discount travel agents known as 'consolidators' can be found throughout Canada and the USA in the yellow pages, major daily newspapers and in free cosmopolitan weeklies.

Council Travel is the USA's largest student travel organization, with around 60 offices. Contact its head office (☎ 800-226-8624, w www.counciltravel.com) to find the

Rua Visconde de Piraja 550, Ipanema, Rio de Janeiro. In Argentina, try ASATEJ (☎ 011-4315-14570), Florida 835, 3rd floor, Oficina 319-B, Buenos Aires.

The following are some sample high-season roundtrip fares:

Caracas	US$650
	(479,140 Venezuelan bolívares)
Guatemala City	US$300
	(2361 Guatemalan quetzals)
Mexico City	US$665
	(6097 Mexican pesos)
Rio de Janeiro	US$1205
	(1205 Brazilian reais)
San José	US$455
	(151,092 Costa Rican colones)
San Salvador	US$199
	(1741 El Salvadorian colones)

The UK & Continental Europe
London remains the discount travel capital of Europe and it's here that the 'bucket shops' will find you the best deals to Belize. Good sources for cheap flights are the advertisements in the weekend sections of the *Independent* and the *Times,* and in free magazines, such as *TNT.* Good budget travel agencies include STA Travel (☎ 0870-240 1010, w www.statravel.co.uk) and Usit Campus (☎ 020-7730 3402, w www.usit campus.co.uk), both of which have branches throughout the UK. High-season roundtrip tickets from London and other European cities ranges from about US$1100 to US$1400 (UK£761/€1240 to UK£969/€1579).

Most flights to Belize City from Europe go through London. Good budget-oriented travel agents elsewhere in Europe include the following:

France
Voyages Wasteel (☎ 08 03 88 70 04 in France only, fax 01 43 25 46 25) 11 rue Dupuytren, 756006 Paris
Germany
STA Travel (☎ 030-311 0950, fax 030-313 0948) Goethestrasse 73m 10625 Berlin
Italy
Passaggi (☎ 06-474 0923, fax 06-482 7436) Stazione Termini FS, Gelleria Di Tesla, Rome

one nearest you. STA Travel (☎ 800-777-0112, w www.statravel.com), another good budget-ticket seller, also has offices in most major US cities.

Travel CUTS (☎ 800-667-2887, w www.travelcuts.com) is Canada's national student and budget travel agency with offices throughout the country.

Here are some sample roundtrip fares from various North American cities. Keep in mind, these are average, high-season, full fares – with a little research and flexibility, you can probably get a cheaper flight.

Chicago	US$660
Dallas/Fort Worth	US$560
Los Angeles	US$680
Miami	US$410
New York	US$616
Toronto	US$650 (C$1009)
Vancouver	US$700 (C$1087)

Mexico, Central & South America
The following are reputable discount-ticket sellers, some affiliated with Council Travel or STA Travel. In Guatemala, ISYTA (☎ 502-332-7629), 11 Calle 0-49 Zona 10, Guatemala City; in Costa Rica, Usit Sinlimites (☎ 506-280-5182), 200m east of Pollo Kentucky in San José; in Mexico SETEJ (☎ 52-5-211-07-43), Hamburgo 305, Colonial Juarez, Mexico City.

Venezuela has some of the cheapest airlinks to Central America. In Caracas, IVI Tours (☎ 02-993-60-82), in Residencia La Hacienda, Piso Bajo, Local 1-4-T, final Avenida Principal de las Mercedes, is the agent for STA Travel and often has a range of good deals. The STA affiliate in Brazil is Student Travel Bureau (☎ 021-259-0023),

Switzerland

SSR Voyages (STA affiliate; ☎ 01-297 11 11, W www.ssr.ch) Leonhardstrasse 10, Zurich

Australia & New Zealand

The cheapest way to get from Australia or New Zealand to Belize City is usually via the US (normally Los Angeles). High-season roundtrip fares from Sidney, Melbourne or Auckland to Belize City via Los Angeles average US$1800 to US$2000 (A$3454 to A$3838).

Both Flight Centre (☎ 02-9281 6466, W www.flightcentre.com.au) and STA Travel (W www.statravel.com) are major dealers in cheap airfares in both Australia and New Zealand. Both have offices in numerous cities. Also check the Internet and travel agents' ads in the yellow pages and newspapers.

LAND

Departure Tax

Exit tax at Belizean land border-crossing points is US$13.75 (US$10 departure tax, plus US$3.75 conservation fee). If you are traveling in and out of Belize, hang on to your PACT (Protected Areas Conservation Trust) receipt because you only have to pay the conservation tax once within a 30-day period. You'll still have to pay the departure tax every time you come and go.

Bus

Belize's buses are incredibly efficient and inexpensive and the roads connecting Belize to its neighbors are in good shape. In the north, Belize's Santa Elena borders Mexico's Subteniente López (a short shuttle from the Mexican seaside town of Chetumal). Belize's Northern Transport has hourly buses between Chetumal and Belize City from 4am to 8pm.

Western Transport buses run between Belize City and the Guatemalan border – to Benque Viejo del Carmen (on the Belize side) and Melchor de Mencos (on the Guatemala side) – connecting with Guatemalan buses headed for Flores (the gateway to Tikal). Buses to Benque leave Belize City at least hourly. For details on Belize bus schedules, see the Getting Around chapter.

Car & Motorcycle

It's not unusual to see US license plates on cars in Belize, as driving from the US through Mexico is pretty straightforward. Expensive car-rental rates in Belize also encourage some travelers to bring their own cars, but ultra-expensive gas prices render driving in Belize downright pricey.

If you do drive, take note that almost every car in Belize has a cracked windshield and a grumbling muffler. If you're planning to stay on main highways, your car will probably be safe from too much abuse, but if you venture off the beaten track, be prepared for bumpy, dusty or muddy roads. Always have water and a spare tire, and, if you're traveling deep into the country's back roads, spare gas is a good idea.

Motorcyclists will have to stick to the main highways and should have a good understanding of their bike's mechanical workings, as it's unlikely the mechanics in Belize City will be able to help you.

SEA

Other than private yachts and fishing vessels, the only boats traveling into and out of Belize run between Placencia and Puerto Cortés in Honduras, or between Punta Gorda and Puerto Barrios in eastern Guatemala.

The *Gulf Cruza* (☎ 2-24506 or 6-23236) runs between Placencia and Puerto Cortés, with stops in Big Creek, every Friday, returning Monday morning. The one-way fare from Placencia is US$50.

Scheduled boats ply the waters between Punta Gorda and Puerto Barrios in eastern Guatemala. Requenas Charter Service (☎ 7-22070) offers daily service to Punta Barrios, leaving Punta Gorda at 9am and returning at 2pm. Lancha Pichilingo (☎ 7-22879) also travels this route, leaving Punta Gorda at 4pm and returning at 10am. Charter trips can be arranged from Punta Gorda to these countries, and if enough passengers split the cost the price per person can be reasonable. Refer to the Southern Belize chapter for more details.

Getting Around

AIR

With few paved roads, Belize depends greatly on small airplanes (de Havilland Twin Otters, Cessnas etc) for fast, reliable transportation within the country.

Belize City has two airports. All international flights use Philip Goldson International Airport (BZE), 9 miles (16km) northwest of the city center. The airport has gift shops and a currency exchange, but no storage lockers. (You can store baggage at the marine terminal on Front St in Belize City.) The small Municipal Airport (TZA) is 1½ miles (2.5km) north of the city center, on the shore. Most local flights will stop and pick you up at either airport, but fares are considerably lower from Municipal, so unless you're connecting to an international flight, it's best to use that one.

Two airlines – Maya Island Air and Tropic Air – operate along two main domestic air routes: Belize City-Caye Caulker-San Pedro-Corozal, returning along the reverse route; and Belize City-Dangriga-Placencia-Punta Gorda, also returning along the reverse route. Tickets for both airlines can be booked through most of the hotels and tour agencies within the country.

Maya Island Air (☎ 2-31140, ✉ miatza@btl.net in Belize City; ☎ 25-2219 at Goldson International Airport; ☎ 26-2435, ✉ miaspr@btl.net in San Pedro; ☎ 800-521-1247 in the USA & Canada; ⓦ www.mayaairways.com)

Tropic Air (☎ 2-45671 in Belize City; ☎ 25-2302 at Goldson International Airport; ☎ 26-2012, fax 26-2338 in San Pedro; ☎ 800-422-3435 in the USA & Canada; ✉ tropicair@btl.net, ⓦ www.tropicair.com)

The following list provides information on flights from Belize City. Fares are one way from Municipal/Goldson International airports (fares from Municipal are cheaper):

Caye Caulker (CKR) – 10 minutes, US$26/47. Tropic Air flights to San Pedro stop at Caye Caulker on request. Maya Island Air has flights (continuing to San Pedro) at 6:45am, 7:15am, 8:30am, 11:30am, 2pm, 3pm, 3:30pm and 4:15pm.

Corozal (CZL) – 1 to 1½ hours, US$61/123. There are no direct flights to Corozal – you must first fly to San Pedro. Tropic Air's 9:40am and 2:30pm flights from Belize City to San Pedro continue to Corozal, then return to Belize City from Corozal leaving at 10:30am, 3:30pm and 5:30pm via San Pedro. There's also a San Pedro-Corozal flight at 7:10am, returning at 7:30am. Maya Island Air has flights from San Pedro to Corozal at 7:15am, noon and 4pm, returning at 7:45am, 12:30pm and 4:35pm.

Dangriga (DGA) – 20 minutes, US$31/45. Maya Island Air flies to Dangriga from Belize City at 8am, 10am, 12:30pm, 2:30pm and 4:30pm, returning at 7:35am, 10:10am, 12:10pm, 2:05pm and 4:55pm. Tropic Air flights leave Belize City at 8:30am, 11am, 12:30pm, 2:30pm and 4:50pm, returning 7:45am, 10:20am, 1pm, 2:20pm and 4:45pm.

Flores, Guatemala (FRS) – 50 minutes, US$88. Both Maya Island Air and Tropic Air have flights from Goldson International Airport daily at 8:30am and 2:30pm. Maya Island Air flights return at 9:50am and 3:50pm; Tropic Air returns at 9:30am and 3:30pm.

Placencia (PLA) – 25 to 45 minutes, US$59/70. All flights stop first in Dangriga. Maya Island Air flies to Placencia from Belize City at 8am, 10am, 12:30pm, 2:30pm and 4:30pm, returning at 7:10am, 9:45am, 11:45am, 1:40pm and 4:30pm. Tropic Air flights leave Belize City at 8:30am, 11am, 12:30pm, 2:30pm and 4:50pm, returning at 7:25am, 10am, 12:40pm, 2pm and 4:25pm.

Punta Gorda (PND) – 55 minutes to 1 hour and 10 minutes, US$76/89. Departures from Belize City are the same as for Placencia. Return flights on Maya Island Air leave Punta Gorda at 6:45am, 9:20am, 11:20am and 4:05pm; Tropic Air departs from Punta Gorda for Belize City at 7am, 9:35am, 12:15pm, 1:35pm and 4pm.

San Pedro, Ambergris Caye (SPR) – 15 minutes, US$26/46.50. Tropic Air offers hourly flights from 7am to 5pm daily. Maya Island Air has 12 flights between 6:45am and 5:30pm daily. Maya will run flights later in the evening if major flights from the US to Belize City have been delayed.

BUS

Belize has a fantastic, reliable and affordable bus system that makes getting around the country a breeze. Several bus companies used to run along the major routes in Belize,

INTERNAL AIR ROUTES

but most of them have been gobbled up over the past couple of years by Novelo's Bus Lines, which has developed somewhat of a monopoly on bus travel in Belize. Though there's talk of Belize one day having a central bus station, Novelo's still uses the former companies' terminals in Belize City, and you'll notice many buses still await a Novelo's paint job. The big companies no longer in existence, but whose terminals are still used by Novelo's, include Batty Brothers (now Western and Northern Transport), Venus (now Northern Transport) and Z-line (now Southern Transport).

Most Belizean buses are used US school buses, although some newer 1st-class services are now available. Express and Premier buses, with air-con and more legroom, make far fewer stops; most people find the comfort worth the extra US$1.50 to US$2.

Buses run frequently along the country's three major roads. Smaller village lines tend to run on local work and school schedules, with buses running from a smaller town to a larger town in the morning and returning in the afternoon.

Belize City's bus terminals are located near the Pound Yard Bridge, along or close to the Collett Canal on W Collett Canal St, E Collett Canal St or neighboring streets. This is a run-down area not good for walking at night; take a taxi. Outside Belize City, bus drivers will usually pick up and drop off passengers at undesignated stops if requested. Visit ⓦ www.belizecentral.net/bus_schedule/schedule.html for an automated bus schedule.

Luggage pilfering has been a problem in the past, particularly on the Punta Gorda route. Carry valuables with you on the bus and give your stored baggage to the bus driver or conductor only, and watch as it is stored. Be there when the bus is unloaded and retrieve your luggage at once.

Bus Companies

Novelo's Bus Lines Novelo's (☎ 2-77372, ⓔ novelo@btl.net) operates Western Transport, Northern Transport and Southern Transport, using different terminals in Belize City. The main Novelo's terminal is at 19 W Collett Canal St.

Western Transport buses travel along the Western Hwy to Belmopan, San Ignacio, Benque Viejo del Carmen and the Guatemalan border. These leave from the old Batty's terminal (Western Transport, ☎ 2-72025) at 15 Mosul St in the morning, and from the main Novelo's terminal in the afternoon.

Northern Transport buses travel up the Northern Hwy to Orange Walk, Corozal and Chetumal (Mexico). These leave from the main Novelo's terminal and from the old Venus terminal (Northern Transport, ☎ 2-73354), on Magazine Rd and Logwood St, in the afternoon and from the old Batty's terminal in the morning.

Southern Transport buses travel down the Hummingbird and Coastal Hwys to Dangriga, Placencia and Punta Gorda. Buses depart from the old Venus terminal (Southern Transport, ☎ 2-73937) throughout the day.

Other Bus Companies A few other bus companies operate smaller-scale services throughout Belize. Among them are the following: **James Bus Service** (☎ 7-22049) operates out of Punta Gorda and has daily runs from Punta Gorda to Belize City via Mango Creek, Dangriga and Belmopan.

Jex Bus travels to Crooked Tree, leaving from the Pound Yard Bridge. **McFadzean's Bus** and **Russell's Bus Service** travel to the Community Baboon Sanctuary at Bermudian Landing. McFadzean's leaves from Mosul and Orange Sts; Russell's departs from Cairo St and Euphrates Ave.

Destinations

Here are details on buses from Belize City to major destinations. Travel times are approximate, as the length of a ride depends upon how many times the driver stops to pick up and drop off passengers along the way. Prices listed are one-way fares for regular/express buses:

Belmopan – 52 miles (84km), 1 hour, US$3.50/5. Almost every bus heading south and west stops in Belmopan, leaving Belize City at least every half hour from 5am to 10:15pm.

Benque Viejo del Carmen/Western Border – 81 miles (131km), 3 hours, US$5.50/7. Western Transport operates daily buses from Belize City to Benque Viejo del Carmen and the western border (stopping in Belmopan and San Ignacio) every half hour from 5am to 9pm. Buses depart from the old Batty Brothers terminal (5am to 10:15am) and from the main Novelo's terminal (11am to 9pm).

Chetumal (Mexico) – 100 miles (160km), 4 hours, US$4.50/6. Northern Transport runs frequent northbound buses from Belize City to Chetumal's Nuevo Mercado via Orange Walk and Corozal from 4am to 7pm. From the old Batty's terminal, nine buses depart hourly between 4am and 11:15am. From the main Novelo's terminal, nine buses depart hourly between noon and 8pm. From Chetumal, 26 buses travel to Belize City at least hourly from 4am to 6:30pm.

Corozal – 96 miles (155km), 3 hours, US$3.75/4.50. See Chetumal, above. In addition, from the old Venus terminal, 17 buses depart half-hourly between noon and 8pm.

Dangriga – 195 miles (170km), 3 to 4 hours, US$5/7. Southern Transport has hourly buses from Belize City to Dangriga (and back) from 6am to 5pm. Most buses go via Belmopan and the Hummingbird Hwy, although some take the shorter but unpaved Coastal Hwy. James Bus Service runs the Belize City-Belmopan-Dangriga-Punta Gorda route daily at 5am, 9am, 10am and 3pm, with an additional bus at 9am Monday, Saturday and Sunday. It returns from

Dangriga at 9:30am Monday, Wednesday, Thursday and Saturday; 4pm Tuesday and Friday; and 11am Sunday.

Flores (Guatemala) – 146 miles (235km), 5 hours. Take a bus across the western border to Melchor de Mencos (see below) and transfer to a Guatemalan bus. Some hotels and tour companies organize minibus trips, which are more expensive but much faster and more comfortable.

Melchor de Mencos (Guatemala) – 84 miles (135km), 3¼ hours, US$6/7.50. Western Transport offers 13 morning buses to Melchor, across the border. Buses leave from the old Batty's terminal around every half hour between 4am and 10am, and return from Melchor at 11:30am, noon, 1pm, 2pm, 3pm and 4pm. Buses also leave from the main Novelo's terminal hourly from 11am to 9pm, returning at least hourly from 4am to 11:30am.

Orange Walk – 58 miles (92km), 2 hours, US$2.25/3. Northern Transport runs frequent northbound buses from Belize City to Orange Walk en route to Corozal or Chetumal. See those entries, above, for details.

Placencia – 161 miles (260km), 4 hours, US$10/12. There is no direct bus service to Placencia, but you can take a morning Southern Transport bus to Dangriga, then catch the connector bus to Placencia. Buses travel from Dangriga to Placencia Monday to Saturday at 12:15pm, 3:30pm and 5:15pm and on Sunday at 12:15pm and 5:15pm. A bus returns from Placencia to Dangriga daily at 5:30am, 7am and 1:30pm. Northern routes leave Placencia at 5:30am and 6am. The 5:30am bus stops in Hopkins.

Punta Gorda – 210 miles (339km), 8 to 10 hours, US$11/13. Southern Transport has buses from Belize City to Punta Gorda at 6am, 8am, noon and 3pm; buses return north at 3am, 4am, 5am and 10am. James Bus Service runs the Belize City-Belmopan-Dangriga-Punta Gorda route (see the Dangriga section, earlier). Return buses depart Punta Gorda at 6am, 8am and noon daily, with an extra bus at 11am on Thursday, Friday and Sunday.

San Ignacio – 72 miles (116km), 2½ hours, US$5/7. See the Benque Viejo del Carmen/Western Border entry, earlier.

CAR

Belize has three good asphalt-paved two-lane roads: the Northern Hwy between the Mexican border near Corozal and Belize City; the Western Hwy between Belize City and the Guatemalan border near Benque Viejo del Carmen; and the Hummingbird Hwy from Belmopan to Dangriga. Most other roads are narrow one- or two-lane dirt roads; many are impassable after heavy rains. The Southern Hwy is paved in patches but remains slow going.

Anyone who drives a lot in Belize has a 4WD vehicle or a high-clearance pickup truck. But if you plan on sticking to the main roads and you're traveling during the dry season, you will be fine renting a car, which will cost about US$20 a day less than a 4WD.

Sites off the main roads are often accessible only by 4WD vehicles, especially during the rainy season between May and November. After heavy rains in Belize, you can get profoundly stuck in floodwaters or mud even with 4WD, and getting winched out is expensive. Wet conditions aren't the only challenge; in mountain regions the dry soil is loose and rocky, making it hard to keep traction on steep roads.

Plenty of fuel stations are available in the larger towns and along the major roads. At last report, leaded gasoline was going for about US$3 per US gallon (US$0.79 per liter). You can gas up with regular, premium (unleaded) and diesel fuel throughout Belize.

Mileposts and highway signs record distances in miles and speed limits in miles per hour (mph), although many vehicles have odometers and speedometers that are calibrated in kilometers.

10mph = 16km/h
20mph = 32km/h
30mph = 48km/h
40mph = 64km/h
50mph = 80km/h

Road Rules

Although Belize is a former British colony, cars drive on the right side of the road here. Road signs pointing the way to towns and villages are often few and far between. Keep track of your mileage so you know when your turnoff is approaching, and don't be afraid to ask people for directions.

Watch out for sudden changes in road conditions, especially in the south; an overly quick transition from pavement to dirt could cause you to lose control of your vehicle. Be prepared to slow down for double speed-control bumps (called 'sleeping policemen') along the approaches to towns and intersections.

All paved roads in Belize are two-lane (one in each direction), and you'll soon learn that Belizeans aren't timid about passing, even on busy stretches of road. Next you'll learn that if you want to get anywhere, you're going to have to play the passing game, too. Major roads are used by vehicles of all sizes and speeds – from lumbering sugarcane trucks to swift new SUVs.

Be safe by using your turn signals when you're ready to pass, always heeding no-passing zones (double solid lines) and keeping an eye out for fast-approaching vehicles behind you. If you're in doubt about whether you have room to pass, don't take a risk – there will be other opportunities.

Use of seat belts is required. If you are caught not wearing yours, the fine is US$12.50.

Petty theft can be an issue – keep your vehicle locked at all times and do not leave valuables in it, especially not in plain view.

Rental

Generally, renters must be at least 25 years old, have a valid driver's license and pay by credit card or leave a large cash deposit. Most rental agencies will not allow you to take a rental out of the country without first signing a release. The release allows you to leave Belize, but be forewarned that your insurance will not cover you or the car in other countries.

Most car-rental companies have representatives at Belize City's Goldson International Airport; many will also deliver or take return of cars at Belize City's Municipal Airport or in downtown Belize City.

Car rental is expensive in Belize. Rates are around US$80 to US$88 per day (US$482 to US$498 per week), 15% tax included, with unlimited mileage. A Loss Damage Waiver (loosely known as 'insurance') costs an addi-

tional US$14 per day, tax included. The big-name car companies will always quote you a high price, but if you're persistent you can usually find a good deal buried beneath. The smaller, locally owned companies (such as Crystal or JR's) will usually be more amenable to negotiating their rates. The following, whose Belize City offices are listed, offer good customer service and quality vehicles, most with air-con:

Budget Rent-a-Car (☎ 2-32435, 2-33986, 800-283-4387 in the USA, e jmagroup@btl.net, w www.budget-belize.com), 771 Bella Vista

Crystal Auto Rental (☎ 2-31600, fax 2-31900, e crystal@btl.net, w www.crystal-belize.com), Mile 1½ Northern Hwy

JR's Auto Rental (☎ 2-75098, fax 2-71565), 157 Neal Pen Rd

National Rental Car (☎ 2-31650, 2-32637, fax 2-32637), 12 N Front St

Thrifty Car Rental (☎ 2-71271, fax 2-71421, w www.thrifty.com), at Fabers Rd and Central American Blvd

Note that you won't need to rent a car for travel on any of the cayes. Bicycles and electric golf carts, available for rent on Ambergris Caye and Caye Caulker, are sufficient.

Insurance

Liability insurance is required in Belize, and you must have it for the customs officer to approve the temporary importation of your car into the country. You can usually buy the insurance from booths at the border for about US$1 per day. The booths are generally closed Sunday, meaning no insurance is sold that day and no temporary import permits are issued. If you're crossing the border with a car, try to do it on a weekday morning.

HITCHHIKING

In Belize it's not the least bit unusual to see a pickup truck overflowing with local workers piled into the back. Because the highways are so straightforward, and the destinations fairly obvious, drivers will not hesitate to slow down and allow anyone – even strangers – to jump aboard. In fact, many people use this pile-into-the-pickup-truck method as a viable way to commute to and from work. For tourists, it's a little different, though if you hold your hand up and look friendly, it's likely that you'll soon get a ride.

Hitchhiking is never entirely safe in any country and in Belize, like anywhere, it's imperative that you listen to your instincts and travel smart. Travelers who decide to hitchhike should understand that they are taking a small but potentially serious risk. You're far better off traveling with at least one other person, and never hitchhike on secondary roads or at night. Also keep in mind that buses in Belize are efficient and cheap; you might decide that a bus is a safer and more comfortable bet.

BOAT

Motor launches zoom between Belize City, Caye Caulker and Ambergris Caye frequently every day. This boat trip is usually fast, windy and bumpy. That said, it's a great way to transition from the Belize City bustle into the cool cruise of the cayes. You will be in an open boat with no shade for at least 30 minutes, so provide yourself with sunscreen, a hat and clothing to protect you from the sun and the spray. If it rains, the mate will drag out a plastic tarp that passengers can hold above their heads, or you can just get wet and wait for the sun to dry you off.

The marine terminal has luggage-storage lockers, but they're expensive at US$1/hour or US$5/day. You might be better off asking a hotel if they'll store your bags.

Schedules

The Belize Marine Terminal (☎ 2-31969), on N Front St at the north end of the Swing Bridge in Belize City, is the main dock for boats to the northern cayes. The terminal building also holds the small Maritime Museum, open 8am to 5pm (closed Monday).

The efficient Caye Caulker Water Taxi Association (☎ 2-31969 in Belize City, ☎ 22-2992 on Caye Caulker, ☎ 26-2036 in San Pedro) operates fast, frequent launches between Belize City, Caye Caulker and San Pedro on Ambergris Caye, with stops on request at Caye Chapel and St George's Caye. Against the wind, the trip to Caulker takes 30 to 45

minutes. The San Pedro ride takes 45 minutes to an hour. Trips cost US$7.50 to Caye Caulker, US$12.50 to San Pedro. See the Northern Cayes chapter for schedules.

Also serving the cayes and usually slightly cheaper, Triple J Boating Service (☎ 2-33464) runs boats to Caye Caulker and San Pedro from the Court House Wharf behind the Supreme Court building. Triple J boats leave daily at 9am. Thunderbolt boats also travel to the cayes, leaving from the Texaco gas station on N Front St, daily at 9am.

ORGANIZED TOURS

Belize has a well-developed network of tour providers, and organized tours can be arranged through local hotels or tour offices at great prices. Additionally, a number of international organizations conduct adventure tours or nature-watching tours in the country. You can find well-trained local tour guides through the Belize Tour Association (☎ 14-4859, e belizeguide@hotmail.com). The following are a few reputable companies that offer or can arrange tours:

International Zoological Expeditions (☎ 5-22119, fax 5-23152; ☎ 508-655-1461, fax 508-655-4445 in the USA; w www.ize2belize.com) runs wildlife expeditions and university research projects from base lodges on South Water Caye and in Blue Creek Rainforest Preserve near Punta Gorda.

Island Expeditions (☎ 5-23328; ☎ 800-667-1630 in North America; w www.islandexpeditions .com) also offers multi-activity adventure-travel packages, including tours from Belize to Tikal.

Maya Travel Services (☎ 2-31623, fax 501-2-30585, e mayatravel@btl.net, w www.mayatravel services.com) is an incredibly helpful organization, whether you want to book tours, plan an itinerary or ask obscure questions about Belize. It can set up a variety of both mainland and cayes tours.

S&L Travel and Tours (☎ 2-77593, fax 2-77594, e sltravel@btl.net) sets up trips to all of the inland sights including Crooked Tree, Lamanai, the Baboon Sanctuary, Altun Ha and Tikal.

Slickrock Adventures (☎ 800-390-5715, fax 435-259-6996 in the USA, w www.slickrock.com) offers a variety of sea- and river-kayaking tours, augmented with diving, snorkeling, mountain-biking and hiking.

Belize City

pop 49,050

Ramshackle, colorful and alive with Caribbean-style hustle and bustle, Belize City is a great place to explore. Here, unlike in more tourist-oriented areas, you'll have a good opportunity to meet Belizeans going about their everyday lives.

Highlights

- Taking in the colonial architecture and cooling sea breezes of the Fort George District

- Visiting the Swing Bridge – the only working bridge of its type in the world and the center of activity in Belize City

- Enjoying traditional Belizean cuisine, from the ubiquitous rice and beans to lobster and other seafood

- Touring the streets of downtown Belize City – a real-time lesson on the country's history

Belize City page 73
Central Belize City
pages 76-77

In the past, travelers to Belize joked that the best thing to do in Belize City was to leave. Stories of street crime and harassment have caused many to skip the city altogether and head straight to a safe haven in the cayes or the Cayo District. But much has been done in recent years to make the streets safer.

Belize City isn't a picture-postcard seaside village. It's a mostly gritty seaside city and one with a fascinating native and colonial past that is apparent everywhere you look. In the center of town, business, Belizean-style, is conducted in Victorian buildings situated along narrow streets. Gingerbread detailing competes with less-graceful window bars on residential clapboard houses. Glimpses of the sea or the river surprise you at the end of most streets, and frigate birds cruise serenely overhead.

As the center of Belize, the city has a style and energy that you won't find elsewhere in the country, amid a cultural blend that you'll find nowhere else in Central America. It attracts a large concentration of high-achievers and a dense concentration of the many ethnicities that blend together to create Belize's vibrant, evolving culture. This is where the country is run, where policy is shaped, where the innovations in business and culture are created.

History

Originally the nation's capital, Belize City was built on the site of a Mayan fishing village. Popular lore has it built on a landfill of mahogany chips and rum bottles, both ingredients generated by the Baymen (British pirates) in the 1700s. It was the first European settlement on mainland Belize, and became Belize's official seat of government after Spanish forces invaded St George's Caye in 1779. (The Baymen won St George's Caye back in 1798, but it was never to be the capital again.) Belize City served as a trading post for loggers, who would spend months in the bush, then return to the city to get paid and to spend their wages on rum and relaxation.

During its tenure as capital, the city endured a multiplicity of disasters, including fires, epidemics and, most profoundly, hurricanes.

After Hurricane Hattie ravaged the city in 1961, the government moved inland to Belmopan, the country's current capital. That said, the prime minister still lives in Belize City, and most events and announcements of nationwide significance still originate here, usually from the conference rooms of the Radisson Hotel.

Orientation

Haulover Creek, a branch of the Belize River, runs through the middle of the city, separating the commercial center (bounded by Albert, Regent, King and Orange Sts) from the slightly more genteel residential and hotel district of Fort George to the northeast. Hotels and guest houses are found on both sides of the creek.

The Swing Bridge joins Albert St with Queen St, which runs through the Fort George District and the pleasant Kings Park neighborhood. It seems as though everything and everybody in Belize City crosses the Swing Bridge at least once a day.

The Belize Marine Terminal, used by motor launches traveling to Caye Caulker and Ambergris Caye, is at the north end of the bridge. The Northern and the Western Hwys originate in Belize City.

Belize's bus stations are near W and E Collett Canal Sts near Cemetery Rd and Orange St. See the Getting Around chapter for details.

Information

Tourist Offices The Belize Tourism Board (BTB; ☎ 2-31910/13, fax 2-31943, e btbb@btl.net), in the Central Bank Building on Gabourel Lane, is open 8am to noon and 1pm to 5pm Monday to Thursday, till 4:30pm Friday.

The Belize Tourism Industry Association (☎ 2-75717, 2-71144, fax 2-78710, e btia@btl.net), 10 N Park St, on the north side of Memorial Park in the Fort George District,

can provide information about its members, including most of the country's hotels, restaurants, tour operators and other travel-related businesses. Hours are 8:30am to noon and 1pm to 4:30pm Monday to Thursday, till 4pm Friday.

Money Scotiabank (☎ 2-77027), on Albert St at Bishop St, is open 8am to 1pm Monday to Thursday, 8am to 4:30pm Friday. Nearby, the Atlantic Bank Limited (☎ 2-77124), 6 Albert St at King St, is open 8am to 3pm Monday, Tuesday and Thursday, 8am to 1pm Wednesday and 8am to 4:30pm Friday (closed for the noon hour).

Also on Albert St you'll find the prominent Belize Bank (☎ 2-77132), 60 Market Square – entrance facing the Swing Bridge – open 8am to 1pm Monday to Thursday, 8am to 4:30pm Friday, and Barclay's Bank (☎ 2-77211), 21 Albert St, open 8am to 2:30pm Monday to Thursday, 8am to 4:30pm Friday.

Post & Communications The main post office is in the Paslow Building at the north end of the Swing Bridge, at the intersection of Queen and Front Sts. Hours are 8am to noon and 1pm to 5pm Monday to Saturday.

Belize Internet Café (☎ 2-72951, fax 2-72923), 4 S Park St across from Memorial Park, is open 8am to 9pm Monday to Saturday. Snacks and juices are available. It's US$5 per hour, US$4 if you're a student. You can also check your email (no snacks though) at Angelus Press (☎ 2-35777), 10 Queen St, for US$5.40 an hour. It's open 7:30am to 5:30pm Monday to Friday, 8am to noon Saturday. In the high-rent district, IBTM Business Center & Internet Café (☎ 2-32668), in the lobby of the Princess Hotel & Casino, offers free instant coffee and online access for US$10 an hour; it's open 7am to 10pm.

Travel Agencies The following tour operators will handle travel arrangements and organize tours throughout the country.

Belize Global Travel Services (☎ 2-77363, 2-77364, w www.belizenet.com/gat.html), 41 Albert St

Discovery Adventures (☎ 2-30748), 5916 Manatee Dr

Jaguar Adventures (☎ 2-36025, **w** www.jaguarbelize.com), 4 Fort St – affiliated with Hugh Parkey's Belize Dive Connection and located in the Fort Street Guesthouse

Maya Travel Services (☎ 2-31623, **w** www.mayatravelservices.com), Belize City Municipal Airstrip

S&L Tours (☎ 2-77593, 2-75145, **e** sltravel@btl.net), 91 N Front St

Bookstores Books are sold at Angelus Press (☎ 2-35777), 10 Queen St, open 7:30am to 5:30pm Monday to Friday, 8am to noon Saturday. They are primarily a stationery and office-supply store.

The Book Center (☎ 2-77457), 4 Church St above Thrift Town, caters to students, so there is a fine selection of scholarly texts alongside best-sellers and a wide assortment of magazines. It's a good choice for maps and books on history, culture and the environment.

The Papagayo Gift Shop in the Belize Biltmore Plaza Hotel (☎ 2-33374), Mile 3 (Km 5) Northern Hwy, and the Radisson Fort George Gift Shop (☎ 2-33333) both carry a good selection of paperback fiction and Belizeana.

Cultural Centers The Bliss Institute (☎ 2-72458), on Southern Foreshore, and the House of Culture (☎ 2-73050), on Regent St, often hold special performances and cultural events. Call for schedules.

The Mexico-Belize Cultural Center (☎ 2-34593, 2-34594, mexbzinst@btl.net), at Wilson St and Barracks Rd, conducts art exhibitions and cultural events throughout the year. Spanish language courses are also offered on a trimester system.

Laundry Stan's Laundry, 22 Dean St, between Albert and Canal Sts, charges US$5 per load. Most hotels can arrange laundry service for you at similar prices.

Luggage Storage Luggage can be safely stored at the Belize Marine Terminal for US$1 per hour.

Medical Services Karl Heusner Memorial Hospital (☎ 2-31548) is on Princess Margaret Dr in the northern part of town. Belize Medical Association (☎ 2-30302/03/04), 5791 St Thomas St, is a private hospital in Belize's Kings Park District. Both offer 24-hour emergency services.

Many people – locals and travelers alike – fly to Houston, Miami or New Orleans for treatment of serious illnesses or injuries.

Emergency Belize City's emergency police numbers are ☎ 911 and ☎ 2-72210. For non-emergencies call ☎ 2-44646 or ☎ 2-72222. The tourist police can be reached 24 hours a day at ☎ 2-72222 ext 401 and ☎ 2-79770 from 9am to 5pm.

For the fire department or ambulance call ☎ 90. If that number is busy, for the fire department call ☎ 2-72579 or for medical emergencies ☎ 2-31548 or ☎ 2-31564. For sea or river emergencies call ☎ 25-2174.

Dangers & Annoyances Yes, there is petty crime in Belize City, but it's not necessary to run for your room at the stroke of dusk, as some doomsayers will tell you. Take the same commonsense precautions that you would in any major city. Don't flash wads of cash, expensive camera equipment or other signs of wealth. Don't leave valuables in your hotel room. Don't use or deal in illicit drugs. Don't walk alone at night, and avoid deserted streets, even in daylight.

It's always better to walk in pairs or groups and to stick to major streets in the city center. Special care should be taken on Front St south of the Swing Bridge and on Handyside St between Queen and Front St, both areas are known to be favorites with muggers after dark. Ask your hotel operator or a shopkeeper for advice on the safety of a particular neighborhood or establishment, and when in doubt, take a cab.

The BTB is deeply motivated to make sure that Belize builds a reputation for safety. To this end it was recently successful in lobbying for the creation of a tourism police force of 50 to patrol heavily touristed areas, mostly in the Fort George and city center areas. Additionally, the regular municipal

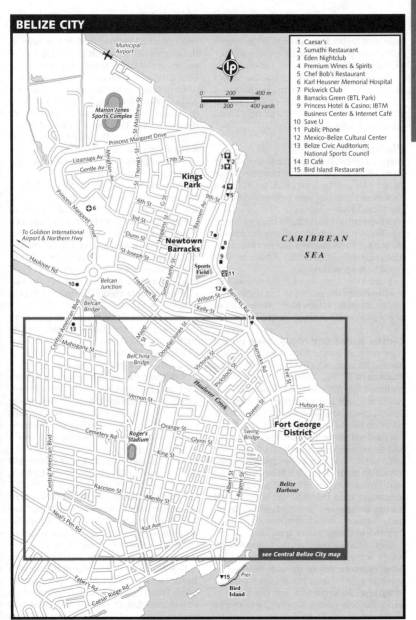

BELIZE CITY

1 Caesar's
2 Sumathi Restaurant
3 Eden Nightclub
4 Premium Wines & Spirits
5 Chef Bob's Restaurant
6 Karl Heusner Memorial Hospital
7 Pickwick Club
8 Barracks Green (BTL Park)
9 Princess Hotel & Casino; IBTM
  Business Center & Internet Café
10 Save U
11 Public Phone
12 Mexico-Belize Cultural Center
13 Belize Civic Auditorium;
   National Sports Council
14 El Café
15 Bird Island Restaurant

Municipal Airport

Marion Jones Sports Complex

Princess Margaret Drive

Lizarraga Av.

Gentle Av.

17th St

Kings Park

St Matthew St.

St Thomas St.

Meigham Av.

G St.

Bayman Av.

9th St

Princess Margaret Drive

6th St.

3rd St.

Hopkins St.

Dunn St

St-Joseph St

Newtown Barracks

To Goldson International Airport & Northern Hwy

Haulover Rd

Belcan Junction

Belcan Bridge

Freetown Rd

Simon Lamb St.

Sports Field

CARIBBEAN SEA

Barracks Rd

Wilson St.

Kelly St.

Central American Blvd

Mahogany St.

BelChina Bridge

Mapp St.

Douglas Jones St.

Haulover Creek

Victoria St.

Pickstock St.

Barracks Rd

Eve St.

Vernon St.

Cemetery Rd

Roger's Stadium

Orange St.

Glynn St.

Queen St.

Swing Bridge

Hutson St.

Fort George District

King St.

Albert St.

Regent St.

Belize Harbour

Raccoon St.

Allenby St.

Neal's Pen Rd

Kut Ave

Central American Blvd

see Central Belize City map

Faber's Rd

Caesar Ridge Rd

Pier

Bird Island

0   200   400 m
0   200   400 yards

police force has developed a higher profile over the past few years. If you're hassled or scammed, report any incidents to the tourist police (see phone numbers above) so they will be aware of trouble spots and patterns.

Tourist police act as roving ambassadors of assurance around town, zipping about on bikes and making sure you're OK. They'll greet you with a friendly 'you all right?' and escort you down dodgier streets.

Walking Tours

As you'll find with most of the towns and villages of mainland Belize, the charms of Belize City are best taken in by having a walk around, making sure to stop and talk to the locals. Following are a few suggested walking routes that include highlights and significant buildings in each neighborhood. Wear a hat and sunscreen and stay hydrated; when you're away from the offshore breezes you'll heat up mighty quick.

Mind your toes, those holes you see all over town are the homes to land crabs who forage about for scraps and garbage, sort of like pigeons with pinchers instead of wings.

Central Belize City A good place to start your tour of Belize City is at the Belize Marine Terminal, which houses the **Maritime Museum** (☎ 2-31969; admission US$4/2 adults/ students with ID; open 7am-5pm daily). If you're a visual learner instead of a reader this might not be good value for you – the exhibits consist of dusty dioramas and skeletons and rather static photos, but the signage and text covering wildlife, boats, fishing and other sea-related topics is lively and informative. Rumor has it that it will be closing and moving to a location on Caye Caulker. More interesting than the museum is the crowd waiting to head out to the islands – a lively mix of students, commuters, merchants, families and, of course, fellow travelers.

Next, head south across the **Swing Bridge**, which is the heart and soul of Belize City. Most everyone passes through this part of town on a daily basis. The bridge, a product of Liverpool's ironworks, was built in 1923 and is the only remaining working bridge of its type in the world. Its operators manually

rotate the bridge open usually at 5:30am and 5:30pm daily, just long enough to let tall boats pass and to bring most of the traffic in the city center to a halt. It's quite a procedure, and if you're in the right place at the right time, you might even get to help out.

Depending on the season there may be a collection of wooden sailboats racked up at the base of the bridge, piled high with small dugout canoes. They belong to local fisherfolk, usually from the north, who come down to ply the waters of the south. For each canoe there's an angler, so it makes for a crowded trip out to sea.

From the Swing Bridge, walk south along Regent St, one block inland from the shore. The large, modern **Commercial Center**, to the left, just off the Swing Bridge, replaced a ramshackle market dating from 1820. The ground floor holds a *food market*; offices and *shops* are above. This market hasn't really caught on with the vendors yet and you'll find more and better wares for sale on the sidewalks around the market than in its interior.

As you start down Regent St, you can't miss the prominent **Court House**, built in 1926 as the headquarters for Belize's colonial administrators. It still serves municipal administrative and judicial functions.

Battlefield Park is on the right across from the Court House. Always busy with vendors, loungers, con artists and other slice-of-life segments of Belize City society, the park offers shade in the sweltering midday heat, although you may find the hassle factor a high price to pay.

Turn left just past the Court House and walk one long block to the waterfront street, called Southern Foreshore, to find the **Bliss Institute** (☎ 2-72458, Southern Foreshore; open 8am-5pm Mon-Thur, 8am-4pm Fri; closed Sat & Sun, check for special performances or schedules). Baron Bliss was an Englishman with a happy name and a Portuguese title who came here on his yacht to fish. He seems to have fallen in love with Belize without ever having set foot on shore. When he died – not too long after his arrival – he left the bulk of his wealth in trust to the people of Belize. Income from the trust has paid for roads, market buildings, schools, cultural centers and many other worthwhile projects over the years.

The Bliss Institute, Belize City's prime cultural institution, is home to the National Arts Council, which stages periodic exhibits, concerts and theatrical works. Also inside is a small display of artifacts from the Mayan archaeological site at Caracol.

Continue walking south to the end of Southern Foreshore, once the neighborhood of Belize's most prominent citizens, then over to Regent St and south to the **House of Culture** (☎ 2-73050, Regent St; admission US$2.50; open 8:30am-4:30pm Mon-Fri, closed Sat & Sun). Built in 1814, it's one of the oldest buildings in Belize City. It sustained severe damage from the hurricane of 1931 and Hurricane Hattie in 1961. Formerly called the Government House, this was the residence of the governor-general until Belize attained independence within the British Commonwealth in 1981. This is also the spot where, on September 21 of that year, the Belizean flag was raised to signify independence from Britain. Today it holds the tableware and furniture once used at the residence, along with exhibits of historic photographs and occasional special exhibits. The admission price is a bit steep for the modest exhibits, but you can stroll the pleasant grounds for free. Displayed in the garden is a skiff from the fleet of Baron Bliss.

Down beyond the House of Culture you'll come to **Albert Park**, which gets nice sea breezes and has a well-maintained playground. Albert St ends at a footbridge that leads to **Bird Island**, a small recreation area with a basketball court (US$2.50 per hour) and an *open-air restaurant* that serves snacks and cool drinks. Bird Island is accessible only by foot.

Inland from the House of Culture, at Albert and Regent Sts, is **St John's Cathedral**, the oldest Anglican church in Central America, built in 1812 with bricks brought from Europe as ballast. It's often under renovation because of weather and termite damage. Notable inside is the ancient pipe organ and the Baymen-era tombstones offering a sad history of Belize's early days and the toll taken on the city's early settlers. A block southwest of the cathedral is **Yarborough Cemetery**, where you'll see the graves of less prominent early citizens – an even more turbulent narrative of Belize, dating back to 1781.

Walk back to the Swing Bridge north along historic Albert St, which has long been the city's main commercial thoroughfare. Note the unlikely little **Hindu temple** between South and Dean Sts, with offices for Amerijet and FedEx on its 1st floor. Head left for two blocks on any of the side streets (King St might be a good choice, because you can pop into Dit's for a snack) to view the Southside Canal, one of the few remaining canals in Belize City. The canals used to carry waste to the sea via Haulover Creek. Enclosed toilets, called 'long drops,' were suspended over the canals for comfort and privacy. Luckily, the canals no longer serve as sewers, but still provide drainage for the city streets.

Fort George District Cross the Swing Bridge heading north and you'll come face-to-face with the wood-frame **Paslow Building**, which houses the city's main post office. Go straight along Queen St to see the city's quaint wooden **central police headquarters**. At the end of Queen St, look left to see the old Belize prison (overshadowed by the imposing, modern, concrete Central Bank building – home of the BTB). Plans are afoot to build a national museum on this site.

You'll see magnificent frigate birds soaring over the city.

CENTRAL BELIZE CITY

PLACES TO STAY
4 Freddie's Guest House
6 Downtown Guesthouse
8 North Front Street Guest House
21 Belcove Hotel
23 Isabel Guest House
41 Fort Street Guesthouse; Jaguar Adventures
44 Chateau Caribbean Hotel
57 Colton House
58 Great House; Smokey Mermaid Restaurant
59 Radisson Fort George Hotel; St George's Dining Room; Baymen's Tavern

65 Seaside Guest House
71 Coningsby Inn
73 Hotel Mopan

PLACES TO EAT
5 Scoop's Ice Cream Parlor
10 Nerie's Restaurant
11 Pete's Pastries
15 Mars Restaurant
51 Macy's
61 Dit's Restaurant
64 Three Amigos
70 Ocean Restaurant & Bakery

OTHER
1 French Honorary Consul
2 Ghane Clock Tower
3 Methodist Church
7 Belize Tourism Board
9 American Airlines
12 Catholic Church
13 Angelus Press (Internet Access)
14 Central Police Headquarters
16 US Embassy
17 Venus Bus Station (Northern Transport-pm buses; Southern Transport-all buses)
18 Fuel Station
19 James Bus Stop
20 Batty Brothers Bus Station (Northern & Western Transport-am buses)
22 Paslow Building; Main Post Office
24 Commercial Center; Big Daddie's
25 Belize Marine Terminal; S&L Tours; Maritime Museum
26 Canadian Embassy
27 Image Factory Art Foundation
28 Belize Tourism Industry Association
29 Mexican Embassy
30 Chinese Embassy
31 Novelo's Bus Station (Northern & Western Transport-pm buses)
32 Jex and MacFadzen's Bus Stop
33 Barclay's Bank
34 Belize Bank

35 Taxi Stand
36 Court House
37 Boat Dock for Triple J & Gulf Cruza
38 Program for Belize
39 Special Affects
40 Mirab Department Store
42 National Handicrafts Centre
43 Internet Café; Dana's Café
45 Thrift Town; Book Center
46 Ro-Mac's
47 Brodie's
48 BTL Telephone Office
49 Bliss Institute
50 Farmer's Market
52 Scotiabank
53 Atlantic Bank Limited
54 Tourist Village; Cruise Ship Dock
55 Belize Audubon Society
56 Taiwanese Embassy
60 Hugh Parkey's Belize Dive Connection
62 Belize Global Travel Services; Grupo TACA; American Express
63 Italian Honorary Consul
66 Baron Bliss Tomb
67 Stan's Laundry
68 Methodist Church
69 Hindu Temple; FedEx
72 Continental Airlines
74 St John's Cathedral
75 House of Culture
76 Playground

Douglas Jones St
BelChina Bridge
Central American Blvd
To Western Highway
Vernon St
Unidos Alley
Magazine Rd
Johnson St
Woods St
Logwood St
17
Mosul St
20
Lakeview St
Banak St
19
Orange St
18
Constitution Park
Pound Yard Bridge
32
Cemetery Rd
Cemetery Rd
31
Cairo St
Collett Canal
Roger's Stadium
King St
Gibnut St
50
Hiccatee St
Iguana St
W Collett Canal St
E Collett Canal St
Dean St
Dolphin St
Bocatora St
Basra St
Raccoon St
Allenby St
Armadillo St
Amara Ave
Euphrates Ave
Tigris St
Kut Ave
Kut Ave
Tanomah St
Mex Ave
Racecourse St

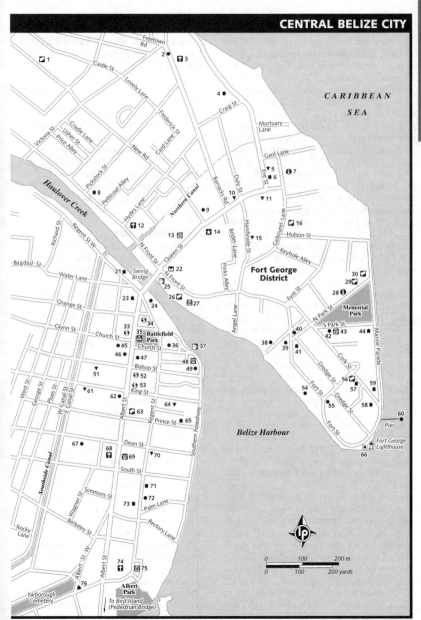

CENTRAL BELIZE CITY

After making a right on Gabourel Lane you'll pass by the **US embassy**. The original structure, on the corner of Gabourel and Hutson, has an interesting history. Originally, it was built in 1866 in New England. It was dismantled and sent to Belize on a freighter as ballast, then reassembled in this very spot. It was privately owned by American PW Shufeldt until the 1930s, when he sold it to the US government. It's taken its licks – several hurricanes and, even more profoundly, generations of termites – but it has been restored and repaired as needed. (Read *Our Man in Belize,* by Richard Timothy Conroy, for a description of the damage Hurricane Hattie did to this building in 1961.) This is among the last wooden embassy structures in the world.

A left at Hutson St will take you to the sea, where if you head south (a right turn) on Marine Parade you'll pass breezy **Memorial Park**, the Chateau Caribbean Hotel and the Radisson Fort George Hotel. At the southern tip of the peninsula you'll reach the **Baron Bliss Tomb**, next to the Fort George lighthouse. A small park here offers good views of the water and the city; kiddies will enjoy the playground at the back.

Walking back to the Swing Bridge along Fort St (which eventually turns into Front St) you'll pass the **Belize Audubon Society** (☎ 2-35004, **w** *www.belizeaudubon.org, 12 Fort St*) offering information on national parks and wildlife reserves throughout the country.

Across the street is the new **Tourist Village** (scheduled to open in early 2002), where passengers from cruise ships disembark. Inside you'll find shops and services designed especially for the cruise traveler.

The **Image Factory Art Foundation** (☎ 2-34151, 91 N Front St; free admission, donations suggested; open 9am to noon & 1:30pm to 6:30pm Mon-Fri, 9am to noon Sat, closed Sun), near the Marine Terminal, displays work by Belizean artists as well as special exhibits on art, history, culture, even hurricanes. Opening receptions are held either on the first or last Friday of the month. Cocktails are served on the Foundation's deck, which looks out on Haulover Creek; call to check schedules. There's also a gift shop here, where you can purchase original art.

Kings Park & Newtown Barracks Another nice option for a short walk is to stroll up Eve St to Newtown Barracks. Starting from Queen St at the police station, take a left onto Eve St. This is a nice seaside stroll of smaller houses. Eve St merges with Barracks Rd, and a wide modern promenade will take you by El Café (a good place to stop for a coffee), past the Belize-Mexico Cultural Center and the Princess Hotel to Barracks Green (also known as BTL Park). This is where Charles Lindburgh landed *Spirit of St Louis* in 1927 as part of a Central American promotional tour extolling the virtues of air travel. The streets west of Barracks Rd make up the modern upscale Newtown Barracks District.

Organized Tours

From Belize City you can book tours to all the country's major sites. See the relevant chapters for greater descriptions of the following sites.

Tours can be arranged through your hotel or by contacting one of the tour operators listed in the Information section, earlier in this chapter. Sites can be visited in combinations depending on their proximity to one another. Altun Ha, Crooked Tree and the Baboon Sanctuary are often packaged as a combination. These are within easiest reach of Belize City, and an early morning tour of any of these sites is a good option if you're leaving Belize on an afternoon flight. The Belize Zoo is also a good quick trip, but day trips can be arranged all the way west to Xunantunich or south to the jaguar reserve at Cockscomb Basin Wildlife Sanctuary. Prices range from US$60 to US$150 per person per tour, depending on distance and number of stops. Other day-trip options from Belize City include a canal trip to Gales Point, dive or snorkeling tours out to the reef, or the Lamanai River Trip (US$80).

Day trips to Tikal (reached by air) can be arranged through Maya Island Air or Tropic Air. See the Getting Around chapter for contact information.

Many of the taxi drivers in town also serve as tour operators, and they're likely to present you with their business card and give you a sales pitch as you enter their cab. These cabbies/tour guides can be quite knowledgeable and personable and may suit you well if you want a customized tour of Belize, probably for about US$100 per day. They're also a good window into the day-to-day life of Belizeans, and are more likely to offer candid information and first-hand recommendations than tour leaders in more structured groups. Cabbies are known to the hotel staff, if you feel that you need a personal recommendation. Also, always make sure your guide has a BTB license.

Hugh Parkey's Belize Dive Connection (☎ 2-34526, fax 2-78808, W www.belizediving .com) specializes in dive trips. Most divers base themselves at the cayes, but it is actually quicker to get out to some of the key dive sites from Belize City, so this is a good option for divers passing through Belize not heading out to the islands or coastal towns. A two-tank dive at the barrier reef is US$90, a three tank dive to Turneffe sites is US$140, and the Blue Hole trip with three dives is US$175. Parkey can also arrange fishing trips: A half day is US$600 for four anglers and two passengers, a full day is US$750.

Swimming

If you're not comfortable trying to sneak into a hotel pool, the **Pickwick Club** (☎ 2-44477, 2-31546, 160 Barracks Rd), near the Princess Hotel, allows guests to use its pool for US$7.50. This is more of a family center than a place for a peaceful swim and a sunbathe, but it's a friendly place and good for meeting the local kids and moms.

Places to Stay

Note that a 7% lodging tax will be added to the cost of your room. In addition, some hotels will tack on a service charge, often around 10%. Prices listed here are base prices, not including tax or service charge; when settling on the cost of a room, be sure to ask about additional charges.

Places to Stay – Budget

The BTB keeps an eye on the city's lowest-budget lodgings and occasionally shuts

down those it deems unworthy. Travelers on a flophouse budget should call first to make sure the place they're thinking of staying is open for business.

North Front Street Guest House (☎ 2-77595, 124 N Front St) Singles/doubles/triples/quads US$9/14/17.50/24.50. This grim little number is often recommended to back-packers, although few stay for more than one night! The front-facing balcony looking out on N Front St and beyond to Haulover Creek has a backwater flair that will appeal to aspiring desperadoes/ettes. It's convenient to the Swing Bridge and the water-taxi terminal. There are eight rooms, two toilets and two showers to choose from. There was a cluster of flophouses in this area but in a fit of spring cleaning the BTB closed them down – this is the only one so far that has managed to reopen.

Downtown Guesthouse (☎ 2-32057, 5 Eve Street) US$6 for a bunk in a dorm room, singles/doubles with shared bath US$7.50/12.50-15, with private bath & TV US$15/20. Interiorly as grim as the North Front Street Guest House, this one is located on a more respectable street and is brightened considerably by the kid sounds coming from the neighboring school and a maternal management style.

Seaside Guest House (☎ 2-78339, e seaside belize@btl.net, 3 Prince St) Bunks US$11, singles/doubles/triples US$18/28/36, all share one bath and two toilets. There are six guest rooms, two with a twin bed and a bunk bed to accommodate three guests, and one dorm room with seven beds. This is the best of the budget guest houses and it's usually necessary to book well in advance. The Seaside has been around for many years. Formerly operated by Friends Services International, a Quaker service organization, it has been sold to new owners who appear to be carrying on the tradition of offering good, helpful service and a safe, happy haven for travelers. You'll feel looked after here, and the staff is more than willing to help you get your bearings when you first arrive in town. The new owners have taken advantage of the sea view afforded by an open lot next door and built a verandah.

Freddie's Guest House (☎ 2-33851, 86 Eve St) Doubles with shared/private bath US$22.50/25. This is a well-run, quiet guest house on a pleasant residential street. Three guest rooms (two share a bath) are located at the basement level of a private home, and there are separate entrances for each room. It's best to make reservations well in advance, as it's often full.

Belcove Hotel (☎ 2-73054, e belcove@ hotmail.com, 9 Regent St W) Six singles/ doubles with shared bath US$15/20, two with private bath US$20/25, one deluxe room with air-con, bath and TV US$40. In the past, Regent St W had a notorious reputation as the place to go when you really wanted to get mugged, but recently it's cleaned up its act. This has made the Belcove Hotel a more viable option for travelers. It's an old hotel, but with friendly, family-style management, remodeled rooms, comfortable beds and tiled baths. Its atmospheric riverside location – on the banks of Haulover Creek overlooking the Swing Bridge – will help you imagine what it was like in Belize City 100 years ago. A member of the tourist police is stationed at the top of the street and the Belcove has a security guard who will help make sure you make it in the door safe and sound. Next door is Marlin's, a rough-and-tumble fishermen's bar, worth a visit if you're staying here.

Coningsby Inn (☎ 2-71566, e coningsby inn@btl.net, 76 Regent St) Singles/doubles US$23/30. Centrally located in a modern building, this new motel offers 10 sparkling rooms with cable TV, air-con and a nice common area with a big-mouth bass that you can play with all you like. Guests can use the kitchen, and there's a good-value restaurant as well.

Isabel Guest House (☎ 2-73139, 3 Albert St) Singles/doubles/triples US$22.50/27.50/35. This clean, pink, family-run establishment is at the intersection of Albert and Regent Sts, above Matus Store, but it's entered by a rear stairway reached through a dark alley – not a good option for solo travelers. To get there walk around the Central Drug Store to the back of the building and follow the signs. It offers three large attic rooms with garret-style peaked ceilings. One huge room has three double beds. All the rooms have private bath and are fan cooled; there's a cavernous common area.

Places to Stay – Mid-Range

Colton House (☎ 2-44666, fax 2-30451, w www.coltonhouse.com, 9 Cork St) Singles/ doubles US$55/65, garden apartment US$75. You'll still find the best deal in town at this charming establishment near the Radisson Fort George Hotel. The graciously restored wooden colonial house was built in 1928 and has withstood three major hurricanes (although Hurricane Hattie deposited it on the other side of Memorial Park; it was rolled back on barrels). Each room has a different decor, most have glossy wood floors, and all have air-con, a ceiling fan, private bath and private access from the wraparound porch. Morning coffee is served. There is a garden apartment with a kitchenette and cable TV. Credit cards are not accepted.

Hotel Mopan (☎ 2-77351, fax 2-75383, w www.hotelmopan.com, 55 Regent St) Singles/doubles/triples with fan US$30/40/45, with air-con US$40/50/60, all with private bath. This big, old, Caribbean-style wood-framed place has 15 basic but spacious and comfortable rooms. They've recently been remodeled and painted in fashion colors (boysenberry, ecru etc), with black-and-white photos on the wall. The best rooms are on the top floor: You'll get a rooftop view of the city. This place is a favorite with student groups and long-term visitors and it's often full – you're sure to meet an interesting bunch of folks if you stay here.

Villa Boscardi (☎/fax 2-31691, w www .villaboscardi.com, 6043 Manatee Dr, Button-wood Bay) Singles/doubles with private bath US$55/65, including breakfast. Located in a quiet suburb between Belize City and the airport, this is a small, charming retreat converted from a family home. Built with all Belizean materials, the rooms are simple, chic and comfortable. There is one private bungalow with a king-size bed; the other four rooms – two with king beds, two with queen – are on the ground floor of the house (the owners live upstairs). The floors and bathrooms are tile. Guests have kitchen and laundry access. With plenty of advance warning, the owners' two vehicles are available for rent: a 4WD Montero for US$78 a day, and the family four-door for US$45, insurance and tax included, gas extra. On weekdays, courtesy shuttle service is available. There is a salon on the premises offering massage, facials and waxing.

Fort Street Guesthouse (☎ 2-30116, fax 2-78808, **e** fortst@btl.net, **w** www.fortst.com, 4 Fort St) Singles/doubles with shared bath US$64/75, with private bath US$64/87. Prices include breakfast. If you would prefer life to be more like a Graham Greene novel, this creaky, old Victorian guest house is just the place for you. The establishment emanates a dim, sleepy ambience, especially from the upper-level louvered verandah. It's spacious enough to have a deserted feel even when it's full. There are six guest rooms; four have two double beds and shared bath, two smaller rooms have private bath. Air-con has not yet come to the Fort Street Guesthouse, but the ceiling fans are powerful and the windows are constantly rattled by sea breezes.

Chateau Caribbean Hotel (☎ 2-30800, fax 2-30900, **w** www.chateaucaribbean.com, 6 Marine Parade) Singles/doubles/triples US$69/79/89, deluxe doubles US$95, all with air-con. Flanked by the sea and Memorial Park, this hotel was at one time a gracious Belizean mansion and at another a hospital. Registration and the bar and dining room are in this original building, with charming colonial façade and brilliant views of the Caribbean, but you're in for a letdown when you walk in – furnishings, ambience and menu don't live up to the exterior. There are 25 basic, frayed rooms in a modern annex; the best rooms are the two deluxe top-floor rooms, which have extra space and private balconies.

Places to Stay – Top End

Radisson Fort George Hotel (☎ 2-33333, fax 2-73820, **e** radexec@blt.net, 2 Marine Parade) Singles/doubles with air-con US$159-179/169-189. The city's highest-end hotel has 102 conservatively decorated rooms with all the comforts. While offering world-class service,

the Radisson Fort George has managed to avoid the cultural detachment that often comes with such a package. Fear not, you will pay US prices for the privilege of staying here. There are three classes of room: Club Tower (the fanciest option, located in a glass tower at the tip of the Fort George peninsula), Colonial (in the original hotel structure) and Executive (the least expensive rooms, located across the street from the main hotel, with no view). You'll be in the thick of things: Most of the major press conferences and government events that occur in the country take place on the grounds, and visiting VIPs usually choose to bunk here. Besides two swimming pools, a health club, a good restaurant and a bar, the Fort George has its own dock used by fishing boats and cruise vessels.

Great House (☎ 2-33400, fax 2-33444, **w** www.greathousebelize.com, 13 Cork St) Singles/doubles with air-con US$110/120. In a gorgeous three-story, colonial-style mansion, built in 1927 on a piece of prime Fort George real estate, the Great House offers 12 charmingly decorated, spacious rooms with 'American-style' amenities such as cable TV (good-sized screen), in-room telephones, refrigerators, even a fruit basket. The views from the upper-floor verandah are hard to beat. Its flaw is that the service is somewhat remote and impersonal, especially when compared to the neighboring Colton House and Radisson Fort George.

Princess Hotel & Casino (☎ 2-32670, fax 2-32660, **w** www.princessbelize.com, Barracks Rd) Singles/doubles US$170/180. This 115-room-and-growing hotel northeast of the city center in the Kings Park neighborhood has gone through a slew of owners. Formerly it was the Fiesta Inn Belize and before that the Ramada Royal Reef. New management has aspirations of making it the premier hotel in the region by providing ample conference facilities and attempting to woo resort-loving vacationers to base in Belize City. This plan has its skeptics. Every room has a sea view, but other than the luxury suites, which have balconies, the rooms are sealed up tight for air-conditioning and the result is more than a tad stuffy. There is a swimming pool, a marina, a casino and Belize City's only movie theater, and there are plans to open a bowling alley (see Entertainment, later in this chapter, for details).

Places to Eat

Belize City's restaurants present a well-rounded introduction to Belizean cuisine, as well as options for reasonably tasty foreign meals. The basic and ubiquitous Belizean dish of rice and beans with stewed chicken is inexpensive and delicious. Lobster (when in season) and shrimp will be at the high end of the price spectrum. Conch (when in season), snapper and other fish fillets are good, moderately priced seafood choices.

Belizeans usually eat their large meal in the afternoon, so later in the day you may find that restaurants have run out of, or are no longer serving, their traditional menu items. While most restaurants list very liberal hours, you'll find the freshest meals and best service if you turn up during traditional mealtimes.

You won't see chain fast food in Belize, which is a refreshing change from other developing countries. In fact, 'fast' and 'food' are not words that go together much in this country, so be patient and treat mealtimes as leisure time.

See the shopping section, later, for a listing of grocery stores.

Cafés *El Café* (☎ 2-34153, 122 Eve St) Pastries & Mexican snacks US$1.50-3. Located in a pleasant neighborhood, this establishment is part café, part art gallery. Draws include claims of the best coffee in town, a nice seaside spot and a good place to hang with the local art scene. Coffee drinks – yes you can get a latte here – range from US$1 to US$3.

Dana's (☎ 2-72951, 4 S Park St) Prices US$1-2.50. Open 8am-8pm daily. Located in the Internet Café, this friendly place serves delicious fruit juices (US$1), as well as burgers and sandwiches (US$1-1.75), in a spare but pleasant air-conditioned environment.

Scoop's Ice Cream Parlor (☎ 2-44699, 17 Eve St) Cones US$1.50-3.50. Never mind

that it's located beneath a pathology lab, you'll be happy you ventured into this ice-cream parlor. There's a large array of choices, from tropical flavors to the ever-popular Oreo cookie crunch – all made on the premises.

Big Daddie's (☎ 2-70932, 2nd floor, Commercial Center) Meals US$2.50-4. You'll get hearty meals at low prices here. Lunch is served cafeteria-style starting at 11am and lasting until the food is gone. Prices vary by size of portion; expect food like breakfasts of fry jacks, eggs, beans and bacon (US$3.50) and burgers (US$2).

Pete's Pastries (☎ 2-45864, 41 Queen St) Prices US$2-4. Open 9:30am-5pm Mon-Sat, 9:30am-1pm Sun. In a tiny building at the corner of Eve St, Pete's is a good bet for lunch if you're on a tight budget. The menu varies daily, but you're likely to have a satisfying choice of barbecued or stewed meats and sandwiches, as well as cakes and pies.

Restaurants *Mars Restaurant* (☎ 2-39046, 11 Handyside St) Meals US$3.50-7.50. Open 7am-6pm daily. A good bet for traditional Belizean breakfasts and lunches, this is a long-time favorite in a new location. Handyside St gets rough after dark, so it's a better choice for daytime meals.

Bird Island Restaurant (☎ 2-76500, on Bird Island at the end of Albert St) Lunch & dinner US$2.50-8. Open daily for lunch 10am-2:30pm, dinner 5:30pm-9:30pm. A nice open-air restaurant in a parklike setting, this is a great lunchtime spot, popular with local office workers, although there are more mosquitoes here than you'll find at the in-town spots. If you're lucky you'll be able to catch a basketball game at the neighboring court. Bird Island serves enormous glasses of fruit juice for US$2.

Three Amigos (☎ 2-74378, 2-B King St) Lunch US$4-6, dinner US$8-14. Open 11:30am-2:30pm & 5:30pm-9pm Sun-Thur, 11:30am-2:30pm, 5:30pm-10pm Fri & Sat. Formerly GG's Café and Patio, this is a favorite with travelers for its tasty food, friendly staff and clean, comfortable dining areas. You'll have a choice of sitting in the cool, tiled dining room – perfect for escaping the midday heat – or out on the patio, best for the evening meal. For lunch, try a burger (US$4) or big plate of rice and beans with beef, chicken or pork (US$4). There are imaginative dinner courses such as grilled seafood and shellfish (US$14) and pastas (US$8), and soups and salads run US$5-6.

Nerie's Restaurant (☎ 2-34028, Queen St at Daly St) Meals US$3-6. Open 7:30am-10pm Mon-Sat. This two-level restaurant is a favorite with expats and locals. The menu contains all your favorite Belizean dishes, from chicken (US$3.50) to gibnut (US$6), along with a delicious chicken in mole sauce (*chirmole;* US$3) and daily specials. The best spot is upstairs on the balcony, where you can gaze on the hustle and bustle of Queen St. The upper level converts to a bar and nightclub on some nights.

Macy's (☎ 2-73419, 18 Bishop St) Prices US$5-8. Open 11am-9:30pm Mon-Sat. This place offers consistently good Caribbean Creole cooking, friendly service and decent prices. The menu changes daily, but you're always likely to get some chicken (US$5), fish fillets (steamed US$7.50, fried US$6) and stewed beef or meatballs. Boar, gibnut and deer often make appearances on the menu. If you're feeling adventurous you may want to try armadillo or wild boar.

Dit's Restaurant (☎ 2-33330, 50 King St) Prices US$1-5. Open 8am-9pm daily. This is a homey place with a loyal local clientele, who are gently reminded by a sign at the counter 'It's nice to be important, but it's more important to be nice.' Huge portions are served at low prices: rice and beans with beef, pork or chicken for US$3, and burgers for US$1.75. Mexican snacks like *salbutes,* (fried tortillas with meat and cheese), *panades* (savory pastries), *garnaches* (corn cakes) and tamales are available at around US$0.50 each (order a few, they're small). There are also yummy cakes and pies for US$1 a slice. This is a great place to stop in for a snack any time of day. There's boil-up and barbecue (US$3-4) on Friday and Saturday.

Ocean Restaurant & Bakery (Ocean Tea Palace; ☎ 2-70579, 46 Regent St) Prices US$3.50-7.50. This is a good bet for Chinese

food: The chef/proprietor makes his own noodles, eschews lard and serves delicious stir-fries and rice and noodle dishes. There are good vegetarian options here.

Sumathi Restaurant (☎ 2-31172, 190 Barracks Rd) Meals US$7-13. Open 11am-11pm Mon-Sat, 1pm-11pm Sun. Belize City's Indian restaurants have been playing musical chairs. This restaurant is under the same management as Memories of India off Queen St, but has moved into the old location of Sea Rock. Although they specialize in southern Indian cuisine, all the usual suspects – curries, biriyanis, tandooris – are on the menu. Check for fresh seafood dishes.

The Victoria House (☎ 2-32302, fax 2-32301, ☒ biltmore@btl.net, in the Belize Biltmore Plaza Hotel, Mile 3 (Km 5) Northern Hwy) Meals US$6-18. Many locals will recommend this restaurant as the best in town, and visitors often agree. You'll see things on the menu here that you won't any place else in Belize. Menu items range from burgers and rice and beans, all the way to pastas, seafood and European entrées. Daily specials, such as catfish parmesan, are imaginative without being too over the top and are always prepared with the freshest ingredients.

St George's Dining Room and *Baymen's Tavern* (☎ 2-77400 for both, Radisson Fort George Hotel, 2 Marine Parade) Meals US$15-50. Open 8am-10pm daily. These two Radisson Fort George restaurants offer broad à la carte menus as well as buffet dinners and theme nights, although the options tend toward stodgy and the prices are high.

Smokey Mermaid Restaurant (☎ 2-34759, Great House Hotel, 13 Cork St) Meals US$12-50. Open 6:30am-10pm daily. This restaurant, across the street from St George's, has similar prices but is less formal. Its terraced patio is a lovely place to relax at the end of the day, and the menu offers plenty to choose from – your best bets are the pasta and seafood dishes. The menu is long, but not terribly imaginative.

Chef Bob's Restaurant (☎ 2-36908, Barracks Rd) US$6-25. Open 11:30am-2pm & 6pm-10:30pm Mon-Fri, 6pm-10:30pm Sat, closed Sun. Gaining in popularity in the Newtown Barracks part of town, Chef Bob from Italy has dressed up a standard cinder block building with a mix of Italian decorations and murals and Belizean knickknacks. The eclectic decor matches the menu. You can get soups and salads (US$6), pub food like scotch egg and fish-and-chips, Mexican-American-style burritos, tacos and quesadillas (US$6-20), falafel, pastas and seafood (US$12-20) and surf-and-turf (US$24). Wednesday night is sushi night. Not the best value in the city, but if you're yearning for variety this is your place.

Entertainment

No matter if you're a local or a visitor, you'll find that in Belize City your social life will center around hotel bars. Friday happy hours at the **Belize Biltmore** or the **Radisson Fort George Hotel** offer a microcosm of the Belize City social life.

When touring acts come through town they'll usually play at the **Belize Civic Auditorium** (☎ 2-72051, 2-72092, 2-75335, Central American Blvd, south of the Belcan Bridge) for the younger set, then play one of the hotels to a more sedate or older group. You can call the Civic Auditorium to see what's on, but posters announcing major events are usually hung all over town (including at hotels and guest houses), so you probably won't have to work that hard.

Cultural events, such a performances of the Belize National Dance Company, are mostly held at the Bliss Institute. Again, notices of performances are posted all over town.

Note that the bar and nightclub scene in Belize City changes rapidly, so take this info with a grain of salt and ask around to get the freshest information on the hot spots.

The **Princess Hotel & Casino** has a number of entertainment venues that have come under some criticism for not being welcoming to locals, an unusual practice for Belize City hotels. There is a casino here with 400 slot machines, several gaming tables and a floor show with Russian dancing girls kicking it up daily at 9pm and 10pm. Nonguests must show US$100 to enter. Cash is converted to tokens at the door. Also on the premises is a **movie theater** (☎ 2-37162) showing first-ish run films. Movies usually start at 6pm and 9pm, with matinees at 3pm Saturday and Sunday. There are also plans to build Belize's first bowling alley (unless you count coconut bowling in Placencia).

Eden Nightclub (☎ 2-34559, 190 Barracks Rd) and its neighbor, **Caesar's** (where you have the choice of using the little Cleopatra's or the little Marc Antony's room), are the spots for dancing all night. They're open Thursday to Saturday and don't get going until around midnight.

Nightfall in Belize City can bring lots of interesting action, much of it illegal or dangerous. Be judicious in your choice of nightspots. If drugs are in evidence, there's lots of room for trouble, and as a foreigner you'll have a hard time blending into the background.

Spectator Sports

Major sporting events are held at the Marion Jones Sports Complex. For a schedule of what's on here, and other places in the city, call the **National Sports Council** (☎ 2-72051, 2-72092, 2-75335, Belize Civic Auditorium, Central American Blvd south of the Belcan Bridge).

Shopping

Albert St is the main shopping area in town, where you'll find groceries, appliances and clothing for sale. There's also the big, largely empty **Commercial Center** (☎ 2-72117, Albert St at Haulover Creek), built on the site of Belize City's old open-air market. Inside you'll find some souvenir stands as well as some housewares and product vendors, although there are as many stands outside on the surrounding streets as inside the center. It's open 6am to 6pm Monday to Saturday.

Groceries Ro-Mac's (☎ 2-77022, 27 Albert St) is a good place to load up on food and other supplies, and it's centrally located to the south-side hotels.

Brodie's (☎ 2-74472, 2 Albert St) This is similar to Ro-Mac's, with some English-language books and magazines. There's also a larger Brodie's near the Belcan Junction.

Save-U *(☎ 2-31291, Central American Blvd at Belcan junction)* Open 8am-9pm Mon-Sat, 8am-2pm Sun and holidays. This is a large, modern store, convenient for loading up on supplies before heading out of town.

There's a ***farmer's market*** by Novelo's Bus Terminal, at Roger's Stadium, at 5am to around midday on Tuesday, Friday and Saturday mornings. It's excellent for finding fresh vegetables.

Premium Wines & Spirits *(☎ 2-34984, 2-36992, ℮ price@btl.net, 166 Barracks Rd)* Open 8am-noon & 1:30pm-5pm Mon-Fri. This place has good prices on local and imported libations.

Souvenirs *National Handicrafts Centre* *(☎ 2-33636, 2 S Park St)* Open 8am-5pm Mon-Fri, 8am-4pm and by appointment Sat. This is ground zero for Belizean souvenirs, carrying the work of 540 Belizean craftspeople, and it's often a stop for tour buses routed through the city. Things to buy include ironwood carvings, slate carvings, rosewood bowls, jewelry carved from cohune palms, original oil paintings by Belizean artists, Mayan *jippy jappa* baskets, some Mayan textiles, and the usual souvenir knickknacks. Information on events going on around the city is usually posted on the door.

Special Affects *(☎ 2-35973, 1 Fort St)* Open 9am-5pm Mon-Sat. This is another fun gift shop, near the National Handicrafts Centre. It has Belizean handicrafts as well as tropical souvenirs brought in from Mexico. Here's the place to get a coconut postcard, stylish shirts and sarongs.

The ***Image Factory Art Foundation*** *(☎ 2-34151, 91 N Front St)* Free admission, donations suggested; open 9am-noon & 1:30pm-6:30pm Mon-Fri, 9am-noon Sat. Near the Marine Terminal, this museum also offers a small selection of art, handicrafts and books with an alternative bent.

Mirab Department Store *(☎ 2-32933/66, 2 Fort St)* Open 9am-5:30pm Mon-Sat. Belize's first upscale department store carries household appliances, furniture for home and patio, electronics and gift items.

The central Fort George location makes it nice for a visit, if only to enjoy the turbo aircon system. It offers a glimpse of middle-class Belizean life that you won't see at regular travelers' haunts.

Getting There & Away

Air Belize City is served by two airports, the Philip Goldson International Airport (BZE) and the Municipal Airport (TZA). The Municipal Airport is closer to the city, and flights into and out of Belize City are much cheaper (nearly half) from the Municipal Airport than from the international terminal. (See the Getting Around chapter for details.)

Bus Bus terminals are located around the Collett Canal, near Roger's Stadium. For schedules to all points, see the Getting Around chapter.

Car & Motorcycle A couple of main streets get you out of town. To reach the Western Hwy (which leads to the turnoffs for the Hummingbird and Manatee Hwys) you must exit via Cemetery Rd, which bisects a fantastic, huge, ramshackle cemetery. (Most of the graves are above the ground because of the high water table and frequent flooding – it's a good reminder to drive safe.) To get to Cemetery Rd from the northern parts of Belize City, take Princess Margaret Dr or Freetown Rd to Central American Blvd. Cross the bridge and continue to Cemetery Rd, then turn right.

If you're south of Haulover Creek, from Albert St, take King St to E Collett Canal St, go right for two blocks to Vernon St, turn left over the canal and continue to Central American Blvd St, go left one block and take a right onto Cemetery Dr.

Reaching the Northern Hwy and the Philip Goldson International Airport is a tiny bit more straightforward. From the Swing Bridge, head east on Queen St, take a left onto Barracks Rd and veer left again onto Freetown Rd just past the Ghane Clock Tower. Freetown Rd turns into Haulover Rd past the Belcan Junction traffic circle; continue on Haulover to the Northern Hwy.

Boat The Caye Caulker Water Taxi Association connects Belize City with Caye Caulker and San Pedro on Ambergris Caye. By request boats will take you to St George's Caye and Caye Chapel as well. Boats usually stop at Caye Caulker and continue on to San Pedro, although if there are enough passengers to fill a boat for each destination the stopover is eliminated. The trip to Caye Caulker takes about 35 minutes, to San Pedro 45 minutes. The boats are open, have fast twin engines, and hold around 40 people each. Captains usually do their best to avoid rainstorms, but sometimes they're inevitable. When they happen, passengers huddle together under large tarps to stay dry.

Getting Around

There is no regular municipal bus system within Belize City.

To/From the Airports Unfortunately, there is no public transportation into and out of either airport, nor is there a shuttle service. The taxi fare to or from the international airport is US$17. You might want to approach other passengers about sharing a cab to the city center.

It takes about half an hour to walk from the air terminal the 2 miles (3km) out to the access road to the Northern Hwy, where it's easy to catch a bus going either north or south.

Taxis from the Municipal Airport into the city are usually around US$2.50 per person.

Car & Motorcycle Driving in Belize City is no more hectic than driving in any major city. Be aware that there are a number of one-way streets in the city. Also, there are recessed gutters at the edge of most of the roads so you'll need to take extra care when parking. Street smarts prevail here – lock your doors and don't leave valuables in your car, especially in plain view.

Taxi Trips by taxi within Belize City (including to and from Municipal Airport) cost US$2.50 for one person, US$6 for two or three and US$8 for four. If you phone for a cab instead of hailing one on the street, the price may go up, as it will if you're going outside the city center. Secure the price in advance with your driver and, if in doubt, check with hotel or restaurant staff about what the cost should be before setting out.

Around Belize City

People who come to Belize and spend their whole trip on the cayes miss out on the country's many other adventurous and interesting places. You don't have to travel far to see birds, monkeys, ruins or just a different perspective. Frequent buses leaving from Belize City make exploring the inland areas immediately west and north of the city easy and rewarding. With a little planning, you could hit one or two of the places in this chapter on an easy day trip from the cayes or Belize City.

Highlights

- Gazing at black howler monkeys in the tree canopy at the Community Baboon Sanctuary
- Bird-watching at Crooked Tree Wildlife Sanctuary
- Getting face-to-face with a jaguar at the Belize Zoo
- Visiting the stunning ruins at Altun Ha

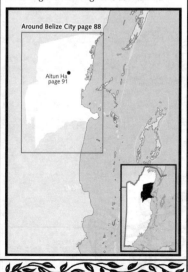

Around Belize City page 88

Altun Ha page 91

Heading up the Northern Highway

On the way out of Belize City, the Northern Hwy passes the airport heading northwest on its route inland. Just north of Ladyville, a dirt road splits off toward the village of Bermudian Landing and the Community Baboon Sanctuary, where your chance of seeing howler monkeys is virtually assured. Near the community of Sand Hill, the Northern Hwy splits again, the vector to the right becoming the Old Northern Hwy, a partially paved, bumpy road heading to the ruins of Altun Ha. Bypassing that turnoff and continuing north, you'll come to signs for the Crooked Tree Wildlife Sanctuary, where the resident and migrant bird population is one of the most diverse in Central America.

If you kept going along the Northern Hwy, you'd come to Orange Walk and Corozal, where sugarcane waltzes in endless rows and the sugar industry continues to sweeten the economy.

COMMUNITY BABOON SANCTUARY

No real baboons inhabit Belize, but Belizeans use that name for the country's indigenous black howler monkeys. Though howler monkeys live throughout Central and South America, the endangered black howler exists only in Belize.

The Community Baboon Sanctuary (☎ 2-12181, ℮ baboon@btl.net; admission US$5; open 8am-5pm daily), in the village of Bermudian Landing, is unique in that it's completely voluntary. This grassroots conservation initiative is fully dependant on the cooperation of private landowners. Led by American zoologist Robert Horwich, a small group of local Creole farmers signed an agreement in 1985 that would protect the howler monkeys' habitat where it butted up against their lands.

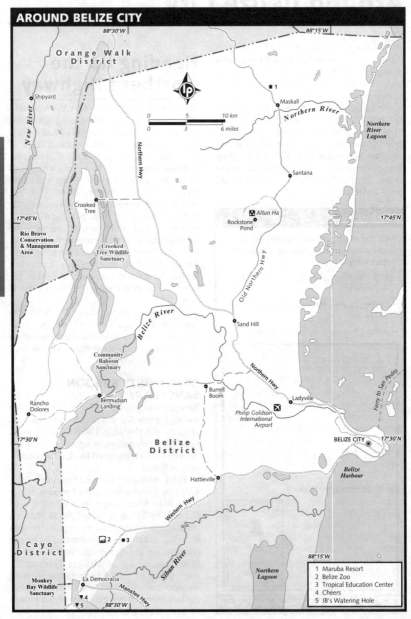

AROUND BELIZE CITY

AROUND BELIZE CITY

Orange Walk District

Shipyard

New River

Northern Hwy

Maskall

Northern River

Northern River Lagoon

Santana

17°45'N

Crooked Tree

Rockstone Pond

Altun Ha

17°45'N

Rio Bravo Conservation & Management Area

Crooked Tree Wildlife Sanctuary

Belize River

Sand Hill

Old Northern Hwy

Community Baboon Sanctuary

Burrell Boom

Northern Hwy

Ladyville

Ferry to San Pedro

Rancho Dolores

Bermudian Landing

Philip Goldson International Airport

17°30'N

Belize District

BELIZE CITY   17°30'N

Hattieville

Belize Harbour

Western Hwy

Sibun River

Cayo District

2   3

Northern Lagoon

88°15'W

Monkey Bay Wildlife Sanctuary

La Democracia

4

5

Manatee Hwy

88°30'W

1 Maruba Resort
2 Belize Zoo
3 Tropical Education Center
4 Cheers
5 JB's Watering Hole

0   5   10 km
0   3   6 miles

88°30'W   88°15'W

To date, 160 landowners from the eight villages surrounding the 20-sq-mile (52-sq-km) sanctuary have voluntarily pledged to protect riparian forest and maintain forest buffer zones around their farmland in order to keep the large monkey habitat in the middle intact.

Managing the Sanctuary

The sanctuary garnered some of its first monies from the World Wildlife Fund and went into a management association with the Belize Audubon Society. But according to Fallet Young, who helped found the sanctuary, the relationship wasn't beneficial to the surrounding villages.

In the past, councils set up to manage the sanctuary, made up of men elected from surrounding villages, had been riddled with conflict. Hot tempers led to bad, ineffective management and, for a while, it seemed the sanctuary was in trouble.

That's when the women stepped in. Led by Jesse Young, the local Women's Conservation Group took over full management of the sanctuary in the late 1990s. Since then, the group has procured funding from national groups like Programme for Belize and Protected Areas Conservation Trust. They now have a computer, phone, fax, a small restaurant and some money to invest in upkeep of the sanctuary. Partial support for the sanctuary comes from outside funding, but a lot of it comes from tourists who, the hope is, will continue to support the economies of the surrounding villages by buying local baked goods and crafts, paying for guides, homestays and admission to the sanctuary.

The Sanctuary Today

The result of so much community cooperation is a thriving broadleaf-forest habitat where a growing population of howlers feeds, sleeps and – at dawn and dusk – howls (loudly and unmistakably). Black howlers are vegetarians and spend most of the daylight hours cruising the treetops in groups of four to eight, led by a dominant male. Various fruits, flowers, leaves and other tidbits keep them happy. As long as

visitors keep to small groups and stay quiet and respectful of the habitat, the monkeys don't seem to mind humans lurking below.

At the sanctuary's small museum and visitor's center, you can learn all about the black howler and the 200 other species of wildlife found in the reserve. A guided nature walk is included with your price of admission. Tours of the villages surrounding the sanctuary are available, as are canoe trips and night hikes.

Places to Stay & Eat

The sanctuary can set up *village homestays* for you, but it's best to arrange these in advance. Be sure to ask lots of questions about whether meals are included, what types of rooms, cost etc. You can *camp* on the sanctuary grounds (US$5 per person) or stay at one of the two rustic (though not cheap) options listed below.

TOM BOYDEN

Black howler monkeys are called baboons in Belize.

Nature Resort (☎ 14-9286, fax 21-2197, e *naturer@btl.net, next to the visitor's center)* Double cabanas with shared/private bath US$27/32, with bath & kitchenette US$43-57. This resort is the best and friendliest place to stay, with rustic cabins that are well maintained. You might consider staying here if you want to get up really early to see the howler monkeys when they're most active.

Howler Monkey Lodge (☎ 2-12158, e *jungled@btl.net)* Cabanas US$40. This resort, formerly the Jungle Drift Lodge, is downright unfriendly and appears to be more interested in catering to group tours than individuals. The grounds here are nice, but US$40 for a small cabana with shared bath seems excessive.

Getting There & Away

The Community Baboon Sanctuary lies 26 miles (42km) west of Belize City in the village of Bermudian Landing – an easy day trip from Belize City or the cayes. You can book an organized tour or arrange for a taxi in Belize City (roundtrip taxi fare will be about US$75).

If you're driving, turn west off the Northern Hwy at the Burrell Boom turnoff (Mile 13). From there it's another 12 miles (20km) of dirt road to the sanctuary. Note that if you're heading to western Belize after visiting the sanctuary, you'll save time by taking the 8-mile (13km) cut from Burrell Boom south to Hattieville on the Western Hwy, avoiding Belize City traffic.

Russell's and McFadzean's operate buses to Bermudian Landing, but the schedules are such that it's necessary to spend the night and leave early the next morning. Russell's buses leave Belize City weekdays at 12:15pm and 4:30pm and Saturday at noon, 1pm and 4:30pm. McFadzean's bus leaves daily at 12:30pm. All buses return from Bermudian Landing at 5:30am and 6am.

Another option is to catch one of the frequent Northern Transport buses heading to the Mexican border, get off at Burrell Boom and hitch the 13 miles (8km) into the sanctuary, though beware this route does not see much traffic.

ALTUN HA

Northern Belize's most famous Mayan ruin is Altun Ha *(Archaeology Department in Belmopan ☎ 8-22106; admission US$2.50; open 9am-5pm daily)*, 34 miles (55km) north of Belize City along the Old Northern Hwy. The site is near the village of Rockstone Pond, 10 miles (16km) south of Maskall.

Altun Ha (Mayan for 'rockstone pond') was undoubtedly a small (population about 3000) but rich and important Mayan trading town, with agriculture also playing an essential role in its economy. Altun Ha had formed as a community by at least 600 BC, perhaps even several centuries earlier, and the town flourished until the mysterious collapse of Classic Mayan civilization around AD 900. Most temples you will see date from Late Classic times, though burials indicate that Altun Ha's merchants were trading with Teotihuacán in Preclassic times.

Of the grass-covered temples arranged around the two plazas here, the largest and most important is the **Temple of the Masonry Altars** (Structure B-4), in Plaza B. The restored structure you see dates from the first half of the 7th century and takes its name from altars on which copal was burned and beautifully carved jade pieces were smashed in sacrifice. Excavation of the structure in 1968 revealed many burial sites of important officials. Most of the burial sites had been looted or desecrated, but two were intact. Among the jade objects found in one of these was a unique mask sculpture portraying Kinich Ahau, the Mayan sun god; as of now, this is the largest well-carved jade object ever uncovered from a Mayan archaeological site. (Look for the jade head illustration in the corner of Belizean banknotes.)

In Plaza A, Structure A-1 is sometimes called the **Temple of the Green Tomb**. Deep within it was discovered the tomb of a priest-king dating from around AD 600. Tropical humidity had destroyed the king's garments and the paper of the Mayan 'painted book' that was buried with him, but many riches were intact: shell necklaces, pottery, pearls, stingray spines used in bloodletting rites, jade beads and pendants, and ceremonial flints.

Modern toilets and a drinks stand are on site.

Places to Stay & Eat

Options and amenities here are few and far between. Occasional kiosks along the route sell water and snacks, but you might want to bring refreshments along and picnic at Altun Ha.

Mayan Wells Restaurant (☎ 2-12039, 1½ miles/2.4km from ruins) Open 11am-5pm Tues-Sat. This restaurant, on the road to Altun Ha, is a popular stop for lunch or refreshments. Traditional Belizean lunches of rice, beans and stewed chicken (US$5) are served in a pleasant outdoor setting. *Camping* is allowed on the premises and bathroom and shower facilities are available. Campsites cost US$5.

Maruba Resort (☎ 3-22199, fax 2-12049, ☎ 713-799-2031 in the USA, e maruba@ flash.net, w www.maruba-spa.com, Mile 40½ Old Northern Hwy) Rooms range from US$130-425 (standard single to jungle treehouse suite), meals extra. This luxury 'jungle spa,' 2 miles (3.2km) north of the village of Maskall, is decorated with an artist's fine eye. The lush grounds are well-manicured and the staff is exceedingly welcoming. Amenities include a Japanese mineral bath and full spa indulgences, including 'mud therapy.' The resort also offers a slew of tours. You can get here by following the Old Northern Hwy from Belize City, or by private or charter boat going up the Northern River from the cayes.

Getting There & Away

The easiest way to visit Altun Ha is on one of the many tours running daily from Belize City or San Pedro on Ambergris Caye.

To get here in your own vehicle, take the Northern Hwy 19 miles (31km) northwest from Belize City to the town of Sand Hill, where the highway divides – the new paved highway continues northwest and the old one heads northeast to the ruins. The old road is narrow and potholed, passing through jungle and the occasional village.

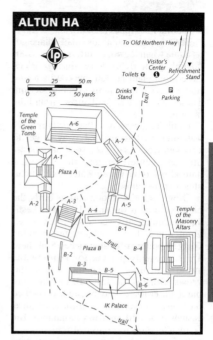

Follow it for about 10½ miles (17km) – about 45 minutes – and look for the sign on the left pointing to the ruins, which are about 2 miles (3.2km) west off this junction. Note that the Old Northern Hwy is not busy; a breakdown could be problematic, and hitchhiking is usually disappointing.

If you're firmly committed to public transportation, you can catch a Russell's bus headed for Maskall, north of Altun Ha, but you won't be able to get there and back on the same day. Buses depart Belize City daily at 1pm, 3:30pm and 5:30pm. The bus returns from Maskall at 5:30am, 6:30am and 7:30am. The trip takes about 90 minutes and costs US$1.50 each way.

CROOKED TREE
pop 1000

A swift 33 miles (53km) up the Northern Hwy, midway between Belize City and Orange Walk, is the turnoff to the fishing and farming village of Crooked Tree and the Crooked Tree Wildlife Sanctuary, which are another 3½ miles (5.5km).

The story goes that this small village got its name when logwood cutters in the 1700s floated up the Belize River through Black Creek to a giant lagoon marked by a tree that seemingly grew in every direction. These 'crooked trees' still grow around the lagoon.

Until the causeway to the Northern Hwy was built in 1984, the only way to get to Crooked Tree was by boat, so it's no wonder life here centers around the lagoon, a natural reservoir whose water level fluctuates with the rains.

Other than the lagoon and its birds, the big draw here is the annual **Cashew Festival**, held on the first weekend in May, to celebrate the cashew nuts harvested from the village's bounty of cashew trees. Soils here are supposedly perfect for growing the sweet fruit upon which the cashew nut grows. During the festival, cashews are parched, cracked and roasted, or turned into cashew cake, cashew jelly, cashew juice, cashew wine and cashew-you-name-it. The festival features live music, storytelling and lots of eating. The harvest season continues into July.

Crooked Tree Wildlife Sanctuary
In 1984 the Belize Audubon Society was successful in having 5 sq miles (12 sq km) around the village declared a wildlife sanctuary *(Belize Audubon Society ☎ 2-35004, fax 2-34985, e base@btl.net, 3½ miles/5.5km west of the Northern Hwy; admission US$4; open 8am-4pm daily)*, principally because of the area's wealth of migrant and resident birds. A small visitor's center (no ☎) right at the entrance to town can give you information and a map of Crooked Tree.

Migrating birds flock to the rivers, swamps and lagoons here each year during the dry season (December to May). The best time of year for wildlife-watching is in May, when the water in the lagoon drops to its lowest level and the animals must come farther out into the open to reach their food supply.

Bird-watchers, don your binoculars and telephoto lens and get ready to witness an orgy of ornithological bliss. Herons, ducks, kites, egrets, ospreys, kingfishers and hawks are just a smattering of the 275 bird species seen here. Jabiru storks grace the area, eating fish, shells and snakes and nesting in winter. With a wingspan of up to 8 feet (2.5m), the jabiru is the largest flying bird in all the Western Hemisphere. Habitat destruction throughout its range had the jabiru on the brink of extinction, but protected wetlands in Belize have given it a shot at survival. Crooked Tree sees the country's highest concentration of these magnificent birds.

Black howler monkeys, Morelet's crocodiles, coatis, iguanas and turtles also live among the mango and cashew trees at Crooked Tree.

Day trips to Crooked Tree are possible, but it's best to stay the night so you can be here at dawn, when the birds are most active. Trails weave through the village and you can spot plenty of species on your own, but you'll get farther and see much more on a guided boat tour. In fact, for those interested in viewing birds and other wildlife, a guided nature tour of this sanctuary is among the most rewarding experiences in Belize.

Boat tours cost US$70 for one to four people (less per person for larger groups). You can also arrange a nature walk (US$4/ hour for one to four people) or canoe rental (US$10). Arrangements can be made through the visitor's center or your hotel.

The hotels in Crooked Tree can also arrange day trips to Altun Ha, the Community Baboon Sanctuary or Lamanai (US$20-40 per person, depending on the size of the group).

Places to Stay & Eat
It's pretty easy to find your way around Crooked Tree. A big signpost is the closest thing the village has to street signs. Most places lack proper addresses, so just follow the directions on the signpost, or ask someone – the townsfolk are friendly and happy to help.

JB's Restaurant (no ☎, go right at the signpost, look for the blue hut on your left) Meals US$3. Open 10am-10pm daily. The menu features a hearty plate of rice and beans with chicken or beef (whichever is on the stove) and cold Belikins.

Rhaburn's Rooms (☎ 25-7035) Singles/doubles US$10/15. Meals US$3. Get to these homestay-style accommodations by turning left at the main signpost, past the police station and church. Go left at the end of the field until you get to a gate; go through it to the light brown house. The four rooms here, above the main house, are very small but clean. Though they haven't been in the room-letting business for long, owners Owen and Maggie Rhaburn are friendly and welcoming.

Sam Tillett's Hotel & Tours (☎ 21-2026, ⒺSamhotel@btl.net) Singles/doubles US$20/30, slightly nicer rooms US$40, luxury Jabiru Suite US$50. Meals US$5. All rooms have private bath with weak water pressure. Sam's bird tours are in demand – he's known throughout the country as the 'king of birds.' The cabana restaurant serves good meals to guests only.

Paradise Inn (☎ 25-7044, fax 23-2579, north end of village) Single/double cabanas US$38/49. Breakfast US$3, lunch US$4, dinner US$7. Also enjoying a considerable reputation among birders, the Crawford family has simple cabanas with nice lagoon views. The restaurant gets high marks with travelers, though be sure to check that it's open.

Bird's Eye View Lodge (☎ 25-7027, fax 2-24869, Ⓔ birdseye@btl.net, south end of village) Dorm rooms/singles/doubles/triples/quads US$15/40/60/70/80. Breakfast & lunch US$7, dinner US$10. This lodge is a bit of a walk from the village, but it's got large, clean rooms facing the lagoon. Birding groups often stay here to do nature walks and boat tours from the lodge. Canoes are also available for rent here.

Getting There & Away

The road to Crooked Tree village is 33 miles (53km) up the Northern Hwy from Belize City, 25 miles (40km) south of Orange Walk. The village is 3½ miles (5km) west of the highway via a causeway over Crooked Tree Lagoon.

If you want to take a bus roundtrip to Crooked Tree, you'll have to spend the night

there. Jex Bus offers service daily departing Belize City for Crooked Tree village at 10:30am, 4:30pm and 5:30pm; return trips leave Crooked Tree at 6am, 6:30am and 7am. A Novelo's bus leaves Belize City from the old Batty's terminal at 15 Mosul St at 4pm and departs Crooked Tree at 6am. The one-way fare is US$1.75.

If you start early from Belize City, Corozal or Orange Walk, you can bus to Crooked Tree Junction and then walk along the causeway to the village (about an hour). You could also hitchhike this route, although traffic is infrequent.

Heading out the Western Highway

Heading west from Belize City along Cemetery Rd, you'll pass right through Lords Ridge Cemetery and soon find yourself headed out of town on the Western Hwy. In 15 miles (25km) you'll pass Hattieville, founded in 1961 after Hurricane Hattie wreaked destruction on Belize City, and in another 13 miles (21km) you'll come to one of Belize's best inland treasures – the Belize Zoo.

Buses run at least hourly along the Western Hwy and upon request will drop you at the zoo or anywhere else along the highway. If you kept going along the Western Hwy, you'd end up in Belmopan, the nation's capital, or still farther, in the outdoor-adventure hub of San Ignacio.

BELIZE ZOO

Anyone visiting should make a trip to this delightful natural zoo (☎ 8-13004, Ⓔ belize zoo@btl.net, ⓌWww.belizezoo.org, Mile 29 (Km 46) Western Hwy; admission US$7.50/3.75 adults/children; open 8am-5pm daily, closed major Belizean holidays). When a documentary film entitled Path of the Raingods was shot in Belize, Sharon Matola was hired to take care of the animals. By the time filming was over, the animals had become partly tame and Matola was left wondering what to do with her 17 semi-wild charges, knowing they were unlikely to survive if released back into the jungle.

In 1983, Matola founded this zoo, which displays native Belizean wildlife in natural surroundings on 29 acres (12 hectares) of tropical savanna. On a self-guided tour (45 to 60 minutes) you'll see more than 125 native animals, including jaguars, ocelots, black howler monkeys, peccaries, vultures, storks, crocodiles, tapirs and gibnuts. One of the stars is April, a Baird's tapir who draws hundreds of people every year to celebrate her birthday (on the first Friday in April).

One of the zoo's central goals is to make Belizeans sensitive to the value of preserving native wildlife. To this end, there are signs throughout the park imploring visitors not to hunt, skin or eat the wild relatives of the zoo's residents. Matola keeps busy running outreach and educational programs. You can easily see many animals here that you'd otherwise only ever see in movies or on brochures. Try to come early in the morning or in late afternoon, when the animals are most active and the tourists scarce.

The zoo is on the north side of the highway (a sign marks the turnoff). It's just a five-minute walk from the highway to the visitor's center, which has displays and information about the programs and animals. The 'Wild Ting' gift shop has some good books and souvenirs.

Tropical Education Center

Across the highway from the zoo, the Tropical Education Center (☎ 8-13003, fax 8-13010, e tec@btl.net, Mile 29 (Km 46) Western Hwy; open 8am-5pm daily) sits on 84 acres (34 hectares) of pine savanna in the Sibun River watershed. The center is governed by the Belize Zoo and is primarily used for environmental education, hosting school groups and scientists who come to learn more about the area's wildlife and natural history.

On the site, a nature trail meanders through the savanna, and treetop platforms let you view wildlife and birds. You can rent a canoe and go for a paddle on the Sibun for US$30/40 (half/full day) per canoe. You can also join the fun Nocturnal

Zoo Tour (US$10 per person) to see what all the zoo's critters are up to at night.

You can *camp* on the grounds (US$6 per person) or stay in one of the three *dormitories* (US$17.50) or *guest houses* (US$35), which have fans, running water and flush toilets. *Meals* (US$6) are available for groups only, although you can use the kitchen for US$1.

MONKEY BAY WILDLIFE SANCTUARY

This sanctuary (☎ 8-13032, e mbay@btl.net, w www.watershedbelize.org, Mile 31½ (Km 50) Western Hwy) stretches across 1070 acres (433 hectares) nestled up against the Sibun River. Across the river is **Monkey Bay National Park**, a remote 2250 acre (911 hectare) preserve that was established in 1992. Together with the park, the sanctuary creates a sizeable wetlands corridor in the Sibun River Valley. Though there aren't many monkeys around today, the park and sanctuary are named for a troop of howler monkeys that used to live in a giant guana-caste tree growing along a bend in the river.

The sanctuary is a nonprofit organization dedicated to teaching 'ecology education,' a phrase that sanctuary founder Matthew Miller suggests goes way beyond just learning about natural history. He says truly understanding a place's ecology includes getting intricately involved in the everyday life of the community.

In addition to intercultural exchange programs featuring village homestays, the sanctuary runs a variety of ecology field courses, including a 14-day canoe trip on the Sibun and Belize Rivers.

The range of tours offered here is extensive, and it's best to email the sanctuary before you come to find out what's happening when you're there. If you're just stopping by, you can rent canoes (US$20 for 24 hours), swim in the river, check out the sanctuary's library or walk around the grounds. The sanctuary is completely solar powered, the water comes from rainwater catchment, and all organic waste is composted. You can *camp* (US$5 per person) or stay in the *dorm-style bunkhouse*

(US$7.50). *Meals* are also available here (US$4-6), but call in advance so they know you're coming.

Places to Stay & Eat

Competing for customers, just southwest of the zoo and the village of La Democracia on the Western Hwy, are two eateries. Both are fun, festive places often filled with just-off-the-plane travelers happily adjusting to the fact that they're on holiday. Each serves Belizean, Mexican and American dishes accompanied by ice-cold Belikins, all at moderate prices.

Cheer's (☎ 14-9311, Mile 31.25 (Km 50) Western Hwy) Meals US$2.50-8. Open 7am-9pm daily. You wonder where all the people come from, but this open-air restaurant is always bustling.

JB's Watering Hole (☎ 81-3025, fax 81-3026 ⓦ www.jbbelize.com, Mile 32 (Km 52) Western Hwy) Meals US$4-7. Open 8am-8pm daily. Traditionalists prefer JB's because it's been there longer, although the eponymous JB is long gone. Still, it's a festive, friendly place decorated with British military paraphernalia. The kitchen serves up good burgers and specialties, like the gringo tamale (US$5.50).

JB's also rents out *rooms* in cabins with private bath for US$25/35 single/double, plus US$15 for each additional person.

Northern Cayes

Of the dozens of islands or cayes (pronounced 'keys'), large and small, that dot the blue waters of the Caribbean off the Belizean coast, the two most popular with travelers are Caye Caulker and Ambergris Caye. Caulker is commonly thought of as

Highlights

- Snorkeling the Hol Chan Marine Reserve and Shark Ray Alley for a crash course in reef sea-life
- Diving among the pristine coral fields at Lighthouse Reef and Turneffe Atoll, or thrill-seeking your way down the Blue Hole
- Enjoying the freewheeling, active Caribbean lifestyle of San Pedro, on Ambergris Caye (La Isla Bonita for you Madonna fans)
- Whiling away a few days on Caye Caulker, a relaxed, budget-oriented hideout
- Taking a boat trip north to Bacalar Chico, a new marine reserve once frequented by seafaring Maya

the low-budget island, where hotels and restaurants are less expensive than on resort-conscious Ambergris, though with Caulker's booming popularity, its residents are fighting to keep the distinction.

Both islands have an appealing, laid-back Belizean atmosphere. Other common denominators include unbelievably blue water offshore, fresh seafood at every meal, grass shacks for all comfort levels, a party atmosphere when you're ready for one and spectacular sunrises and sunsets delivered daily.

No one's in a hurry here, and everyone is friendly. Island residents include Creoles, Mestizos and a few transplanted North Americans and Europeans. They operate lobster- and conch-fishing boats, hotels, little eateries and island businesses supplying the few things necessary in a benevolent tropical climate. One of the delights of these cayes, indeed of all of Belize, is that the locals enjoy their natural treasures as much as visitors do. They'll keep an eye out for you and are genuinely concerned with your enjoying their home/island. Somehow, folks on both islands have managed to avoid becoming jaded.

Comparing costs to other Central American destinations, you'll be in for some sticker shock, but when compared to other Caribbean destinations, Belize's Caribbean spots are quite reasonable.

Considerations for Responsible Diving

The popularity of diving is placing immense pressure on many sites. Please consider the following tips when diving and help preserve the ecology and beauty of reefs.

- Do not use anchors on the reef, and take care not to ground boats on coral. Encourage dive operators and regulatory bodies to establish permanent moorings at popular dive sites.
- Avoid touching living marine organisms with your body or dragging equipment across the reef. Polyps can be damaged by even the gentlest

Tube sponges in various colors and sizes

Stingrays are actually gentle – unless in danger.

It's a design of nature that many creatures, like this bearded scorpion fish, blend into their surroundings.

Red-lored parrot

King vultures are the largest of their species.

Protected, jaguars thrive in Belize.

Collared peccaries are common in the forests of Belize.

Head to Half Moon Caye to see red-footed boobies.

Red ginger flower by the New River

contact. Never stand on coral, even if it looks solid and robust. If you must hold on to the reef, only touch exposed rock or dead coral.

- Be conscious of your fins. Even without contact, the surge from heavy fin strokes near the reef can damage delicate organisms. When treading water in shallow reef areas, take care not to kick up clouds of sand. Settling sand can easily smother the delicate organisms of the reef.

- Practice and maintain proper buoyancy control. Major damage can be done by divers descending too fast and colliding with the reef. Make sure you are correctly weighted and that your weight belt is positioned so that you stay horizontal. If you have not dived for a while, do a practice dive in a pool before taking to the reef. Be aware that buoyancy can change over the period of an extended trip: Initially, you may breathe harder and need more weight; a few days later, you may breathe more easily and need less weight.

- Resist the temptation to collect or buy coral. Aside from the ecological damage, taking home marine souvenirs depletes the beauty of a site and spoils the enjoyment for others. The same goes for marine archaeological sites (mainly shipwrecks).

- Be sure to take home all of your trash and any litter you may find as well. Plastics, in particular, are a serious threat to marine life. Turtles can mistake plastic for jellyfish and eat it.

- Minimize your disturbance of marine animals. In particular, do not ride on the backs of turtles, as this causes them great anxiety.

Shark Ray Neighborhoods Most visitors to Belize agree that a visit to one of the shark and stingray habitats off Caye Caulker or Ambergris is quite an exhilarating experience, especially if you're new to snorkeling. Encouraged by chum from tour operators, nurse sharks and southern stingrays have been tamed to the extent that they'll swim up to boats and around the legs of snorkelers. As you arrive on the scene at one of these spots (Caulker's is called Shark Ray Village, Ambergris' Shark Ray Alley), the animals will rush your boat, anxious to meet you and see what kind of snacks are on offer. You're welcome to stay in the boat for this, but most adventurous visitors jump in the water to see the animals up close. Some of the sharks and rays are tame enough to be held, so you'll be able to pet them (the

Vital Statistics

You'll usually dive from a 20- to 26-foot twin-engine shallow draft skiff that can hold up to 15 people. Temperatures average in the 80s – quite comfortable – and for diving, a shorty suit is usually all you'll need. Full-day dives usually get going at around 9am. For local dives you'll usually do your surface interval back at San Pedro, or at a snorkeling site.

rays feel like velvet, the sharks like sandpaper) and even cradle them in your arms for a photo op. If you stand still, the rays and sharks will brush up against you like friendly cats. Nurse sharks look intimidating when you first see them, especially under water, where everything looks bigger, but at closer inspection, you'll see that they're kind of cute. They eat by suction (hence the name) and will make a huge slurp when they get too close to the surface when sucking up their snacks.

There is some danger associated with these creatures. Keep in mind that they are wild animals – treat them with respect and follow the directions of your tour guide. Nurse sharks have rows of small, sharp teeth in their mouths. They're usually used for crushing shellfish, but they could be harmful if your hand or fingers were to find their way into a mouth – don't point at a nurse shark or dangle any body parts off the boat. The rays have stingers at the end of their tails, which they won't use unless they're stomped on. Humans are not to wear fins in these habitats to better avoid unfortunate stomping incidents.

Snorkeling Tips

The spots at Hol Chan and Shark Ray Alley on Ambergris Caye can be rewarding even to the greenest snorkeler. Following are some tips for spotting underwater wildlife.

Trying to cover a lot of ground is fun because the flippers give you superhuman speed, but if you want to commune with a fish, you'll need to stay still and blend in.

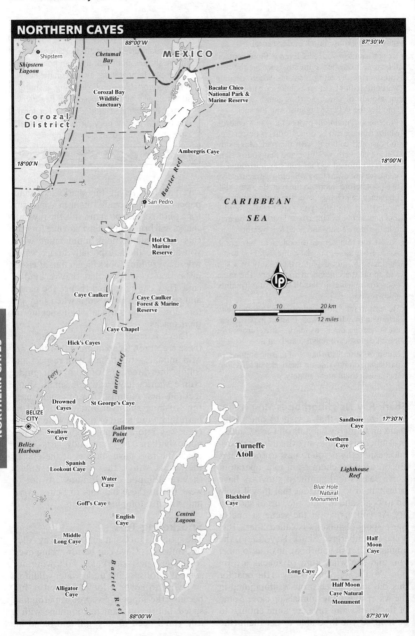

NORTHERN CAYES

Beaches

The shorelines of Caulker and Ambergris seem to be constantly shifting at the mercy of Caribbean hurricanes. Recent Hurricanes Mitch and Keith deposited a respectable amount of sand on the islands and cleared quite a bit of brush and vegetation away from the shore: There are more sandy strips of land around than in years past. While sitting on the sand is quite pleasant now, swimming isn't so much. Because the shoreline is protected by reef, the coastlines don't get pounding surf, so sea grass (essential for preserving sea life and preventing erosion) grows well in the waters just off the shore. This keeps the water closest to shore muddy and a little murky. Swimming in the cayes happens mostly from docks. All shoreline and docks are public access here, and you are allowed access to the sea from all of the docks, so don't be shy.

When you get to a spot that looks promising, stay still: If you don't seem threatening, the animals will come out to have a look at you. Be patient, often it takes time for your eyes to adjust. Learn to look for the fish: It's a primary responsibility of some of them to maintain camouflage, so you need to look carefully. It's a good idea to stick with a guide when you start out, as they'll be able to point out animals and show you where to look for them. Once you know what to look for, it becomes easier to spot things. It is immensely rewarding when you find something on your own. Your best bet is to seek out areas of coral that are unbroken, healthy and colorful – fish are attracted to the nutrients of live, healthy coral.

Inspect your gear carefully before you check it out. Just like a rental car, you're responsible for any dents or scratches, so it's best to be aware of the condition of your equipment before you head out. Look for broken or chipped flippers and broken straps on your mask, and make sure the seal is good around your mask. Your mask should fit snugly on your face; your nose and forehead should not come in contact with the mask lens if you press on it.

AMBERGRIS CAYE & SAN PEDRO
pop 4500

The largest of Belize's cayes, Ambergris (am-**ber**-griss, sometimes am-**ber**-jis) lies 36 miles (58km) north of Belize City. It's about 25 miles (40km) long, and its northern side almost adjoins Mexican territory.

Most of the island's population lives in the town of San Pedro, near the southern tip, and, in fact, the entire island is often referred to as San Pedro. The barrier reef is only a half mile (0.8km) offshore here. In the morning, before the workday noises begin, stand on one of the docks on the town's east side – you can hear the low bass roar of the surf breaking over the reef.

More than half of the tourists who visit Belize fly straight to San Pedro and use it as their base for excursions elsewhere. Even so, San Pedro is certainly no Cancún, though there has been some small-scale development in recent years.

Ambergris has an engaging, laid-back atmosphere. You'll see plenty of 'no shirt, no shoes – no problem!' signs. San Pedro has sandy streets, lots of Caribbean-style wooden buildings (some on stilts) and few people who bother to wear shoes. Everyone is

The Name Ambergris

The commonly accepted theory is that Ambergris is named for the blubbery gray substance manufactured in the intestines of sperm whales and used in perfume production. It used to wash up on the island in great quantities, before sperm whales were hunted into oblivion in the late 1800s and early 1900s. A less scatological theory has the name derived from the semi-precious Amber stone, but this one doesn't get much attention.

friendly, and, for the most part, each visitor is welcomed as a person, not a source of income.

That said, Belizeans and travelers do have a love-hate relationship with San Pedro. Some think it's too crowded and overrun by foreign intruders, but the island has willingly taken on tourism and gracefully handles crowds.

The crowds it draws are people passionate about being in the water. Water sports are the name of the game on Ambergris. The streets of San Pedro tend to be deserted in early afternoon, filling up again after the diving and snorkeling boats return in late afternoon. Then visitors relax and rejuvenate for the evening's festivities. In addition, tours and attractions are accessible, safe and well managed here. It may be too settled and 'resorty' for some, and indeed if your motivation is purely to make your money last, this may not be the place for you. But, think about it – there are 640 hotel rooms on the island – that's one hotel in Cancún – so when put in perspective, it's still pretty relaxed on old Ambergris Caye.

History

Ambergris Caye started life as a Mayan trading post and part of the Yucatán Peninsula. Mayans dug the narrow channel at Bacalar Chico (only a mile long and little more than a canoe's width across) around 1500 years ago, separating Ambergris from Mexico and opening up a better trade route

to mainland Belize. As with the Maya on the mainland, the inhabitants here gradually relocated to the bush as contact with the Europeans became more frequent. The Baymen likely gave the island its seafaring name in the 1600s and, according to lore, used the coves, alongside French and Dutch pirates, as hideouts when ambushing Spanish ships. European contact with Ambergris declined when the Baymen turned from pirating to logging in the mid-1700s.

Ambergris wasn't significantly populated until the War of the Castes in the Yucatán first forced Mestizos, then Maya, across Bacalar Chico and onto the island. San Pedro (named for Peter, the patron saint of fishermen) was founded in 1848. While fishermen lived in relative peace on the island, its ownership was bandied about by wealthy British mainlanders who intended to farm the land but never quite made a go of it. The land was in foreclosure in 1873 when it was purchased by James Hume Blake. The Blake family converted much of the island to a coconut plantation, conscripting many of the islanders to work the land by demanding rent from them to stay in their homes. This coconut business thrived through the 1930s, but by the 1950s it had been all but destroyed by a series of hurricanes that hit the island. The 1960s formally broke the Blake family stronghold on Ambergris Caye when the Belize government forced a purchase of Ambergris Caye and redistributed the land to the islanders.

While the coconut industry declined, the island's lobster industry began to develop. Before the 1920s, the area's spiny lobsters were considered a nuisance because they ruined fishing nets. The market for these shellfish skyrocketed once refrigerated ships came to the island and were able to transport the fresh catch to the mainland.

The lobster catchers of San Pedro formed cooperatives to eliminate price-fixing by the key players in the industry and eventually built a freezer plant on their island, making lobster fishing a viable means of income for the islanders. This brought people off the coconut plantations and into their boats, further dooming the coconut industry.

GREATER SAN PEDRO

PLACES TO STAY
1 Mata Chica Resort; Mambo
   Restaurant
2 Journey's End
4 Captain Morgan's Retreat
5 Capricorn Resort and Restaurant
6 El Pescador Lodge
14 Corona Del Mar
15 Coconuts Caribbean Hotel
16 Villas at Banyan Bay
18 Banana Beach Resort
19 Victoria House

PLACES TO EAT
3 Rendezvous
8 Sweet Basil
9 Hideaway Sports Lodge
11 Carmen's Kitchen at Woody's
   Wharf
13 La Margarita

OTHER
7 Palapa Bar
10 Internet Café
12 Crazy Canuck's Bar
17 La Diosa Day Spa

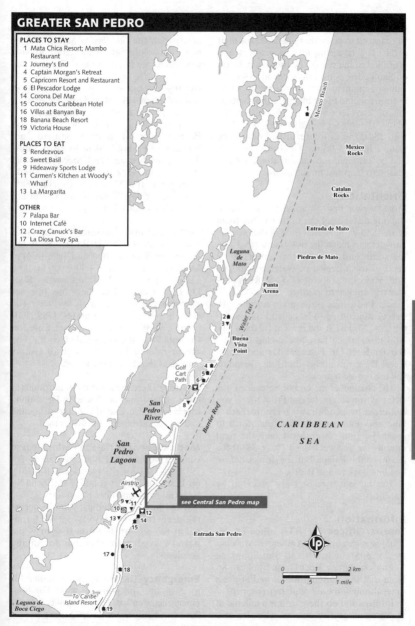

Mexico Beach

Mexico
Rocks

Catalan
Rocks

Entrada de Mato

Piedras de Mato

Laguna
de
Mato

Punta
Arena

Water Taxi

Buena
Vista
Point

Golf
Cart
Path

San
Pedro
River

Barrier Reef

CARIBBEAN

SEA

San
Pedro
Lagoon

Airstrip

see Central San Pedro map

Entrada San Pedro

Laguna de
Boca Ciego

To Caribe
Island Resort

0   1   2 km
0   .5   1 mile

NORTHERN CAYES

Inevitably, the waters close to Ambergris Caye became fished out, and San Pedranos were forced to go farther out to sea for their catch. The resulting loss of product and profit led to the rise of the tourism industry on San Pedro, as fisherfolk began to see the value of augmenting their income by acting as tour, fish and dive guides for the smattering of travelers who began visiting the island. The lobster industry peaked in 1984, with 184,000lb of lobster fished out of the waters. In 1992–93 the yield was 18,000lb. The government recently created a lobster season to help sustain the industry.

Orientation

Most of San Pedro's services are within walking distance of each other in the town center and within a half mile of the airstrip. However, to reach the hotels and resorts to the south and north of the center, you'll need to use wheeled or water transportation. Minivan taxis cost US$2.50 for a one-way trip anywhere in town.

San Pedro has three main north-south streets, which used to be called Front St (to the east), Middle St and Back St (to the west). Now these streets have tourist-class names – Barrier Reef Dr, Pescador Dr and Angel Coral Dr, respectively – but some islanders still use the old names.

The channel at the end of Pescador Dr is as far as you can go by car. From there, you can cross by hand-drawn ferry to reach a bike and golf-cart trail that runs north to Journey's End resort. Most take the road only as far as Sweet Basil (☎ 26-3870) for lunch, or the Palapa Bar for drinks, before heading back to San Pedro.

The far north resorts are accessed by water taxi.

Information

Tourist Offices The BTB office (☎ 26-2605) is at the smallish Ambergris Museum (☎ 26-2605), at the Island Sun Shopping Center on Barrier Reef Dr and Pelican St. Note that this museum was closed at press time, although there are plans to reopen.

Information on the island is available at w www.ambergriscaye.com. The site also features some details on all of Belize and a lively message board. The town's weekly newspaper, the *San Pedro Sun,* is full of news and helpful information for both visitors and locals. It comes out on Friday.

Money You can exchange money easily in San Pedro, and US cash and traveler's checks are accepted in most establishments.

Atlantic Bank Limited (☎ 26-2195), on Barrier Reef Dr, is open 8am to 2pm Monday to Friday, 8:30am to noon Saturday. Cash advances are US$5. Across the street and a block down is Belize Bank, open 8am to 1pm Monday to Thursday, 8am to 4:30pm Friday, 8:30am to noon Saturday. Cash advances are US$7.50.

Post & Communications The post office is on Buccaneer St, off Barrier Reef Dr. Hours are 8am to noon and 1pm to 5pm Monday to Friday (until 4:30pm on Friday).

Coconet's (☎ 26-2834), on Barrier Reef Dr, open 8am to 9pm daily, has Internet equipment and a surprisingly lively bar. The rates are US$2.50/15 minutes, US$5/half hour, US$10/hour. The Internet Café, on Coconut Dr at the south end of town, offers similar rates and is convenient for visitors staying at that end of the island.

Laundry There are several Laundromats at the southern end of Pescador Dr; among them are Belize Laundry & Dry Cleaning and J's Laundromat. It's US$5 a load.

Medical Services The San Carlos Medical Clinic, Pharmacy & Pathology Lab (☎ 26-2918, 26-3649, for emergencies ☎ 14-9251), on Pescador Dr just south of Caribeña St, treats ailments and does blood tests.

The Lions Club Medical Clinic is across the street from the Maya Island Air terminal at the airport. Right next door is the island's hyperbaric chamber for diving accidents.

Emergency The emergency number for medical, fire and police is ☎ 90. For non-emergencies call ☎ 26-2022 (police), ☎ 26-3668 (medical) and ☎ 26-2372 (fire).

CENTRAL SAN PEDRO

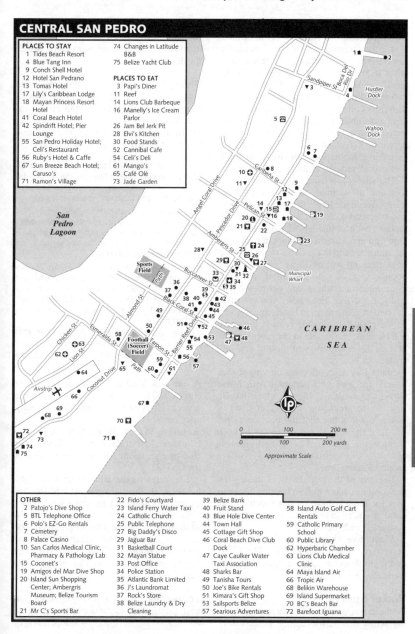

PLACES TO STAY
1 Tides Beach Resort
4 Blue Tang Inn
9 Conch Shell Hotel
12 Hotel San Pedrano
13 Tomas Hotel
17 Lily's Caribbean Lodge
18 Mayan Princess Resort
    Hotel
41 Coral Beach Hotel
42 Spindrift Hotel; Pier
    Lounge
55 San Pedro Holiday Hotel;
    Celi's Restaurant
56 Ruby's Hotel & Caffe
67 Sun Breeze Beach Hotel;
    Caruso's
71 Ramon's Village

74 Changes in Latitude
    B&B
75 Belize Yacht Club

PLACES TO EAT
3 Papi's Diner
11 Reef
14 Lions Club Barbeque
16 Manelly's Ice Cream
    Parlor
26 Jam Bel Jerk Pit
28 Elvi's Kitchen
30 Food Stands
52 Cannibal Cafe
54 Celi's Deli
61 Mango's
65 Café Olé
73 Jade Garden

OTHER
2 Patojo's Dive Shop
5 BTL Telephone Office
6 Polo's EZ-Go Rentals
7 Cemetery
8 Palace Casino
10 San Carlos Medical Clinic,
    Pharmacy & Pathology Lab
15 Coconet's
19 Amigos del Mar Dive Shop
20 Island Sun Shopping
    Center; Ambergris
    Museum; Belize Tourism
    Board
21 Mr C's Sports Bar

22 Fido's Courtyard
23 Island Ferry Water Taxi
24 Catholic Church
25 Public Telephone
27 Big Daddy's Disco
29 Jaguar Bar
31 Basketball Court
32 Mayan Statue
33 Post Office
34 Police Station
35 Atlantic Bank Limited
36 J's Laundromat
37 Rock's Store
38 Belize Laundry & Dry
    Cleaning

39 Belize Bank
40 Fruit Stand
43 Blue Hole Dive Center
44 Town Hall
45 Cottage Gift Shop
46 Coral Beach Dive Club
    Dock
47 Caye Caulker Water
    Taxi Association
48 Sharks Bar
49 Tanisha Tours
50 Joe's Bike Rentals
51 Kimara's Gift Shop
53 Sailsports Belize
57 Searious Adventures

58 Island Auto Golf Cart
    Rentals
59 Catholic Primary
    School
60 Public Library
62 Hyperbaric Chamber
63 Lions Club Medical
    Clinic
64 Maya Island Air
66 Tropic Air
68 Belikin Warehouse
69 Island Supermarket
70 BC's Beach Bar
72 Barefoot Iguana

NORTHERN CAYES

Hol Chan & Shark Ray Alley

Hol Chan Marine Reserve (Hol Chan is Mayan for 'little channel') was the first marine reserve established in Central America. Just 4 miles (6.5km) south of San Pedro, it's the most popular snorkeling and diving site in Belize, and rightly so, because it's swarming with fish of all shapes and sizes. The park encompasses about 5 sq miles (8 sq km) of protected area, dotted with coral formations, at depths to 30 feet. Shark Ray Alley is usually visited in combination with Hol Chan and is now considered part of the marine reserve.

The site is a terrific introduction to the reef and the animals to be seen in these waters. You'll see larger fish such as groupers and barracudas, as well as schools of thousands of colorful smaller fish darting around. Don't go expecting seclusion. On busy days the water around the area becomes a virtual boat parking lot, as these are the most popular spots to visit. Instead, think of this as an aquarium where you get to jump in and join the fish. The earlier you get there the better; going there at lunchtime is also a good option for avoiding crowds, but there will be more marine life in the morning. The best guides will show you around and find critters for you.

Shark Ray Alley offers an amazing chance to get up close and personal with nurse sharks and southern stingrays, who will swim right up to greet you in 6½ feet (2m) of water. You'll notice that the boat operators will feed the fish. This is necessary to keep them in the protected areas and on view, although the animals can get aggressive around feeding time.

Because of the popularity of these sites, the coral has taken quite a beating. Do your part for conservation by not touching any coral; if you're unsure in your flippers, give yourself a wide berth.

Most dive shops and boat operators make day and afternoon trips to Hol Chan, and night dives are also an option. The entrance fee is US$5.

Water Sports

Ambergris is good for all water sports, including scuba diving, snorkeling, sailboarding,

boating, swimming, deep-sea fishing and sunbathing. Just about any local can put you in touch with someone organizing watersports trips.

Diving Many island hotels have their own dive shops, which rent equipment, provide instruction and organize diving excursions, sometimes in conjunction with the San Pedro shops. Following is a list of reputable independent dive shops in San Pedro.

Amigos del Mar Dive Shop (☎ 26-2706, fax 26-6264, e amigosdive@btl.net), on the dock east of Lily's Caribbean Lodge, rents scuba and snorkeling gear and leads diving and fishing trips.

Blue Hole Dive Center (☎ 26-2982, fax 26-2981, e bluehole@btl.net) offers a variety of snorkeling and diving trips, including overnight excursions, and is known for the competence and professionalism of its staff.

Coral Beach Dive Club (☎ 26-2013, fax 26-2864, e forman@btl.net) arranges a variety of trips, including overnight boat excursions on its Offshore Express. It's not the island's fanciest dive operation, but it gets high marks from experienced divers.

Patojo's Dive Center (☎ 26-2283, fax 26-3797, e patojos@btl.net) is a small, family-run operation offering knowledgeable and personal service.

A one-tank local dive, without equipment, costs US$35; with two tanks US$50. Night dives to Hol Chan cost US$35. BCD (buoyancy control device), mask and fins rent for around US$15. Full-certification courses take three to four days and cost US$350, including equipment. Resort dives are offered for US$125.

Day trips to the Blue Hole and Lighthouse Reef (three dives) cost US$165, and overnights (offered by the Coral Beach Dive Club) include five dives for US$250. Multi-night trips can also be arranged. Day trips to Turneffe Atoll (three dives) cost around US$150. See the Other Northern Cayes section, later in this chapter, for details on these sites.

Snorkeling There are plenty of snorkeling and picnicking excursions to be made around the island (US$20-45, depending on

Diving & Snorkeling from Ambergris Caye

It's best to be flexible about where you want to go. Rather than request a specific site, let your dive operator know what you would like to see or do, and they'll do their best to accommodate you under the current conditions.

Dive masters usually choose the site based on weather conditions. On stormy or windy days you're likely to stay within the reef where the water is calmer and the visibility is better. Another variable is the price of fuel, which can fluctuate dramatically. In order to keep prices consistent and competitive, dive operators usually frequent sites closer in to San Pedro when the price of gas is high.

An old-timer rule of thumb is that if you can see the waves breaking over the reef from the shore, stay inside of it. Of course, you may not have the luxury if you've only got a week or two on the islands.

Site names can be confusing, since dive shops, and even dive masters, sometimes have different names for the same sites. However, as a rule of thumb, the sites are usually named for the landmark closest to them. So, for example, you'll have Victoria Tunnels across from the Victoria House. One of the most popular sites is Tacklebox, named for the former Tacklebox Bar, where Sharks Bar is now.

Formations to be seen on the local dives are similar – you'll see the terms cuts, canyons, tunnels and caverns in the name of some of the sites. Canyons or cuts are deep dramatic grooves cut into the coral by the surf. Caverns or tunnels are created when coral formations on either side of the canyons grow together – they're known in dive vernacular as 'swim-throughs.' Swimming through and between these formations alongside schools of colorful fish can be an extraordinary experience.

Sea life off the cayes ranges from tiny nudibranchs, banded coral shrimps, brittle staffs, tube worms and tunicates living in coral crevices to large animals like groupers and sharks, which are best seen near cuts with strong currents. Several varieties of sharks ply these waters, so you're sure to see a nurse shark and probably will see a reef shark. There are also lemontip and hammerheads. Oceanic white tip are sometimes spotted by lucky divers and snorkelers.

Following is a list of some of the local sites where you'll likely be taken to see various underwater attractions.

Most Popular Sites
Tacklebox, Tres Cocos, Tuffy Canyons, Cypress Canyons and Amigos Wreck are the most popular sites due to their wide variety of coral formations and marine life.

Best to See Large Animals
Sites near cuts are usually good for seeing large, hungry fish, which are attracted to the area by the current and the variety of tasty marine life that comes into the cuts. These include Mata Cut and Punta Azul.

Best for Coral-Viewing
Tuffy Cut maintains a terrific variety of coral, including staghorn, elkhorn, brain, lettuce and gorgonian fans.

Best to See Turtles
You'll have a good chance of seeing turtles around Tacklebox during March and April.

Best Wreck
Amigos Wreck is a 60-foot tug boat intentionally sunk to provide a marine habitat. Living in and around it are several nurse sharks and moray eels. Between Coral Garden Canyons and Sandbox Canyons, it's the only wreck on the local reef. This is a popular dive site because the variety of marine life you'll see here is a sure thing. Sure thing, too, are the crowds.

the number of stops you make). Most popular is undoubtedly Hol Chan Marine Reserve south of the island. Popular stops north of San Pedro include Basil Jones and Mexico Rocks, where the land meets the reef. The going rental rate for a snorkel, mask and fins is US$8. Check with the shops listed in Diving, above.

Manatee-Watching The best manatee-watching (US$75) is south of Ambergris Caye and Caye Caulker, in a habitat off Swallow Caye. Trips out to this site usually include a few snorkel stops along with the manatee viewing. If you're planning to spend time on Caye Caulker as well as San Pedro, this trip might be better done from Caye Caulker, since the location is closer, and you'll pay less and spend less time getting to and from the sites.

Sailing & Kayaking Sailsports Belize (☎ 26-4488, ⓦ www.sailsports.net) rents sailboards (US$20 per hour) and sailboats (US$30 per hour); lessons are available.

Kayaks can be rented from the dock at Fido's (☎ 14-1429). Waters between the shore and the reef can be treacherous with traffic, so it's recommended that kayaks be used to explore the lagoon side of the island. Fido's also arranges parasailing outings (US$50 for a single trip, US$90 for tandem).

Swimming While sandy beaches are plentiful, sea grass at the waterline makes entry from the shore not terribly pleasant, so you'll mostly be swimming from piers.

All beaches are public, and most waterside hotels and resorts are generous with their lounge chairs on slow days. The pier at Ramon's (see Places to Stay) is a great spot for swimming. Another good spot is the beach in front of the Banana Beach Lodge. Current from a cut in the reef has created an area here where there is less beach grass than elsewhere in the area.

Fishing San Pedro draws anglers and fly-fishing enthusiasts anxious to take a crack at Belize's classic tarpon flats, which cover over 200 sq miles (324km). Anglers come to attempt a Grand Slam: catching bonefish, permit and tarpon all in one day. In addition, wahoo, sailfish, snook, snapper, barracuda and grouper also bite. The fishing is mostly on a catch and release basis.

Deep-sea fishing isn't the greatest draw in Belize – people come here for the reef. There are, however, stories of giant marlin caught out in the deep beyond.

Costs for fishing start at US$135 for a half day, US$185 for a full day, for one to two people. Charters carrying one to six people cost US$350 for a half day, US$650 for a full day.

Other Activities
La Diosa Day Spa (☎ 26-3558, on Coconut Dr south of town), offers massage and beauty treatments, such as salt scrubs and facials, in a pleasant and peaceful environment. Several different types of massage are available, from Swedish massage to ayurvedic treatment to acupressure. Treatments cost around US$60/hour. There is also an aroma bar and soap deli, where you can purchase custom-blended unguents based on your skin type and mood.

Organized Tours
Boat Tours Any hotel, travel agency or dive shop can fill you in on tours. Most have offices in the village, although you'll likely make arrangements by phone. In addition to the following, there are independent operators who can arrange smaller, lower-priced tours for you. Ask for references from your hotel operator, and don't do business with any unlicensed tour operator.

Excalibur Tours (☎ 26-3235)
Seaduced by Belize (☎ 26-2254)
Searious Adventures (☎ 26-4202, after 6pm ☎ 26-2690)
Tanisha Tours (☎ 26-2314)

The **Rocky Point Snorkel Trip and Barbeque** is not to be missed. Boats leave early in the morning and head to snorkel stops including Blue Point, Basil Jones and Mexico Rocks. You'll go ashore at a beach around Mexico Rocks (different tour operators have different spots), and while you relax, your tour leader catches lunch, which is then barbecued on the beach. Fresh catch, which can include fin fish, lobster or conch, depending on the season, is steamed in aluminum pans over an open fire, usually with tomatoes, onions or peppers. Price (US$55-75), includes lunch and soft drinks. Local operators running this trip include **Dino Gonzales** *(☎ 26-2224)*, and **Tulu** at the Coral Beach Dive Shop *(☎ 26-2817)*. Note that this day trip heads north, so it does not visit Hol Chan or Shark Ray Alley.

Bacalar Chico National Park & Marine Reserve is a newly created national marine park at the northern tip of Ambergris Caye. The highlight of the tour is a visit to the channel dug 1500 years ago by sea-trading Maya; it separated Ambergris Caye from Mexico's mainland. There's a nature trail and some small Mayan ruins to explore above ground, and pristine coral and plentiful marine life in the sea, not to mention manatees, turtles, crocodiles and plenty of birds.

The trip makes a stop at Rocky Point, notable as one of the only places in the world where land meets reef. It's now a World Heritage Site.

Tour operators don't make daily runs to Bacalar, so you'll need to plan in advance for this trip. It's intended to be an alternative to the increasingly crowded Hol Chan Marine Reserve, but its distance – about 90 minutes from San Pedro – has kept the number of visitors down. When the seas are rough, tour boats travel up the west side of the island to reach the sites. Day trips cost US$75, plus a US$2.50 entrance fee. Tours can be arranged from the operators listed below.

The aptly named *Rum Punch II* *(☎ 26-2340, 26-2817)* is a wooden sailboat (you'll see it from shore, as it has a distinctive punch-colored sail) that runs sunset cocktail cruises (US$15) up to the Capricorn Resort (for more cocktails), as well as snorkel trips with a couple hours' stop on Caye Caulker (US$45).

Those with a more technical interest in sailing may want to board the *Me Too* catamaran from the Yacht Club pier for an excursion to Caye Caulker, with a couple of snorkel stops in between (US$50). Contact **Hustler Tours** *(☎ 26-2538).*

Mainland Tours Many visitors to Belize use San Pedro as their base and make excursions by plane or boat to other parts of the country. Following is a selection of tours to the mainland that are offered from San Pedro.

Altun Ha, the closest ruin from the cayes, is one of the most popular stops on day trips from San Pedro. If you have one day and wish to see a wide sample of mainland attractions, you can choose an Altun Ha trip paired with a couple of other stops (US$60 to US$75).

One trip pairs Altun Ha with a stop at the exotic Maruba Jungle, accessed by a river boat. The long pause at Maruba can be filled with lunch, then swimming or horseback riding (at extra cost). Lunch is pricey at the nearby spa, and if you're watching your budget, it's OK to bring a pack lunch. (See the Around Belize City chapter for more on Altun Ha.)

If you're interested in seeing some wildlife and moving at a quicker pace, you might combine Altun Ha with a trip to the Community Baboon Sanctuary at Bermudian Landing or the Crooked Tree Wildlife Sanctuary, or both. The Belize Zoo and Altun Ha are also packaged together, but it's a long drive between the two. (See the Around Belize City chapter for descriptions of these sites as well.)

Altun Ha is lovely, but there isn't the detail and significance and architectural variety as **Lamanai**. If you want a closer look at Mayan history and ruins, consider the Lamanai River Trip (US$125), which takes you up the Lamanai River (lots of bird and croc spotting), past the Mennonite village of Shipyard, and to the ruins of Lamanai – a large and important trading post that flourished during the Late Pre-Classic Mayan era. (See the Northern Belize chapter for a description of this trip.) This is a great tour, but it makes for a long day trip in a variety of vehicles – ocean boat, then van, then river boat, then back again. If your passenger's skills aren't as keen as your desire to walk

NORTHERN CAYES

among these ruins, you'll want to give this one a pass.

Another option is one of the excellent cave-tubing adventures offered by **Ian Anderson's Caves Branch Tours** (US$90 to US$125). Tours combine a tube float and a tour of a cave, where you'll see pottery shards and other evidence of the ancient Maya. At some point your guide will ask that you turn off all head lamps and flashlights, and the group will spend a few spooky moments in total darkness. For those craving an extra dose of adrenaline, try the Black Hole Drop. See the Southern Belize chapter for details.

Half-day tours to Altun Ha, the Community Baboon Sanctuary and the Belize Zoo can also be arranged for US$45.

Mayan Island Air and Tropic Air offer trips (by air) to the **Tikal** ruins in Guatemala. See the Getting There & Away chapter for details.

Tours all the way west to **San Ignacio, Xunantunich** and the **Mountain Pine Ridge** are also on the menus of San Pedro tour operators. You'll spend most of your time getting to and from these sites from San Pedro, and it's recommended that you spend a few days in the region instead of trying to visit from the cayes.

Your hotel, or the tour operators listed above, offer all of these trips on a near-daily basis.

Places to Stay

Wherever you stay, you'll never be more than a minute's walk from the water. All but the cheapest hotels accept major credit cards. Listed below are winter, peak-season rates, not including the 7% room tax. Rates usually drop 10-15% during the low season, May through November.

Competition for guests in San Pedro is fierce, and some hotels offer taxi drivers commissions for bringing in guests. Often this commission is tacked onto the cost of your room, so you're likely to save money if you make reservations in advance or show up unescorted. You'll also avoid being taken on a lodging tour of the island if you tell your cab driver that you have reservations

in advance. Most hotels on the island now have strict cancellation policies to dissuade guest-pirating by cab drivers.

Places to Stay – San Pedro

Budget *Hotel San Pedrano* (☎ 26-2054, fax 26-2093, e sanpedrano@btl.net, Barrier Reef Dr at Caribeña St) Singles/doubles/triples/quads with fan US$25/30/38/43, with air-con US$35/40/48/53, all with private bath. This hotel has six rooms (three with air-con) and fills up quickly in high season. It's best to book in advance. Most rooms don't have ocean views, but you can always sit out on the wraparound porch.

Tomas Hotel (☎ 26-2061, 12 Barrier Reef Dr) Doubles without/with air-con US$25/ 32, all with private bath. This family-run place offers seven light, airy rooms (some with tub). This hotel and the San Pedrano, in the same block and related by family, represent the best budget options in town. They're off the beach, but close enough to allow plenty of breeze, and the rooms are well-ventilated.

Conch Shell Hotel (☎ 26-2062, e conch shell@btl.net, at the eastern end of Caribeña St) Nine rooms, all with fan and private bath, low season/high season US$25/50. Another old, small hotel right on the beach, this is a good low-season option, but the value drops when the price doubles.

Ruby's Hotel (☎ 26-2063, fax 26-2434, Barrier Reef Dr) Two rooms with shared bath (single or double) US$16, two rooms with twin bed & private bath US$17.50, 12 rooms with private bath US$30, on the oceanfront with private bath US$47.50. You pay for location and tradition in this wooden, red-trimmed perennial. While there are only a few low-priced rooms, the amenities – thin walls, tired mattresses, indifferent staff – reflect its budget reputation. That said, it attracts return visitors year after year, and the choice waterfront rooms must be reserved well in advance.

Mid-Range Some of the following hotels charge an additional 10% or 15% for service, in addition to the 7% government room-tax.

Coral Beach Hotel (☎ 26-2013, fax 26-2864, Barrier Reef Dr at Black Coral St)

Singles/doubles/triples US$45/65/85, all with air-con. This is a simple hotel also offering good-value dive packages. The rooms here aren't anything special, but, like the dive operation, the place has a loyal clientele who rave about the friendly service and tasty food.

Lily's Caribbean Lodge *(☎ 26-2059, fax 26-2623, e lilies@btl.net, Barrier Reef Dr at Caribeña)* Singles/doubles/triples US$50/60/70, all with air-con & refrigerator. This old hotel faces the sea and offers 10 clean, basic rooms; several (especially those on the top floor) have good views.

Spindrift Hotel *(☎ 26-2018, 26-2174, fax 26-2251, Barrier Reef Dr at Buccaneer St)* Doubles with fan/air-con US$47/66, rooms with sea view US$83, two one-bedroom beachfront apartments US$110. This modern, concrete affair, with 24 rooms of various sizes, is in a good location right in the center of town on the beach.

Changes in Latitude B&B *(☎/fax 26-2986, Coconut Dr)* Singles/doubles with private bath & air-con US$80/85. South of the airport, just north of the Belize Yacht Club, this trim two-story guest house has six rooms with tiled floors and bathrooms arranged along the periphery of the ground floor, and a deck upstairs. It's just a short block inland from the beach and has a nice garden area and sea views from the upper deck. The owner has a wealth of knowledge about the area and is happy to help set up any adventure. Punta dance presentations (and lessons) are often arranged for guests. Breakfast is included, and there's a common kitchen area with a refrigerator, stove and microwave. Rooms are comfortable but small, so if you plan on sticking close to home, you might want to choose a place with more sitting area or a better verandah. Guests enjoy the social interaction and camaraderie here.

Tide's Beach Resort *(☎ 26-2283, fax 26-3797, e patojos@btl.net)* Doubles/triples with fan US$80/90, with air-con US$100/110, all with private bath & refrigerator. Sea-facing rooms do not have air-con – it's unnecessary because of the near-contact breeze. Recently built by the owners of Patojos Dive Shop, this two-story hotel has

eight spacious rooms with new fixtures and a friendly, family atmosphere. It's just far enough north so as to eliminate foot traffic, yet close enough to reach town in less than 10 minutes.

Coconuts *(☎ 26-3500, 26-3677, 26-3514, fax 26-3501, w www.coconutshotel.com, Coconut Dr)* Singles/doubles/triples/quads US$85/95/105/115, includes breakfast. One of the best values on the island, this smallish, solidly built concrete hotel gets high marks for friendly, attentive service and comfortable, down-to-earth atmosphere. The rooms are spacious and airy, and outside are tidy, sandy grounds, comfortable deck chairs and wide porches for enjoying the sea breeze. Amenities include air-con and cable TV. It's a mile (1.6km) south of the village (about a 20-minute walk). There's a nice swimming dock next door at Corona Del Mar, and guests have use of the pool at Banana Beach Resort, Coconut's sister hotel.

San Pedro Holiday Hotel *(☎ 26-2014, fax 26-2295, w www.ambergriscaye.com/holidayhotel, Barrier Reef Dr)* Singles & doubles US$103-113, triples US$125-135; the higher-priced rooms have air-con. In the south part of the town center, the San Pedro has rooms in three cheery, pink-and-white wooden buildings, all facing the sea. It's a cute and fun place to spend a few days – you'll be right in the thick of things. However, while well appointed (air-con, ceiling fans, patios and some refrigerators), the rooms are plain and the walls are thin – you pay for the location.

Top End *Sun Breeze Beach Hotel (☎ 26-2191, fax 26-2346, w www.sunbreeze.net)* Standard singles/doubles US$110/120, deluxe with Jacuzzi, refrigerator and oceanfront view US$140/150. This generic two-story concrete building, across Coconut Dr from the airport, has a sandy inner court and swimming pool opening toward the beach, and shady, tiled porticos set with easy chairs, popular for lounging. The interior looks like a standard American motel room. Each of the 34 air-conditioned rooms has two double beds, cable TV, private bath, ceiling fan and phone. Conveniently located across from the airstrip, it's fronted by the only paved road in San Pedro.

Corona Del Mar (☎ *26-2055, fax 26-2461,* **w** *www.ambergriscaye.com/coronadelmar, Coconut Dr*) Doubles with queen beds & air-con but no sea view US$110, with sea view US$135, double/triple/quad one-bedroom suites US$135/150/165, each additional person US$15. Breakfast is included. Run by a couple of retired Americans who have lived on the island for years, this good-value spot offers friendly, casual service.

The hotel is on a small seafront plot, and the owners have made the most of it by building up. West-facing rooms are high above the other buildings in the area, providing nice views, even though they're not of the sea. The rooms are well-ventilated and comfortably decorated, and there's plenty of space for sharing, especially in the apartments. Free coffee and rum punch are served all day. There's a nice swimming dock in the front and plenty of spots for lounging. The stairs to the upper floors are steep and not suitable for those with mobility problems.

Blue Tang Inn (☎ *26-2326,* ☎ *866-337-8203 in the USA,* **w** *www.bluetanginn.com*) Doubles US$100-140, depending on view. A pleasant retreat on the north side of town, the Blue Tang has spacious rooms. The porch at the top level offers a birds-eye view of the beach, and the pool is private and inviting. Some rooms have spa tubs.

Mayan Princess Resort Hotel (☎ *26-2778, fax 26-2784,* **e** *mayanprin@btl.net, Barrier Reef Dr*) Double suites US$125. A modern condominium building in the center of town on the beach, this hotel has suites with kitchenettes, air-con, cable TV and open terraces, but the place still has a bunker-like feel to it.

Ramon's Village (☎ *26-2071, fax 26-2214, Coconut Dr*) Doubles US$150-185. Ramon's, south of the town center, at the sea, offers 60 rooms in two-story thatched-roof cabanas facing a good beach with a nice swimming dock. There's also a dive shop, excursion boats, Jet Skis, sailboards, lounge chairs for sunbathing, a casual, busy bar, a recently re-modeled swimming pool that curves through the grounds…this place has everything, and

it's very well maintained. Rooms come in a variety of styles and settings, and those farther away from the beach have the lowest rates. Some cabanas have sea views, many have sitting porches, and all come with at least a king-size bed or two double beds. The higher-priced rooms have kitchenettes and sitting rooms.

This gets a high rating for resort amenities and proximity to town, although some have complained that it could be located on a beach anywhere. Ramon's is putting in a stand of colonial-style cabins across Coconut Dr for those who aren't interested in the grass-shack experience. They'll rent for around US$125. Bicycles and golf carts can be rented.

Places to Stay – North Island

North Island is where you want to go if you really want to get away from it all. These resorts are mainly accessible by boat (especially after dark when the hand ferry no longer runs), and visitors tend to leave only when they're heading out to sea. If you're interested in an active social life, stay in town or south.

Mata Chica Resort (☎ *21-3010, fax 21-3012,* **e** *matachica@btl.net*) Doubles US$210-275, luxury villa US$550. Extravagantly decorated and managed by an Italian couple who set out to bring la dolce vita to Ambergris Caye, this is the chicest place on the island. There are 11 luxurious thatched-roof *casitas,* each decorated in a tropical-fruit theme. If it looks familiar, maybe it's because it served as the girl's dorm for the *Temptation Island* set. If you're not staying, you can still visit for dinner at Mambo, the resort's equally high-end restaurant (see Places to Eat).

El Pescador Lodge (☎ *26-2398,* **w** *www.el pescador.com*) Seven-night fishing packages cost US$2250 for in-room and on-board double occupancy; seven-night non-fishing packages cost US$1345 for double occupancy. This charming old-time fishing lodge is hoping to draw couples and families by opening a swimming pool and offering land-based activities as well as fish-based ones. There are family-style meals served in the dining room to encourage mixing, and an inviting wrap-around porch encourages lounging. Some large rooms have three double beds to accommodate groups or families.

Capricorn Resort (☎ 26-2809, W www .ambergriscaye.com/capricorn) Single/doubles US$120/150. The three cabins seem rustic but have all the comforts: air-con, spacious bathrooms, wide porches. Popular with honeymooners, Capricorn is relaxed and intimate by day, but it heats up for a few hours during dinner when people from town boat up to enjoy the excellent restaurant.

Captain Morgan's Retreat (☎ 888-653-9090 in the USA, W www.belizevacation .com) Single/double rooms US$160/225, one-bedroom villas (single or double) US$240. This resort recently came to fame as the scene of a lot of the action in the first round of the *Temptation Island* series. It's got all the fixings for a no-holds-barred tropical vacation. The set designers updated some of the rooms to a stylish tiki look for the show. There's a hot tub and a big, wide, cold swimming pool. Bedrooms are decorated with Mayan-themed art, and each room has a CD player. Fishing poles, kayaks, bikes, canoes and snorkel gear are provided for guests. There are 15 casitas, 16 one-bedroom villas and three two-bedroom villas.

Journey's End (☎ 26-2173, 26-2397, ☎ 800-460-5665 in the USA, W www.journeysend resort.com) Non-seafront/seafront rooms US$115-185/215, three-bedroom villa US$510. This all-inclusive resort is the largest on the island at 50-plus acres. Popular with divers and families, it's billed itself as offering 'a barefoot adventure.' Guests reach it by launch (a 12-minute ride from San Pedro), and once they arrive, some might not feel the need to venture back. There's a pool and a good bar and restaurant.

Places to Stay – South of Town

The following places include resorts over a mile south of town, which is outside of a 20-minute walk to reach San Pedro. Down here you get seclusion without isolation, and a number of services and restaurants have cropped up so you can still get out without committing to heading all the way into town.

Banana Beach Resort (☎ 26-3890, W www .bananabeach.com) December 21 to Easter Sunday poolside/oceanfront/deluxe ocean-front one-bedroom apartments US$125/150/175, the rest of the year US$100/120/150. With a freshwater swimming pool and one of the best swimming beaches on the island, Banana Beach is becoming a popular spot. The rates are terrific for what you get – a one-bedroom apartment with a well-appointed kitchen, cable TV, telephone and a foldout couch in the living room. Extra twin beds can be added if necessary. It's a great option for families. Two levels of rooms are arranged around a courtyard swimming pool. The oceanfront rooms have private terraces, the deluxe rooms are slightly larger, but the floor plan is roughly the same. The rooms are furnished with wicker furniture, and the courtyard is landscaped with tropical plants in colorful Yucatecan ceramic pots.

Caribe Island Resort (formerly called Chateau Caribe; ☎ 26-3233, W www.ambergris caye.com/caribeisland) One-room suites US$115-130 double, depending on view; junior suites US$140-165; two- to three-room suites, some with two levels, US$225-335, some sleep up to nine. Quite a stretch (3 miles/5km) from town, this place is bright and shiny and gets good marks for service. The multi-bedroom suites are popular with families. All rooms have kitchens, tiled floors, Mayan-inspired interiors and wide, breezy verandahs. Prices increase during the Christmas and New Year's holidays. There's a large pool, and guests have use of bicycles, kayaks and sailboats.

Victoria House (☎ 26-2067, fax 26-2429, ☎ 800-247-5159 in the USA, W www.victoria house.com) Doubles US$155-235, suites US$300-325, two/three bedroom villas US$580/760. Two miles (3km) south of the airport, on the beach, this elegant resort is one of the oldest on the islands, but management often makes changes to keep the place fresh. A pool was recently added, and the rooms have lately been remodeled with a white-on-white color scheme to accent their rich mahogany interior; mosquito nets add to the exotic, romantic feel of the rooms. Here you're away from it all, but San Pedro is a quick 10-minute bike, shuttle-van or golf-cart ride away (use of bikes is free for hotel guests; golf carts can be rented). The beach and grounds are beautifully kept, shaded by vegetation and a healthy stand of palm trees that have withstood hurricane and disease. Amenities include a dining room, bar and dive shop. Meal plans are available.

Belize Yacht Club *(☎ 26-2777, fax 26-2768,* e *bychotel@btl.net, Coconut Dr)* Suites US$165-400. This hotel, on Coconut Dr south of the airport, has several two-story Spanish-style buildings arranged around a small swimming pool and set amid well-manicured lawns stretching down to the beach. Its air-conditioned one- to three-bedroom suites have full kitchens, but the atmosphere is on the stuffy side, and the rooms are in need of updating, especially in light of newer, comparatively priced hotels on the island.

Villas at Banyan Bay *(☎ 26-3739,* w *www .banyanbay.com)* Ocean-view units US$200, oceanfront US$225. This large timeshare resort has well-appointed, spacious, two-bedroom, two-bath apartments with tiled floors and hardwood interiors. Dive packages are available.

Places to Eat – San Pedro

San Pedro restaurants are used to catering to tourists, and it's easier to get fed at irregular hours here, but like the rest of the country, your best bets for freshness and good selection will be at traditional mealtimes.

Several small cafés in the town center serve cheap, simple meals. The best places for low-budget feasting are the stands in front of the park, where you can pick up a plate of stewed chicken with rice and beans, barbecue and other delicacies for under US$2, then enjoy it while watching a rousing game of pick-up basketball.

Ruby's Caffe *(☎ 26-2063, Coconut Dr)* Prices US$4-7. This is a tiny place, next to Ruby's Hotel on Barrier Reef Dr, with good cakes and pastries, but unpredictable hours.

Manelly's Ice Cream Parlor *(☎ 26-2285, Barrier Reef Dr at Pelican St)* Scoops start at US$1.50. Open 10am-10pm daily. Manelly's serves traditional, delicious homemade ice cream, as well as yogurt and nonfat choices.

Celi's Deli & Restaurant *(☎ 26-2014, Barrier Reef Dr)* Café prices US$1.50-5. Open 6am-6pm daily. Restaurant prices US$10-20. Open for lunch 11am-2pm, dinner 5:30pm-9pm daily. Celi's Deli, just north of the San Pedro Holiday Hotel, serves food to go – fried chicken, sandwiches, ice cream and homemade banana bread. On the beach side, Celi's Restaurant, known for its ceviche, specializes in seafood and attracts a good-sized crowd, despite it's high prices.

Café Olé *(☎ 26-2907, Coconut Dr)* Breakfast & lunch US$4-7, dinner US$12-20. Open 7am-4pm. Dinner begins at 5:30pm daily. This café, across from the airport, has a deli offering olive oils, cheeses and wine and serves meals in a coffeehouse atmosphere. Walk in for breakfast (served all day) and lunch. It's a good break from Belizean cuisine, and prices are reasonable considering the novelty of ordering cappuccino (US$3.50), French toast (US$6), bagels with cream cheese (US$3.50) or panini (US$5). Danishes and croissants are made on the premises. To enjoy dinner here, you must make reservations and preorder the day or morning before; only five tables are served. The menu changes daily and will include a pasta dish and fresh fish.

Elvi's Kitchen *(☎ 26-2176, Pescador Dr)* Dishes US$5-25. Hotel staff will recommend Elvi's, near Ambergris St, for seafood and traditional Belizean dishes. The atmosphere is somewhat canned and the prices are above average, but you can get everything from chicken, rice and beans to a full lobster dinner with wine. Mixed drinks are available but expensive. Be sure to ask about items not priced on the menu – they're sometimes out of scale and you may get a surprise.

Reef *(Pescador Dr between Pelican & Caribeña Sts)* Meals US$5-9. Open for lunch 11am-2pm, dinner 5pm-10pm daily. If you're yearning for traditional Belizean and Mexican fare at traditional prices, try this thatched-roofed, sand-floored eatery. The decor is nautical kitsch, the staff is attentive but down-to-earth, and the portions are ample. If you think all rice-and-bean dishes taste alike, try the Reef, and you'll learn to be a connoisseur.

Jade Garden *(☎ 26-2506, Coconut Dr)* Meals US$5-18. San Pedro's Chinese restaurant is a 10-minute walk south of the airport. It has a long menu with OK Chinese dishes along with some traditional Belizean dishes.

Jam Bel Jerk Pit *(☎ 26-2594, Ambergris St)* Dishes US$5-7. Open 11am-3pm & 6pm-11pm daily. Jam Bel, next to Big Daddy's Disco, serves spicy, hot Jamaican dishes at reasonable prices. There's a nice rooftop patio, and the chef is willing to spice the food according to your tolerance. Jerk shrimps are a favorite.

Cannibal Cafe *(☎ 26-3706, Barrier Reef Dr at Black Coral St)* Breakfast US$4, lunch & dinner US$5-10. Open 7:30am-9pm Mon-Sat. This is a lively beachside café serving moderately priced breakfasts, lunches and early dinners. Popular menu items include the Cannibal Sandwiches – fish, shrimp, chicken or beef wrapped in a tortilla with cheese and salsa (US$5-7). Tropical drinks are served up at the bar.

Papi's Diner *(☎ 26-2047, on Pescador Dr at Sandpiper St)* Breakfast US$1.50, lunch & dinner US$2-10. Open 7am-10am & 11am-10pm daily. This small, friendly place is a good budget option on the north side of town. It has elaborate main courses, but the bargains are in the burgers, chicken and pork chops.

Caruso's *(☎ 26-3347)* Mains US$10-15. Open 6pm-10pm daily. In an open patio at the Sun Breeze Beach Hotel, this place serves passable seafood pastas; it's best to stick to the basics.

Mango's *(☎ 26-2859, Barrier Reef Dr)* Dishes US$4-13. Open 11am-11pm Thur-Tues, closed Wed. Right on the beach, just south of Ruby's, Mango's cuisine combines Caribbean and Louisiana Creole, reflecting the owners' background. Most menu items – po' boys, tropical grilled chicken breasts and fresh green salads are in the US$4-8 range, and more elaborate dishes such as

Beach Barbecues

Following are a few of the regular beach barbecues that are held around town. Get there on the early side and expect chicken, lobster (in season), pork ribs and steak, served with cole slaw or potato salad, a rice-and-bean combo and fresh fruit.

Ramon's *(☎ 26-2071, at Ramon's Village)* US$10-15 a plate. Starting at 6pm Tues & Sat. This is more upscale than most of the beach barbecues: The food is pulled off the grill before guests arrive, so there's no waiting, but you're a bit detached from the barbecue proceedings. Prices here are listed in US dollars.

BC's Beach Bar *(☎ 25-3289)* US$5-7. From 11am to 3pm Sun. One of the best, this barbecue feels like it happened spontaneously, even though it's been a weekly event for quite some time. Get here early, as the food sometimes runs out before 2pm.

Lions Club Barbeque *(At the Lions Club Pavilion on Barrier Reef Dr at Pelican St)* US$3-5. Fri & Sat from 5:30pm. Here you get to gather with travelers and townspeople alike and contribute to a good cause – the San Pedro Hospital, for which construction is often delayed. This is a terrific value. Chicken is always served, and fish and shellfish sometimes appear on the menu as well.

Crazy Canuck's Bar *(☎ 26-2870)* US$7. Starting at 6pm Sun. This one's hosted by the folks at Carmen's Kitchen and there are good seafood options.

Celi's *(☎ 26-2014)* US$8-12. Starting at 6:30pm Wed. There's usually live music playing, and the tables are set up on the beach. Folks usually wander over after the chicken drop at the Pier Lounge.

jambalaya and seafood can cost around US$12. Fruit smoothies can be had here for US$3.50.

Places to Eat – North Island

Sweet Basil *(☎ 26-3870)* Lunches US$7-10. Open 10am-5pm Tues-Sun, closed Mon. A

NORTHERN CAYES

quarter mile north of the river, this high-end gourmet deli is only open for lunch. It sells sandwiches and imported cheeses and meats and is the prime destination for folks making a bike or golf-cart excursion to the north side of the island. The restaurant is set in a wooden, Victorian-style home, with flowery and tropical gardens.

The latest thing in fine dining is to take a moonlight water-taxi ride up to one of the resort restaurants at the island's north end. Meals are pricey at these places, but menus are often unusual and feature excellent seafood preparations. Each restaurant has its own distinction, but what makes them really special is the starlit ride to and from dinner. The taxi-ride is usually US$7-10 roundtrip per party. Note that dinner arrangements must be made in advance, and seating usually starts around 7:30pm.

Mambo Restaurant (☎ 21-3010) Meals US$25-45. Open daily. This place serves food with a Mediterranean flair. Fanciful, tropical decor will make you think you've been transported elsewhere. Be sure to stroll around the grounds, because this is what over-the-top tropical paradise is all about.

Rendezvous (☎ 26-3426) Meals US$17-35. Open daily. This restaurant serves French-Thai fusion, with a heavy emphasis on Thai seafood curries, stir-fries and grilled foods. It also makes its own wine. A vineyard on Ambergris? No, the grape juice is bought in concentrate and fermented on the premises.

Capricorn (☎ 26-2809) Meals US$20-45. Closed Wed. This restaurant's nouvelle cuisine is considered to be among the best in Belize. Here you'll have the choice of eating inside in a small dining room (close to the action in the kitchen), or outside on the patio; both areas are lit by festive twinkling lights. Stone-crab cakes, grilled steaks and seafood crêpes are featured on the menu and prepared with French-influenced methods and sauces.

Places to Eat – South of Town
Hideaway Sports Lodge (☎ 26-2141, Coconut Dr) Mains US$5-12. Open 7am-10pm daily. Run by a pack of pack-a-day Texans who know their Tex-Mex, this place serves enchi-

ladas that you'll write home about. It has a cute country dining room with wooden booths and red-checkered tablecloths, but it can get smoky inside.

Carmen's Kitchen at Woody's Wharf (☎ 26-2055) Meals US$5-10. Open Tues-Sun for breakfast 7am-10am, lunch 11:30am-3pm, dinner 6pm-10pm; open Monday for breakfast only 7am-10am. The well-rounded menu at this casual and friendly restaurant includes standard breakfast items, burgers, quesadillas, grilled fish and lobster, conscientiously prepared and reasonably priced.

La Margarita (☎ 26-2222, Coconut Dr, south of the airport) Meals US$8-16. Open 5:30pm-9:30pm Wed-Mon, closed Tues. Convenient to hotels south of San Pedro, festive La Margarita offers passable Tex-Mex-style cuisine prepared with fresh ingredients. Nachos are US$5-7.50, and mains like enchiladas and fajitas, served with rice and beans will cost US$8-12.50 depending on your choice of chicken, beef or seafood.

Entertainment
Sipping, sitting, talking and dancing are parts of everyday life on Ambergris. Many hotels have comfortable bars, often with sand floors, thatched roofs and reggae.

Bars *Coconuts Bar* A tiny open-air shelter in front of the Coconuts hotel is a nice spot to grab a drink and a conversation. The staff is friendly, and there's a welcoming bunch of regulars.

Sharks Bar (☎ 26-3235) You can count on reggae throbbing from this over-the-water fisherfolk's hangout all day and into the night. It's near the Caye Caulker Water Taxi Dock, in the former location of the beloved, departed Tackle Box Bar. The fish pen at the end of the wharf has been restored, though no animals were in captivity at press time.

Fido's Courtyard Bar (☎ 26-3176, Barrier Reef Dr & Pelican St) Open 11am-midnight daily. This is the central party spot, decorated with seafaring memorabilia – you'll find a place like this in any resort town. Everyone is welcome, and there is live music Thursday to Saturday nights. It's also a good place to clue in to the other activities around town.

BC's Beach Bar (☎ 26-3289) On the beach in a palapa between Ramon's Village and the Sea Breeze Beach Hotel, BC's stays open late and is usually filled with sun-crisped expatriates enjoying Jimmy Buffett on the jukebox. The Sunday afternoon barbecue is a hot ticket.

Mr C's Sports Bar Here's where sports-loving locals and travelers come to enjoy major sporting events. Across from Fido's, towering over Barrier Reef Dr, this third-floor establishment contains four massive TVs and a couple of pool tables. On the ground floor is the open-air Reef Rock Café, which attracts its share of holiday merrymakers.

Pier Lounge In the Spindrift Hotel, this place holds a chicken drop every Wednesday at 7pm. It's not nearly as bad as it sounds – no chickens are injured in the process, although their dignity takes a beating. A grid with numbers is spread on the sand, participants place bets on the grid. The winning number is the one the chicken poops on.

Discos ***Big Daddy's Disco*** This black-lit nightspot, near San Pedro's church, often features live reggae, especially in winter.

Jaguar Bar (☎ 26-4077, on Barrier Reef Dr across from the town square) This jungle-themed bar features papier-mâché dioramas for decor and keeps irregular hours, but you can usually count on it rocking late into the night on weekends.

Ahhh, the suspense at Pier Lounge!

Barefoot Iguana US$7.50 cover. Like Jaguar and Big Daddy's, this place gets going late (after 10pm). The music is good and loud, the decor fanciful, with an indoor waterfall and other rain-foresty touches. Barbecue stands are set outside to feed late-night revelers.

Palace Casino (☎ 26-3570, Pescador Dr at Carabeña St) Opens at 6pm, closed Wed. With low ceilings, slots, blackjack tables and a seedy ambience, this should satisfy those who need a little gambling with their vacations.

Shopping
Groceries *Island Supermarket* (☎ 26-2972) This is a large, modern, air-conditioned market. Visitors from the US will find plenty of their favorite snacks, but will pay the same, if not more, for them here than at home. If you like buying in bulk, across the way is the Belikin warehouse, where you can pick up a case of beer for US$22.

Rock's Store (☎ 26-2044, Black Coral St) Open 6:30am-10pm Mon-Sat, 7am to 1pm Sunday. This place offers a smaller selection but lower prices than the Island Supermarket.

Fresh vegetables can be purchased at the *fruit stand* on Barrier Reef Dr, next to the Coral Beach Hotel.

Souvenirs Plenty of *gift shops* in the hotels and on Barrier Reef Dr sell key chains, T-shirts and beachwear. Cottage Gift Shop, on Barrier Reef Dr, has a particularly good selection; it's open 9am to 9pm.

One of the best shopping spots is ***Belizean Arts*** (☎ 26-3019, Fido's Courtyard), open 9am-9pm daily, which sells ceramics, wood carvings and paintings alongside affordable and tasteful knickknacks. Look for their fragrant orange-peel candles, a new offering on the Belize crafts scene. Also in Fido's Courtyard is ***Amber*** (☎ 26-3101), open 9am-9pm Mon-Sat, 10am-2pm & 5pm-9pm Sun, selling handmade jewelry produced on the island. ***Kimara's Gift Shop*** (☎ 26-4001), open 8am-9pm daily, is part gift shop, part junk shop.

NORTHERN CAYES

Check for good prices on last year's souvenirs, slate and jadestone amulets and bottles retrieved from the sea.

Getting There & Away

Both Maya Island Air (☎ 26-2435) and rival Tropic Air (☎ 26-2012) offer several flights daily between San Pedro and the Belize City airports and to Corozal. See the Getting Around chapter for details.

The Caye Caulker Water Taxi Association (☎ 26-2036; Caye Caulker main office ☎ 22-2992) runs boats between San Pedro, Caye Caulker and Belize City. Boats to Belize City via Caye Caulker leave from the Shark's dock in San Pedro at 8am, 9:30am, 11:30am, 1pm and 2:30pm (also 4:30pm on weekends and holidays). Boats leave Belize City for San Pedro at 9am, 10:30am, noon and 3pm. Cost is US$12.50 one way, US$22.50 roundtrip. Boats leave Caye Caulker for San Pedro at 7am, 8:30am, 10am, 1pm and 4pm; fare is US$7.50 each way, US$12.50 roundtrip.

Getting Around

You can walk into town from the airport in 10 minutes or less, and the walk from the boat docks is even shorter. Cabbies (☎ 26-2934, 26-2038, 26-2041) drive minivans, and a ride from the airport costs US$2.50 to any place in town, US$5 to the hotels south of town.

San Pedranos get around on foot, bicycle or golf cart, although the truck and minivan population is increasing. You can rent golf carts at Polo's EZ-Go Rentals (☎ 26-2467, 26-3542), at the northern end of Barrier Reef Dr, or at Island Auto Golf Cart Rentals (☎ 26-2790), across from the airstrip. Two-seaters cost US$10 for one hour, US$30 for four, US$35 for eight, US$50 for 24 and US$225 per week. You can rent bikes at Polo's EZ-Go or Joe's Bike Rentals (☎ 26-5371) for rates around US$6 for a half day, US$9 for 24 hours.

The Island Ferry (☎ 26-3231) operates an Ambergris-only water-taxi service north and south from the Fido's Courtyard dock. In high season boats depart every two hours from 8am to 4pm and hourly from 6pm to 10pm, stopping at the north end resorts. This service runs less frequently in low season. Prices average US$10 a stop. Arrangements can be made for custom runs at US$20. North island resorts also frequently run their own shuttle service to and from San Pedro at little or no cost for guests.

CAYE CAULKER
pop 750

Caye Caulker remains a budget-travelers' mecca. It's long been part of a classic tourist route that involves Tulum in Mexico and Tikal and Antigua in Guatemala. Proud of this heritage, Caulker retains the shacky, low-rent charms that have drawn travelers here for near on 20 years: There is a tradition of sitting and staying a while. Lately, however, a couple of upscale resorts have cropped up.

Even though it's a hanging-out kind of place, there are some activities available to keep those who are used to covering a lot of territory from going stir crazy. Guest houses are basic and haven't seen many improvements beyond what is required by the BTB. Hotels don't have restaurants or pleasant grounds; instead, visitors take to the village for entertainment. This, and the fact that it's tiny, makes for more of a traveling community. Water is the name of the game here; snorkel tours are the most common day-trips. It is possible to plan inland tours from Caulker, but there is much less movement back and forth to the mainland than on Ambergris Caye.

Approaching Caye Caulker from Belize City, you glide along the eastern shore, where dozens of wooden docks jut out to give moorings to boats. Off to the east, about a mile (1.6km) away, the barrier reef is marked by a thin white line of surf.

Caye Caulker lies some 20 miles (32km) north of Belize City and 15 miles (24km) south of San Pedro. The island is about 4 miles (6.5km) long and only about 650 yards (600m) wide at its widest point. Mangrove covers much of the shore, and coconut palms provide shade. The village is on the southern portion of the island. Actually Caulker is two islands now: Hurricane Hattie carved 'the Split' through the island just north of the village. It's a popular swimming area now. North of the Split is mostly unde-veloped land, although much of it has been parceled and sold off to long-term Caulker residents, and there is talk of developing it for tourism some day. However, part of the north island was recently declared a nature reserve.

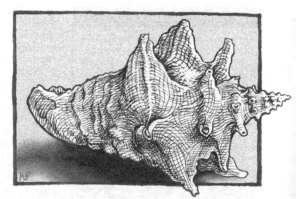

You disembark and wan-der ashore to find a place of unpaved 'streets.' The town government has carefully placed 'Go Slow' and 'Stop' signs at the appropriate places, even though there are usually no vehicles in sight and everyone on Caulker naturally goes slow and stops fre-quently. Virtually constant sea breezes keep the island comfortable, even in Belize's sultry heat. If the wind dies, the heat imme-diately becomes noticeable, and sand flies and mosquitoes may become pesky.

You'll share the streets with tame, good-sized iguanas fairly tolerant of the pa-parazzi – a nice couple live in the cemetery. Many gardens and paths on the island have borders of conch shells, and every house has its catchment, or large cistern, to gather rainwater for drinking.

History
Caye Caulker was a fishing settlement and popular in the days of the British bucca-neers as a place to stop for water and to work on their boats. Like Ambergris Caye, it grew in population with the War of the Castes, and is known mainly as a Mestizo island. It was purchased in 1870 by Luciano Reyes, whose descendants live on the island. Reyes parceled the land out to a handful of families, who sub-parceled them to their growing families as the years went by. In fact, to this day, descendants of those first land owners still live in the general

vicinities of those original parcels. Caye Caulker remains a fishing village to this day, although tourism and guiding is becoming increasingly important for the economy.

Caulker was one of the first islands to establish a fishermen's cooperative in the 1960s, allowing them to receive fair prices for the lobster and other sea life pulled from their waters.

Orientation
Caulker has been growing and is now a village with a Front, Middle and Back St. What was previously known as Back St is now Middle St, and Way Back St (formerly no more than a path) has been promoted to Back St. Time marches on. The dock street runs east-west through the center of the village. The distance from the Split in the north to the village's southern edge is little more than a half mile (0.8km). Plans to fill in the Split and develop the north part of the island are afoot.

Most of the tour operators are clustered on either side of Front St north of the dock street. There is little to no difference in prices among tour operators. In fact, most work closely together consolidating tours on slow days and juggling overflow during busier seasons. You'll be touted on your way up and down the street.

North of the dock is where most of the action and nightlife is. Budget travelers

The Name Caulker

The name Caye Caulker probably morphed from it's Spanish name, Hicaco, with encouragement from seafarers who stopped here to work on their boats (corking or caulking their hulls). You'll see it labeled Caye Corker on some maps. Hicaco is the Spanish name of the palm trees that were once prevalent on the islands.

You'll see signs referring to Caulker as La Isla Carinosa (dear little island). Most say this was manufactured in response to Ambergris' nickname La Isla Bonita (beautiful island).

looking for a more social environment usually settle here. The south side is quieter – cheaper, more traditional restaurants and hotels are located here. Secluded beachside hotels are available south of the cemetery, mostly accessed by beach path.

Used to be that most of the tourist facilities were on the east side of the village, but that's changed, with a few hotels and a restaurant cropping up 'to the back.' Here you'll get lovely sunsets and seclusion, but you'll pay with a longer walk into civilization and extra bugs. This area is ironically referred to as the suburbs and considered to be the territory of 'non-local' residents.

Information

South of the village, on the site of the Caye Caulker Mini Reserve (☎ 22-2251), is the Belize Tourism Industry Association (BTIA) office. You can get information on the island's flora and fauna, then put your new knowledge to work as you stroll along a short interpretive trail. Hours for the visitor's center are irregular, but the trail is always open. Rumor has it that the Belize Maritime Museum, now located at the Water Taxi terminal in Belize City, may move out here someday.

Atlantic Bank Limited, on Middle St, is open 8am to 2pm Monday to Friday and 8:30am to noon Saturday. Cost for a credit-card advance is US$5.

The post office is located on Back St, three blocks south of the dock street. Hours are 8am to noon and 1pm to 5pm Monday to Thursday, till 4:30pm Friday. The *Internet Bar* on Front St charges about US$1.50 for 15 minutes.

Caye Caulker has a few Web sites, including W www.gocayecaulker.com, W www.cayecaulker.org and W www.cayecaulker.com. They're helpful for planning what to do and provide some descriptive information on many of the island's guest houses, restaurants and tours.

You can leave your luggage at the Caye Caulker Water Taxi office as you look for a place to stay.

The Caye Caulker Health Center (☎ 22-2166) is on Front St, two blocks south of the dock street. Service is free, but donations are welcome.

There are a number of families in town with laundry services (US$5 a load is the going rate), such as the one next door to Jolly Roger's fruit stand on Front St, south of the dock street. There's a coin laundry on the north side of the dock street.

Water Sports

The best guides will get in the water with you to point out interesting coral formations. They also know where to find the best critters, since many of the animals have territories and favorite spots.

Several places in town rent water-sports equipment. You can get snorkeling gear (US$5) or sea kayaks (US$20 half day), or take out a Hobie Cat sailboat (US$20/50 per hour/half-day).

Diving Common dives made from Caye Caulker include two-tank dives to the local reef (US$55); two-tank dives in the Hol Chan area (US$68); three dives off Turneffe (US$100) and trips to the Blue Hole (US$160, including equipment). Prices are roughly the same from each dive operator, but there may be differences in level of service, quality of equipment and quantity and quality of meals. Check with other divers, and inspect boats and equipment before choosing your dive operators.

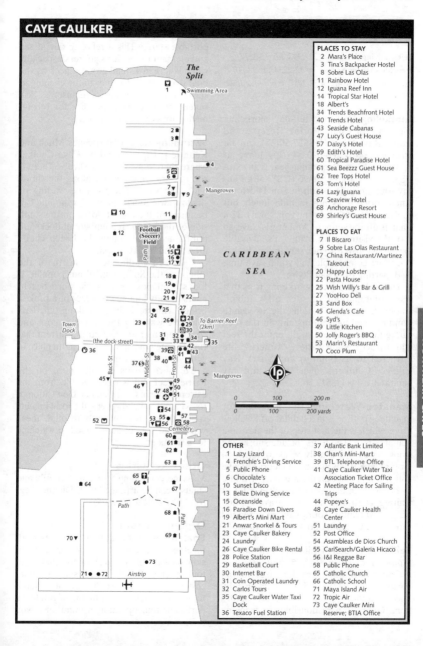

CAYE CAULKER

The Split

Swimming Area

Mangroves

CARIBBEAN

SEA

Football (Soccer) Field

Path

Town Dock

(the dock street)

Back St

Middle St

Front St

To Barrier Reef (2km)

Mangroves

Cemetery

Path

Path

Airstrip

| 0 | 100 | 200 m |
| 0 | 100 | 200 yards |

PLACES TO STAY
2 Mara's Place
3 Tina's Backpacker Hostel
8 Sobre Las Olas
11 Rainbow Hotel
12 Iguana Reef Inn
14 Tropical Star Hotel
18 Albert's
34 Trends Beachfront Hotel
40 Trends Hotel
43 Seaside Cabanas
47 Lucy's Guest House
57 Daisy's Hotel
59 Edith's Hotel
60 Tropical Paradise Hotel
61 Sea Beezzz Guest House
62 Tree Tops Hotel
63 Tom's Hotel
64 Lazy Iguana
67 Seaview Hotel
68 Anchorage Resort
69 Shirley's Guest House

PLACES TO EAT
7 Il Biscaro
9 Sobre Las Olas Restaurant
17 China Restaurant/Martinez Takeout
20 Happy Lobster
22 Pasta House
25 Wish Willy's Bar & Grill
27 YooHoo Deli
33 Sand Box
45 Glenda's Cafe
46 Syd's
49 Little Kitchen
50 Jolly Roger's BBQ
53 Marin's Restaurant
70 Coco Plum

OTHER
1 Lazy Lizard
4 Frenchie's Diving Service
5 Public Phone
6 Chocolate's
10 Sunset Disco
13 Belize Diving Service
15 Oceanside
16 Paradise Down Divers
19 Albert's Mini Mart
21 Anwar Snorkel & Tours
23 Caye Caulker Bakery
24 Laundry
26 Caye Caulker Bike Rental
28 Police Station
29 Basketball Court
30 Internet Bar
31 Coin Operated Laundry
32 Carlos Tours
35 Caye Caulker Water Taxi Dock
36 Texaco Fuel Station
37 Atlantic Bank Limited
38 Chan's Mini-Mart
39 BTL Telephone Office
41 Caye Caulker Water Taxi Association Ticket Office
42 Meeting Place for Sailing Trips
44 Popeye's
48 Caye Caulker Health Center
51 Laundry
52 Post Office
54 Asambleas de Dios Church
55 CariSearch/Galeria Hicaco
56 I&I Reggae Bar
58 Public Phone
65 Catholic Church
66 Catholic School
71 Maya Island Air
72 Tropic Air
73 Caye Caulker Mini Reserve; BTIA Office

NORTHERN CAYES

Dive shops on Caye Caulker include the following:

Belize Diving Service (☎ 22-2143, fax 22-2217)
Frenchie's Diving Service (☎ 22-2234, fax 22-2074)
Paradise Down Divers (☎ 22-2437, ℮ paradisedown @btl.net)

Snorkeling Half- and full-day snorkeling trips to Hol Chan Marine Reserve and Shark Ray Alley (US$17.50/25) can be arranged daily. Half-day trips leave at 9:30am and 2pm. Snorkeling gear is an extra US$5, as is park entrance (US$2.50). Full-day tours include a stop in San Pedro for lunch (price does not include lunch, but you're welcome to bring your own). Hol Chan is off the shore of Ambergris Caye, so if you're visiting both islands, it's advisable to save the trip for your stay in San Pedro. Prices are comparable, but you'll save time by departing from San Pedro.

There are also local snorkeling trips that visit combinations of sites off Caulker, among them Coral Gardens, the Swoosh (a stand of coral near an opening in the reef, where the current and swells enter the reef and attract a good variety of marine life attracted to its bounty) and Shark Ray Village, Caulker's own shark and ray habitat. Cost is US$12.50.

Manatee-Watching The best bet for manatee-spotting is in a habitat off Swallow Caye, which is the first stop of the day on a manatee tour. The tours include snorkeling stops as well, and usually break for lunch on Goff's Caye. Boats pass by St George's Caye and Gallows Point on the way back. Be sure to bring a sun hat, as this involves a lot of waiting, chatting with other travelers and bubble-watching. Tours can be arranged through any Caulker boat-tour operator.

Sailing A handful of sailboats, including the **Stone Crab** (☎ 16-3146, ℮ jimmystours@hotmail.com) take travelers out to the various sites (US$12.50). Boats usually leave around 11:30am and return before 5pm. Guests are responsible for bringing

their own food and drinks. The boats typically carry a nice big ice chest and a good portable stereo. This a relaxing day at sea and pleasant for novice seafarers, especially when you're in a small group. Check by the boat dock before 10am or in the evening to speak to the boat skippers themselves. Ask other visitors or your hotelier for recommendations on the best tours.

Swimming Recent Hurricanes Mitch and Keith left strips of sand on Caye Caulker where there once were sea shrubs. There is still sea grass underwater along the shore, which doesn't make for nice wading or shallow swimming. The best swimming can be found at the end of docks on the south side of the island (remember, all docks are public access, although the beach chairs aren't) and from the Split.

Caulker's public beach, north of the village at the Split, is small but popular. It looks a bit post-apocalyptic since beach-goers usually lounge on pieces of a broken bridge with steel girders poking out. That said, the water at the beach is cool and clean, kept that way by a strong current that runs through the Split, and it's a fun place to get to know the locals.

The surf breaks off the shore on the barrier reef and is easily visible from the eastern shore of Caye Caulker. Don't attempt to swim out to it, however – the local boaters speed their powerful craft through these waters and are not accustomed to watching for swimmers.

Other Activities
Massage, combining Swedish with reiki and shiatsu, can be arranged with Dianne Siegfried (☎ 21-4059, 16-0295).

Organized Tours
Boat Tours Most boat/tour operators work together, combining clients onto one boat on slow days or selling overflow to other boat/tour operators on other days, since it's more cost effective for them to bring a full boat out to sea. This can be disappointing if you had a particular tour operator in mind, or if you

Manatee Conservation

Over the past 10 years manatee-watching off Swallow Caye has become a popular offering for tour operators on Caye Caulker and in San Pedro and Belize City. As traffic to the area increased, so too did the stress and strain on the manatee population. Chocolate Heridia was one of the first Caulker fishermen to begin ferrying backpackers on his fishing boat from Belize City to the island. He later pioneered these trips to Swallow Caye and took notice of the impact increased traffic has had on the manatees.

Today he devotes himself to manatee conservation and has been tireless in his efforts to protect the manatee habitat around Swallow Caye. Guidelines have been put in place to protect the gentle creatures, while encouraging them to stay in the area and be on view for visitors. Swimming with manatees is now forbidden by the Belize Forestry Department, and signs have been posted to dissuade boat operators from using their motors near the manatees and from speeding through the area. (Propeller injuries are one of the chief causes of death to manatees).

While these guidelines are in place, not all boaters and tour operators who visit the island respect them. Chocolate and other conservationists are working to have a permanent caretaker established in these waters. They are also working to protect the sea grass around Swallow Caye – essential for these vegetarian animals – and for a ban on spearfishing in the area.

were hoping for a small group. If you prefer a smaller group, you might want to gather a group and arrange for a charter instead of being grouped together on a general tour.

When booking boat tours discuss price, number of people on the boat (they can become crowded), duration, areas to be visited and the seaworthiness of the boat before committing. The boat and motor should be in good condition. Even sailboats should have motors in case of emergency (the weather can change quickly here).

The following are among the tour operators plying the waters off Caye Caulker and touting tours from storefronts on Front St:

Anwar Snorkel & Tours (☎ 22-2327)

Carlos Tours (☎ 22-2093)

Chocolate's (☎ 22-2151, e chocalate@btl.net) Chocolate is the pioneer of the manatee tours and still does them occasionally, but he leaves the snorkeling-only trips for the other boats.

EZ-Boy (☎ 22-2349)

Ras Creek Ras (as in Rastafarian) operates a palm-frond-covered houseboat out to the reef. His tours attract a lively party-loving crowd. Make arrangements with Ras in the mornings on the main dock.

Land Tours Nature and bird-watching tours (US$13) can be arranged through **Ellen McRae** (☎ 22-2178, CariSearch/Galleria Hicaco, Front St) or **Dorothy Beveridge** (☎ 21-2079, Seaing is Belizing). Beveridge starts with the interpretive trail at the Caye Caulker Mini Reserve (☎ 22-2251) and combines bird-watching with a mangrove tour.

Mainland tours can be also be arranged from Caulker, but they don't run as frequently as those from Ambergris. The most popular is the Altun Ha river trip, which stops at Maruba Resort for lunch, swimming and horseback riding (US$60). This can be arranged through the tour operators listed in Water Sports, earlier, or your hotel. (See the Around Belize City chapter for more on Altun Ha.)

Places to Stay

The rates listed below do not include the 7% room tax.

You'll be affronted with touts offering to show you around the island and help you find a place to stay as soon as you leave the boat. Some find this a perfectly reasonable way to find a place to sleep, while others are irritated by the fact that the touts won't take

NORTHERN CAYES

you to places that don't pay commission and will often tell you a place is full if you make a specific request that doesn't reward them.

If you're particular about where you stay, or you're on a tight budget, you're going to be better off calling when you arrive to see if a place has rooms available, then arranging for taxi service to check the hotel out and see if it's for you. There is a BTL office with a bank of public phones on Front St at the dock street.

Places to Stay – North of the Dock Street

Budget *Tina's Backpacker Hostel (☎ 22-2351, Front St)* Bunks US$7.50. The cheerfully decorated façade, roomy front yard and wide, hammock-filled verandah reflect an equally cheerful guest roster. Folks say that this is what a hostel's all about. You'll meet budget travelers from all over, enjoying the relaxed atmosphere and unlimited kitchen privileges. The upstairs bathroom isn't for the faint of heart – it's shared by guests occupying the 11 bunks in the three upstairs rooms. Downstairs is a bit better – only eight guests in two rooms share one bathroom.

Albert's (☎ 22-2277, Front St) Singles/doubles US$7.50/10. Eight cramped but clean rooms share two bathrooms. Rooms are close to Front St, and there's lots of foot traffic, so if you're a light sleeper you might consider someplace else.

Tropical Star Hotel (☎ 22-2374, W www .startours.com, Front St) Singles or doubles US$17.50-42.50, depending on the view; all with private bath. This two-story wood-and-masonry guest house, toward the village's north side, has a nice porch for sitting and is popular with vacationing Belizeans. It's affiliated with the higher-priced Tropical Paradise Hotel on the south end of town.

Rainbow Hotel (☎ 22-2123, fax 22-2172, Front St) Singles or doubles US$30-35, depending on location; rooms with air-con US$43; apartments (four people maximum) US$15 per person. Rooms in this two-story bunker-like concrete building are plain and clean but cell-like, especially

What's That Smell?

Caye Caulker has a couple of sources for water. Water for taps and showers is usually rainwater collected in cisterns that sit on the roofs of houses. Desalinated seawater or ground water is used for toilets, drainage and sometimes laundry. This accounts for the acrid and off-putting smell that rises from many toilets and drains, which some travelers mistake for a sewage smell. To help keep the smell at bay, keep your toilet seat closed and put a towel or a plug over your drains, although most are reassured merely by the fact that what they're smelling isn't as foul as they'd imagined.

considering the metal netting over the windows. The two kitchen-equipped apartments are less grim.

Mid-Range *Trends Beachfront Hotel (☎ 22-2094, on the beach, just north of the water taxi dock)* Doubles US$35, one cabana US$45. This happy, turquoise building beckons you from the dock, and even if you don't stay here, it's a nice greeting to what lies in store for you on Caye Caulker. The pink-trimmed building has gracious porches with sea views and the location can't be beat for its birds-eye view of the dock area. If you're more about interior comforts, this probably isn't the place for you – the walls are thin and the mattresses could use a freshening up.

Mara's Place (☎ 22-2156) Singles or doubles US$25. This lively establishment is in a good location near the Split. Rooms have cable TV.

Sobre Las Olas (☎/fax 22-2243, Front St) Doubles with fan/air-con US$25/47.50. This place, perpetually under construction and seemingly always empty, has 12 rooms (four with fans, eight with two beds and air-con). Some rooms have cable TV.

Chocolate's (☎ 22-2151, e chocolcate@ btl.net, Front St) On the north side of town, this place has one lovingly-crafted, mahogany-lined room, built over their gift shop, renting for US$60 a night. The terrace overlooks Front St, great for people-watching. Arrangements for this room should be made well in advance.

Top End *Iguana Reef Inn* (☎ 22-2213, fax 22-2000, W www.iguanareefinn.com, west side) Junior suites US$95, deluxe rooms US$110. Some will say it's not the 'real' Caye Caulker, but plenty others will welcome the amenities offered at the island's most upscale accommodation. Solidly built and chicly decorated, the most expensive hotel on the island is also one of the best values: Rooms are spacious and comfortable, beds are big, decor is chic but subdued, and service is friendly and efficient.

Plans are in the works for a sunset bar and Caulker's first pool. There are eight junior suites with a sitting area, fold-out bed, refrigerator, mini-bar, air-con and spacious tiled bathroom with tub. Deluxe rooms have separate sitting rooms. Also, the location is good – set back from the center of town you'll avoid foot traffic and noise, but still be minutes away from Front St. It's perfect for honeymooners wanting the funkiness of Caulker alongside the comfort of a resort.

Places to Stay – South of the Dock Street

Budget *Daisy's Hotel* (☎ 22-2123, Front St) Singles/doubles US$8.50/12.50, all with shared bath. Close to the seaside, this hotel has 12 rooms sharing three bathrooms.

Edith's Hotel (☎ 22-2161, Middle St) Singles or doubles with shower US$20. This is a tidy, proper hotel with tiny rooms with private bath, centrally located on a quiet street.

Tom's Hotel (☎ 22-2102, beachside south) Singles/doubles US$17.50/22.50 for rooms with shared bath, US$30 for rooms & cabins with private bath. This big, well-kept place is the best budget option south of town off the seaside footpath. There are 20 simple rooms with shared bath, 15 larger rooms with private bath in a newer building, and a handful of comfortable

cabins. All the buildings are painted a glaring white and situated on an equally glaring stretch of sand.

Lucy's Guest House (☎ 22-2110, near the Caye Caulker Health Center) Two rooms with shared bath US$12.50, seven rooms with private bath US$25. This guest house is not on the shore, but the duplex-style rooms are arranged around a tranquil garden with ample porches and a tree swing for enjoying the fresh air.

We have received more than one report from travelers of things disappearing from the guest rooms at *Ignacio's Beach Cabanas*. The price and location here are desirable, but if you stay, do not leave cash or valuables in your room.

Mid-Range *Tree Tops Hotel* (☎ 22-2008, fax 22-2115, W www.treetopsbelize.com, beachside south) Doubles with shared/private bath US$25/30. This friendly hotel is the best value on the island. Owners Doris and Terry Creasey run a tight ship and take great pride in making sure their guests experience the best Caye Caulker has to offer. Each of the four cheerful, well-appointed rooms has a fridge and TV and unique decor. Two sea-facing rooms have private bath and two rooms with shared facilities face west. Reserve in advance, as it's nearly always full. The buildings are set back from the beach, with a nice garden for sitting.

Tropical Paradise Hotel (☎ 22-2124, fax 22-2225, W www.startours.com, Front St) Rooms US$25-35; tightly packed cabins range from US$40 with fan to US$50 with fan and cable TV, US$70 with air-con, cable TV and refrigerator. Its central location at the end of Front St brings plenty of guests to this densely packed property. One gets the impression that the owners don't feel they need to offer much by the way of services or amenities to compete for business. The restaurant is dependable.

Seaview Hotel (☎ 22-2205, fax 22-2105, e seaview@aol.com, beachside south) Doubles US$40. This low-key sleeper on a quiet stretch of beach offers four rooms with private bath and fan, two of which have sea views. Guests can enjoy the sea from a palapa at the end of the dock here. It's small and gets good word of mouth, so it's best to reserve in advance.

Anchorage Resort (☎ 22-2391, fax 22-2304, e anchorage@btl.net, beachside south) Doubles with private bath US$45. Constructed on the site of Caye Caulker's first resort, this place has comfortable, modern, hotel-style rooms of concrete construction. Rooms have two double beds, private balconies and cable TV; it's a bargain for the price.

Sea Beezzz Guest House (☎ 22-2176, beachside south) Rooms US$40-60, with private bath. Open Nov-April only. This is a solid two-story house on the shore with a nice patio garden in front. It's safe, secure and comfortable, and offers dining-room service for all three meals.

Trends Hotel (☎ 22-2094, Front St) Doubles with no air-con/air-con US$20/30. This hotel is under the same ownership as the Trends Beachfront Hotel, but has lower prices in congruity with its distance from the water. Rooms in this cheerily-painted concrete building are secure and tidy and worth the price.

Shirley's Guest House (☎ 22-2145, w www.shirleysguesthouse.com, beachside south) Rooms with shared/private bath US$45/60; cabins with private bath US$80. On the south side near the airstrip, this secluded place (adults only) has nice cabins and duplexes in a quiet garden setting.

Top End **Seaside Cabanas** (☎ 22-2498, e seasidecabanas@hotmail.com, on the beach, south of the water taxi dock) Dorm beds US$10, deluxe rooms US$100. This hotel has six spacious rooms in a two-story building and six dark-wood bungalows. Judging from the exterior, you would think that this was a regular bungalow-style hotel that could be found anywhere along the shoreline. Management here, however, has paid attention to the details and put in nice amenities like thick cotton sheets, good solid walls, reading lamps, big comfy beds, air-con (although you won't need it nine

times out of 10) and cable TV. It's the place for travelers who want to be close to the action, but are willing to pay for some extra comforts.

Lazy Iguana (☎ 22-2350, e momiller77@aol.com) Doubles US$75. On the island's southwest side, this place is off the beaten track, but tall enough to provide a good view of the island and the sea. Four rooms are for rent and a rooftop patio offers 360-degree views of the island.

Places to Eat

You'll find prices here higher than on the mainland, though not as high as the restaurants in San Pedro. Seafood is your best bet.

Do your part to avoid illegal lobster fishing: Don't order lobster outside its mid-June to mid-February season, and complain if you're served a 'short' (a lobster below the legal harvest size).

Glenda's Cafe (Back St) Prices US$2-4. Open 7am-10am for breakfast, 11am-3pm for lunch Mon-Fri, closed Sat & Sun. The best cheap breakfast in town is on the island's west side. Full breakfasts of eggs, bacon or ham, bread and coffee (US$3) are on the menu, and burritos and tacos (US$2) are offered for lunch. Get there early for breakfast, as they usually run out of menu items – and interest – around 9am.

Cindy's Café Breakfast US$3-7. This breakfast spot serves organic coffee, espresso drinks with soy milk, granola, yogurt and breads made on the premises. At press time Cindy's was not in its permanent location. Ask around for the latest on her locale.

Coco Plum (☎ 22-2226, off Back St near the airstrip) Breakfast & lunch US$4-6. Open 7:30am-3:30pm Tues-Sun; check hours in low season. This is by far the most unusual restaurant on the island due to its peaceful surroundings and Euro-conservationist vibe. It's off the beaten track but worth the walk if you're after whole-wheat pancakes or breads for breakfast (the chefs/owners are firm believers in roughage) or gourmet pizzas for lunch or, quite possibly, the best cappuccino in Belize. Maps to Coco Plum have been thoughtfully placed in a basket on Front St to help travelers find their way. The garden is a living museum of the plants in Belize; check out the ceiba tree at the entrance.

For box lunches (US$3-5) try the **YooHoo Deli** (☎ 22-2232, Front St), open 10am-6pm Wed-Mon. There's eat-in breakfast and lunch, too, and fresh-brewed coffee all day. If you're leaving early in the morning for a tour, it's best to call the day before to arrange for a takeaway meal.

Sand Box (☎ 22-2200) Breakfast US$3-4, lunch US$2-5, dinner US$5-10. Open 7am-10pm daily. Serving all three meals (and gallons of Belikin), this is the island's most popular place to dine. For dinner, the specials board may include fish with spicy banana chutney (US$7) or the less-expensive barbecued chicken or pastas (including vegetarian lasagna). The food's delicious, but it will come quicker if you check in at the side of the bar for your menu. Atmospheric touches include barstools with names engraved in them, sand floors and illuminated glass buoys, but the best decor is the clientele. This is the island's unofficial seat of government and where you'll meet Caye Caulker's characters and eavesdrop on some island gossip. At press time the Sandbox was up for sale, which may lead to changes.

Il Biscaro (☎ 22-2045, Front St) Meals US$5-10. Open 7am-9pm Wed-Mon. Caulker's Italian restaurant serves up hearty breakfasts with espresso drinks in the morning and plates of pasta and seafood for dinner.

Pasta House (Front St) Breakfast US$5, Dinner US$7-10. Open for breakfast 7am-11am; dinner 6:30pm-10pm daily. New on the scene, this place serves granola, breads, yogurt and espresso drinks for breakfast. Pizzas and ample plates of pasta – toppings change daily – are served up at dinner. The pleasant outdoor setting is as much an attraction as its well-priced meals.

Happy Lobster (☎ 22-2064, Front St) Mains US$10-15. Open 6:30am-10pm Thur-Tues. This is Caye Caulker's answer to not-

so-great, expensive seafood with a nice view from an elevated patio. It's good for catching breezes on a hot day.

Wish Willy's Bar & Grill Dinner US$7-12. Opens at 6pm most days. This scene is not to be missed, if you're patient and not too hungry. The 'dining room' at Wish Willy's consists of a deck and a shed made romantic with white tablecloths, candlelight and ultra-hip background music. Willy, a Belizean who's spent some time stateside, takes care of the service, and Maurice, the strong-silent type, runs the grill. The menu will be rice, salad and whatever's fresh. Unpaired females consistently get the best service and prices. There's also a haphazard bar in Willy's living room that heats up after the diners have left. Guests from all over the world have graffitied the wall here. One scribe summed the place up accurately: 'Willy, dude, the service was slow and you forget my order. Fucking wicked. I can't wait to come back.'

Jolly Roger's BBQ (no ☎, Front St) Dinner US$5-10. Opens at 6:30pm Mon-Sat. This is definitely the most unusual setup on the island. Roger, the truly jolly proprietor, has a small drum barbecue set up on the east side of Front St, his dining room is on the west side. You'll hang out with Roger's wife and kids as you enjoy your meal. This place has visitors coming back night after night for its delicious meals and warm, welcoming environment. During the day you can buy fresh fruit juice for US$2.50 a liter, delivered in a re-purposed water bottle. Stop by late in the afternoon to see what Roger's got planned for the grill.

Sobre Las Olas Restaurant (☎ 22-2243, Front St) Meals US$8-12. This restaurant draws raves for its shrimp barbecue and complaints for uneven food quantity. Have a look at what's on offer before you make your decision about sitting down.

Marin's Restaurant (☎ 22-2104, Middle St) Meals US$5-10. You'll get hearty Belizean fare, seafood dishes, burgers and other sandwiches here. There are good indoor and outdoor options, and the sand floor is festive.

Little Kitchen *(☎ 22-2401, Front St)* Dishes US$2-4. Good, cheap, ample meals are offered at Little Kitchen. Mexican snacks – tostadas, salabutes and tacos – are served all day. In the evening there's catch of the day and other specials served with traditional rice and beans. Prices depend on the size of the portions.

Syd's *(☎ 22-2994, Middle St)* Dishes US$0.50-6. Like Little Kitchen, this is a great place for hearty, good-value Mexican-style dishes. Try a couple of tostadas for lunch (US$0.50 each) or the steamed fish for dinner (US$4).

Oceanside *(☎ 22-2033, Front St)* Dinner US$5-8. Open 10am-midnight Sun-Thur, 10am-2am Fri-Sat. Caye Caulker's fast lane, this place has good, cheap standard menu items prepared with care and doled out in generous portions. The space, however, is more for drinking and making new friends than it is for dinner, so if you're after quiet or romance (with someone you already know), choose elsewhere.

Tropical Paradise Hotel Restaurant *(☎ 22-2124, Front St)* Breakfast US$3, lunch US$3-5, dinner US$4-15. Open for breakfast & lunch 7am-2pm; dinner 6pm-10pm Mon-Sat. This restaurant has been operating at the end of Front St for years – the service and cuisine are a bit tired. You can order curried shrimp or lobster (US$12) or choose from among many lower-priced items.

China Restaurant/Martinez Takeout *(☎ 22-2018, Front St)* Lunch US$1-4, dinner US$4-6. Sharing counter space, these two businesses serve passable Chinese food and Mexican dishes like tacos and burritos, alongside Belizean rice-and-bean dishes.

Entertainment

The ***Oceanside*** *(☎ 22-2033, Front St)* often hosts live bands. Its Saturday karaoke night is the place to be. There are lots of TVs here – islanders and visitors alike gather for televised sporting events. The meals are cheap and good.

I&I Reggae Bar is the happening reggae bar, and its construction resembles an adult jungle gym. The main structure is a three-level tree house, with swings for chairs and a good sound system. There's a putting green and a makeshift weight machine on the ground floor, and a slab on the main floor that serves as the platform for body shots.

Lazy Lizard *(☎ 22-2368, at the Split)* mainly serves beer to swimmers and other hangers-about, but it has some menu items as well.

The ***Sand Box*** *(☎ 22-2200, Front St)*, ***Wish Willy's*** *(off Front St)* and ***Popeye's*** *(☎ 22-2032, on the beach)* attract their fair share of thirsty travelers.

The ***Sunset Disco*** *(☎ 22-2312)*, on the west side of the island, gets going Thursday to Saturday after 11pm.

Shopping

Caye Caulker Bakery *(Middle St)* Under US$1. Open 7:30am-noon & 2pm-7pm Mon-Sat. This is the place to pick up fresh bread, rolls and similar goodies.

Other picnic supplies are available at ***Chan's Mini-Mart*** *(☎ 22-2165, Middle St & the dock street)* and ***Albert's Mini-Mart*** *(☎ 22-2277, Front St)*.

There is a sprinkling of gift shops along Front St, which offer the traditional beach-resort fare. Of particular note is ***Chocolate's Gift Shop*** *(☎ 22-2151)*, where Annie Seashore sells lovely and unusual Indonesian dresses and Guatemalan textiles that she gathers on yearly shopping trips. Another place for out-of-the-ordinary souvenirs is the ***Coco Plum Giftshop*** *(☎ 22-2226)*, where you'll find specially commissioned handicrafts, such as cassava castanets, carved bowls and baskets.

Getting There & Away

Air Maya Island Air (☎ 22-2012) and Tropic Air (☎ 22-2040) offer regular flights between Caye Caulker, Ambergris Caye and the Belize City airports. See the Getting Around chapter for details.

Boat The Caye Caulker Water Taxi Association (☎ 22-2992, ☎ 2-31969 in Belize City) runs boats from Caulker to Belize City at 6:30am, 7:30am, 8:30am, 9:30am, 10am, noon, 1pm and 3pm (also at 5pm on week-ends and holidays). Boats leave Belize City's Marine Terminal for Caye Caulker at 9am, 10:30am, noon, 1:30pm, 3pm and 5pm. The ride takes 30 to 40 minutes, depending on the weather. The fare is US$7.50 one way, US$12.50 roundtrip.

Boats to San Pedro on Ambergris Caye run at 7am, 8:30am, 10am, 1pm and 4pm, re-turning at 8am, 9:30am, 11:30am and 2:30pm (also 4:30pm on weekends and holidays). The ride takes 20 to 30 minutes. Fare is US$7.50 one way, US$12.50 roundtrip.

Water taxis also run to St George's Caye and Caye Chapel, but you must request these stops and arrange pick-up in advance. It's best to make these trips in the morning.

Getting Around

Caulker is so small that most people walk everywhere. If need be, you can rent a bicycle or golf cart (US$20/hour) or use the golf-cart Rainbow Taxi Service (☎ 22-2123), which costs US$2.50 for a one-way trip any-where on the island, except to and from the airstrip, when you'll pay US$2.50 per person.

OTHER NORTHERN CAYES

Most visits to the other northern cayes are made by day trip from Caye Caulker or San Pedro, usually as part of a snorkel or dive trip. Serious divers and fishers, and some-times honeymooners looking for solitude, often choose to stay at the outlying resorts on the smaller cayes.

Caye Chapel

Just south of Caye Caulker, Caye Chapel features an exclusive **18-hole golf course** *(☎ 2-28250)* and a super-deluxe corporate retreat center. Golfing is open to the pub-lic when no one is retreating (9/18-holes US$50/75, clubs and cart included). You must also arrange boat transportation to the island, which will probably cost about US$25 from San Pedro or Caye Caulker. From Belize City, Caye Caulker Water Taxi will stop here on request, but you must arrange in advance for the taxi to pick you up at the end of the day.

St George's Caye

Offshore, 9 miles (14km) from Belize City, St George's Caye was the Belize settlement's first capital (1650–1784) and site of the deci-sive 1798 battle between British settlers and a Spanish invasion force. Today it holds va-cation homes for the Belize elite, one diving resort and an R&R compound for the British Army. The island is pretty and his-torically important, but its significance can easily be absorbed while riding by on a boat. If you must, you can arrange for a water taxi to drop you at the island. Be sure to make arrangements to have them pick you up again before you disembark. There's a small gift shop on the island in case you want to buy a T-shirt to prove you were there. At press time, the lone restaurant on the island had closed.

Turneffe Atoll

The Turneffe Islands together comprise the Turneffe Atoll, one of the three atoll reefs in Belize's waters. The atoll is 30 miles (49km) long and 10 miles (16km) wide. Turneffe is usually visited by day trip – it's within easy reach of Caulker, Ambergris and Belize City to the north and Glover's Reef and Hopkins to the south. Placencia dive boats even occasionally make the trip to Turneffe Elbow, the southern tip of the islands.

The atoll is alive with coral, fish and large rays, and the terrain is quite varied: You can enjoy wreck, wall and current diving, as well as protected shallow areas abundant with coral (perfect for novice divers and snorkelers). On rough days it's favored by San Pedro dive operators because the trip out is made behind the reef, protecting pas-sengers from choppy open seas that must be crossed to reach the other outer reef sites. The most popular sites are around the Elbow, where the current attracts big hungry fish in large numbers and affords one of the only drift dives in Belize. Other sites include Rendezvous, Hollywood and Cabbage Patch (with an impressive stand of brain coral). Fishing enthusiasts are attracted by the flats, which are ideal for saltwater fly-fishing.

NORTHERN CAYES

The atoll hosts a couple of resorts catering to single-minded divers and fishers: **Turneffe Island Lodge** (☎/fax 21-2011, ☎ 14-9564, W www.turneffelodge.com), on the southern tip, and **Blackbird Caye Resort** (☎ 888-271-3483 in the USA, W www.black birdresort.com), on the western side. Both offer fishing and diving packages starting at around US$1600 per week, based on double occupancy.

Lighthouse Reef Atoll

Lighthouse Reef, made up of six cayes, is the farthest atoll from the Belize shore and offers some of the country's best underwater visibility. The famous Blue Hole is one of the most popular and unusual dive sites in the region. There is spectacular wall diving here, as well as some opportunities for on-land exploring.

In addition to what's described below, other top sites in Lighthouse Reef are self-defining and include North Long Wall, Gorgonian Wall, Manta Wall and the Zoo. Half Moon Caye Wall is probably the best of the lot for its variety of coral formations along the wall and within canyons and swim-throughs. Of particular interest is a field of garden eels found on the sand flats near the wall. Snorkelers don't despair, the shallows around these sites are interesting as well.

Blue Hole In the center of Lighthouse Reef, the Blue Hole is the country's best-known dive site and often appears in tourist brochures touting Belize's marine wonders. It's a sinkhole of vivid blue water around 400 feet (122m) deep and 1000 feet (305m) across. The dive itself is somewhat gimmicky – you drop quickly to 130 feet (40m), where you swim beneath an overhang, observing stalactites above you and, usually, a school of reef sharks below you. Ascent begins after eight minutes because of the depth.

This trip is usually combined with other dives at Lighthouse Reef, and experienced divers will tell you that those other dives are the real highlight of the trip out. But

judging from its popularity – all the dive shops make a run to the Blue Hole at least twice a week – plenty are willing to make the deep descent, gimmick or not. There are reef sharks in the Blue Hole, and some dive masters make a practice of chumming the sharks so that you can get a closer look at them. This can be an exhilarating event, but it can also be overwhelming, especially when you're at 130 feet where it's necessary to ascend very slowly and carefully.

Note that on day trips the Blue Hole will be your first dive, which can be nerve-racking if you're unfamiliar with the dive master and the other divers, or if you haven't been underwater for a while. It is recommended that you do some local dives with your dive masters before setting out cold on a Blue Hole trip. An alternative is to take an overnight trip to the reef. Coral Beach Dive Club (see Diving in the Ambergris Caye section, earlier in this chapter) offers a five-dive overnight trip for US$220.

Half Moon Caye A bird sanctuary and home to the rare red-footed booby, this is the most visited of the atoll's cayes. Underwater visibility can extend more than 200 feet (60m) here. The caye has a lighthouse, excellent beaches and spectacular submerged walls teeming with marine flora and fauna. Standing less than 10 feet (3m) above sea level, the caye's 45 acres (18 hectares) hold two distinct ecosystems. To the west is lush vegetation fertilized by the droppings of thousands of seabirds, including some 4000 red-footed boobies, the wonderfully named magnificent frigate bird and 98 other bird species. The east side has less vegetation but more coconut palms. Loggerhead and hawksbill sea turtles, both endangered, lay their eggs on the southern beaches.

A nature trail weaves through the southern part of the island to an **observation platform** (admission US$5) that brings viewers eye level with nesting boobies and frigate birds. Along the path you'll see thousands of seashells, many inhabited by hermit crabs

Pancakes for sale at a Belize City market

No longer the capital, Belize City is still the hub.

Belize City's court house was built in 1926.

Preparing coconuts builds strong muscles.

Haulover Creek splits the land mass of Belize City in two.

CAROLYN MILLER CARLSTROEM

Thatched-roof cottages also come in luxury style. Blancaneaux Lodge, western Belize

JOHN ELK III

Dock by the Lamanai Outpost Lodge on the New River, northern Belize (unnerving when you first notice them moving!). Accommodations are unavailable, but *camping* is allowed in designated areas, and showers and toilets are provided. The lighthouse at sunset is utterly beautiful. Organized boat trips stop at Half Moon Caye and the nearby Blue Hole.

Other Lighthouse Reef Cayes Northern Caye, another small but lovely caye, is home to the *Lighthouse Reef Resort (☎ 800-423-3114, fax 863-439-2118 both in the USA, ⓦ www.scubabelize.com)*, which attracts divers who wish to roll out of bed and into the sea. Seven-night fishing and diving packages start at US$1500.

The remaining four cayes, Sandbore, White Pelican, Long Caye and Hat Caye, are popular with mosquitoes and crocodiles, and are mostly admired from afar by humans.

Northern Belize

The northern Belize most commonly seen by visitors is farmland. Vast sugarcane fields grow alongside the paved, swift Northern Hwy, and off on the side roads. Mennonites, Maya and Mestizos tend efficient multi-purpose farms. Head deeper into the region and you'll hit jungle in the hilly west and mangrove swamp along the convoluted Caribbean shoreline.

Highlights

- Taking a boat tour up the New River and through the jungle to the magnificent ruins at Lamanai
- Experiencing the true rain forest at Río Bravo Conservation & Management Area
- Lapping up the saltwater breeze in the Spanish-influenced town of Corozal
- Escaping to a timeless world in the sleepy seaside village of Sarteneja

OTHER MAPS
Northern Belize page 131

Orange Walk and Corozal are the region's two major towns. Orange Walk is the commercial center for area farming as well as the starting point for river tours to Lamanai, a Mayan ruin site known for its historical interest and for the exotic river journey that most travelers take to reach it.

Corozal is Belize's northernmost town of appreciable size and is a gateway for travelers going to and from Mexico's Yucatán Peninsula. It's a pleasant seaside town offering an eclectic combination of Mayan, Mexican and Caribbean cultures, and its sea breezes are a refreshing escape from the area's inland heat. At Cerros, across the bay from Corozal, a small Mayan fishing settlement became a powerful kingdom in Late Preclassic times.

The north has several significant biosphere reserves. Largest is the Río Bravo Conservation & Management Area, a giant preserve of tropical forests, rivers, ponds and Mayan archaeological sites in the western part of the Orange Walk District. Way up in the Corozal District, Shipstern Nature Reserve is a remote and wild protected area near the tiny fishing village of Sarteneja.

While sugar extraction and processing is by far the number one industry here, most of this land was settled not by farmers looking for lush pastures, but by refugees fleeing war in the Yucatán. The War of the Castes (from the Spanish *Guerra de Castas)* began in 1847 and lumbered on in a series of bloody battles until 1901. One of the war's main points of contention involved the caste system, essentially a class system that shoved the indigenous Maya to the bottom of the socioeconomic ladder under Spanish and later British rule.

A treaty ratified in 1897 defined Belize's northwestern border. The number of Caste War settlers, along with the area's proximity to Mexico, gives northern Belize a unique Spanish influence.

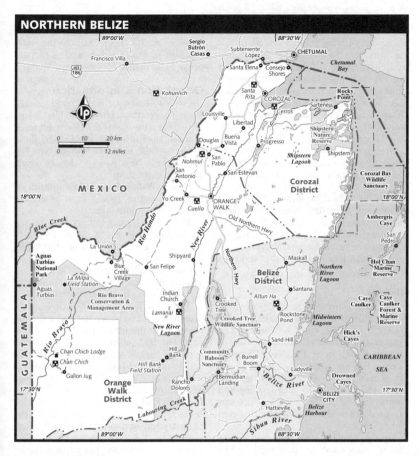

ORANGE WALK
pop 16,000

The agricultural and social center of northern Belize, Orange Walk is 58 miles (94km) north of Belize City. The town serves the region's farmers (including many Mennonites), some of whom grow citrus fruits and papaya. The name of the game here, however, is sugarcane and its byproducts – sugar, molasses and rum.

Orange Walk's Tower Hill Sugar Refinery became the only one in Belize after the Libertad refinery near Corozal shut its doors in 1983. Tower Hill now processes about a million tons of cane per year. Cane grows quickly, and the fertile soil and sunny, warm weather grants farmers two harvestable crops a year. It's a dependable crop that is especially noted for its high sucrose content.

Despite its fruitful yield, Belize's most prolific cash crop remains plagued with financial instability, mostly due to plummeting world sugar prices and the resulting demand for bolstered production, which has been hindered by an archaic quota system.

Farmers can't grow enough, the refinery can't produce enough, and the world market isn't paying enough (for more, see the boxed text 'Sweet & Sour Sugar Industry'). Still, Tower Hill employs about 500 workers, and most of Orange Walk's inhabitants work in jobs relating to cane production. Two types of rum are distilled in Orange Walk: Caribbean and Rum Master, both of which are cheap and readily available throughout the country.

Orange Walk is not highly developed for tourism, but does have a few modest hotels and good restaurants. The town's got a rough-and-tumble feel and though it's a friendly place, don't be surprised if you see the odd guy staggering drunk in the streets (did we mention the rum?). Another option, if you're spending a few days in the region, is to base yourself in Corozal about 41 miles (66km) north. Buses between the two towns are plentiful.

History

British mahogany cutters in Belize (then British Honduras) helped make Orange Walk one of Belize's first settlements. The loggers shipped raw mahogany out of Orange Walk, along the New River to Corozal Bay and eventually to Belize City. When mahogany exports started to decline, the residents turned to corn farming and tapping sapodilla trees for chicle, which was exported and used for making chewing gum and rubber.

Orange Walk's first real population 'boom' happened in the 1850s when refugees fleeing Yucatán's War of the Castes began spilling over to settle in British Honduras. The indigenous Maya were already resentful of British and Spanish encroachment and had spent the majority of the 1800s defending their lands. The War of the Castes (1847–1901) simply fueled the cause.

The ruins of two British forts in Orange Walk – Fort Mundy and Fort Cairnes – serve as unfortunate reminders of the often horrific conflict. In 1872, the British garrison held off a final attack by the Icaiche Maya by killing their leader and severely weakening their army's power. This battle stands as

the last armed resistance by Maya peoples in Belize. Today, an old flagpole in front of Orange Walk's town hall is the only remnant of Fort Cairnes, while Independence Plaza marks the site of Fort Mundy.

Orientation & Information

It's easy to find your way around Orange Walk. The Northern Hwy, called Queen Victoria Ave in town, serves as the main road. The center of town is shady Central Park, on the east side of Queen Victoria Ave. The slow-moving New River snakes by along the east side of town.

Orange Walk lacks an official tourism information center, though most hotels can provide local information.

The Sandy Hunter Library (☎ 3-22167), on Hospital Crescent at the north end of town, has a good collection of local books and magazines.

On Main St a block east of Central Park you'll find Scotiabank (☎ 3-22194) and right across the street Belize Bank (☎ 3-22019).

The post office (☎ 3-22345) is in the Sub-Treasury Building beside the police station, across from the library on Hospital Crescent. The BTL office (☎ 3-22196), on the corner of Park St and Lovers' Lane, is open 8am to noon and 1pm to 5pm weekdays.

Check email or surf the 'net at Orange Walk Information & Technology Center in the Town Hall across from Central Park. It's open 2pm to 9pm weekdays, 1pm to 7pm Saturday and 3pm to 9pm Sunday. You can also try the K&N Print Shop (☎ 3-22473), on Queen Victoria Ave just north of the Mi Amore Hotel. It's open 8am to noon, 2pm to 5pm and 7pm to 9pm daily. Both charge US$3 per hour.

The town hospital (☎ 3-22073) is in the northern outskirts, readily visible on the west side of the Northern Hwy.

Archaeological Sites

Cuello Close to Orange Walk and with a 3000-year history, Cuello (**kway**-yo) is the earliest-known settled community in the Maya world, although there's unfortunately little to show for it. The Maya of Cuello were excellent pottery makers and prolific

Sweet & Sour Sugar Industry

For three centuries, industry in Belize meant one thing: mahogany. Extraction of the magnificent hardwood led Belize's export commodities, and the country's financial stability seemed to dangle on the trees' branches. When over-cutting brought forestry to its knobby knees, Belize put all of its agricultural resources into another crop: sugarcane.

The promise of the sugar industry was foreshadowed in the mid-1800s when a handful of farmers started producing sugar and rum for England on a small scale. In 1935, with the opening of the Libertad refinery near Corozal, the industry started weighing in. But massive sugar production didn't get underway until a British company, Tate & Lyle, purchased the refinery in the early 1960s.

The crisis that followed is a pattern seen in countries throughout the world. Suddenly, Belize once again had an industry controlled by a single corporation that was fully dependant on a mono-crop agriculture and intensely vulnerable to market whims.

But the 1970s sugar boom put dollar signs in everyone's eyes. Throughout northern Belize, peasants turned into pillars of prosperity and the boom significantly, finally, increased the standard of living for Maya-Mestizos. Sugar had become big business and, unlike mahogany, sugarcane never seemed to run out. Cane grows easily in the hot climate; the crop is harvestable every six months, giving farmers two solid crops a year.

That same decade, ecological consequences started becoming clear; an almost total reliance on cane meant a greater reduction in diversified farming. The money was in cane, so farmers, always in a race to grow and produce more in order meet production targets, practiced slash-and-burn agriculture and ever expanded the boundaries of their farms. Where before they grew food to feed their families and villages, they now grew cane.

Farmers could not keep up with demand when the sugar boom reached its height in 1980. By then most farmers were full-fledged *cañeros*, whose crops were devoted entirely to cane.

In the early 1980s, world sugar prices plummeted. Widespread recession in developed countries led to lower sugar demands. The dramatically lower sugar price meant more cane had to be produced at a fraction of the cost just to keep up.

The Libertad refinery was shut down in 1983. Now, Orange Walk's Tower Hill refinery processes all of the country's cane. The market crash proved the instability of the industry and that survival is always at the mercy of the world market.

Though the sugar industry is the primary business in northern Belize, it continues to lose money. Refinery workers haven't seen a raise in a decade, and sugar prices remain low, resulting in a deteriorating supply. Now, more than ever, the industry needs to diversify.

Cane is used primarily to make refined sugar, but it is also processed into rum and molasses. A movement is under way promoting the co-generation of bagasse, a byproduct of processed cane. Bagasse, researchers contend, could be developed into an alternative electric energy source. The government and Belize Sugar Industries (BSI) are seriously researching the possibility of co-generation. There's even talk of reopening the Libertad refinery, to process enough bagasse to allow Belize to export energy. Meanwhile, citrus fruits, banana, papaya and farmed and fresh seafood augment sugar as the country's main export.

NORTHERN BELIZE

farmers, and though archaeologists have found plenty here, only Structure 350, a nine-tiered, stepped pyramid, will draw your interest.

The site is on private property owned by the **Cuello Brothers Distillery** (☎ 3-22141, *San Antonio Rd – also called Yo Creek Rd*), 2½ miles (4km) west of Orange Walk (take Bakers St out of town). The distillery, on the left (south) side of the road, is unmarked except for a gate; the site is through and beyond it. It's free to explore, but ask permission at the distillery gate. A taxi to

Cuello from Orange Walk will cost about US$10 roundtrip.

Nohmul 'Great Mound' in Mayan, Nohmul (noh-**mool**) was a much more important site than Cuello. The vast site covers more than 7 sq miles (18 sq km), though most of it is now overgrown by grass and sugarcane. Though the ruins themselves aren't exactly spectacular, the view from Structure 2, a lofty acropolis and the site's tallest building, is. You can see clear across the Orange Walk District, over endless fields of cane.

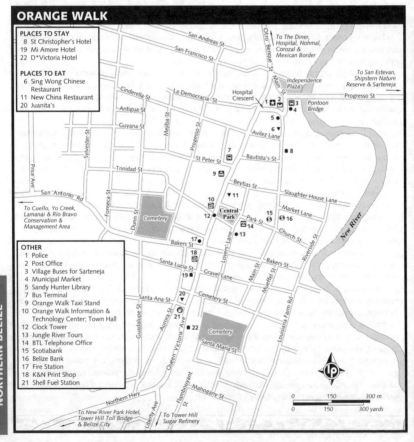

ORANGE WALK

PLACES TO STAY
8 St Christopher's Hotel
19 Mi Amore Hotel
22 D*Victoria Hotel

PLACES TO EAT
6 Sing Wong Chinese Restaurant
11 New China Restaurant
20 Juanita's

OTHER
1 Police
2 Post Office
3 Village Buses for Sarteneja
4 Municipal Market
5 Sandy Hunter Library
7 Bus Terminal
9 Orange Walk Taxi Stand
10 Orange Walk Information & Technology Center; Town Hall
12 Clock Tower
13 Jungle River Tours
14 BTL Telephone Office
15 Scotiabank
16 Belize Bank
17 Fire Station
18 K&N Print Shop
21 Shell Fuel Station

To The Diner, Hospital, Nohmal, Corozal & Mexican Border

To San Estevan, Shipstern Nature Reserve & Sarteneja

To Cuello, Yo Creek, Lamanai & Río Bravo Conservation & Management Area

To New River Park Hotel, Tower Hill Toll Bridge & Belize City

To Tower Hill Sugar Refinery

0   150   300 m
0   150   300 yards

From the northern edge of Orange Walk, drive 9.6 miles (15.5 km) north on the Northern Hwy to the village of San Jose. On the north end of the village look for the sign directing you 1.3 miles (0.8 km) west to Nohmul. The dirt road forks slightly twice – keep your eyes on the odometer and stay right; the actual site is not well marked. Getting to the site is tricky without a car, though you could take a bus to San Jose, and walk the dirt road. A taxi from Orange Walk will cost about US$15 roundtrip.

Places to Stay

Juanita's (☎ 3-22677, 8 Santa Ana St) Single or double with shared bath US$10. Popular for its restaurant, Juanita's four very basic but clean rooms, all of which come with a double bed and fan, make it the cheapest place to stay in town.

St Christopher's Hotel (☎/fax 3-21064, e rowbze@btl.net, 10 Main St) Single/double/triple with fan US$27.50/32.50/37.50, with air-con US$37.50/42.50/47.50. Despite the rather garish salmon-pink building, this decently priced hotel offers the best value in Orange Walk. The clean, quiet rooms come with private bath, tiled floors and cable TV. The off-street riverside rooms are the nicest.

Mi Amore Hotel (☎ 3-22031, fax 3-23462, e miamore@btl.net, 19 Queen Victoria Ave) Single/double/triple with fan US$19.50/29/35, with air-con single & double/triple US$42.50/53.50. All 12 rooms here have private bath and most have TV. Rooms are tidy and comfortable, but the noisy disco on the ground floor pounds out loud music until 3am on Friday, Saturday and Sunday nights.

*D*Victoria Hotel* (☎ 3-22518, fax 3-22847, e dvictoria@btl.net, w www.d-victoriahotel.com, 40 Queen Victoria Ave) Single or double with fan US$22.50, single/double/triple with air-con US$37.50/43/53.50. This is another good value, where all of the 34 spacious, clean rooms have TV and private bath with good showers. The bonuses here are the outdoor swimming pool, friendly staff and hammocks out back. On weekends, the hotel's lounge can be noisy, so ask for a room away from the action.

New River Park Hotel (☎ 3-23987, fax 3-23789, e newriver@btl.net, Northern Hwy) Doubles with fan/air-con US$25/45. Meals US$4-12. On the east side of the Northern Hwy, 4 miles (7km) south of Orange Walk just north of the Tower Hill toll bridge, this hotel backs onto the New River, one of the put-in spots for boat tours traveling to Lamanai. Though in need of some repair, the hotel's spacious rooms are quiet, and the ones with air-con on the upper floor come with balconies. The terrace restaurant attracts both locals and tourists.

Places to Eat

Pick up cheap local grub or fresh produce from the occasional vendors set up around Central Park, or stop by the *Municipal Market*, where you can get homemade rice and beans, tortillas and Mexican food from one of the many stalls. The market is on the north end of Main St, where it turns into Hospital Crescent.

Juanita's (☎ 3-22677, 8 Santa Ana St) Prices US$2.50. Open 6am-2pm & 6pm-9pm daily. You can tell by the dedicated locals who flock here that the food is good. A simple place near the Shell fuel station, where everything is a cheap US$2.50, Juanita's serves eggs and bacon at breakfast, rice and beans and other local favorites, like cow-foot soup, the rest of the day.

The Diner (☎ 3-22131, 37 Clark St) Meals US$7-12. Open 7am-10pm daily, until midnight Fri & Sat. This is the favorite local hangout for breakfast, lunch and dinner. It's off the beaten track a bit but worth it for its creative menu and cool, leafy setting. Sit and drink cold Belikins under the big thatched-roof palapa and enjoy the special of the day, which could be anything from beef fajitas to steamed garlic shrimp. Go north and turn left just before the hospital, then bear right (follow the signs) and go about a quarter mile (400m). If you don't have a ride, it's about a 20-minute walk from the center of town. The Diner also rents out a couple of unimpressive rooms for US$20.

Like everywhere else in Belize, an influx of Taiwanese and Chinese immigrants has blessed Orange Walk with several Chinese restaurants. Following are a couple of the nicest.

New China Restaurant (☎ 3-22650, on Queen Victoria Ave half a block north of Central Park) Dishes US$3-7. Clean and usually busy with locals, this restaurant offers generous portions and lots of vegetarian options at great prices. Try the vegetable chop suey (US$3) or the pineapple lobster (US$6.50).

Sing Wong Chinese Restaurant (☎ 3-20018, 13 Main St at Avilez Lane) Dishes US$5-12. With slightly higher prices, this large, clean restaurant boasts a full bar and large menu, with everything from basic chow mein (US$5) to seafood (US$11).

New River Park Hotel (☎ 3-23987, Northern Hwy) Breakfast US$4-5, lunch & dinner US$4-12. Open 8am-11pm daily. You can eat inside or on the terrace at this hotel restaurant that serves up good standard breakfasts such as eggs, bacon and potatoes. The rest of the day the menu features burgers, sandwiches and steak or seafood dinners.

Getting There & Away

Novelo's Northern Transport buses (☎ 3-22858) run regularly south to Belize City and north to Corozal and Chetumal (Mexico). Buses run at least hourly in both directions, with additional runs in the early morning and late afternoon to accommodate work and school schedules. All buses traveling along the Northern Hwy stop briefly in Orange Walk.

The old peach-colored bus stand at Queen Victoria Ave at St Peter St is now defunct; Novelo's currently uses the old Terry's Cafe (the old 'Coke' sign is still there), across St Peter St at 45 Queen Victoria Ave. By bus, it takes about two hours to reach Belize City (58 miles/92km) and an hour to get to Corozal (41 miles/66km). For more bus information see the Getting Around chapter.

Orange Walk Taxi (☎ 3-22050) is next to the old bus stand. A one-way taxi from

Orange Walk to Belize City is around US$65; to Corozal it's about US$35.

LAMANAI

By far the most impressive site in this part of the country, Lamanai *(admission US$2.50; open 8am-5pm daily year-round)* is in its own archaeological reserve on the New River Lagoon near the small settlement of Indian Church. The vast site is Belize's second-largest Mayan site (next to Caracol), and the trip up to Lamanai, by motorboat up the New River, is an adventure in itself.

Take a sun hat, sunscreen, insect repellent, shoes (rather than sandals), lunch and a beverage (unless you plan to take a tour that includes lunch).

History

As with most sites in northern Belize, Lamanai ('Submerged Crocodile' in Mayan) was occupied as early as 1500 BC, with the first stone buildings appearing between 800 BC and 600 BC, making it the longest known occupation of the Mayan era. Lamanai flourished in Late Preclassic times, growing into a major ceremonial center with immense temples long before most other Mayan sites. Excavations at Lamanai have uncovered representations of crocodiles on pottery pieces, figurines and on buildings, indicating that the crocodile was an important figure.

Unlike at many other sites, Mayas lived here until the coming of the Spanish in the 16th century (Spanish records show that the Maya called the New River 'Dzuluinicob,' meaning 'foreign men'). The Spaniards found a thriving community. The ruined church (actually two of them) nearby attests to the fact that there were Maya here for the Spanish friars to convert. Convert them they did, but by 1640 the Maya rebelled against Christianity and reverted to their ancient forms of worship.

British interests later built a sugar mill, now in ruins, at Indian Church. Archaeological excavations here started as early as 1917, but large-scale digging, by David Pendergast of Canada's Royal

Ontario Museum, began in 1974. Major excavation efforts continue today, but the painstaking work of uncovering the more than 800 structures found here would take several lifetimes, not to mention massive amounts of funding.

New River Voyage
Most visitors opt to reach Lamanai on a spectacular boat ride up the New River from the Tower Hill toll bridge south of Orange Walk. On this trip, available only as part of an organized tour (see that section, later), you motor 1½ hours upriver, between riverbanks crowded with dense jungle vegetation. En route, your skipper/guide points out the many local birds and will almost certainly spot a crocodile or two. Along the way you pass a molasses barge (which carries molasses to Belize City) and the austere Mennonite community at Shipyard. You might see a traditional fisherman in a dugout canoe, but other than that you'll feel immersed in the jungle and quite removed from civilization. Perhaps this is why, when finally you come to New River Lagoon – a long, broad expanse of water – and the boat dock at Lamanai, your imagination is reeling and ready to absorb Mayan civilization.

Touring Lamanai
Landing at Lamanai, you'll sign the visitor's book, visit the museum (no ☎), and pay the admission fee. The museum exhibits some figurative flint stones, beautiful examples of pottery and obsidian and jade jewelry. From the museum, you'll wander into the dense jungle, past gigantic guanacaste, ceiba and *ramón* (breadnut) trees, strangler figs, allspice, epiphytes and examples of Belize's national flower, the black orchid. In the canopy overhead you might see (or hear) one of the groups of resident howler monkeys. A tour of the ruins takes 90 minutes minimum, more comfortably two or three hours. The time you'll spend at the sight depends on your guide and the size of the group. If you want to stay longer, just ask your guide for a little extra time.

'The Mask Temple'(N9-56) To the north along a jungle path, Structure N9-56, built and modified between 200 BC and AD 1300, has a huge stylized mask of a man in a crocodile-mouth headdress 13 feet (4m) high emblazoned on its southwest face. Archaeologists have dug deep into this structure (from the platform level, high on the east side) to look for burials and to document the several earlier structures that lie beneath. To date, they've found a tomb containing the remains of a man adorned with shell and jade jewelry. Nearby, the remains of a woman found in a second tomb suggest a succession of leaders – perhaps a husband and wife, or brother and sister.

Near this structure are a small temple and a ruined stela that once stood on the temple's front face. Apparently some worshipers built a fire at the base of the limestone stela and later doused the fire with water. The hot, stone stela, cooled too quickly by the water, broke and toppled.

'Lag' (N10-43) Structure N10-43, the tallest temple on the site, is a massive building rising 125 feet (33m) above the jungle canopy. Other buildings along La Ruta Maya are taller and in better shape, but this one was built well before the others; its construction began in about 100 BC. Excavations show that the grand ceremonial temple was constructed on a site that was primarily residential, indicating a rather dramatic shift in power to this part of the community. In today's terms, this equates to a palace being built in the middle of a working-class neighborhood. Check out the ancient pulley system used by the Maya. Over the next few years, you'll likely witness excavation work happening at this structure.

Ball Court Not far from N10-43 is Lamanai's ball court; it's smallish compared to those at other Mayan sites, but it boasts one of the largest ball-court markers found anywhere. A ceremonial vessel containing liquid mercury was found beneath the marker. The mercury probably came from Guatemala.

Stela 9 East of the ball court, this Late Classic stela represents Lord Smoking Shell. The date depicted on the stela celebrates the conclusion of the *tun* (year), as well as the anniversary of the lord's reign. The remains of five children – ranging in age from newborn to eight – were found buried beneath the stela. Archaeologists believe the burial must have been highly significant, since offerings are not usually associated with the dedication of monuments.

'Temple of the Jaguar' (N10-9) Part of a complex of residential buildings, this Early Classic temple (Structure N10-9) has a succession of modifications that attests to the Maya at Lamanai's longevity and perseverance in traditional ways, even after European influence. Archaeologists have found evidence that the community here continued to thrive at a time when other Mayan cities were already in rapid decline.

Lamanai Outpost Lodge

This reclusive jungle lodge *(☎ 2-33578, fax 2-12061,* e *lamanai@btl.net,* w *www .lamanai.com)* is a five-minute boat ride south of Lamanai. Perched on a hillside sloping down to the lagoon, the well-kept lodge, bar and gorgeous open-air dining room enjoy panoramic views. The 18 thatched-roof *bungalows (single/double/ triple/quad US$105/125/145/165),* each with fan, private bath and verandah, are cozy and perfectly suited to the casual jungle atmosphere. Breakfast costs US$8, lunch US$12, dinner US$22. Owners Mark and Monique Howells, originally from Australia, employ 37 Belizeans at the lodge, most of whom live in nearby Indian Church.

Archaeologists, ornithologists, botanists and naturalists in residence at the lodge lead tours, give lectures or work in the lodge's lab. Activities include river excursions (the nighttime spotlight safari is a highlight), wildlife walks and tours of Lamanai.

All-inclusive multi-day packages are available, as are education-adventure programs that allow guests to participate in archaeological or jungle-habitat research. Transfers from Belize City can be arranged by land or air.

Organized Tours

The Novelo brothers (all five of them) have excellent reputations as guides and naturalists. Their company, **Jungle River Tours** *(☎ 3-22293, fax 3-22201,* e *lamanaimaya tour@btl.net, 20 Lovers' Lane, Orange Walk),* near the southeast corner of Central Park, offers excursions to Lamanai (US$40 per person), which include lunch, beverages and the guided tour along the river and at the ruins. The tour group meets at 9am at the office in Orange Walk, though by prior arrangement the boat will pick you up at the New River Park, St Christopher's, Mi Amore or D*Victoria Hotels. The tour returns at around 4pm. Reservations are required.

Reyes & Sons *(☎ 3-23327)* runs tours departing Jim's Cool Pool, just north of the toll bridge, at 9am daily (be there by 8:30am). They offer a boat ride and guided tour (US$40 per person, though the price drops if you've got a bigger group).

Note that the Lamanai entrance fee (US$2.50) is not included in the price of either tour.

It's possible to get an early bus from Belize City to Orange Walk, get out at the Tower Hill toll bridge and be in time for the morning departure of the boats to Lamanai. Be sure to call and reserve space with a tour company first, so they know to pick you up. In the evening you can catch a return bus to Belize City at the bridge or, preferably, in Orange Walk.

Getting There & Away

Though the river voyage is much more convenient and enjoyable (see Organized Tours, above), Lamanai can be reached by road (36 miles/58km) from Orange Walk via Yo Creek and San Felipe. Allow at least an hour to travel the bumpy roads. Bus service from Orange Walk is limited (it's primarily for people coming from villages to town for marketing).

The Mennonites

It almost seems like an aberration, an odd sight inspired by the hot sun, or maybe just a blurry result of too much sweat dripping in your eyes. But the vision of women in wintry frocks and blond men with blue eyes, blue denim overalls and straw cowboy hats is not something your imagination has conjured up: You're looking at Belizean Mennonites.

Distantly related to the Amish in Pennsylvania, Belize's Mennonite settlers stem from an enigmatic Anabaptist group that dates back to 16th-century Netherlands. Like the Amish, the Mennonites have strict religion-based values that keep them isolated in agricultural communities. Speaking mostly an obscure guttural German, the Mennonites run their own schools, banks and churches. Traditional groups reject any form of mechanization or technology, believing instead in old-world ideas. They are devout pacifists and will at all costs reject the political ideologies (including paying taxes) that have, throughout history, been thrust upon them.

Adhering to their philosophies and values has not been easy for the Mennonites, who have a long history of shuffling about the world trying to find a peaceful environment where they could be left alone. Their stringent beliefs first drove them out of the Netherlands to Prussia and Russia in the late 1600s. In the 1870s, when the Russian government insisted on military conscription, the Mennonites upped and moved to Canada. They rebuilt communities in isolated parts of Saskatchewan, Alberta and British Columbia. There they stayed until after WWI, when the Canadian government, backed by anti-German sentiment and post-war patriotism, demanded English be taught in Mennonite schools, and the Mennonites' exemption from conscription was being seriously reconsidered. Again the most devout Mennonites moved on, settling now in Mexico's harsh highlands. But things didn't work out in Mexico either – by the 1950s the Mexican government insisted the Mennonites join Mexico's social security program, and once again the Mennonites packed up.

The first wave of about 3500 Mennonites settled in Belize (then British Honduras) in 1958. Unlike other countries, Belize was happy to have them. So far, diversifying agriculture in Belize had been a bit of a bust, with locals importing everything from meat and poultry to tomatoes and eggs. The Mennonites were known for their industriousness and farming prowess, and there was plenty of land, so the doors were opened wide and they stepped on in.

Throughout Mennonite history, there have been splinter groups who, while maintaining many of the fundamental religious ideals, have rejected others. This is true of some of the factions that settled in Belize. Progressive Mennonites, many of whom came from Canada, speak English and have no qualms about using tractors to clear their land, or pickup trucks to shuffle their families about. These groups are found in Blue Creek near Orange Walk, or at Spanish Lookout in the Cayo District, and are downright wealthy compared to most Belizeans. Ardent fundamentalist and conservative groups, such as the one in Shipyard near Orange Walk or at Barton Creek in the Cayo District, still use horse-drawn buggies to get around, and shun electricity.

Belize has been good to the Mennonites and the Mennonites have been good to Belize. Mennonite farms now supply most of the country's dairy, eggs and poultry. Furniture-making is also a Mennonite specialty and you'll often see them selling their goods at town markets.

RÍO BRAVO CONSERVATION & MANAGEMENT AREA

Protecting 260,000 acres (105,200 hectares) of tropical forest and its inhabitants, the Río Bravo Conservation & Management Area (RBCMA) encompasses a whopping 4.6% of Belize's total land. Owned and managed by the private, nonprofit Programme for Belize (PFB), the RBCMA supports a myriad of forest types along with astonishing biodiversity in plant, bird and animal life – including 392 bird species (more than half of the total species count in Belize), 380 tree species and 70 species of mammal, including all five of Belize's cats (jaguar, jaguarundi, ocelot, puma and margay). In fact, Río Bravo is said to have the largest concentration of jaguars in all of Central America. Some 50 species of bat live here, along with a creepy-crawly array of spiders and scorpions. If you're looking for true, wild tropical rain forest, this is the place to come.

In addition to the wealth of plant and animal life here, over 60 Mayan sites have been discovered on the land. The preeminent site is **La Milpa**, the third-largest Mayan site in Belize, believed to have been founded in the Late Preclassic period. Archeologists from Boston University are conducting ongoing excavations at the site.

Though none of the RBCMA's funding comes from the government, the reserve is set up as a sort of national park whose goals are ecosystem protection, along with re-

search and sustainable-development projects. The long-term goal of PFB is to create a sustainable reserve that generates income without upsetting the integrity of the land. Projects to date include agro-forestry (tree reproduction and sustainable logging), micro-propagation of orchids, carbon sequestration and community development in villages traditionally dependent on reserve lands. Tourism accounts for a sizeable chunk of funding, and thousands of visitors – including local and international school groups – come each year to learn about the ecosystem, conservation and environmental awareness.

History

Archeologists figure Mayas lived in the area as early as 800 BC. When Spanish expeditions first came through what is now the RBMCA in the early 1600s, the Maya were

Chicle & Chewing Gum

Chicle, a pinkish to reddish-brown gum, is actually the coagulated milky sap, or latex, of the sapodilla tree *(Achras zapota)*, a tropical evergreen native to Central America. *Chicleros* (chicle workers) enter the forest and cut large gashes in the sapodillas' trunks, making a pattern of V-shaped cuts high up the trunk of the tree. The sap runs from the wounds down the trunk, where it's collected in a cloth container at the base. After being boiled, it is shaped into blocks, called *marquetas,* for shipping. Repetitive cutting often kills the tree, and, thus, chicle harvesting tends to result in the serious depletion of sapodilla forests. Even if the tree survives the first round of cuts, a typical tree used for harvesting chicle has a life span of just 10 years.

First used as a substitute for natural rubber (to which the sapodilla is related), by about 1890 chicle was best known as the main ingredient in chewing gum (including the ever-popular Chiclets).

As a result of war research for a rubber substitute during the 1940s, synthetic substitutes were developed for chicle. Now chewing gum is made mostly from these synthetic solutions. However, in the northwest of Belize, chicleros still live in the forests harvesting the sap for gum. Though the chicle-tapping method hasn't changed, the decreased demand for natural chicle alleviates the pressure of overharvesting sapodilla trees. To check out some real chicle gum, visit **w** www.junglegum.com.

still accessing the same riverine trade routes, though by then their population, like at other inland Mayan sites, had been seriously depleted.

By the mid-18th century, mahogany logging camps dominated the area, and the loggers – Baymen – were continually attacked by the Maya who resented the woodcutters' presence. Logging companies fought hard against Mayan resistance, and the industry eventually won.

By the mid-1800s, the Belize Estate and Produce Company (BEC) owned almost all of the land in northwestern Belize. The company carried out major extractions of mahogany and Mexican cedar, which they would float through the river system out to the coast. With the advent of rail systems and logging trucks, operations flourished until over-cutting and a moody market finally prompted BEC to stop cutting trees.

In addition to logging, intensive chicle tapping by *chicleros* took place throughout the 20th century. The chicle was exported and used to make chewing gum (including Chiclets) until synthetic gums proved cheaper. (You can still see slash scars on chicle trees throughout the RBCMA.)

Belizean businessman Barry Bowen purchased the land in the mid-1980s. He quickly sold off massive chunks to Yalbac Ranch (owned by a Texan cattle farmer) and to Coca-Cola Foods. Meanwhile the Massachusetts Audubon Society was looking for a reserve for migrating birds. Coke donated 42,000 acres (1700 hectares) to support the initiative, and Program for Belize was created to manage the land. Coke had plans to develop citrus farms throughout what is now the RBCMA, but outcries from environmentalists prompted Coke to reconsider. In 1992, Coke donated another 52,000 acres to PFB through the Nature Conservancy. Bowen also donated some land and PFB bought the rest, bringing today's total to 260,000 acres (105,200 hectares).

La Milpa Field Station

It's a long trek out here, so most visitors who come to Río Bravo stay overnight at one of the two field stations in the reserve.

Hill Bank Field Station is used primarily for school groups, while most independent travelers will stay at La Milpa Field Station, which also puts up educational and research groups. The La Milpa Field Station, on the road to Gallon Jug and Chan Chich, has an education center, on-site medicinal trail, access to hiking trails and the nearby La Milpa archaeological site.

Accommodations are in four-person *dorm rooms* (US$76 per person) or in gorgeous *cabanas* (US$92 per person) that come complete with private bath, running water, fresh linens and mosquito nets over the beds. There are plenty of hammocks in which to kick back and listen to birdsong. The price includes all meals and two guided tours.

Visiting and transportation arrangements must be made in advance through Programme for Belize (☎ 2-75616, fax 2-75635, e pfbel@btl.net, 1 Eyre St, Belize City). PFB can also arrange inexpensive transportation. If you're driving on your own, ask for specific directions and definitely fill up on gas in Orange Walk before setting out. The drive takes about 3½ hours on bumpy roads, so be sure your spare has air.

CHAN CHICH LODGE

In western Orange Walk District, Chan Chich Lodge (☎/fax 2-34419, e info@chanchich.com, w www.chanchich.com) is truly a destination unto itself; in fact, many of its visitors take a charter from Belize City and spend their entire trip here. Its setting is incredible: Thatched cabanas share space with partially excavated ruins in the central plaza of a Mayan archaeological site. Single/double *cabanas* cost US$145/165, meals cost US$40 per person; an all-inclusive package (including meals and activities) runs US$265/385. Each of the 12 cabanas has a private bath, fan, two queen-size beds, a verandah and bottled water. No more than 32 guests (mostly families and couples) stay here at one time, which keeps it uncrowded and helps maintain the truism that you're really in the middle of nowhere.

The lodge offers guided walks and activities throughout the day, and 9 miles (15km) of trails invite independent exploration.

While you may not see jaguars during your visit, you'll definitely feel their presence, and you are likely to see coatis, warries, deer, howler and spider monkeys and an array of bird life. Resident ornithologists have identified more than 350 bird species here. One of Belize's first eco-lodges, Chan Chich remains among the most luxurious, though it maintains a casual, shorts-and-T-shirt atmosphere.

The lodge lies between the settlement of Gallon Jug and the Guatemalan border. It's best reached by chartered plane from Belize City (about US$210 per person roundtrip), though you can also drive in on an all-weather road (130 miles/210km, three and a half hours from Belize City).

Gallon Jug

One of the activities available from Chan Chich is a tour of Gallon Jug, a small village essentially fabricated in 1986. Like most of the land surrounding Chan Chich, Gallon Jug is owned by Barry Bowen, the Belikin beer brewer and Coca-Cola distributor often described rather overtly as 'the richest man in Belize.' Of his 130,000-acre (52,000-hectare) parcel of tropical rain forest, Bowen set aside 3000 acres (1214 hectares) for experimental farming under the name of Gallon Jug Agro-Industries. The sense of organization and intention here is hard to ignore; everything growing in the mani-cured and orderly fields is deliberate and very controlled. Projects to date include growing corn, soybean, sugarcane, cacao and organic coffee beans. Another program hopes to raise the quality of local beef by artificially inseminating local cows with the sperm of imported English Hereford cattle. Ask at Chan Chich if you are interested in touring Gallon Jug.

COROZAL & AROUND
pop 10,000

Corozal is a prosperous farming town blessed with fertile land and a favorable climate for agriculture (sugarcane is the area's leading crop). It's a popular stop with travelers busing their way to or from Mexico, and many choose to base here

when exploring northern Belize. Two May-an ruins vie for attention here, as do some good budget hotels and excellent eateries. If you've been traveling inland, breezy, watery Corozal offers a welcome respite from the heat. Parkland runs all along the waterfront and there are many places to jump in the water and cool off.

Due to its proximity to Mexico and settle-ment by Caste War refugees, Spanish is the predominant language here, though most residents also speak English and Creole.

History

Corozal's Mayan history is long and impor-tant. On the town's northern outskirts are the ruins of a Mayan ceremonial center once called Chetumal, now called Santa Rita. This center controlled trade routes from the coast along modern-day Mexico's Río Hondo and Belize's New River. Unlike most Mayan sites, Santa Rita's structures were not elevated, so most of the ruins lie buried beneath the town of Corozal. Across the bay, Cerros was also a substantial coast-al trade center and is one of the most im-portant Late Preclassic sites discovered in Belize. Today the Cerros Maya Archeologi-cal Reserve covers 53 acres of land over-looking Chetumal Bay.

Mayas have been living in the Corozal area since about 1500 BC (modern Corozal dates from only 1849). When refugees from the War of the Castes in the Yucatán fled across the border to safe haven in British-controlled Belize, they were still exposed to random attacks by Maya Indians. The refugees built Fort Barlee for protection and founded a town and named it Corozal after the Spanish word for cohune palm, which is a strong symbol of fertility. Today the post office complex sits on the fort's foundation. A colorful mural by Belizean-Mexican artist Manual Villamor depicting Corozal's history enlivens the lobby of the town hall. (If the town hall is closed, which it often is, you can still see the mural by peeking through the window).

For years Corozal had the look of a typical Caribbean town, with adobe and thatched-roof homes. Then Hurricane Janet roared through in 1955 and blew away many of the old wooden buildings on stilts. Much of Corozal's wood and cinderblock architecture dates from the late 1950s.

A sugar refinery located in Libertad, just a few miles south of Corozal, was closed in 1985 after falling victim to declining sugar prices. Though the ministry of the sugar industry toys with the idea of reactivating the Libertad refinery, it sits like an industrial skeleton, and the town of Libertad is a veritable ghost town. The Corozal economy is still based on sugar, however, with many of its residents involved in farming cane, all of which is now processed in Orange Walk.

Orientation & Information

Though founded by the Maya, Corozal is now arranged around a town square in the traditional style of a Mexican town. You can easily walk to any place in town.

The main road through town is 7th Ave, which briefly skirts the sea before veering inland through town. The main plaza is bordered by 4th and 5th Aves, and by 1st St S and 1st St N.

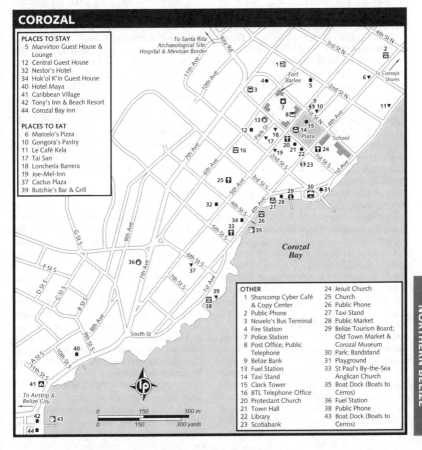

COROZAL

PLACES TO STAY
5 Marvirton Guest House & Lounge
12 Central Guest House
32 Nestor's Hotel
34 Hok'ol K'in Guest House
40 Hotel Maya
41 Caribbean Village
42 Tony's Inn & Beach Resort
44 Corozal Bay Inn

PLACES TO EAT
6 Marcelo's Pizza
10 Gongora's Pastry
11 Le Café Kela
17 Tai San
18 Lonchería Barrera
19 Joe-Mel-Inn
37 Cactus Plaza
39 Butchie's Bar & Grill

OTHER
1 Shancomp Cyber Café & Copy Center
2 Public Phone
3 Novelo's Bus Terminal
4 Fire Station
7 Police Station
8 Post Office; Public Telephone
9 Belize Bank
13 Fuel Station
14 Taxi Stand
15 Clock Tower
16 BTL Telephone Office
20 Protestant Church
21 Town Hall
22 Library
23 Scotiabank
24 Jesuit Church
25 Church
26 Public Phone
27 Taxi Stand
28 Public Market
29 Belize Tourism Board; Old Town Market & Corozal Museum
30 Park; Bandstand
31 Playground
33 St Paul's By-the-Sea Anglican Church
35 Boat Dock (Boats to Cerros)
36 Fuel Station
38 Public Phone
43 Boat Dock (Boats to Cerros)

Corozal Bay

To Santa Rita Archaeological Site, Hospital & Mexican Border

To Consejo Shores

To Airstrip & Belize City

0   150   300 m
0   150   300 yards

Built in 1886, the old town market and custom house – one of only 11 buildings spared by Hurricane Janet – now houses a museum and the BTB information office (☎ 4-23176). It's open 9am to 4pm daily and dispenses a free self-guided nature map of Corozal's trees and shrubs.

The Belize Bank (☎ 4-22087), on the northeast side of the plaza, is open for currency exchange 8am to 1pm Monday to Thursday, 8am to 4:30pm Friday. Scotiabank (☎ 4-22046), on 4th Ave half a block south of the plaza, is open 8am to 1pm Monday to Thursday, 8am to 4:30pm Friday.

Corozal's post office (☎ 4-22462) is on the site of the old Fort Barlee on 5th Ave, across from the plaza. It's open 8:30am to noon and 1pm to 4:30pm Monday to Thursday, and 8am to 4pm Friday. The BTL office (☎ 4-22196) is on 6th Ave between 2nd and 3rd Sts S. It's open 8am to noon and 1pm to 4pm weekdays, and 8am to noon Saturday.

The best place in town to check email or surf the Web is at Shancomp Cyber Café & Copy Center (☎ 4-23429, e shancomp@ btl.net), 26 2nd St N. It's open 8am to 9pm daily. Internet access costs US$3.30 per hour.

A small but pleasant library (☎ 4-23751), beside the town hall on the south side of the plaza, is open 9am to 7pm weekdays, 9 am to 1pm Saturday.

Corozal's Hospital (☎ 4-22076) is just a few miles northwest of town along the road to Santa Rita.

Laundry service is available at Nestor's Hotel (☎ 4-22354), 123 5th Ave. You can drop off your stuff in the morning and pick it up in the afternoon for US$1.25 per pound.

Archaeological Sites

Santa Rita Called Chetumal by the Maya, this coastal city sat astride important trade routes from the coast to two major rivers – modern Mexico's Río Honda and modern Belize's New River. These rivers were vital to the local Maya, but also proved essential to residents as far off as Petén in Guatemala. Trade items included honey, vanilla and cacao. Because of its position at the two river mouths, Santa Rita had its share of wealth. It was an important site, believed to have been established in 2000 BC, though its heyday was during the Postclassic period, which meant the Maya occupied the site when Spanish explorers arrived.

Despite its prominence, however, there isn't much of the city left to see. Excavations in the early 1900s found jade and pottery artifacts, most of which were dispersed to museums, and the site's important frescoes have long been destroyed. Much of Santa Rita lies buried beneath the town site of Corozal. When Corozal expanded from a tiny village into a bustling town, many of the covered mounds became road fill and the stones of the ancient temples were used for building house foundations.

Santa Rita's one restored **Mayan temple** *(admission free; open daylight hours daily)* is in a small, tidy park just over half a mile (1km) northwest of the bus terminal in Corozal. Go north on the main highway just under half a mile (800m) and bear right just before the statue. After about another 100 yards (90m) turn left and go straight for about two-tenths of a mile (320m) to the site. The 'hill' on the right is actually a temple. There is no visitor's center.

Cerros This site *(Cerro Maya; open 8am-5pm daily)* was an important coastal trade center that flourished in Late Preclassic times. Today, the site is at the heart of the sprawling Cerros Maya Archeological Reserve sitting on a peninsula overlooking Chetumal Bay. Its proximity to the New River made it a valuable trade center for Lamanai especially, and it acted as a major gateway into other inland Mayan communities. Unlike at other Mayan sites, little subsequent construction from the Classic and Postclassic periods covers the original structures here. Thus, the site has given archaeologists important insights into Mayan Preclassic architecture.

Climb Structure 4, a temple more than 65 feet (20m) high, for stunning panoramic views. Though the site is still mostly a mass of grass-covered mounds, the center has been cleared and consolidated, and it's easy to see how the plaza structures were designed to fit together. Also notable are the canals that ring the site, which have remained mysteriously clear of vegetation through the ages.

You can drive to Cerros via a rough dirt road that's only accessible in the dry season. Ask in town for specific directions.

Many people opt to take a boat to the site. A few guides specialize in boat trips that include guided tours of the site. Two of the best in town are **Stefan Moerman** (☎ 4-22833) and **Jose Majil** (☎ 4-20100). You can call the guides directly or set up trips through most hotels. The cost is usually US$25 per person, though the more people you have, the cheaper the trip is. You can also charter a boat (US$50) or arrange for a fisherman to take you over to the site to explore independently. The boat trip takes about 15 minutes; then you walk 10 minutes to the site.

Bacalar Chico

Stefan Moerman also runs a snorkeling and bird-watching tour (1-2/3-4/5-6 people US$200/250/300) to Bacalar Chico (also called Boca Bacalar Chico), a national marine park at the northern tip of Ambergris Caye. The park, accessed through a channel dug 1500 years ago by sea-trading Maya, is a splendid alternative to the congested snorkeling spots visited from San Pedro. Marine life is plentiful, the coral pristine. For more see the Northern Cayes chapter.

Places to Stay – Budget

Caribbean Village (☎ 4-22752, 7th Ave at 11th St S) Tent sites US$5 per person, single or double US$20. South of town, across the main road from the sea, this no-frills budget option has windowless white-walled palapas, or you can pitch your tent on the large swath of grass shaded by coconut palms.

Central Guest House (☎ 4-22358, fax 4-23335, e cghczl@yahoo.com, 22 6th Ave) Single or double (one bed) US$12.50, double (two beds) US$15. A short walk from the plaza, this simple, cheap place has

rather dark and dismal rooms with shared bath. Bonuses include a cooking area and a large common area.

Nestor's Hotel (☎/fax 4-22354, e nestors @btl.net, 123 5th Ave S) Single & double/triple & quad US$20/30. This lively spot makes a large part of its money from its restaurant-bar and video machines. Rooms are small but come with private bath and fans in every room. This is an easy place to meet other travelers. The bar can get noisy, so ask for a room away from the action.

Marvirton Guest House & Lounge (☎ 4-23365, 16 2nd St N) Single/double/triple US$25/27.50/32.50. This small, family-style guest house is quiet and clean. Rooms have private bath. There's also a small restaurant and bar.

Hotel Maya (☎ 4-22082, fax 4-22827, e hotelmaya@btl.net, w www.hotelmaya .com, 7th Ave between 9th & 10th Sts S) Single/double/triple with fan US$25/31/40, single/double with fan & TV US$30/37.50, with air-con & TV US$42.50/50. This friendly place is the longtime budget favorite, where the 17 aged but clean and breezy rooms come with private bath and good showers. The adjoining eatery serves good, cheap meals at breakfast, lunch and dinner (US$3.25-8).

Places to Stay – Mid-Range

Hok'ol K'in Guest House (☎ 4-23329, fax 4-23569, e maya@btl.net, w www.corozal.net, 89 4th Ave) Singles/doubles/triples/quads US$32/40/45/50. Given the Mayan name for 'rising sun,' this modern hotel is the best value in town. The comfortable rooms are designed to catch sea breezes, and each has two double beds, a bathroom, cable TV and a patio, complete with hammock. The large common room has a sink, fridge and bookshelf full of tradable books. Co-owned by a former Peace Corps worker, this favorite spot also has a nice dining room and patio.

Tony's Inn & Beach Resort (☎ 4-22055, fax 4-22829, e tonys@btl.net, w www .tonysinn.com, Corozal Bay Rd) Doubles with fan/air-con/TV & air-con US$30/65/70. This popular resort, about a mile (1.6km) south of the plaza on the shore road, has landscaped grounds and lawn chairs set to enjoy the view of the bay. It has 24 well-used rooms in a motel-style building, with cable TV, a restaurant and an outdoor bar.

Corozal Bay Inn (☎ 4-22691, e relax@ corozalbayinn.com, w www.corozalbayinn .com, Corozal Bay Rd) Singles/doubles/ triples/quads US$42/52.50/63/73.50. Next door to Tony's, this friendly family-run place has spacious rooms with kitchenettes, hammocks and lots of good sea breeze. Hospitable staff, the Some Place Else palapa bar and an outdoor swimming pool are major bonuses.

Places to Eat

For fresh fruit stop by the ***public market***, on 4th Ave at 3rd St S, where local farmers sell their produce early every morning.

The ***Hok'ol K'in Guest House***, ***Hotel Maya***, ***Corozal Bay Inn*** and ***Tony's Inn & Beach Resort*** have good restaurants with both indoor and outside seating.

Gongora's Pastry (☎ 4-23631, 1st St N, beside Belize Bank) Baked goods US$1-2. Open 6:30am-4pm. Stop by this great local bakery to pick up fresh bread or delicious baked goods.

Marcelo's Pizza (☎ 4-23275, 25 4th Ave) Pizza slice US$1, whole pizza US$6. Open 10am-11pm daily. There are good ooey-gooey American-style pizzas served up at this friendly spot.

Lonchería Barrera (no ☎, 1st St S & 5th Ave) Dishes US$1-3. Open 11am-9pm daily. Offering traditional Mexican food at unbeatable prices, the tiny, family-run Barrera serves tostadas for US$0.25 and burritos for US$0.50. It's off the west corner of the square.

Joe-Mel-Inn (☎ 4-22526, 5th Ave at 2nd St S) Dishes US$2-5. Open 6:30am-5pm Mon-Fri, 6:30am-2:30pm Sat. Here you'll find truly terrific Mexican and Belizean specialties including cow foot soup, tamales and some of the very best rice and beans in Belize. The only thing bad about this place is that it's not open for dinner.

Cactus Plaza (☎ 4-20349, 6 6th St S) Meals US$3-4. This roadside kiosk-style restaurant serves up authentic Mexican

food and fresh fruit juices. You can also get fresh fruit margaritas, which, along with a pool table, help make it a lively spot at night.

Nestor's Hotel (☎/fax 4-22354, 123 5th Ave S) Breakfast US$2-4, lunch & dinner US$2.50-9.25. Kitchen open 7am-9pm daily, bar open until 11pm. Inexpensive, large portions of excellent Belizean and American fare make this a splendid choice for a meal. Even if you're not eating, this popular watering hole is a good place to meet both locals and fellow travelers.

Tai San (no ☎, Park St between 1st and 2nd Sts S) Dishes US$3-10. Open 9am-9pm daily. The favorite Chinese restaurant in town is also a favorite local hangout, where the loud music and cold Belikins seem to take precedence over the food. The menu features standard Cantonese dishes, served in large portions.

Butchie's Bar & Grill (☎ 4-23141, 3rd Ave between 6th & 7th Sts S) Meals US$4-6. Open noon-10pm Wed-Sun, 3pm-10pm Mon & Tues. Right on the edge of Corozal Bay, Butchie's open-air seating is best for sipping a cold Belikin, munching on a snack of ceviche or playing pool. The full menu features fairly average burgers, steak and seafood.

Le Café Kela (☎ 4-22833, 37 1st Ave between 2nd & 3rd Sts N) Crêpes US$3.50, meat & seafood US$4-8.50. Open 11am-8:30pm Mon-Sat. Set in a palapa with lovely landscaping, Kela blends traditional Belizean dishes with French cuisine. Here you'll find the best crêpes in Belize, along with pastas, steak and seafood. Everything is made to order, so service seems slow but worth it for what you get. Though it's outside, Kela is immaculate. The excellent food and ocean breeze make this the best place in town to eat.

Getting There & Away

Air Corozal has its own airstrip (code CZL) south of the town center, reachable by taxi (US$4). It is only an airstrip, with no shelter or services, so there's no point in arriving too early for your flight. Taxis meet all incoming flights.

Maya Island Air (☎ 4-22082) and Tropic Air (☎ 4-20356) each have three flights daily between Corozal and San Pedro (20 minutes, US$35 one way). Maya Island Air flights leave daily at 7:45am, 12:30pm and 4:30pm; purchase tickets at the office in the Maya Hotel. Tropic Air flights depart at 7:30am, 10:30am and 3:30pm; purchase tickets from the office at the airstrip. From San Pedro you connect with flights to Belize City and onward to other parts of the country. For details, see the Getting Around chapter.

Boat A few tour guides lead boat trips and provide water taxi service across Chetumal Bay. A couple of the best guides are Stefan Moerman (☎ 4-22833) and Jose Majil (☎ 4-20100). Among the more popular trips, including the tours to Cerros and Bacalar Chico, are the tours to Sarteneja (US$75 roundtrip).

A water taxi, the *Lady Lowe* (☎ 4-12011), offers shuttle service to San Pedro leaving from the Corozal Bay Inn dock daily at 6am. The same taxi leaves San Pedro for Corozal daily at 4pm.

Bus Most of the frequent buses traveling between Chetumal (Mexico) and Belize City stop in Corozal at the Novelo's bus terminal (☎ 4-22132), at the corner of 7th Ave and 1st St S.

Buses leave Corozal and head south via Orange Walk for Belize City every hour from 4am to 2pm, and at least every 90 minutes after that. Likewise, buses travel between Belize City and Corozal hourly (96 miles/155km, 2¼ to 2¾ hours), with extra runs in the afternoon to accommodate work and school schedules.

Crossing the Border Corozal is 8 miles (13km) south of the border point at Santa Elena (Belize) and Subteniente López (Mexico); from there, it's another 7 miles (12km) to Mexico's Chetumal. Most people opt to take a bus from Corozal through to Chetumal, which takes about 45 minutes depending on border traffic. Otherwise, you have to hitch a ride or hire a taxi (expensive at US$12) from Corozal to Santa Elena and

cross the border on foot. From Subteniente López, minibuses shuttle to Chetumal's Minibus Terminal all day.

You'll have to pay a US$10 departure tax and US$3.75 conservation fee when you leave Belize (total US$13.75). If you're on the bus, you'll get off at the border, pay the fee, show your passport and get back on the bus. If you're driving, you'll have to show your vehicle registration or car-rental agreement, along with your passport.

Customs is pretty lax on your way into Mexico, but coming from Mexico to Belize is usually more controlled. If you look like you've been on the road a while, don't be surprised if customs asks to search your bags.

CONSEJO SHORES

Just 7 miles (11km) northeast of Corozal, a small European and North American expatriate community centers around the retirement developments at Consejo Shores. The development neighbors the tiny Consejo Village, which sits on a peninsula on the shores of Chetumal Bay.

The brainchild of Canadian Bill Wildman, Consejo Shores underwent its initial development as a luxury-style community in the 1970s. Wildman thought the area would boom with retirees. It boomed briefly, but poor road conditions and a bout of sketchy security has slowed growth in recent years. Still, low property taxes, sunny weather and large lots have attracted about 200 gringos to the area. There's not much to do here, except walk the beach, swing in a hammock or – like many folks – look at real estate.

CasaBlanca by the Sea (☎ 4-38018, fax 4-38003, ℮ info@casablanca-bythesea.com, ⓦ www.cbbythesea.com, Consejo Village) Single/double rooms US$50-70/65-80, suites US$120/130. This modern guest house sitting along the breezy shore is a good place to kick back and do absolutely nothing. Clean rooms come with air-con or fans and the restaurant serves up good Belizean seafood.

SARTENEJA & AROUND
pop 1600

Sarteneja is a tiny traditional fishing village east of Corozal. It is not an easy place to get to (see Getting There & Away, below), which means Sarteneja doesn't make it onto many itineraries – it's a great option for travelers who really want to get away from it all. In town there's not much to do but gaze at the turquoise sea and make friends with the townspeople, although it's possible to arrange boating and fishing trips. The name Sarteneja (sar-ten-**eh**-ha) comes from the Mayan 'Tzaten-a-Ha,' which means 'water between the rocks,' a phrase that describes some of the old sinkholes, or cenotes, used by the Maya as water wells.

Shipstern Nature Reserve

This huge nature reserve (*3 miles south of Sarteneja; admission US$5; open 8am-5pm daily*) is owned by the International Tropical Conservation Foundation, based in Switzerland, and under the management of the Belize Audubon Society (☎ 2-34533, fax 2-34985, e base@btl.net). The park covers approximately 22,000 acres (9000 hectares) of hardwood forest, saline lagoons, savannah wetlands and mangrove swamps. Some 250 bird species are known to exist in the reserve, and coatis, peccaries, tamanduas and other wild creatures put in frequent appearances. You might even see jaguar tracks.

The entrance fee includes a visit to the small museum, a 45-minute guided nature walk and a tour of the butterfly breeding farm. Because of the profusion of wildlife and dense unmarked trails, you must have a tour guide to go farther into the reserve. Guides charge US$2.50 per hour and usually provide excellent insight into the reserve's flora and fauna. You can also take an all-day tour that includes a boat trip, birding and hiking (US$50 per person), and you can arrange for overnight trips deep within the reserve. While this remote area is light on tourists (don't be surprised if you're the only one around), it's unmistakably heavy with mosquitoes; bug spray, long sleeves and pants are recommended.

Places to Stay & Eat

Fernando's Seaside Guesthouse (☎ 4-32085, N Front St) Doubles US$25. Breakfast

US$3.50, lunch & dinner US$6-9. This immaculate, friendly and delightful sea-breezy guest house has three rooms, each with a sparkling private bathroom.

Krisami's Bayview Lodge (☎ 4-32283, fax 4-32247, e krisamis@btl.net, N Front St) Doubles US$60. Meals US$5-10. Down the road, south of Fernando's, this lodge rents modern, tiled motel-style rooms with aircon and private bath. Nearby, Krisami's also rents two cabanas. The restaurant serves meals to guests.

Richie's (☎ 4-32031, N Front St) Prices US$4. Open 3pm-11pm daily. This is a good dining option in a palapa just north of Fernando's. Richie will also cook for you outside of opening hours by special arrangement. Meals include stewed chicken, rice and beans and various Mexican dishes.

Last Resort (☎ 4-12009, e donna@ belizenorth.com, W www.belizenorth.com, Copper Bank) Cabins with electricity and fans US$17.50 per night, US$105 per week, all with shared bath. This remote resort, created by Enrique Flores and Donna Noland, is 25 miles (40km) west of Sarteneja, in Copper Bank Village. It's a low-key, low-budget getaway with 10 thatched-roof cabins arranged at the mouth of a lagoon. It's best for visitors who are planning to stay and sit awhile. You can swim in the lagoon, or arrange fishing or snorkeling tours. Buses serve the village from Orange Walk and Corozal, or you can get to the resort by boat from Corozal for US$50. Call the Last Resort to arrange transportation.

Getting There & Away

Sarteneja is 40 miles (64km) northeast of Orange Walk. If you're driving, you'll head out over the bridge on north part of Orange Walk. The road will take you through the village of San Estevan and the Mennonite community of Little Belize. At Mile 23 (Km 37), veer right to reach Sarteneja and Shipstern. (The left road will take you through Progresso to Copper Bank and the Last Resort.) The bumpy but scenic drive takes about 90 minutes in good weather. Village buses run from Orange

Walk to Sarteneja and Copper Bank Monday to Saturday.

You can now drive to Sarteneja from Corozal by catching the hand-cranked car ferry from Corozal to Copper Bank. From there you can drive the 25 miles (40km) to Sarteneja. A charter boat from Corozal to Sarteneja takes 45 minutes and costs US$75.

Cayo District (Western Belize)

As you travel west from Belize City, the topography takes a dramatic and refreshing turn. Way in the distance, the purple-hued,

Highlights

- Venturing deep into the jungle to the Mayan ruins of Caracol, climbing to the top of Caana and marveling at the green jungle canopy
- Swimming, tubing, crawling and hiking through ancient caves
- Relaxing at one of the many jungle lodges
- Experiencing pine forest, refreshing river pools and lush waterfalls in the Mountain Pine Ridge

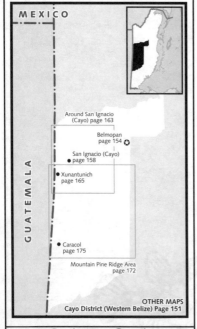

MEXICO

Around San Ignacio
(Cayo) page 163

Belmopan
page 154 ✪

San Ignacio (Cayo)
● page 158

● Xunantunich
page 165

GUATEMALA

● Caracol
page 175

Mountain Pine Ridge Area
page 172

OTHER MAPS
Cayo District (Western Belize) Page 151

jagged crags of the Maya Mountains seem to suddenly bloom out of the flat land. This is the Cayo District – western Belize – where the country's highland peaks rise to over 3000 feet (900m). This beautiful, unspoiled mountain terrain is dotted with waterfalls, caves and Mayan ruins, and teeming with wild orchids, colorful parrots, keel-billed toucans and other exotic flora and fauna – prime territory for adventure seekers.

Today, the thriving farming and holiday center is in many ways, still a child finding its way. For much of its existence, the Cayo District was considered (especially in terms of tourism) to be a last frontier, a patch of impenetrable jungle way out west. Though the Western Hwy was built in the 1930s, paving wasn't completed until the 1980s, when the first lodge-owners bought land and started their endless wrestles with the jungle. The district's cultural mix – Spanish-speaking Mestizos, Maya, Creoles, Garifunas, Chinese, Lebanese and British, Canadian and American expats – does wonders to keep things interesting.

Belmopan, the nation's sleepy capital, is perhaps more helpfully regarded as a de facto transportation hub, with buses stopping here before sliding south down the Hummingbird Hwy, or winding along the Western Hwy to San Ignacio and the Guatemalan border.

San Ignacio, the beating heart of the Cayo District and an undeniable ecotourism hub, is surrounded by rivers, lush broadleaf rain forest and, oddly, pine forest. This is a place where you can be pampered at a high-end jungle lodge or get grimy and dirty climbing through a cave.

Throughout the reign of the Mayan Empire, the Cayo District hummed with powerful kingdoms and ceremonial centers. Take an adventurous visit to the ancient metropolis of Caracol, or check out easy-to-access sites like Xunantunich, El Pilar and Cahal Pech.

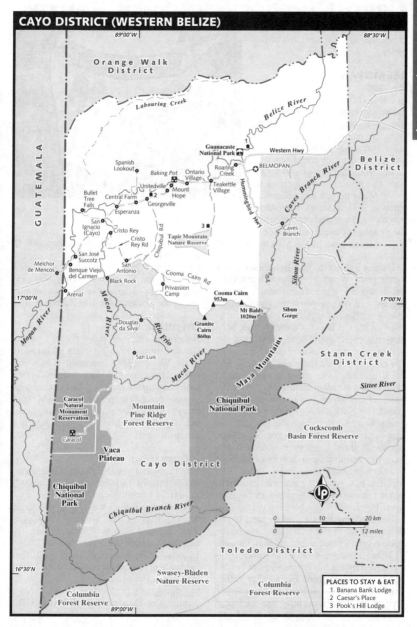

CAYO DISTRICT (WESTERN BELIZE)

Orange Walk District

Labouring Creek

Belize River

GUATEMALA

Spanish Lookout

Baking Pot

Ontario Village

Roaring Creek

Guanacaste National Park

Western Hwy

BELMOPAN

Belize District

Caves Branch River

Unitedville

Mount Hope

Teakettle Village

Central Farm

Bullet Tree Falls

Georgeville

Esperanza

San Ignacio (Cayo)

Cristo Rey

Chiquibul Rd

Tapir Mountain Nature Reserve

Hummingbird Hwy

Caves Branch

Sibun River

Cristo Rey Rd

Melchor de Mencos

San José Succotz

San Antonio

Benque Viejo del Carmen

Black Rock

Cooma Cairn Rd

Privassion Camp

Cooma Cairn 953m

Mt Baldy 1020m

Sibun Gorge

Arenal

Macal River

Rio Frio

Granite Cairn 860m

Douglas da Silva

San Luis

Mopan River

Macal River

Stann Creek District

Sittee River

Maya Mountains

Caracol Natural Monument Reservation

Caracol

Mountain Pine Ridge Forest Reserve

Chiquibul National Park

Cockscomb Basin Forest Reserve

Vaca Plateau

Cayo District

Chiquibul National Park

Chiquibul Branch River

0   10   20 km
0   6   12 miles

Toledo District

Swasey-Bladen Nature Reserve

Columbia Forest Reserve

Columbia Forest Reserve

PLACES TO STAY & EAT
1 Banana Bank Lodge
2 Caesar's Place
3 Pook's Hill Lodge

The area's numerous and popular forest lodges make great base camps for your explorations of the region.

BELMOPAN
pop 7000

In 1961, Hurricane Hattie all but destroyed Belize City. Perhaps it was government paranoia or just proactive planning, but certain that killer hurricanes would come again and that Belize City could never be secure from their ensuing destruction, the government decided to move. Many people were skeptical when in 1971 it declared its intention to build a model capital city in the geographic center of the country – a small place nobody went to called Belmopan.

During its first decade Belmopan was a lonely place. Weeds grew through cracks in the streets, a few bureaucrats dozed in new offices, and insects provided most of the town's traffic. The capital has been slow to come to life but the gradually growing population is friendly and content. Most of the government ministries are based here, and a few embassies liven the place up (including the British High Commission, although the US embassy is still in Belize City). With the vision of Belmopan as a government hub, a grand new National Assembly was built to resemble a Mayan temple and plaza. It was supposed to house the government offices, but the buildings, together looking something like a drab college campus of concrete bunkers, provide insufficient space. The result is a variety of government offices lacking uniformity and spread throughout town. Belmopan is also home to the national police academy training center, and if you strike a match in Belize, it'll probably be the Toucan brand, made right here in Belmopan.

Though the majority of the workforce is employed by the government, most people opt to commute from Belize City rather than move into Belmopan's quiet suburbia. This is most noticeable at the end of a working day, when the mass exodus of government workers catching buses out of town makes the otherwise slow capital come to life. Unless you have business with the government, you'll probably stay only long enough to have a snack or a meal at one of the market stalls near the bus station.

And then there was a city.

Orientation

Belmopan, about 50 miles (80km) west of Belize City, less than 2½ miles (4km) south of the Western Hwy and about a mile east of the Hummingbird Hwy, is a small place easily negotiated on foot. Most of the buildings are placed along a ring road that encircles the town. The regional buses stop at the bus depot at the Market Square, which is the town's hub.

Information

Brochures and basic tourist information are available from the Ministry of Tourism (☎ 8-23394), 14 Constitution Dr.

The Belize Bank (☎ 8-22303), 60 Market Square, is open 8am to 1pm Monday to Thursday and 8am to 4:30pm Friday. The nearby Scotiabank is open 8am to 2:30pm Monday to Thursday and 8am to 4:30pm Friday. You can use foreign ATM cards here (but not at Belize Bank).

Belmopan's post office (☎ 8-22122) is behind the Department of Natural Resources building, near the police station.

Belmopan Vault

If you take a tour of any of the archaeological sites in Belize, you will likely hear your guide mention that most of the uncovered artifacts have been shipped away to museums in foreign countries, or locked deep inside the mysterious Belmopan Vault. The bulk of Belize's archaeological treasures that haven't been taken from the country are in Belmopan, stored in a vault at the government's Department of Archaeology awaiting the much-anticipated opening of a national museum in Belmopan.

With a long history of funding problems, security issues and political red tape, the museum project became somewhat of a political volleyball that kept getting spiked to the ground. Its failure seemed inevitable. Meanwhile, some of the world's most impressive and priceless Mayan artifacts are outside of Belize, or sitting like forgotten orphans on a shelf in the Belmopan Vault. Used to be you could visit the vault, but now viewing is restricted to archaeologists and special groups.

But things are finally starting to look up. Thanks to a supportive government, a new museum building in Belmopan and an injection of US$10 million for archaeological projects, the museum just might one day open its doors.

Architect and archaeologist John Morris was seconded from the Department of Archaeology to his new post as the coordinator for the Belize Museum Project. At his desk in the future museum building, which sits by itself on a dirt road in Belmopan, Morris says the current government has a lot more prerogative than past administrations when it comes to culture.

'It always comes down to money,' Morris says. 'Now that we have the money, it's an issue of disbursement of funds.' He says once the museum building undergoes some structural changes and the big issues involving museum management have been addressed, the 24,000-sq-foot museum will be one of a kind. 'It's an ambitious project,' says Morris, 'but once it's accomplished, it will truly be a gem.'

Archaeologists with the Tourism Development Project, which is devoted to boosting 'archeo-tourism' in Belize, have been working hard at recovering Mayan artifacts from museums and private collections in other countries. 'This stuff belongs in Belize,' Morris says, 'and it's slowly, finally, making its way home.' All of the recovered artifacts will join the contents from the vault to be put on permanent or rotating display in the new museum.

Morris gets a twinkle in his eye when he starts thinking about the museum in the realm of possibility. 'It's a long time coming,' he says, giddy at the prospect of a permanent museum dedicated to the ever-evolving discovery of the ancient Maya.

So when will this thing open? 'If I'm an optimist, I'd say they'll be cutting the ribbon in December 2002,' Morris says with a smile. 'The cynic in me, however, says it'll be more like fall 2003.'

The BTL office (☎ 8-22193), on Bliss Parade across from the Civic Center, is heavily air-conditioned, so even if you don't have to use the phone, it's a good place to escape the heat. Its hours are 8am to noon and 1pm to 4pm weekdays, 8am to noon Saturday.

Techno Hub (☎ 8-20061), in the bus terminal, offers Internet access for US$1.50 per 15 minutes or US$4.50 per hour. Though noisy, with the whirring and bleeping of arcade games, it's a convenient place to check email from 8am to 6pm Monday to Saturday.

The Angelus Press bookstore (☎ 8-23861, fax 8-22948, w www.angeluspress.com) sells guidebooks and regional titles. It also has a copy and fax center. It's open 7:30am to 5:30pm weekdays, closed weekends.

Betty's Laundromat & Fast Food (☎ 8-20743), 3 Caracol St, is open 9am to 8pm daily (sometimes closed on Sunday). Do-it-yourself laundry costs US$4 to wash and

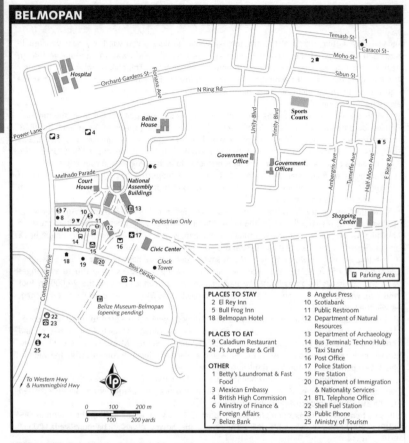

BELMOPAN

PLACES TO STAY
2 El Rey Inn
5 Bull Frog Inn
18 Belmopan Hotel

PLACES TO EAT
9 Caladium Restaurant
24 J's Jungle Bar & Grill

OTHER
1 Betty's Laundromat & Fast Food
3 Mexican Embassy
4 British High Commission
6 Ministry of Finance & Foreign Affairs
7 Belize Bank
8 Angelus Press
10 Scotiabank
11 Public Restroom
12 Department of Natural Resources
13 Department of Archaeology
14 Bus Terminal; Techno Hub
15 Taxi Stand
16 Post Office
17 Police Station
19 Fire Station
20 Department of Immigration & Nationality Services
21 BTL Telephone Office
22 Shell Fuel Station
23 Public Phone
25 Ministry of Tourism

dry, or you can drop your stuff off for US$5 per load. If you're planning to eat, think again. Despite the name there's not much fast food offered here.

There's a public restroom on the north side of the market square, charging US$0.25.

The Belmopan Hospital (☎ 8-22264), the only emergency facility between Belize City and San Ignacio, is on the north end of town.

Government Offices

In the National Assembly buildings, the **Department of Archaeology** (☎ 8-22106, fax 8-23345) contains a vault full of artifacts gathered from ancient archaeological sites throughout Belize. The vault's contents will be displayed in the long-awaited museum (see the boxed text 'Belmopan Vault'). Until then, the vault remains closed to the public, though you can get a hint of what's inside by the meager display in the office hallway. Stop by the department to find out which sites are currently undergoing excavations, or to pick up brochures (they cost US$1). Also ask about the status of the museum.

Nearby, the **National Archives** *(☎ 8-22097, fax 8-23140)* keeps a good collection of old photographs, newspapers and other historical documents, used mostly for research. The **Department of Natural Resources** *(☎ 8-22249)*, in the big building directly behind Market Square, is a good source for topographic and land maps, though most are fairly out of date. Other ministries in the National Assembly buildings and the area include the Ministry of Health *(☎ 8-22325)*, the Ministry of Finance & Foreign Affairs *(☎ 8-22167)*, the Ministry of Human Development & Women *(☎ 8-22161)* and the prime minister's office *(☎ 8-20399)*.

Places to Stay

Belmopan is a town for bureaucrats and diplomats, not one for budget travelers, making good places to stay few and far between.

El-Rey Inn (☎ 8-23438, fax 8-22682, e *hibiscus@btl.net, 23 Moho St)* Singles/doubles US$19.50/24.50. This exceedingly basic place gets mention for its private baths, clean rooms and relative affordability. Rooms have fans, but no air-con.

Belmopan Hotel (☎ 8-22130, fax 8-23066, e *gsosa@btl.net, 2 Bliss Parade)* Singles/doubles/triples with bath US$43.50/50/57.50. This 20-room hotel is convenient to the Market Square bus terminal. Its restaurant is open for all three meals and the outdoor pool offers refreshing respite from Belmopan's heat. The spacious though dark and worn rooms come with air-con and TV.

Bull Frog Inn (☎ 8-22111, fax 8-23155, e *bullfrog@btl.net, 25 Half Moon Ave)* Singles/doubles US$48/63. With 23 rooms, a bar and good restaurant, the Bull Frog is Belmopan's nicest place to stay. Its cheerful but over-priced air-conditioned rooms have private bath and cable TV.

Places to Eat

If you're looking for a snack, you can't go wrong noshing at the *market stalls* set up around Market Square. Vendors sell plenty of tasty, low-cost munchies, drinks and fresh fruit.

Bull Frog Inn (see Places to Stay) Breakfast & lunch US$4-6, dinner US$7-10. Kitchen open 7am-9:30pm daily. The hotel's popular restaurant serves up Belizean and Mexican fare, along with gringo standbys like steak and potatoes. On weekend evenings things liven up with karaoke or DJ music.

Caladium Restaurant (☎ 8-22754, Market Square) Meals US$4.50-10. Open 7:30am-8pm Mon-Sat, closed Sun. This restaurant, just opposite the bus station on the north side of Market Square, offers a good variety of Belizean specials, burgers and seafood.

J's Jungle Bar & Grill (☎ 8-22175, Constitution Dr) Meals US$3-11. Open 10am-midnight daily, to 3am Thur. This small, groovy spot near the Shell Station and Ministry of Tourism plays great music and offers an interesting menu. Try the molasses and chipotle pork chops (US$9) or beef tenderloin (US$8). On Thursday night, when the rest of Belmopan is slumbering away, J's has karaoke, dancing and occasional bands.

Getting There & Away

The Novelo's bus station *(☎ 8-23031)* is in the middle of Market Square. Thanks to its location near a major highway intersection, Belmopan is a stop for virtually all buses operating along the Western and Hummingbird Hwys. That makes it easy to get in and out of the city. Buses head to and from Belize City every half hour or so between 5am and 7pm. See the Getting Around chapter for details.

GUANACASTE NATIONAL PARK

At the junction of the Western and Hummingbird Hwys, Guanacaste National Park, *(Belize Audubon Society ☎ 2-35004, Mile 55 (Km 88.5) Western Hwy; admission US$2.50; open 8am-4:30pm daily)* is Belize's smallest national park. The 52-acre (21-hectare) nature reserve around the confluence of Roaring Creek and the Belize River is named for a giant guanacaste tree on its southwestern edge. Somehow, possibly thanks to the odd shape of its trunk, the tree survived the axes of canoe makers and still rises majestically in its jungle habitat. Festooned with bromeliads, epiphytes, ferns and dozens of other varieties of plants, the great tree supports a whole ecosystem of its own.

The guanacaste, or tubroos tree, is the national tree of Costa Rica (in Belize that honor goes to the mahogany) and is one of Central America's largest trees. Its light wood was used by the Maya to make dugout canoes. The tree is identifiable by its wide, straight trunk and broad, flat seed pods that coil up into what looks like a giant, shriveled ear (you'll see fallen 'ears' on trails throughout Belize).

A hike along the park's 2 miles (3.2km) of trails will introduce you to the abundant local trees (including the guanacaste) and colorful birds. Birding gets even better here in winter, when migrating birds fleeing North America come here for warmth. After your hike, you can head down to the river for a dip in the park's good, deep swimming hole.

Places to Stay & Eat

East of Guanacaste National Park and the turnoff from the Western Hwy to Belmopan is *Banana Bank Lodge* (☎ 8-12020, fax 8-12026, e bbl@btl.net, w www.banana bank.com, Mile 47 (Km 76) Western Hwy) Singles/doubles/triples in lodge with fan US$65/75/85, with air-con US$79/99/109, singles/doubles/triples/quads in cabanas US$79/89/119/139, all with breakfast. This wonderful lodge on the north side of the Western Hwy sits on an isolated bluff overlooking the Belize River. Lush green pastures and modern stables house some 60 horses, all of which are loved and in good condition. Experienced equestrians and novices alike can arrange half-day (US$50) or full-day (US$90) riding trips into the jungle.

Each of the thatched cabanas here has a private bath and a unique two-bedroom design. All are decorated with local art, including the work of lodge owner Carolyn Carr. The New Mexico–style lodge rooms include private bath but no air-con. A giant telescope lets you search for planets in the

starry skies, and the lodge's 'zoo' includes two spider monkeys and Tika, the Carr's pet jaguar who appears in most of Belize's tourist brochures.

A rough road leads to the lodge (call for directions) or you can get picked up by one of the lodge's ferry operators. Signs off the highway will lead you to a metal gong on the opposite side of the river. Bang it and someone will come get you in a hand-operated ferry. The lodge can also transfer you to and from Belmopan for US$10.

WEST TOWARD SAN IGNACIO

The Western Hwy continues west through the Cayo District, climbing slowly to higher altitudes through lush farming country. Tiny country towns with odd names such as Teakettle Village, Ontario Village, Mount Hope and Unitedville appear along the way. Mayan ruins are everywhere – even in the small mounds on the sides of the road – like the ones currently being excavated at **Baking Pot** near the village of Mount Hope. At **Teakettle Village**, a dirt road leading south of the Western Hwy skirts the Roaring Creek and the mostly impenetrable Tapir Mountain Nature Reserve. This is the road guides take to Actun Tunichil Muknal, a popular cave tour out of San Ignacio (see the Around San Ignacio section, later in this chapter). The road also leads to Pook's Hill Lodge (see Places to Stay & Eat).

At **Georgeville**, 16 miles (26km) west of Belmopan, you'll see another dirt road heading south. This is the **Chiquibul Rd** (also called Pine Ridge Rd), which heads south into the Mountain Pine Ridge – you'll take this road if you're headed straight from Belize City to one of the Mountain Pine Ridge lodges (see that section, later in this chapter). This road also leads to Barton Creek Cave and the Green Hills Butterfly House (see the Around San Ignacio section). Right on the highway in Georgeville, **Caesar's Place** (see Places to Stay & Eat) has a guest house and one of the country's best gift shops, with a wide selection of Belizean souvenirs and Guatemalan handicrafts at good prices. (It also sells a good collection from its Web site at w www.belizegifts.com.)

Just west of Georgeville is the turnoff north to **Spanish Lookout**, a prosperous Mennonite community 3 miles (5km) north of the highway on the north bank of the Belize River (a free, hand-cranked ferry will take you across the river).

Places to Stay & Eat

Pook's Hill Lodge (☎ 8-12017, fax 8-23361, e *pookshill@btl.net*, w *www.pookshill belize.com, 5 miles/8km south of Teakettle Village*) Single/double/triple cabanas US $95/135/166. Breakfast US$6, lunch US$9, dinner US$16. A dirt road leading off the Western Hwy from Teakettle Village leads to Ray and Vicki Snaddon's beautiful 300-acre estate nestled beside the Tapir Mountain Nature Reserve.

The main lodge surrounds a small Mayan plaza (which is currently under excavation) and the round, thatch-and-stucco cabanas sport wraparound windows and immaculate natural-stone bathrooms. River swimming and forest hiking are free, and horseback riding, river tubing and mountain biking are available for a reasonable charge. Tours can be arranged to all the Mountain Pine Ridge and Cayo attractions at rates similar to those charged in San Ignacio. This is a great place to kick back for a couple of days. Pook's Hill is 12 miles (20km) southwest of Belmopan and 21 miles (34km) east of San Ignacio.

Caesar's Place (☎ 9-22341, fax 9-23449, *Mile 60 (Km 96.6) Western Hwy*) Singles/doubles/triples/quads US$40/50/55/60. Breakfast & lunch US$7, dinner US$14. Basic but clean and comfortable rooms here come with private bath. The meals are notoriously good. The same family owns Black Rock Lodge (see Places to Stay & Eat in the Around San Ignacio section).

SAN IGNACIO (CAYO)
pop 6000

San Ignacio is also called El Cayo, or simply Cayo, – 'the island' in Spanish – for its remote island-like isolation deep in the Macal River Valley. The Macal and Mopan Rivers flow together at Branch Mouth near San Ignacio; together they become the Belize River, which roughly follows the highway east to Belmopan and veers north for a while before spilling into Haulover Creek and the Belize Harbour at Belize City.

Long before roads drove in to San Ignacio, river transportation served an important role. San Ignacio's place at the confluence made it a watery hub for boats carrying mahogany and chicle crops down the river to the coast. Once logging and chicle-tapping fizzled out and roads made access easier, the town and its surrounding areas shifted to agriculture and cattle ranching.

Together with neighboring Santa Elena (population 3600) across the river, this is the chief population center of the Cayo District. That said, it's still a small, slightly grungy town continually redefining itself as tourism takes hold. By day, it's a relaxed, even quiet place. By night, the jungle rocks to music from the town's bars and restaurants.

There's not much sight-seeing to do in town, but San Ignacio makes a good base if you're planning to explore the Mountain Pine Ridge, or if you want to arrange tours on one of Cayo's outdoor adventures such as horseback treks, canoe trips on the rivers and creeks, caving, touring the region's Mayan ruins and hiking in the tropical forests.

San Ignacio, with its selection of hotels and restaurants, is also the logical place to spend the night before or after you cross the Guatemalan border, which is just 9 miles (14km) west.

Orientation

San Ignacio sits in a valley of seven hills on the west bank of the Macal River; Santa Elena is to the east over the Hawkesworth Bridge, San Ignacio's landmark suspension bridge. The town's two bridges are usually both one-way – the newer, northernmost bridge leads traffic into San Ignacio, while Hawkesworth Bridge leads traffic out of town. During the rainy season, however, the new bridge often floods, and traffic is diverted to Hawkesworth Bridge. Burns Ave is the town's main street. Everything in town is accessible on foot.

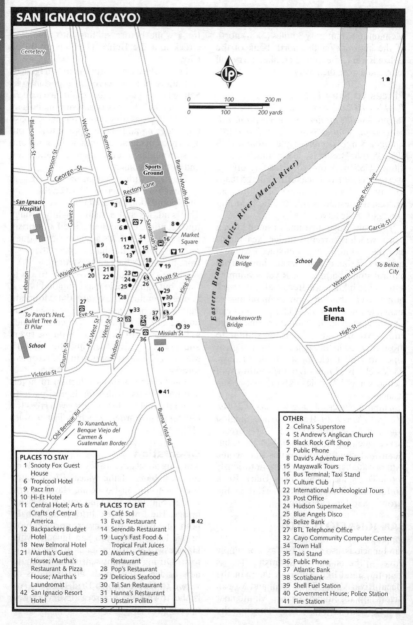

SAN IGNACIO (CAYO)

0   100   200 m
0   100   200 yards

Cemetery

Blancaneaux St
West St
Burns Ave
Simpson St
George St

Sports Ground

Branch Mouth Rd

Rectory Lane

●2

▼3

🚏4

San Ignacio Hospital

Galvez St

5 ●
6 ●

📷7

8 ●

Savannah

Market Square

11 ●   14
12 ●
13 ▼   15

🏣16

▣17

■9

10 ■

18

▼19   New Bridge

Waight's Ave

21 ■
20 ●
22 ●

23 🏣
24 ●   26
25 ●

Wyatt St

Knight St

School

Garcia St

George Price Ave

Belize River (Macal River)

To Belize City

Western Hwy

Santa Elena

Lebanon

▼29
▼30
▼31

27

33

Eve St

Far West St
West St
Hudson St

32 🏛   35 37
34 38

🏧39

36   Missiah St

40

Hawkesworth Bridge

Eastern Branch

High St

To Parrot's Nest, Bullet Tree & El Pilar

School

Church St

Victoria St

● 41

Old Benque Rd

To Xunantunich, Benque Viejo del Carmen & Guatemalan Border

Buena Vista Rd

■ 42

PLACES TO STAY
1 Snooty Fox Guest House
6 Tropicool Hotel
9 Pacz Inn
10 Hi-Et Hotel
11 Central Hotel; Arts & Crafts of Central America
12 Backpackers Budget Hotel
18 New Belmoral Hotel
21 Martha's Guest House; Martha's Restaurant & Pizza House; Martha's Laundromat
42 San Ignacio Resort Hotel

PLACES TO EAT
3 Café Sol
13 Eva's Restaurant
14 Serendib Restaurant
19 Lucy's Fast Food & Tropical Fruit Juices
20 Maxim's Chinese Restaurant
28 Pop's Restaurant
29 Delicious Seafood
30 Tai San Restaurant
31 Hanna's Restaurant
33 Upstairs Pollito

OTHER
2 Celina's Superstore
4 St Andrew's Anglican Church
5 Black Rock Gift Shop
7 Public Phone
8 David's Adventure Tours
15 Mayawalk Tours
16 Bus Terminal; Taxi Stand
17 Culture Club
22 International Archeological Tours
23 Post Office
24 Hudson Supermarket
25 Blue Angels Disco
26 Belize Bank
27 BTL Telephone Office
32 Cayo Community Computer Center
34 Town Hall
35 Taxi Stand
36 Public Phone
37 Atlantic Bank
38 Scotiabank
39 Shell Fuel Station
40 Government House; Police Station
41 Fire Station

Information

Tourist Offices If San Ignacio is the face of the Cayo District, then Eva's Restaurant is its nose. Eva's (☎/fax 9-22267, e evas@btl.net, w www.evasonline.com, 22 Burns Ave), the social center of the temporary and permanent expatriate set, remains the town's best place for information exchange. Owner Bob Jones, who swears he remains an impartial information source, can tell you anything you need to know about tours, guides, prices and places to stay, no matter what your budget. If you stay in San Ignacio for an hour or a week, you'll no doubt find yourself loitering around Eva's.

Money Be forewarned that none of the ATMs in San Ignacio accepts foreign bank cards, though you'll be fine with traveler's checks or US cash. Belize Bank, at 16 Burns Ave, is open 8am to 1pm Monday to Thursday, 8am to 4:30pm Friday and 9am to noon Saturday. Scotiabank, on the corner of Burns Ave and King St, keeps the same hours. Atlantic Bank, at 17 Burns Ave, is open 8am to 2pm weekdays and 8:30am to noon Saturday.

Post & Communications San Ignacio's post office (☎ 9-22049) is on Hudson St near Burns Ave. It's open 8am to noon and 1pm to 5pm Monday to Thursday, and 8am to noon and 1pm to 4pm Friday. The BTL office (☎ 9-22052) is on the corner of Eve and Church Sts. It's open 8am to noon and 1pm to 5pm weekdays.

The best place to go online is Cayo Community Computer Center (☎ 9-23736, e cayo com@btl.net) in the town hall building. The entrance is at Eve and Hudson Sts. It's open 8am to 8pm Monday to Saturday. Internet access costs US$1.50 for 30 minutes. Eva's Restaurant also offers Internet access; costs are US$2.50 for 15 minutes, US$5 for 30 minutes, US$9.50 per hour.

Medical Services The basic San Ignacio Hospital (☎ 9-22066) is up the hill off Waight's Ave, west of the center. For more serious illness or injury, head across the river in Santa Elena to the Hospital La Loma Luz (☎ 9-22087, fax 9-22674), an Adventist hospital and clinic.

Organized Tours

Lodges in the Cayo District operate their own tours and excursions on foot, by canoe and on horseback. But you can also take similar excursions using a cheap hotel in San Ignacio as your base. Many guides and tour operators advertise their services at Eva's Restaurant or at nearby shops on Burns Ave. For more information on the various tours, see the corresponding sections in this book. Here's a sampling of the types of tours (and prices) that are offered:

- Voyages by boat or canoe along the Macal, Mopan and Belize Rivers; favorite goals on the Macal River include the Rainforest Medicine Trail at Ix Chel Farm and the butterfly farm at Chaa Creek. US$25.
- A trip to the Mountain Pine Ridge, which usually includes a picnic and a swim in the pools at Río On, a walk to Thousand Foot (Hidden Valley) Falls and a tour of the Río Frio Cave. US$37.
- An overland trip to the Mayan ruins at Caracol, with quick stops at the above Mountain Pine Ridge sites. US$50.
- Tours to Mayan ceremonial caves where you'll see pottery shards, skulls and other evidence of the Maya. Popular cave trips include Che Chem Ha (US$26 for two), Barton Creek Cave (US$25) or Tunichil Muknal (US$65).
- An excursion to Tikal (Guatemala), either for the day or overnight. US$75 and up.

Places to Stay

Budget San Ignacio has some inexpensive accommodations, which is great if you're staying put for a while to explore the area. Beware, however, that some are in worse shape than others. Though usually full, the following two places on Burns Ave don't put much emphasis on cleanliness.

Central Hotel (☎ 9-24179, 24 Burns Ave) Singles/doubles US$10/12.50. This is one of San Ignacio's cheapest hotels; rooms come without running water.

Backpackers Budget Hotel (no ☎, 22 Burns Ave) Rooms US$10. Above Eva's, this dumpy place has two beds in each of its six rooms and shared bath, but it puts even less emphasis on cleanliness.

Other budget options offer cheap rooms that are cleaner and usually quieter.

Pacz Inn (☎/fax 9-24538, 2 Far West St) Singles/doubles/triples US$10/17.50/20, all with shared bath. This hotel rents five basic but sparkling clean rooms that share two bathrooms. The spacious rooms come with two or three beds, making it good for travelers who want to share costs.

Hi-Et Hotel (☎ 9-22828, 12 West St) Singles/doubles with shared bath US$7.50/ 10. In a bright yellow house, Hi-Et (not at all to be confused with the Hyatt) has small, thinly partitioned rooms, but clean beds and low rates. Five rooms share three bathrooms, and each room has a small balcony.

Tropicool Hotel (☎ 9-23052, 30 Burns Ave) Singles/doubles/triples/quads US$10/ 12.50/15/17.50. Tropicool Hotel has pleasant ground-floor rooms with shared bath. It also has two cabins with private bath and balconies facing a garden for US$25. The rooms are basic, but it's a clean and friendly place.

New Belmoral Hotel (☎ 9-22024, e rain bow@btl.net, 17 Burns Ave) Singles/doubles/ triples with fan US$15/22.50/30, rooms with two queen beds and air-con US$40. Despite the name, there's nothing new about this hotel whose 11 spacious but drab rooms have private bath and cable TV. Its spot on the town's major intersection makes it noisy. Rates for longer stays are available.

Snooty Fox Guest House (☎ 9-22150, fax 9-23556, 64 George Price Ave) Doubles with shared bath US$20, cabins with bath US$35, apartment US$50. This tidy guest house, just across the river in Santa Elena, has clean doubles, cabins and an apartment with two bedrooms and a kitchen. A long stairway leads down to the river.

Mid-Range *Martha's Guest House* (☎ 9-23647, e marthas@btl.net, w www.belize marthasguesthouse.com, 10 West St) Singles/ doubles with shared bath US$24/26, doubles with private bath US$32. This modern home with a family atmosphere has 11 beautiful guest rooms, all of which are unique and accented by mahogany floors or private balconies. Some rooms have cable TV, and hotel amenities include a Laundromat and an excellent ground-floor café.

San Ignacio Resort Hotel (☎ 9-22034, fax 9-22134, e sanighot@btl.net, w www .sanignaciobelize.com, Buena Vista Rd) Singles/doubles/triples US$65/91/104, deluxe units with air-con US$84/110/130. About a half mile (1km) uphill from Government House, this hotel is the closest thing San Ignacio has to an American-style hotel. Queen Elizabeth had a luncheon here in 1994 on her trip to Belize, followed by a nap in room 31, and now it seems the hotel is resting somewhat on its royalty laurels. Its 25 basic rooms are overpriced with timeworn bathrooms. The hotel has a pool, restaurant, bar and disco, and it often fills up with tour groups.

Places to Eat
Lucy's Fast Food & Tropical Fruit Juices (no ☎, Savannah St & Branch Mouth Rd) Fresh juice is sometimes hard to come by in these parts, which makes this friendly kiosk across from the bus station something of a gem. You can get fresh papaya, watermelon or pineapple juice (whatever's in season) for a mere US$0.75.

Pop's Restaurant (☎ 9-23366, West St just south of Martha's) Breakfast US$2-4. Open 6am-2pm & 6:30pm-10pm daily except Wed, when it's not open at night. This small place is a good choice for a filling, slightly greasy breakfast, which is served all day. You can also get a tasty ice-cream cone.

Upstairs Pollito (☎ 9-22019, upstairs at 8 Hudson St) Meals US$1.25-4. Open 7am-3pm & 5:30pm-10pm Mon-Sat (closed Sun). Pollito's friendly owner will welcome you into his little haven of Belizean home cooking. Locals come for the delicious and big portions of rice and beans (US$3-3.50).

Eva's Restaurant (☎ 9-22267, 22 Burns Ave) Breakfast US$2.50-4, lunch & dinner US$3-8. Open 7am-11pm Sun-Thur, 7am-midnight Fri & Sat. British expat Bob Jones and his Belizean wife Nettie feed an army of tourists, archaeologists and locals here at the information and social hub of San Ignacio. The menu features burgers, burritos and Belizean favorites, along with proper British breakfast and daily specials. Service can be downright surly, but the staff is remarkably cool about letting people loiter all day.

Martha's Restaurant & Pizza House *(☎ 9-23647, 10 West St)* Prices US$3.50-10. Martha's popular terrace café serves freshly prepared food for all three meals. Known for its unique pizzas, the menu also features things like granola with fresh fruit and yogurt for breakfast, and a range of delicious sandwiches and dinner dishes with lots of vegetarian options.

Maxim's Chinese Restaurant *(☎ 9-22283, 23 Far West St)* Prices US$3-6. Open 11am-3pm, 5:30pm-midnight daily. If you've got a hankering for Chinese food, this small, dark restaurant comes highly recommended by the locals.

Tai San Restaurant *(☎ 9-22257, 9 Burns Ave)* Prices US$4-10. Open 11am-3pm & 5:30pm-midnight Sun-Thur, 10am-midnight Fri & Sat. This cavernous restaurant gives another Chinese option for food, with a full menu of Cantonese favorites. Next door, with a similar menu and prices, the cafeteria-style ***Delicious Seafood*** *(☎ 9-23402, 11 Burns Ave)* has a louder radio and crowd. It's open 8am-3pm & 5pm-11pm daily.

Serendib Restaurant *(☎ 9-22302, Burns Ave, across from Eva's)* Prices US$4-11. Open 10am-3pm & 6pm-10pm Mon-Sat. Don't let the drab storefront fool you into bypassing this restaurant, serving – of all things – Sri Lankan dishes. The service is friendly, the food is excellent (ranging from simple dishes to steak and lobster), and an outdoor patio in the back makes the atmosphere pleasant.

Hanna's Restaurant *(☎ 9-23014, 5 Burns Ave)* Breakfast US$3-5, Belizean dishes US$2.50-5, Indian dishes US$4-9. Open 6:30am-3pm & 6:30pm-10pm daily. Hanna's serves both Indian and Belizean menus, along with traditional breakfast. Vegetarians will find lots to eat here, while carnivores should sample the tasty beef curry or chicken tika.

Café Sol *(☎ 9-24373, West St)* Meals US$4.50-7. Open 7am-2:30pm & 6:30pm-9pm Tues-Sat, 7am-2:30pm Sun, closed Mon. This refreshing, healthy addition to the Cayo restaurant scene brings with it interesting dinner specials like the portobello mushroom sandwich (US$5) or Thai noodle salad (US$4.50), good breakfasts like cheese-stuffed French toast (US$4) and superb coffee. This place is highly recommended for a quiet dinner or peaceful breakfast.

Entertainment

Blue Angels Disco *(☎ 9-24309, upstairs on Hudson St near Burns Ave)* Cover charge only for bands. Open 8am-3am Fri & Sat, 8am-midnight Sun-Thur. This venue regularly has big-name live music on the weekend. Canned music keeps things rocking on weekdays.

Culture Club *(☎ 9-22349, upstairs at 10 Savannah St)* Cover charge only for special events. Open 3pm-midnight weekdays, 3pm-3am weekends. This popular spot jams to live reggae and world music daily. Especially hot are shows by local punta and Rasta bands or Garifuna drummers.

Cahal Pech Night Club *(☎ 9-23380, top of Cahal Pech Hill)* Open 5pm-midnight Wed & Thur, 5pm-2am Fri & Sat. This gigantic disco-style bar features karaoke on Thursday, DJ music on Friday and bands on Saturday.

Benque Viejo del Carmen, the small town just east of the Guatemala border, often holds weekend dances, attracting people from all over the country, and explodes with action during the Benque Festival held annually in July. Ask in San Ignacio to see if anything's on for the weekend.

Shopping

Groceries The best place to buy fresh fruit is at the ***open-air market*** held every Saturday morning (usually around 7am-noon) in the park behind the bus station. Farmers come from all over the Cayo District to sell their fruits, vegetables, jams and dairy products – you can't get fresher than this.

Celina's Superstore (☎ 9-22247, 43 Burns Ave) Celina's is an all-purpose general store, good for buying groceries, hardware and forgotten camping supplies.

Hudson Supermarket (☎ 9-24623, 5 Hudson St) Open 8am-9pm Mon-Sat, 8am-1pm Sun. Come here for dried goods and groceries.

JULIET COOMBE

Bundles of pencils made in the Cayo District

Souvenirs *Arts & Crafts of Central America (☎ 9-22253, 24 Burns Ave)* This shop sells some Guatemalan crafts, guidebooks, postcards and some kitchy wood carvings. A couple doors north, *Black Rock Gift Shop (☎ 9-23770)* has a smattering of crafts. A small gift shop at *Café Sol* (see Places to Eat, earlier) has a surprisingly good collection of Guatemalan crafts, along with cookbooks, guidebooks and local souvenirs. The best and biggest place to buy souvenirs in the area is at the Caesar's Place gift shop on the Western Hwy east of San Ignacio (see the West Toward San Ignacio section, earlier in this chapter).

Getting There & Around

The Novelo's bus station (☎ 9-23360) is at the corner of Branch Mouth Rd and Savannah St, in front of the market square. Buses run to and from Belize City, Belmopan and Benque Viejo del Carmen nearly every half hour. One-way fares to Belize City are US$2.50 (regular, 2½ hours) or US$3.50 (express, two hours). It costs US$0.50 to get to Benque Viejo del Carmen. For more details, see the Getting Around chapter.

The Savannah Taxi Co-op (☎ 9-22155) is in the bus station and the taxi stand for the Cayo Taxi Drivers Association (☎ 9-22196) is on the traffic circle opposite Government House. Rates can be surprisingly high for short trips out of town (a trip of a few miles can easily cost US$5 to US$10), especially when the buses are so cheap.

Safe Tours Belize (☎ 9-24262, fax 9-22128, **e** dcpil@yahoo.com, **w** www.belizex .com/safetours.htm), across the Hawkesworth Bridge in Santa Elena, rents reliable vehicles. Rental rates are US$75 per day for 4WD Isuzu Troopers, and US$100 per day for full-size passenger vans. Rates include unlimited mileage and air-con, but not the 8% tax. You must put down a US$250 deposit, which you'll get back when you return the vehicle. Be sure to note existing damage before you drive away, otherwise you might get charged for it later.

AROUND SAN IGNACIO (CAYO)

Most of the visited sights in the Cayo District are near San Ignacio, and reached via organized tours or buses from town. The number of activities and tours may seem overwhelming, but keep in mind that the Cayo District is relatively small and nothing is more than a float down the river, or a bumpy dirt road's ride away. This section covers the array of activities and sights in the area.

Archaeological Sites

Mayan sites surround San Ignacio. Only a short climb up the hill out of San Ignacio are the unspectacular but easily accessible ruins of Cahal Pech. Seeing relatively few visitors, El Pilar is just a short distance to

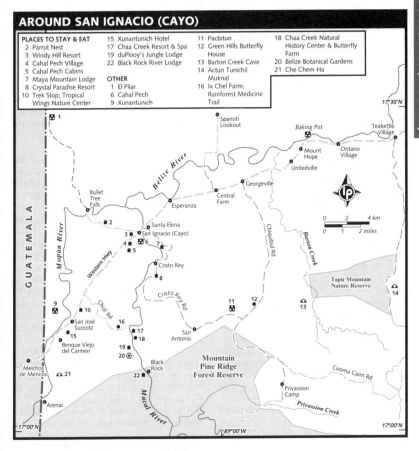

AROUND SAN IGNACIO (CAYO)

PLACES TO STAY & EAT
2 Parrot Nest
3 Windy Hill Resort
4 Cahal Pech Village
5 Cahal Pech Cabins
7 Maya Mountain Lodge
8 Crystal Paradise Resort
10 Trek Stop; Tropical
   Wings Nature Center

15 Xunantunich Hotel
17 Chaa Creek Resort & Spa
19 duPlooy's Jungle Lodge
22 Black Rock River Lodge

OTHER
1 El Pilar
6 Cahal Pech
9 Xunantunich

11 Pacbitun
12 Green Hills Butterfly
   House
13 Barton Creek Cave
14 Actun Tunichil
   Muknal
16 Ix Chel Farm;
   Rainforest Medicine
   Trail

18 Chaa Creek Natural
   History Center & Butterfly
   Farm
20 Belize Botanical Gardens
21 Che Chem Ha

the northwest straddling the Guatemalan border. The impressive and popular site of Xunantunich is farther west along the Western Hwy and is reached by hand-cranked ferry across the Mopan River. Farther afield are the small ruins at Pacbitun and the spectacular site of Caracol (covered in the Mountain Pine Ridge section, later in this chapter).

Cahal Pech Sitting on the top of a hill overlooking San Ignacio, Cahal Pech (☎ 9-24236; admission US$2.50; open 6am-6:30pm daily) is Mopan and Yucatec Mayan for 'Tick City.' It earned the nickname in the 1950s when the site was surrounded by pasture whose cows were riddled with ticks.

Cahal Pech (kah-**hahl** pech) was a city of some importance from 900 BC to AD 800. The 34 buildings here are spread over 6 acres (2.4 hectares) and grouped around seven plazas. Plaza B, about 500 feet (150m) from the museum building and parking area, is the site's largest plaza and also the most impressive. It's surrounded by some of the site's most significant buildings. Off Plaza A, Structure A-1 is the site's tallest pyramid.

Cahal Pech is about a mile (less than 2km) from San Ignacio. A small visitor's center explains some of the history. If you're walking, head up Buena Vista Rd (near the Hawkesworth Bridge); the uphill hike will take you about 45 minutes. You might want to bring water and a picnic lunch and enjoy the views from the hilltop.

El Pilar About 12 miles (19km) northwest of San Ignacio, 7 miles (11km) northwest of Bullet Tree Falls, the Mayan archaeological site of El Pilar (Spanish for 'watering basin') is perched almost 900 feet (275m) above the Belize River. El Pilar was occupied for 15 centuries, from the Middle Preclassic (about 500 BC) through the Late Classic (about AD 1000) periods. Long before political borders, El Pilar stretched into modern-day Pilar Poniente in Guatemala, and the two countries are now working in partnership to preserve the area.

With 25 plazas and 70 major structures, the city was more than three times the size of Xunantunich. Despite ongoing excavations since 1993, headed by Dr Anabel Ford of the University of California Santa Barbara, El Pilar has been left largely uncleared. While seeing El Pilar's greatness requires a certain amount of imagination, six archaeological and nature trails meander among the jungle-covered mounds and make exploration worthwhile.

Though you can explore El Pilar on your own, there is no public transportation to the site, so you'll need a car, tour guide or taxi.

Xunantunich Belize's most accessible Mayan site of significance, Xunantunich *(shoo-nahn-too-neech; no ☎; admission US$5; open 7am-5:30pm Mon-Fri, 7:30am-4:30pm Sat & Sun)* is reached via a free hand-cranked ferry crossing at San José Succotz, on the Western Hwy about 7 miles (12km) southwest of San Ignacio. From the ferry, which comes and goes on demand, it's a hot walk of a mile (2km) uphill to the ruins.

Set on a leveled hilltop above the Mopan River, Xunantunich, built mainly between AD 600 and AD 1000, controlled

the riverside track that led from the hinterlands of Tikal down to the Caribbean. During the Classic period, a ceremonial center flourished here. When Caracol and Naranjo (Guatemala) collapsed around AD 800–850, the much smaller Xunantunich, whose population never topped 10,000, remained partially inhabited. Archaeologists have uncovered evidence that an earthquake damaged the city badly about AD 900, after which the place may have been largely abandoned.

The site's dominant structure, El Castillo (Structure A-6), rises 130 feet (40m) above the jungle floor. Climb to the top of the temple and marvel at the spectacular 360-degree view.

El Castillo underwent two distinct construction phases, the first of which produced the spectacular friezes that encircle the exterior walls. The second phase, oddly, covered up much of the artwork. The temple's west frieze was excavated in 1933 and today is buried behind a fiberglass replica. Work to uncover the temple's east side is ongoing. The name Xunantunich, meaning 'Stone Maiden,' comes from an old story that a maiden appeared one night, then mysteriously dissolved into the stone of El Castillo.

An excellent visitor's center explains Xunantunich's Mayan history, along with its extensive excavation history. A couple of kiosks sell soft drinks and souvenirs. You can hire a guide for a one-hour tour for US$15, but the site can easily be navigated independently.

Xunantunich Hotel (☎ 9-32584, fax 9-23739, e xunhotel@btl.com, on Western Hwy, in San José Succotz) Doubles with fan/air-con US$45/60. This colorful hotel across the road from the ferry to Xunantunich has seven rooms with private bath, a pool and Jacuzzi. Canoe rentals (US$22.50 per day) are available and there's a bar where you can get lunch and refreshments.

Buses on their way between San Ignacio and Benque Viejo del Carmen will drop you at the ferry for the one-way fare of US$0.50. This is also an easy route to hitchhike, though you should use your judgement and women should avoid hitchhiking alone. The

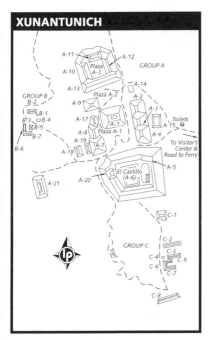

ferry hours are 8am to 5pm; crossing is on demand and free for both foot passengers and cars.

Pacbitun Mayan for 'Stones Set in Earth,' Pacbitun (pahk-be-**toon**) is a small archaeological site, approximately 12 miles (20km) south of San Ignacio via Cristo Rey Rd, near the village of San Antonio. The site seems to have been occupied continuously through most of Mayan history, from 900 BC to AD 900. Archaeologists began work here only in 1971, when they uncovered more than 20 pyramids, eight stelae and several raised irrigation channels. Today only lofty Plaza A has been uncovered and partially consolidated. Structures 1 and 2, on the east and west sides of the plaza, respectively, are worth a look. Within them archaeologists discovered the graves of Maya women of nobility, buried – interestingly – with a variety of musical instruments, perhaps played at their funerals. Pacbitun is

on private land; you can visit by yourself, but you should ask permission from Mr Tzal, whose property you'll pass on the road to the ruins.

Caves

The fascinating activity of cave exploration is relatively new in Belize and cave excavation is even newer. A series of limestone cave systems throughout western Belize is now believed to have been used by the ancient Maya for rituals, ceremonies, sacrificial offerings and burials. Archaeologists say caves throughout the region were believed by the Maya to be gateways to Xibalbá (shi-bahl-**bah**), a nine-tiered underworld where gods resided. As such, findings include hundreds of pottery vessels, remnants of food, fire and even human remains.

Considering this context, a new breed of archaeology – called spelioarchaeolgy – has been born. and it's an exciting time to be in Belize. The folks who explore caves have a few things in common: They're adventurous, athletic and relentlessly curious. You don't have to be a spelioarchaeologist (hell, you don't even have to be able to say it) to explore these caves, but you do have to go on tours. Caves are extremely sensitive and are being dangerously exposed to tourism overload. You can help by not disturbing artifacts and cave formations, and by not going on tours with groups larger than eight people.

In addition to the fascinating Mayan cave history, you'll be awed by the geomorphological structures of the caves themselves, where undulating flowstone decorates the walls, stalactites and stalagmites grow like ancient trees, bats flit in and out of ceiling nooks and darkness prevails.

Barton Creek Cave One of the more popular day trips offered out of San Ignacio is the canoe or tube float through Barton Creek Cave off the Chiquibul Rd. The cave holds spooky skulls, bones and pottery shards. Ten ledges above the river, along with artifacts such as *ollas* (large jars), suggest that this was a place of important ritual activity. Some 28 sets of human remains found in the cave leave archaeologists wondering if the bodies were sacrificial offerings or just burials that played some part of ancestor worship.

On the trip, you'll canoe or ride an inner tube about a mile through the cave, looking at the formations and remaining artifacts. Quite a few companies run tours through the cave. Two independent operators are David Simson of **David's Adventure Tours** (☎ 9-23674), whose office is near the bus station in San Ignacio, or **Michael Waight**, owner of the Snooty Fox Guest House (☎ 9-22150, 64 George Price Ave) in Santa Elena. The half-day trip costs US$25.

Actun Tunichil Muknal Undoubtedly one of the most incredible and adventurous tours you can take in Belize, the trip to Tunichil Muknal (toon-**itch**-all muk-**nahl**) is an unforgettable journey on the edge of the remote Tapir Mountain Nature Reserve. The trip starts with an easy 45-minute hike through trails and creeks (your feet will be wet all day) to the cave opening, a spectacularly wide, misty mouth surrounded by lush jungle. You'll then don your helmet, complete with headlamp, follow your guide into the cave (starting with a frosty plunge into a 20-foot-deep pool), and then hike, climb, twist and turn your way through the cave.

Giant shimmering flowstone rock formations compete for your attention with thick calcium-carbonate stalactites dripping from the ceiling. Phallic-looking stalagmites grow up from the cave floor. Later, you'll follow your guide up into a massive opening, where you'll see hundreds of pottery vessels and shards, along with human remains. One of the most shocking displays is the calcite-encrusted remains of a woman, the cave's namesake – Actun Tunichil Muknal means 'Cave of the Stone Sepulcher.'

Actun Tunichil Muknal was first 'discovered' in the 1970s, but it wasn't fully investigated until Jaime Awe, a Belizean archaeologist, started poking around Belize's caves in the early 1990s. Only then did anyone even fathom the scope of the cave's significance. From 1996 to 2000, researchers found more than 200 pottery

pieces and 14 skeletal remains. Only a few of these artifacts have been removed, keeping the cave something of a living natural museum.

In 1993, a crew for the National Geographic video series 'Journey to the Underworld' filmed scenes in Tunichil Muknal. It garnered even more attention when another crew, this time from *National Geographic Adventure* followed Awe into the cave and published a story in the magazine's July/August 2001 edition.

While all this attention is good for archeotourism in Belize, it may prove not so good for the integrity of the cave. In an effort to keep wear and tear to a minimum, only two tour operators (six guides) are allowed to bring groups into the cave. Trained by Awe, the guides know the cave's history and fragility, but they are also under renewed pressure to keep up with tourist demand. You can help by refusing to go on (or pay for) tours that have more than six to eight guests per guide.

The first company to begin running tours into the cave is the preeminent **Pacz Tours** (☎ 9-22477, arrange tours at Eva's in San Ignacio). The other company allowed to bring groups is **Mayawalk Tours** (☎ 9-23070, 19 Burns Ave, San Ignacio). Most hotels and lodges can book tours for you. The cost of the full-day trip is US$65, including lunch and equipment. Bring shoes (not sandals) and a change of clothes.

Che Chem Ha Antonio Morales' dog was busy chasing down a gibnut when it seemingly disappeared into a rock wall on Morales' property. Dumbfounded, Morales pressed into the 'wall' and discovered it was actually a cave mouth, and inside he found 96 pieces of priceless Mayan artifacts. This happened in 1999 and proved to be the discovery of Che Chem Ha (☎ 9-37013, Mile 8 (Km 13) on Hydro Rd near Benque Viejo del Carmen; tours US$26 for one or two people, US$10 for each extra person).

Morales, who's been farming this land with his family since the 1940s, could have sold the artifacts, or hoarded them and kept the cave a secret, but he knew his find was too important to keep buried. He contacted the government and now, along with his wife Lea, graciously hosts archaeology field camps and tourists. His son William conducts most of the tours through the cave, and the experience is a family affair.

Che Chem Ha is a mix of the word 'Chechemex' a Maya tribe named in honor of the poisonwood tree, which is known for its strength and hardiness, and the Mayan word 'ha,' meaning water. The Morales' lush property boasts creeks and waterfalls.

The cave, which is about 820 feet (250 meters) long, was used by the Maya for food storage and rituals. Today it features narrow passages that wind past intact ceremonial pots to a stela at the end of the tunnel. Bring good shoes, water and a flashlight. The tour takes about 90 minutes. Later, you can hike down to **Vaca Falls** for a swim in the river.

You can also stay at Che Chem Ha in one of the six rustic but tidy thatched-roof, waterless *cabanas*. The price (singles/doubles US$41/80) includes three home-cooked meals. The Morales' can arrange to pick you up in San Ignacio. You can also come on your own by following the Western Hwy to Benque Viejo del Carmen, turning left onto the Hydro Rd (at the Long Lucky Chinese Restaurant) and following it for 8 miles (13km). Look for signs on the left. It's about a 45-minute drive from San Ignacio.

Rainforest Medicine Trail
Formerly called the Panti Medicine Trail, this herbal-cure research center is at **Ix Chel Farm** (☎ 9-23870, 8 miles (13km) southwest of San Ignacio up Chial Rd; admission US$5; open 8am-noon & 1pm-4pm daily).

Don Elijio Panti, who died in 1996 at age 103, was a healer in San Antonio village who used traditional Mayan herb cures. Dr Rosita Arvigo, an American, studied medicinal plants with Don Elijio, then began several projects to spread the wisdom of traditional healing methods and to preserve the rain forest habitats, which harbor an incredible 4000 plant species.

One of her projects was the establishment of the Rainforest Medicine Trail, a self-guiding path among the jungle's natural

cures. Also on the grounds, Granny's Garden features some universal plants such as ginger, amaranth, lemongrass, basil and marigold. Little placards list the plant names, associated myths and medicinal uses.

You can also buy Ix Chel's medicinal tonics at the farm's **Rainforest Remedies** (ⓔ info@rainforestremedies.com, Ⓦ www .rainforestremedies.com; open weekdays 9am-4pm). Drawn from the farm's resources and marketed by the Ix Chel Tropical Research Foundation, which supports traditional Mayan healers and protection of the rain forest ecosystem, the tonics help everything from backaches and colds to traveler's diarrhea and digestive problems. Tonics include 'Belly Be Good' for digestion problems, 'Back Support,' 'Clearing Support' or 'Traveler's Tonic,' cold medicine and special formulas for both men and women. You can also order the tonics from the Web site.

To get to Ix Chel, take the Western Hwy to Chial Rd and follow signs to the Chaa Creek Resort & Spa. One of the most popular ways to get here is on a canoe trip along the Macal River.

Butterfly Farms
Even if you're not particularly into butterflies, a stop at one of the Cayo District's three butterfly farms is very worthwhile. You'll learn about the delicate life cycle of the butterfly, along with the business of breeding butterflies for export.

At **Green Hills Butterfly House** (☎ 9-12017, ⓔ meerman@btl.net, Mile 8 (Km 13) Chiquibul Rd; admission US$4; open 8am-5pm daily), biologists Jan Meerman and

Rosita Arvigo & Don Elijio Panti

In 1969, Rosita Arvigo left Chicago in search of something more meaningful in life. She wound up in southern Mexico, where she lived alongside Maya and Nahuatl Indians. She learned to farm and got her first glimpses at the locals' ability to heal using little more than flowers and plants that grew in their backyards. She returned to Chicago to become a doctor of naprapathy, an offshoot of chiropractic medicine that focuses on therapeutic bodywork.

In 1981, Arvigo, missing the warm weather and still yearning for something else, moved to western Belize with her two children and husband, Greg Shropshire. They bought 35 acres of untamed land, which at the time was only accessible by canoe. Just beyond the property, Arvigo's friends Mick and Lucy Fleming were also wrestling with the challenges of clearing jungle on their own 87 acres of land (which later became Chaa Creek).

In 1982, while trying to carve out a life in Belize, Arvigo met Don Elijio Panti when he was 86 years old. Don Elijio was a natural Maya healer who lived in the village of San Antonio. For decades Don Elijio had healed thousands of patients who traveled from all over Belize to seek his help with physical, emotional and spiritual ailments.

To Arvigo, it seemed Don Elijio had an almost magical power to heal. But she knew from what she'd witnessed in Mexico that this healing power didn't come out of thin air; rather, it came from plants, flowers and the Mayan spirits that lived high on tree branches, under bushes and in the ground. Though Don Elijio was a healer and knew almost everything about the medicinal uses of plants, he could not read or write – his entire bank of knowledge was stored in his head.

Arvigo went on to apprentice with Elijio, gathering plants from the forests and knowledge from the old man's wisdom. She worked with him until his death in 1996, at age 103.

Before Don Elijio's death, Arvigo began working with Dr Michael Balick, director of the Institute of Economic Botany at the New York Botanical Garden. Together, under the Belize Ethnobotany Project, they identified, cataloged and collected 3560 plants, many of which are currently being evaluated by the US's National Cancer Institute for potential use in the fights against cancer and AIDS.

Arvigo set up the Ix Chel Tropical Research Foundation, whose mandate is to preserve traditional healing methods and to conserve the rain forest through research and education. One of the foundation's projects is the Terra Nova Forest Reserve, 6000 acres (2428 hectares) of protected land in the remote Yalbac Hills north of San Ignacio. When forests are cleared for farming or development, foundation workers transplant the trees and shrubs to Terra Nova in the hopes of building a strong enough 'seed bank' that will continue growing in perpetuity.

Today at Arvigo's farm, Ix Chel (named for the Mayan goddess of healing and medicine), the Rainforest Medicine Trail demonstrates to its visitors the medicinal values of Belize's abundant plant life. About 10,000 people visit Ix Chel every year. Arvigo helps run Rainforest Remedies, the farm's store, which sells tinctures of medicinal herbs online and throughout Belize. She teaches workshops, goes on lecture tours, conducts the Bush Medicine Camp for local children and sees an endless stream of patients.

Arvigo's story is told in her fascinating book *Sastun: My Apprenticeship with a Maya Healer*, coauthored by Nadine Epstein, and *Rainforest Remedies: The Maya Way to Heal Your Body & Replenish Your Soul*. To find out about workshops, write to e workshops@ixchelherbs.com.

Tineke Boomsma (the same duo who founded Belize's first butterfly farm at Shipstern Nature Reserve) raise a staggering variety of butterfly species, about a dozen of which are exported to the USA. Knowledgeable guides will walk you through the farm – the largest live butterfly display in Belize – explaining the life cycle of the butterfly, from egg to caterpillar to pupa to butterfly.

Get to Green Hills by turning south onto the Chiquibul Rd off the Western Hwy at Georgeville – Mile 61 (Km 98). This road heads into the Mountain Pine Ridge.

The **Chaa Creek Natural History Center & Butterfly Farm** (☎ 9-12010, e natural history@chaacreek.com, at the Chaa Creek Resort & Spa; admission US$5; open 8am-5pm daily) breeds only the dazzling blue morpho (Morpho peleides), whose pupa are exported for about US$3 each. The tour is interesting and worthwhile, as is the small natural history center, where you'll see displays on archaeology and the early Maya. There's also an excellent collection of the many moths, insects and amphibians that inhabit the area.

You can also learn about butterflies at the **Tropical Wings Nature Center** (☎ 9-32265, Mile 71 (Km 114) Western Hwy; admission US$2.50), where a small butterfly house, museum (complete with an Unpetting Zoo) and medicinal trail are on the site of the Trek Stop (see Places to Stay & Eat).

Belize Botanical Gardens

These, the first botanical gardens in Belize (☎ 9-23101, e gardens@btl.net, w www .belizebotanic.org; admission US$2.50, guided tour US$10; open 7:30am-4pm, next to duPlooy's off Chial Rd), were officially registered in 1997. Today, the bountiful gardens feature more than 150 native orchid species, indigenous heliconias, bay leaf palms and hardwoods. Two ponds attract a variety of waterfowl. Devoted to conservation, education and sustainable agriculture, the gardens are an excellent addition to the Cayo attractions.

Activities

A great way to spend a morning or afternoon is canoeing or tubing on the Macal and Mopan Rivers, which swell in the rainy season, starting in late June. The most popular and affordable trips are offered by **Tony's River Adventures** (☎ 9-23292), which can be booked through Eva's in San Ignacio. An excellent trip is the float down the Macal River, which includes a visit to the Rainforest Medicine Trail at Ix Chel Farm and to the butterfly farm at Chaa Creek (US$20). Many of the lodges also have canoes for guest use.

Horseback riding is another fun way to tour around. **Easy Rider** (☎ 9-23734) has a stable on the outskirts of town. The staff will pick you up in San Ignacio and take you on riding trips for US$25 (half day) or US$40 (full day, including lunch).

For independent types who don't mind sweating buckets in the heat and humidity, mountain biking is a good way to explore Cayo trails, or to get to some of the sites without a car. The **Tropicool Hotel** (☎ 9-23052, 30 Burns Ave in San Ignacio), rents bikes for US$25 (half day) or US$40 (full day). The **Chaa Creek Resort & Spa** (see Places to Stay & Eat, later) rents better-quality bikes for US$30 per day.

Places to Stay & Eat

Around San Ignacio Trek Stop (☎ 9-32265, e susa@btl.net, Mile 71 (Km 114) Western Hwy) Tent sites US$5, with tent rental US$7, cabins US$10 per person. Six miles (10km) west of San Ignacio, this is an ideal spot for backpackers. The rustic but clean and comfortable hand-hewn cabins come with mosquito nets over the beds. Guests share compost toilets and solar-powered hot showers, along with use of kitchen facilities. Camping is safe and comfortable. Meals are available at the Trek Stop restaurant, which is open for all meals from 7am-9pm daily. Nature trails are on the site, as is the Tropical Wings Nature Center, which houses an interpretive center and a small butterfly farm (it's free to guests). The Trek Stop is just off the Western Hwy, so it's easy to hop on a bus into San Ignacio.

Parrot Nest (☎ 9-37008, cell 14-6083, e parrot@btl.net, w www.parrot-nest.com) Tree houses US$25, cabins with shared bath US$32, cabin with private bath US$37.50. Breakfast US$3, dinner US$8. An aptly named establishment, Parrot Nest is 3 miles (5km) northwest of San Ignacio, near the village of Bullet Tree Falls. Guests stay in tree houses built high up in the trees, or in thatched cabins with the Mopan River floating by. This is a great option if you like the idea of a jungle lodge but don't have a big budget. Owners Chris and Theo Cocchi work hard to keep the site welcoming and beautiful. They'll arrange tours, and Chris offers a free shuttle to and from San Ignacio. Optional meals are served outdoors overlooking the river.

Crystal Paradise Resort *(☎ 9-22772, fax 9-12014,* **e** *cparadise@btl.net,* **w** *www.crystalparadise.com, Cristo Rey)* Singles/doubles/triples US$25/39/49. Near the village of Cristo Rey on the road to the Mountain Pine Ridge, this resort was built by a local Belizean family, the Tuts, who are well known in these parts for making thatched roofs (such as the ones here and at the Chaa Creek Resort & Spa). The cabanas come with private bath, fans, verandahs and hammocks. This is a simple place, where the women of the family cook up traditional Belizean meals and the sons lead tours.

Cahal Pech Village *(☎ 9-23740, fax 9-22225,* **e** *daniels@btl.net, on Cahal Pech Hill)* Double cabins with fan/air-con US$45/55. This place, about 1½ miles (2.5km) uphill from the town center, has a large, thatched main building surrounded by 14 small thatched cabins. In summer the place is overrun with archaeology students who spend their days out doing field work. Perched atop Cahal Pech Hill, the cabins enjoy fine views of the town and valley, but without a car the walk to and from town can get tedious. Cahal Pech also has a restaurant open daily for breakfast and dinner.

Cahal Pech Cabins *(☎/fax 9-23380, on Cahal Pech Hill)* Double cabins US$37.50, US$5 each extra person. The nine tidy cabins have two double beds, private bath, fans and patios with hammocks. Some have views over San Ignacio.

Maya Mountain Lodge *(☎ 9-22164, fax 9-22029,* **e** *jungle@mayamountain.com,* **w** *www.mayamountain.com, 9 Cristo Rey Rd)* Room (single or double) with fan/air-con US$49/70, cottage US$100. Breakfast & lunch US$8, dinner US$16. This lodge, just over 1½ miles (2.5km) from San Ignacio, is

a friendly place on beautiful grounds with a refreshing swimming pool. The six rooms and eight thatched cottages all have fan and private bath with hot water. Delicious, home-style meals are served in the verandah restaurant. Bart and Suzi Mickler, the owners, are walking encyclopedias of Belizean jungle lore. In fact, they pioneered many of the tours that are widely offered throughout the region, including at their lodge.

Windy Hill Resort *(☎ 9-22017, fax 9-23080,* **e** *windyhill@btl.net,* **w** *www.windyhillresort.com, Mile 69 (Km 111) Western Hwy)* Singles/doubles/triples/quads US$60/80/95/110. Breakfast US$8, lunch US$10, dinner US$17.50. Windy Hill, about 1½ miles (2.5 km) west of San Ignacio on the Western Hwy, has all the amenities: swimming pool, riding horses, nature trail, canoes ready for a paddle on the Macal River and a full program of optional tours and all-inclusive packages. Accommodations are in 25 cozy wooden cabins with private bath, cable TV and ceiling fans. Rates don't include meals.

Along the Macal River Some of Belize's best lodges lie along the Macal River, reached by Chial Rd off the Western Hwy. Most of these places are remote and self-contained by design. Unless you have a car, you'll be at the mercy of the resort shuttle drivers, who are usually very accommodating to guests. If you drive in yourself, your host lodge will give you exact directions.

Black Rock River Lodge *(☎ 9-22341, fax 9-23449,* **e** *blackrock@btl.net,* **w** *www.blackrocklodge.com, turn off of Chial Rd)* Singles/doubles with shared bath US$40/50, singles/doubles/triples/quads with private bath US$60/70/75/80. Breakfast US$8, lunch US$9, dinner US$16. This remote lodge is situated in the middle of the jungle in the secluded Black Rock Canyon. It's an elegantly rustic place featuring thatched-roof cabanas, solar electricity and solar-heated hot water. For directions or information, ask at Caesar's Place, near Georgeville on the Western Hwy.

Chaa Creek Resort & Spa (☎ 9-22037, *fax 9-22501,* e *chaacreek@btl.net,* w *www .chaacreek.com, 3½ miles (5.6km) on Chial Rd)* Singles/doubles/triples US$140/165/ 195, luxury suites US$180. Breakfast US$10, boxed lunch US$8, dinner US$26. The crème de la crème of Cayo jungle lodges, Chaa Creek blankets the bank of the Macal River right next to Ix Chel Farm and the Rainforest Medicine Trail. Owned and operated by Lucy and Mick Fleming, who stumbled upon the grounds in 1977, Chaa Creek blossomed from an overgrown farm into Belize's first and best jungle lodge. Its beautifully kept thatched-roof cottages are set in tropical gardens and richly decorated with Mayan textiles and local crafts; all have fan and private bath. Along with an array of tours, a state-of-the-art spa now graces the lodge's ongoing list of services.

Chaa Creek also operates the *Macal River Camp*, a budget alternative offering platformed safari-style tents with shared bath. The price (US$50) includes breakfast and dinner. Guests at Macal River Camp have access to the grounds at Chaa Creek Resort & Spa.

duPlooy's Jungle Lodge (☎ 9-23101, fax 9-23301, e *duplooys@btl.net,* w *www.du plooys.com, 4 miles (6.4km) on Chial Rd)* Double occupancy (US$15 per extra person): 'Pink House' US$50, 'Jungle Lodge' US$130, luxury bungalows US$165, 'Casita' US$250. This family-run lodge complex, with a good, casual energy, is on a fairly steep hill; the rooms look out over the tree canopy and are accessed by boardwalk, giving the place a tree house appeal. Guests can enjoy swimming in the Macal River or sunbathing on the resort's white, sandy beach. Free coffee and birding in the mornings start your day off right.

You can also explore the on-site Belize Botanical Gardens (see that entry, earlier in this section) or go on one of the lodge's many tours. Four levels of accommodations are available; rooms in the Pink House have fan and shared bath, standard bungalows and rooms in the Jungle Lodge have fans and private bath. There are also high-end bungalows and the luxury Casita (suitable for families). Optional meal packages cost US$35 per day for three meals.

For other lodges near San Ignacio, see the Mountain Pine Ridge section.

MOUNTAIN PINE RIDGE AREA

South of the Western Hwy, between Belmopan and the Guatemala border, the land begins to climb toward the heights of the Maya Mountains, whose arcing crest forms the border separating the Cayo District from the Stann Creek District to the east and the Toledo District to the south. From San Ignacio, it's about 9 to 13 miles (15km to 21km) to the park gate, depending on which route you take.

In the heart of this highland area – the land of macaws, mahogany, mangoes and jaguars – over 300 sq miles (777 sq km) of tropical pine forest has been set aside as the **Mountain Pine Ridge Forest Reserve**. Unlike the tropical broadleaf forests so prevalent in Belize, whose shallow soil base sits on limestone, much of the Mountain Pine Ridge's soil sits on a superficial level of red clay, beneath which lies solid granite. This infertile soil base makes agriculture almost impossible and harsh seasonal droughts and floods inevitable. This was perhaps a consideration for the Maya who, it appears, traveled through the Pine Ridge but didn't live in it.

Instead of describing a topographic feature, the word 'ridge' here describes the type of forest, which is identified by its most prominent tree – here it's the mountain pine. The sudden and total switch from tropical palms to pine trees is truly bizarre; you'll hear much exclaiming from foreign visitors about the incongruity of this arrangement. Also eliciting exclamations is the destruction of the Pine Ridge habitat caused by the southern pine beetle (see the boxed text).

The high elevation and cooler climate mean relief from both heat and mosquitoes. The reserve and its surrounding area are full of rivers, pools, waterfalls and caves to explore. South of the Pine Ridge on the edge of the Vaca Plateau and nuzzled up against the Guatemala border is the remote

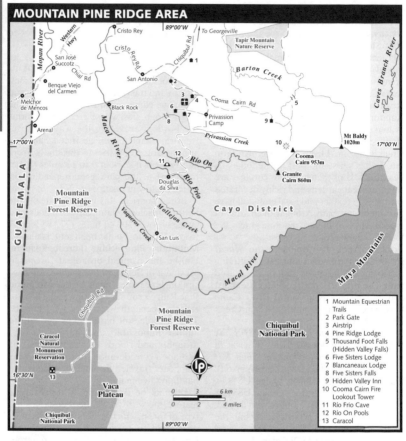

Chiquibul National Park. Some 200,000 acres (81,000 hectares) of wilderness are protected here, including the ruins of Caracol, Belize's largest and perhaps most magnificent Mayan site. Beyond Caracol, an intricate series of karst caves is believed to be the biggest in the Western Hemisphere. The area was not noted by modern researchers until the 1970s and, because of difficult access, most of the cave system remains unexplored.

When visiting the Mountain Pine Ridge and Chiquibul National Park, keep in mind that except for a small presence of forestry

workers in the village of Douglas da Silva, staff at the area lodges, a few archaeologists, occasional British troops on training exercises and a smattering of illegal squatters from Guatemala, this massive area is mostly uninhabited.

Roads into the Mountain Pine Ridge area are few (see Getting There & Away, later in this section). If you've got a car you can explore on your own, otherwise, taking the popular Mountain Pine Ridge tours from San Ignacio is the best way to get to the sites. Also, if you're staying at any of the Pine Ridge lodges, you'll have ample opportunity to explore the area. Before venturing in on your own, find out about road and weather conditions by calling the Forestry Department (☎ 9-23280) on weekdays between 8am and 5pm.

At the entrance to the reserve, a park ranger stops all vehicles and registers names and license plates. This is to control illegal activity and to keep track of who is in the area in case of accidents or bad weather. Chiquibul Rd (also called the Pine Ridge Rd) is the main route running through the Pine Ridge.

Waterfalls & Caves

With the exception of Five Sisters Falls, all of the sites listed below are free to explore.

One of the region's much-touted aquatic highlights is **Thousand Foot Falls** (Hidden Valley Falls). Access it by turning off the Chiquibul Rd onto Cooma Cairn Rd and

following it for 9 miles (14km). Hiking trails surround the falls, and a viewing platform at the top of the cascade is a great spot for catching a Mountain Pine Ridge vista. Despite the name, the falls actually are around 1600 feet (488 meters) high and, despite the height, the thin long stream of falling water isn't that spectacular. Still it's a beautiful, lush spot to hike around and shows a good example of the blending forest ecosystems.

The shorter, fatter **Five Sisters Falls** (☎ 9-23184 at Five Sisters Lodge; admission US$3/1 adults/children; open daylight hours) are accessible by an outdoor elevator ride from Five Sisters Lodge. The five falls cascade over a short drop-off and gather in a tranquil pool. Travelers and locals alike visit this site.

At **Río On Pools**, small waterfalls connect a series of pools that the river has

The Southern Pine Beetles' Path of Destruction

Like a thief in the night or a snake in the grass, a tiny beetle no longer than 0.2 inches (6mm) is devastating Belize's Mountain Pine Ridge forest. Take a look around and you'll see that the pine trees, which are supposed to be green, are now a sickly, fiery hue of red, or they've already fallen dead. The culprit for this mess is the tiny southern pine beetle *(Dendroctonus frontalis)*, which has destroyed more than 90% of the Pine Ridge forest.

The beetles, which only live up to a month, possess sophisticated 'semiochemical' communication systems that they use to move onto a host material – in this case, pine trees – where they feed, mate and reproduce. In her lifetime, a female can produce up to 150 eggs. The beetle in Belize is one of five bark beetles destroying pine forests in the Americas. Extreme weather conditions (such as hurricanes) contribute to the problem and, while the beetles are almost impossible to eradicate, certain methods can be used to slow their path of destruction.

A well-managed forest should be able to survive a pine beetle attack. Sanitation salvaging (removing infested trees), selective logging (creating forest buffer zones) and spraying of insecticides can help control the problem. In Belize, critics say, due to government cutbacks in forestry, slow response and lax management, this approach happened too late.

While today's infestation already promises to annihilate the pine forest trees – a major catastrophe in itself – it's the other ramifications that have resident environmentalists concerned. The ecological changes in the forest affect the Macal River watershed, which supplies residents living along the Macal and Belize Rivers (including Belize City) with freshwater. Soil erosion on an already shallow soil base threatens river flow and wildlife habitat, and the dry, unstable trees make massive wildfires almost a certainty.

While the Forestry Department has major plans underway to replant trees and salvage whatever it can of the remaining forest, it will take at least 25 years for the forest to recover if, in fact, it can.

carved out of granite boulders. The natural pools are refreshing and the smooth slabs of granite rock are perfect for stretching out to dry off. A picnic area and outhouse are the only amenities here. About 2½ miles (4km) south of the pools is the forestry settlement of **Douglas da Silva**. While there's little to do here, it's a good idea to stop by the ranger's station if you are planning on going farther south into the Chiquibul National Park.

Less than a mile (2km) from Douglas da Silva is one of the most popular Pine Ridge attractions. **Río Frio Cave**, a large, easily accessed cavern, was part of a cave system used by the Maya to bury their dead. The river gurgles through the sizeable cave, keeping it cool while you explore, looking at the interesting rock formations. Energetic types can take the easy **Río Frio Nature Trail**, a 45-minute jaunt through the forest, with some good vantage points of the surrounding area. The site has an outhouse and picnic tables. This, along with the Río On Pools, is usually included on Mountain Pine Ridge tours.

Caracol

Some 50 miles (80km) south of San Ignacio and 26 miles (42km) south of Douglas da Silva via Chiquibul Rd lies Caracol *(Department of Archaeology in Belmopan ☎ 8-22106; admission US$5; open 8am-4pm daily),* a vast Mayan city hidden deep in the jungle of Chiquibul National Park. Following a rugged road, this trip takes about three hours (each way) from San Ignacio.

Sitting high on a plateau 500 feet (152m) above sea level, the site – the largest in Belize – is massive, with evidence of 37 miles (60km) of internal roadways and transportation routes. It is estimated that, at its height, Caracol's population topped 150,000 – more than half of Belize's population today. Why such an enormous city developed here, in the middle of the jungle and far from an accessible water source, is one of the big questions that leave archaeologists scratching their heads.

Once you've traveled the long road to Caracol, you'll get to the site's main gate and visitor's center. The site is staffed by guides who will show you around for free (you can tip at your discretion). Keep in mind when touring here that it would take archaeologists several lifetimes to excavate a site this size; an imagination and sense of adventure are essential. There are toilets, but no other services, so be sure to have food, water and, if you're driving, a spare tire.

Mayan History A small population lived at Caracol in the Late Preclassic and Early Classic periods (300 BC to AD 550), but it wasn't until after a series of wars with Tikal and Naranjo (Guatemala) in the Late Classic period (AD 550 to AD 700) that Caracol flourished. A ball court marker (called Altar 21) dedicated in AD 633 by Lord K'an II suggests that his father, 'Lord Water,' defeated Tikal in AD 562 and Naranjo in AD 556. This is an exciting discovery that indicates Caracol could've rivaled (or surpassed) the size and power of Tikal.

Residents of Caracol came from all levels of society, from poor farmers to royalty, though its population was probably dominated by a large 'middle class.'

At its height, the metropolis would've surpassed modern-day Belize City's size and bustle.

Excavation History The ruins were first stumbled upon in 1938 by a mahogany logger named Rosa Mai. That year, commissioner of archaeology AH Anderson named the site Caracol (Spanish for snail), perhaps because of all the snail shells found in the soil. In 1950, Linton Satterthwaite from the University of Pennsylvania excavated 32 stone monuments, two causeways and five ball courts. In 1978–79 Paul Healy from Trent University explored the agricultural terraces. Since 1985, Drs Diane and Arlin Chase from the University of Central Florida have led the Caracol Project, through which the Chases' field schools have conducted surveys and excavations revealing Caracol's massive central core and complex urban development.

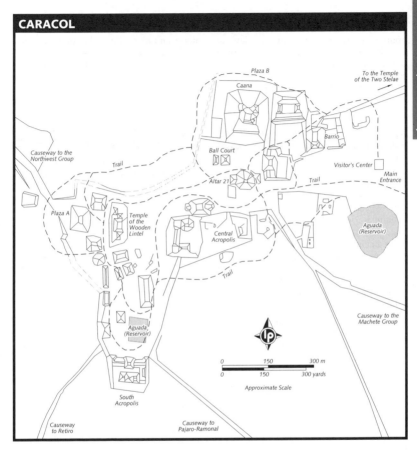

CARACOL

A four-year (2000–4) loan from the International Development Bank has given the Tourism Development Project (TDP; an offshoot of the Ministry of Tourism whose goal is to boost archaeological tourism in Belize) a surge in funding that will allow excavations to continue year-round. More money from Taiwanese investors will go to improving the road in to Caracol. Leading the TDP are Drs Jaime Awe and Allan Moore, Belizean archaeologists who suggest that this is the most exciting time in Caracol's modern history and that in the not-too-distant future, the site could rival Guatemala's Tikal.

Touring the Site A system of trails meanders through Caracol, but Plazas A and B around the Central Acropolis are the most excavated. The big highlight here is **Caana** (Sky-Palace) in Plaza B, Caracol's tallest structure at 141 feet (43m) and the tallest human-made structure in Belize. Caana underwent many construction phases until its completion in about AD 800. There are stone 'beds' throughout the middle portion. High steps narrowing up to the top probably led to the royal family's compound, where Structure B-19 was found to house Caracol's largest and most elaborate tomb (containing a woman's remains). You can climb to the top of Caana and feast upon one of the most magnificent views in all of Belize. Other than the occasional patch-farm fire, it's jungle as far as the eye can see.

The **Temple of the Wooden Lintel**, in Plaza A, was built with zapote wooden cross-beams, which dates the building to the 1st century AD and means it was one of the oldest and longest-used buildings at Caracol. Excavations here revealed a cache containing 684 grams of liquid mercury.

The neat and extensively excavated **ball court** is the site of Altar 21, the marker commemorating Caracol's defeat of Tikal.

Archaeology: Not Just a Thing of the Past

It all starts with a flurry of activity at Eva's Restaurant in San Ignacio. The place is bustling with archaeology students – smoking, eating eggs and getting jacked up on coffee while they wait out the usual Monday morning chaos.

All these people shuffling about are part of the Belize River Valley Archeological Reconnaissance project (BVAR), which is working on archaeological research projects throughout Belize. These people, mostly young Americans, Canadians, British and Belizeans, are waiting for trucks to pick them up and usher them out to their prospective projects. An energetic buzz fills the air and the sun outside heats the day, even though it's just 9am.

I'm waiting for Dr Jaime Awe, Mr Belize Archaeology himself. Awe is supposed to pick me up at 8am and take me three hours through the jungle to the remote site of Caracol, the largest Mayan site in Belize. I tell a couple of people I'm waiting for Awe, that he was supposed to be there at 8am, and they laugh. 'You'll be lucky if you get out of here by noon.' So, relieved I haven't been forgotten, I settle back and watch the flurry and sip another cup of coffee.

Belize Valley Archeology Reconnaissance Project

While I wait, I find out what BVAR's all about. For 12 seasons, the project, under the auspices of the Department of Archaeology, has focused on gaining a regional understanding of the Maya. Instead of just focusing on one specific site, BVAR's objective is to study the settlement pattern in the valley and the relationships among sites, be they geographic, cultural or antagonistic. Not only are the big sites being excavated, but also the small, residential areas that sit under mounds of dirt in backyards throughout modern-day Belize.

One fascinating component of BVAR is the Western Belize Regional Cave Project, which has delved deep into the area's numerous caves to better understand how the prehistoric Maya used them for everything from rituals to ceremonies and sacrifices.

Volunteers come from all over the world to participate in the BVAR field schools. Most of them are archaeology students, but others are simply curious and looking for an injection of adventure.

BVAR is headed up by Awe, who's down here working with the University of New Hampshire. Awe grew up in San Ignacio and spent his childhood exploring the same caves and mounds of dirt he's exploring now. In between, he earned a master's degree from Canada's Trent University and went on to get a PhD from the University of London in England. This was the first PhD in archaeology ever obtained by a Belizean.

For more information on field schools, check out **w** www.bvar.org or write to **e** archeology@bvar.org.

The Road to Caracol

It's 11:30am, the caffeine is percolating overtime in my blood when a crazed-looking British guy pulls up in his white pickup truck and tells me I'll be going to Caracol with him, that Awe will meet

Nearby, an elite group likely lived in the **Central Acropolis**, 'downtown Caracol.' A royal tomb found here contained four sets of human remains, along with more than 20 pottery vessels. Another elite residential area, the **South Acropolis** is worth a look, as are the reservoirs (which caught rainwater) and causeways.

Organized Tours

Most of the tour companies in San Ignacio run tours into the Mountain Pine Ridge, as do all of the area lodges. On a typical tour, you'll pile into a van and visit Río On Pools, Río Frio Cave and one of the waterfalls. The full-day tour is usually around US$35. Ask at Eva's or try International Archeological

Archaeology: Not Just a Thing of the Past

us there. This guy is sweaty from running around San Ignacio, stocking up on supplies to bring to the archaeology camp at Caracol. I learn later that this is Pete Zubrzycki, the site manager at Caracol.

The drive to Caracol is nothing short of gnarly. The bumpy road seems to go on forever and a spinout seems just moments away. But we get there, and when we do, I am instantly awed by the sheer isolation. Caracol is truly in the middle of the jungle, which is why when we pull up to the archaeology camp I am literally shocked at how civilized it all is. A collection of palapa huts encircles the site's former main plaza. In the middle is a makeshift soccer field, a volleyball net and a mess tent big enough to feed an army. Wandering around the perimeter is the camp horse, Tequila.

Awe arrives with more people, supplies and more flurry as the staff take turns reporting the newest crises that have developed at camp. Like the ancient Maya, the workers living at Caracol have no natural water source, so all the water has to be brought in, collected from rainwater, or pumped from faraway creeks. Now, it seems, the camp is dangerously low on water. A couple of workers have minor injuries; there aren't enough beds for everyone; someone forgot the onions in San Ignacio.

It seems, to an outsider, like a rather high level of chaos, but it's undeniable that much work is underway here. Some 100 workers, mostly Belizean, live at the camp, along with a handful of archaeologists, all of whom are working to excavate this giant site, a task that seems akin to looking for a needle in a haystack.

I ask Awe how many structures are believed to be at Caracol. 'A hell of a lot,' he says and, when he sees I'm writing this down, suggests there might be upwards of 55,000. 'Let me put it this way,' he says. 'There are more ancient structures here than there are houses in Belize today.'

Later, after a delicious camp dinner of rice and beans, we are joined by Allan Moore, director of the Tourism Development Project (TDP), which works with the Belize Tourism Board to promote tourism at Belize's many Mayan sites. While Awe oversees the site, Moore keeps track of the money. Most of the workers are watching a movie, brought in by Awe to help fill the emptiness of nights in the jungle. The generator hums with the crickets.

Awe grabs a bottle of rum and pours us all a drink. He explains the TDP. 'It's the first time Belize has made a concerted effort to fund archaeology projects for the purpose of tourism.' He says funds are making year-round excavations at Caracol possible. Awe says that with a little infrastructural development, some road work and international marketing, Caracol could rival Copán in Honduras or Tikal in Guatemala. Awe, whose energy never seems to slow, says 'I want people to come here and experience the adventure of a lifetime.'

The next day I walk around the site and try to comprehend its size and importance. It takes a lot of imagination, but the immediacy of the excavation work, the fact that new discoveries are made here daily, makes me feel both a part of Caracol's history, and its future.

– **Debra Miller**

Tours (☎ 9-23991, fax 9-22760, ⓔ iatours@ btl.net), which runs frequent tours to the Pine Ridge area. You'll find them next door to Martha's on 9 West St in San Ignacio.

Many companies also offer tours to Caracol, though trips are less frequent due to the rugged road. Everald Daily Shuttle Service (☎ 9-22772, 9-12014, ⓔ cparadise@ btl.net) operates out of the Crystal Paradise Resort (see Places to Stay & Eat in the Around San Ignacio section, earlier in this chapter), but will pick you up anywhere in San Ignacio. The trip lasts all day (roughly 8am-5pm) and the US$50 price per person includes stops at Río On Pools, Río Frio Cave and the tour of Caracol, but does not include lunch or the US$5 admission fee to Caracol.

Places to Stay & Eat

The forests and mountains of the Mountain Pine Ridge area are dotted with a handful of small inns, lodges and ranches offering accommodations, meals, hiking, horseback trips, caving, swimming, bird-watching and similar outdoor activities.

A few of these lodges are for the budget traveler; the rest are more expensive, though they offer a good value for the money. Standard room rates are listed below, but most of the lodges also offer money-saving packages that include lodging, meals and tours. It never hurts to ask if discounts and specials are available.

Although you can sometimes show up unannounced and find a room, these are small, popular places, so it's best to write or call for reservations as far in advance as possible.

Unless you have your own transportation, you'll have to depend on taxis or the hospitality of your lodge hosts for transport between San Ignacio and the lodges. Sometimes the lodges will shuttle you at no extra cost, or they'll arrange a taxi for you. The Mountain Pine Ridge lodges are served by the Blancaneaux Lodge airstrip; charter flights are arranged by the lodge.

The only place to *camp* in the Pine Ridge is on an open field in Douglas da Silva

owned by the Forestry Department. Sites are only US$2.50, but they lack shade and there are no amenities nearby. Call ☎ 9-23280 or stop by the ranger's station in Douglas da Silva.

See the map for a general idea of the location of the following lodges. If you decide to drive in on your own, your lodge will provide you with exact directions.

Pine Ridge Lodge (☎ 82-3180, ☎ 800-316-0706 in the USA, ⓔ prlodge@mindspring .com, Ⓦ www.pineridgelodge.com, 5 miles into forest reserve) Cottages with bath (double) US$75, US$15 each additional person. Lunch US$7, dinner US$17.50. This unique eco-lodge rents out spacious, well-maintained cottages with private bath and good hot showers. A visit to the special hammock room is a must. There's no electricity here, but you'll come to love your kerosene lantern and its soft, comforting glow. The restaurant cooks up delicious meals using butane. The lodge's water comes from rainwater catchment or is pumped up from the pristine creek. The lodge is the first one you'll see once you've entered the forest reserve. It's 19 miles (30km) south of San Ignacio.

Blancaneaux Lodge (☎ 9-23878, fax 9-23919, ☎ 800-746-3743 in the USA, ⓔ blodge @btl.net) Single/double cabanas with light breakfast US$120-150/150-180, single/double/triple/quad villas US$275/350/375/400. Lunch US$6-8, dinner US$10-22. This indulgent lodge offers 14 rooms in thatched cabins and luxury villas overlooking waterfalls and beautifully manicured tropical gardens. Formerly a private writing retreat for the resort's owner, director Francis Ford Coppola, the lodge features beautiful tiled bathrooms, open-air living rooms (in the villas) and a decor filled with handicrafts from Belize, Guatemala, Mexico and Thailand. The restaurant serves Italian cuisine (Coppola's own recipes) and wines from the Niebaum-Coppola Estate Winery in California's Napa Valley. A bottle of Coppola's famed Rubicon goes for US$95.

Five Sisters Lodge (☎ 9-23184, fax 9-12024, ⓔ fivesislo@btl.net, west of Blan-

caneaux Lodge) Singles/doubles with balcony & shared bath US$55/65, single/double/triple/quad cabanas with private bath US$85/105/125/140. Breakfast & lunch US$6, dinner US$17.50. This locally owned lodge catering to a range of budgets is named for the five waterfalls that cascade through the property. Cozy hillside cabanas have screened-in porches, bathtubs and mosquito nets. The open-air restaurant overlooks the falls. A hydro-powered tram runs guests down to the river for swimming and sunbathing.

Hidden Valley Inn (☎ 8-23320, fax 8-23334, ☎ 800-334-7942 in the USA, e info@ hiddenvalleyinn.com, w www.hiddenvalley inn.com, Mile 9 (Km 14.5) on Cooma Cairn Rd) Singles/doubles/triples including tax, breakfast & dinner US$140/207/270. Just a few miles from the Thousand Foot (Hidden Valley) Falls, this inn sits on a massive property that straddles the pine forest ecosystem and tropical forest. Endless, well-maintained hiking trails and waterfalls let you explore on your own. Accommodations are in the main lodge or one of the 12 comfortable cottages that come with private bath. There's a restaurant and lounge in the main lodge.

Mountain Equestrian Trails (☎ 81-2041, ☎ 800-838-3918 in the USA, e metbelize@ btl.net, w www.metbelize.com, Mile 8 (Km 13), Chiquibul Rd) Safari-style tents US$20 per person, single/double/triple/quad cabanas US$100/120/140/160. Breakfast US$7, lunch US$10, dinner US$18. Technically just outside of the Mountain Pine Ridge Reserve, MET's topography is broadleaf tropical forest with nary a pine tree in site. Horseback riding is the specialty at this lovely jungle lodge sitting on 150 acres of rolling greenery. Accommodations are in spacious cabanas with private bath and kerosene lamps – there's no electricity. They can arrange tours throughout the area, but the horses draw most guests. Packages are available, as are half-day (US$60) and full-day (US$85 with lunch) rides. You can reach MET by taking the Chiquibul Rd from Georgeville off the Western Hwy, or via the

Cristo Rey Rd from San Ignacio. Call for directions or to arrange transfers.

Getting There & Away

Most people venturing into the Mountain Pine Ridge do so on organized tours or by getting a ride with whichever resort they are visiting. If you have a rental car, it's also possible to drive through the area. Two main roads access the Pine Ridge, from east to west, Chiquibul Rd (also known as the Pine Ridge Rd), which intersects the Western Hwy at Mile 61 (Km 98), near Georgeville, about 6 miles (10km) east of San Ignacio, and Cristo Rey Rd, which turns south off the Western Hwy in Santa Elena (across the river from San Ignacio). The Cristo Rey Rd passes the villages of Cristo Rey and San Antonio. At 13 miles (21km), the Cristo Rey Rd joins the Chiquibul Rd, which continues as far south as Caracol.

All roads in the area are rough and should not be attempted in anything but a high-clearance or 4WD vehicle. Remember, too, that these are active logging roads and big, fast-moving logging trucks should be given the right of way. Roads are sometimes impassable between May and late October. Always check with tour operators in San Ignacio about road conditions; you don't want to drive deep into the jungle only to be turned back. Before attempting the road to Caracol, stop by the ranger's station in Douglas da Silva to get the most current road conditions.

BENQUE VIEJO DEL CARMEN

From San Ignacio it's another 10 miles (16km) southwest down the Western Hwy to the Guatemala border. A sleepy town 2 miles (3km) east of the border, Benque Viejo del Carmen holds few services for travelers: You're better off eating and sleeping in San Ignacio. The town stirs from its normal tropical somnolence in mid-July, when the **Benque Viejo del Carmen Fiesta**, a nine-day religious ceremony, celebrates the town's patron saint with days of music and revelry.

Crossing the Border

Cross early in the morning to have the best chance of catching buses onward. Get your passport (and, if applicable, your vehicle papers) stamped at the Belizean station, then cross into Guatemala. The border station is supposedly open 24 hours a day, but most travelers try to cross during daylight hours. Citizens of most countries do not need a visa to enter Guatemala (check W www.guatemalaweb.com to see if you need a visa). At the border, the guard will stamp your passport, which allows you to be in the county for 30 to 90 days. This visa can be renewed at immigration in Guatemala City for another 30 to 90 days. At the border, you may ask for the 90 days specifically if you know you will be staying for the entire three-month period (it's much easier than having to renew it in Guatemala City).

Be prepared to pay a US$10 departure tax, plus US$3.75 Protected Areas Conservation Trust (PACT) fee when crossing the border. Hang on to your receipt; the PACT fee is valid for 30 days if you cross another border from Belize. On the Guatemala side,

you'll have to pay a fee of 30 quetzals (about US$4).

Two banks at the border will change money, but the itinerant moneychangers often give you a better deal – for US cash. The rates for exchanging Belizean dollars to Guatemalan quetzals and vice versa are poor. Use up your local currency before you get to the border, then change hard foreign currency, preferably US dollars.

Both Transportes Pinita and Transportes Rosalita buses westward to Santa Elena (Guatemala) depart Benque early in the morning. Sometimes available are more comfortable – and more expensive – minibuses (US$10 per person); many travelers feel this is money well spent.

To go on to Tikal, get off the bus at El Cruce/Puente Ixlú, 22 miles (36km) east of Flores, and wait for another bus, minibus or obliging car or truck to take you the final 21 miles (35km) north to Tikal. Note that the flow of traffic from El Cruce to Tikal drops dramatically after lunch. You can also opt to go all the way to Flores and join an organized tour there. See the Excursion to Tikal chapter for more information.

Southern Belize

If you want to explore off the tourist track, this is the place.

Southern Belize, encompassing the districts of Stann Creek and Toledo, presents

Highlights

- Enjoying the lazy life in Placencia from a beachside hut or a world-class resort
- Soaking up Garifuna culture in Dangriga or Hopkins
- Diving and snorkeling the atolls of Glover's Reef
- Touring the present-day Mayan villages of Toledo, great to combine with visits to the atmospheric ancient sites of Nim Li Punit and Lubaantun
- Exploring the rugged terrain of Cockscomb Basin – easy to access on your own or with a guide
- Cooling your heels in Punta Gorda, easily the most remote and unusual of towns in Belize

OTHER MAPS
Southern Belize page 183
Cockscomb Basin Wildlife Sanctuary page 199

Dangriga page 188
Hopkins Area page 195
Placencia Peninsula page 202
Around Punta Gorda-On Land page 214
Placencia Village page 204
Punta Gorda page 210

GUATEMALA

HONDURAS

the country's most diverse topography, including an extensive limestone cave system off the Hummingbird Hwy, the Maya Mountains running through the middle of the area, and miles of virgin rain forest in the south. Within the region are Cockscomb Basin Wildlife Sanctuary, Victoria Peak, the lovely and remote ruins of Toledo – Lubaantun and Nim Li Punit – and the small village of Red Bank and its surrounding forests, which at certain times of the year are inhabited by scarlet macaws.

Out to sea, the barrier reef continues to stretch its way down the coastline, and the farther south you get the fewer other humans you'll have to share it with. Off Dangriga, Tobacco and South Water Cayes and Glover's Reef offer divers and snorkelers nearly virgin reef to explore. From Placencia divers and snorkelers can access Gladden Spit, where it's possible to see migrating whale sharks when the season is right, and Laughing Bird Caye, an area with diverse undersea life. Off Punta Gorda are the Sapodilla and Snake Cayes, still largely undiscovered and teeming with marine life.

There are three major towns in the region – Dangriga, a lively seaside town and the center of Garifuna culture in Belize; Placencia, the region's biggest draw, attracting beach-loving travelers for whom life in the cayes is just too hectic; and Punta Gorda, Belize's southernmost town, largely untraveled (but on the brink of discovery) – and a fascinating mix of Creole, Latin and Mayan cultures.

The Southern Hwy – only partially paved and perpetually under construction – carries travelers through the region. The farther south you travel, the more remote and wild the landscape becomes, the fewer travelers you'll see, and the more adventurous you'll be. It's a somewhat monotonous and jarring route and veteran Belize travelers often recommend that you avoid the aggravation and fly to points south.

Hurricane Iris

On October 8, 2001, Hurricane Iris, a powerful category 4 hurricane, hit southern Belize, most heavily affecting the coastal areas. Hardest hit, the Placencia peninsula and the Mayan villages of Toledo have recovered quite well, but some businesses may not yet be open when you arrive. When making plans in this area, you might want to call ahead and check the status of the establishment you intend to visit.

MANATEE HIGHWAY TO GALES POINT

The mostly unpaved Manatee (or Coastal) Hwy goes southeast from the Western Hwy at Mile 30, at the village of La Democracia, a short distance past the Belize Zoo. Keep your eyes peeled for a gas station on the south side of the road, as this is where you'll turn.

This was long considered the shortcut to Dangriga, but the Hummingbird Hwy takes about the same amount of time now that it's been paved, and when the weather is rainy the still-unpaved Manatee Hwy will take a bit longer. If you're driving south and back, going one direction on Hummingbird and the other direction on Manatee is a nice way to break up the trip. The landscape is much different than what you'll see elsewhere in Belize. Orange dirt road winds through lush farmland, approaching and then passing through limestone formations that rise sharply up from the fields, much like coral rises sharply from the sandy bottom of the sea.

GALES POINT

Gales Point is a sleepy Creole town built along 2½ miles of narrow peninsula jutting into Belize's southern lagoon. This area has a couple of superlative distinctions: One, it has the highest concentration of Western Manatees in the Caribbean. Two, it's the primary breeding ground for 60% of the hawksbill turtles in Belize. There's only one road in and out of the town, and you'll find that you

get to know the townspeople pretty quickly. A Garifuna drummer lives in town and will arrange performances and lessons.

Manatee-Watching

Manatees are attracted to the region for the warm freshwater spring located 200 yards (182m) off the point. They can be seen around the spring and grazing on the sea grass that grows in the lagoon. Manatee tours can be arranged at the Manatee Lodge (see Places to Stay & Eat); a two-hour tour costs US$50 for one to four people. Manatee-watching can be combined with other activities offered by the lodge, such as a southern lagoon or river tour, a jungle hike or a visit to one of the nearby caves. A half-day tour combining one of the above activities with manatee-watching costs US$120 for up to four people. A full-day tour is US$165 and includes a choice of two activities, plus the manatees.

Turtle Tours

Hawksbill, which are protected, as well as loggerhead and green sea turtles, which aren't yet protected in Belize, lay their eggs on 21 miles (34km) of beach across the lagoon from Gales Point.

Leroy and Teri Hogan Andrewin of the **Gales Point Turtle Project** (☎ 21-2031, ✉ letssaveturtles@aol.com) have made nest protection in Gales Point their personal crusade. Recently they've developed a plan to turn their vocation into a paying business venture and are offering tours to the hawksbill nesting areas, where visitors can participate in the steps necessary to protect the turtles' nests and help the hatchlings begin their new lives. The action happens from May to November each year. The project has released up to 15,000 hatchlings into the sea in seasons past.

Early in the season the Turtle Project groups go out and find new nests, build enclosures around them to keep predators away and inspect nests that have already been fortified. Turtles work hard to hide their nests (they lay about 150 to 200 eggs), but a good eye (or nose if you're a raccoon or a skunk) can find them. Later in the

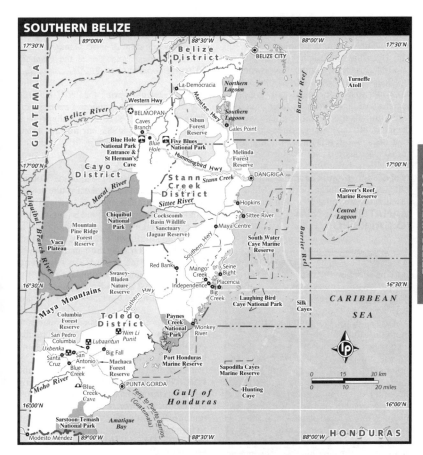

SOUTHERN BELIZE

season, when the turtles are hatching, shells are counted to keep track of the year's turtle reproduction. Newly hatched turtles are tagged and then released into the wild (this usually happens under cover of night).

Group or individual tours can be taken by canoe, (US$50; it will take longer to get in and out) or motorboat (US$75); each tour lasts up to eight hours. Evening tours are conducted during hatching season (canoe/motorboat US$63/86).

This is not for everyone; it's buggy, muddy work, with lots of exposure to the elements, and, obviously, you're not guaranteed a turtle sighting. Though definitely not a soft adventure, it's a rewarding experience for those willing to roll up their sleeves and get up close and participatory with nature.

Other Activities

Snorkeling trips to the reef can be arranged at Manatee Lodge for US$240 for up to four people – you'll take a 10-minute boat ride east on the Bar River, which connects the southern lagoon to the Caribbean Sea. **Cockscomb Basin** is also within reasonable day-trip distance – see that section, later, for more information.

Places to Stay & Eat

Manatee Lodge *(☎ 21-2040, e manatee@btl.net)* Singles/doubles/triples US$87/100/115. Breakfast & lunch US$7.50, dinner US$13.50. Recently under new ownership and located at the tip of the Gales Point peninsula, this is a peaceful spot on a pleasant piece of land and the center of activity for visitors to the area. The grassy grounds stretch out to the water on three sides, and a long dock is offered for swimming. There are 10 spacious and comfortable rooms with nice modern bathrooms. Larger rooms are available for groups. The restaurant is excellent and serves large portions. Meals are based on traditional Belizean dishes and made with fresh ingredients and plenty of green vegetables.

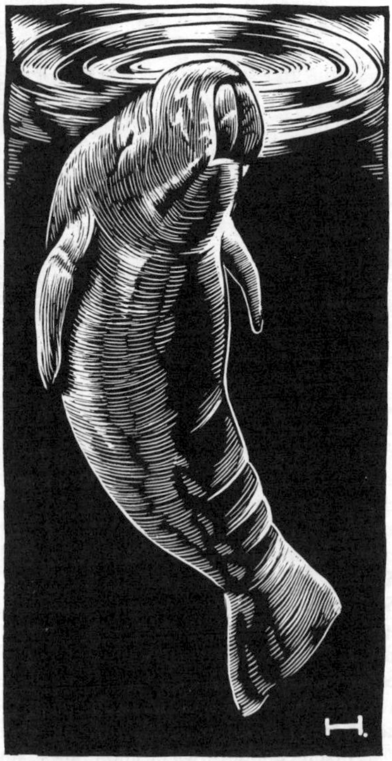

Gales Point is a hot spot for manatees.

Rooms can be rented for US$12.50 a night at ***John Moore's Lodging*** *(☎ 21-2031 community phone or ☎ 21-2040 Manatee Lodge where John leads tours)* or at the ***Women's Village Cooperative*** *(☎ 21-2031 community phone).*

Gentle's Cool Spot *(☎ 21-2031 community phone),* ***Carol's Caribbean Cuisine*** *(☎ 21-2023)* and Mrs T's Kitchen will prepare meals for around US$3. For upscale dining head to the Manatee Lodge.

Getting There & Away

Manatee Hwy (also known as the Coastal Route) is the road you'll take if you're driving to Gales Point. The turnoff is 23 miles (37km) from the Western Hwy, 15 miles (24km) from the Hummingbird Hwy junction.

A 5pm Southern Transport bus leaves Belize City and travels the Manatee Hwy to Dangriga, arriving at the Gales Point junction around 6:30pm. From Dangriga, the Manatee Hwy/Coastal Route bus leaves at 5am and arrives at the Gales Point junction at 6am.

It's also possible to get there by boat from Belize City through a network of canals. Arrangements can be made through Manatee Lodge, or by calling Charlie Usher (☎ 25-2967, cell 14-1350); the price will be around US$165 for up to four passengers. The trip takes you through a riverine mangrove area and the location where *Mosquito Coast* was filmed.

ALONG THE HUMMINGBIRD HIGHWAY

Heading south from Belmopan, the Hummingbird Hwy stretches 49 miles (79km) to the junction of the Southern Hwy and the turnoff to Dangriga. It's a gorgeous and dramatic drive over the Maya Mountains and through foothills and valleys of citrus plantations – probably the most scenic and varied route in Belize. Mile counters on the Hummingbird Hwy run from Mile 55 at the Western Hwy junction to Mile 0 at Dangriga city limits. At Mile Marker 16 (29 miles from Belmopan) you'll crest the hills at a spot aptly named Over the Top, also known as Hummingbird Gap.

At the southern end of the highway you'll go over a few one-lane bridges. This is evidence of an old railway line that ran through the valley in the early 1900s. It fell out of use when the banana industry declined.

Ian Anderson's Caves Branch Tours

Ian Anderson is the pioneer of the Belize cave-tubing trips, and though it's not the cheapest adventure outfit in Belize, it's still one of the best. Caves Branch operates on a 58,000-acre (23,200-hectare) private estate, and only guests of the resort (day or overnight) are allowed on these tours, so the caves aren't overrun. The tour operators, employees of the lodge, are superbly knowledgeable and attentive.

Day trips (US$75 to US$105 per person) are tailored to various levels of activity: You can choose a leisurely tube float down the Caves Branch River; float and climb through ceremonial caves to see evidence of the Maya in pottery shards and other artifacts; or go for a harder adventure where you'll hike, climb and even rappel to reach your destination. Nature walks and night tours are also available.

Showcasing the Caves Branch offerings is the Black Hole Drop (US$105), as seen on the Discovery Channel and the series *Temptation Island*. You'll get trussed up in a harness, then coaxed backward over a cliff to rappel down a seemingly bottomless but actually 300-foot (91m) sinkhole. The exhilarating ride sends you through the forest canopy, past the mouth of a sacred Mayan cave and down into a tropical forest. Be aware that the way to the cave is through steep, rough terrain; often the hike in and out is harder on people than the actual rappel.

Another popular tour, especially with couples, is the overnight expedition, where you can spend a candlelit night alone in a cave (US$215 per person).

To participate in any of these tours you must wear hiking boots (no open-toed shoes). If you don't have your own, you can rent them for US$5.

Day trips can be arranged from San Pedro and Caye Caulker – you'll leave your

island at dawn and return to Belize City just in time to catch the last water taxi home. But to get the full effect of this adventure camp, it's best to spend the night.

Places to Stay & Eat *Ian Anderson's Caves Branch Adventure Company & Jungle Lodge* (☎/fax 8-22800, W www.cavesbranch .com) Tent sites US$5 per person, bunks US$15 per person, double cabanas with shared bath US$68, double cabana suites with private bath US$108. Breakfast & lunch US$12, dinner US$17. Credit cards are not accepted. A good balance of adventure and comfort makes this jungle lodge popular with honeymooners and families. The focus here is on the tours, however, so you'll feel left out and idle if you opt to stick around the lodge during the day.

The jungle has been cleared just enough to allow room for the buildings, giving the grounds an exotic feel, especially at night when the tiki torches are lit. One of the more popular features is the almost open-air jungle showers, with palapas for stalls, buckets with nail holes for showerheads and a seemingly endless supply of warm water. There are three classes of rooms: dorm rooms containing seven bunks each, bungalows built two to a building, and deluxe jungle suites with living rooms and private bath. The shared bathroom facilities here are the best in Belize – clean spacious rooms are lit by kerosene all night and decorated with fresh flowers.

On the premises you'll hear howler monkeys in the middle of the night and see keep-billed toucans in the trees. The management keeps dogs as pets, so there's little chance of running into any sort of ferocious animal, but there has been evidence that jaguars are present in the wilderness around the lodge. Packages and multi-day cave expeditions are available.

Blue Hole National Park & St Herman's Cave

The Blue Hole, focus of the like-named national park *(admission US$4; open 8am-4pm daily)*, is a cenote (a water-filled limestone sinkhole) formed when the roof caved in on a portion of one of the underwater rivers of the Sibun River tributaries. The cenote is 328 feet (98.4m) in diameter and 108 feet (33m) deep. A set of stairs leads into the recession to a swimming hole that is 25 feet (7.6m) deep and the glowing sapphire blue that inspired its name. The river dips back underground through a spooky echo- and bat-filled chamber. A popular stop on the Hummingbird Hwy for visitors and locals, its subterranean cooling systems makes for a refreshing dip, even on the hottest days. It becomes murky and less inviting after a rain.

The visitor's center is about 11 miles (18km) south of Belmopan on the Humming-

bird Hwy (Mile 44). At the center is the trailhead to St Herman's Cave, a large cavern used by the Maya during the Classic period. This is one of the few caves in Belize that you can visit independently, although a guide is required if you wish to venture in farther than a half a mile. A flashlight is a must. Also here is an observation tower and 3-mile (4.8km) network of trails, including a nature walk.

The trail to the Blue Hole itself starts at a parking area about a mile farther down the highway. (Break-ins are not unheard of here, so be cautious with your belongings.) You don't have to stop at the visitor's center if you're just going for a swim; an attendant is posted at the trail to the Blue Hole to collect your money. Most visitors are content just to have a dip in the water and a peak in the cave, however, guides can be arranged at the visitor's center to point out the special features of the cave or to help you out with nature-spotting.

Five Blues National Park

At Mile 32 of the Hummingbird Hwy (22 miles/36km south of Belmopan) is the turnoff to Five Blues National Park *(admission US$4; open 8am-4pm)*, a primitive, community-managed reserve surrounding a cenote that reflects five different shades of blue. Turn left off the highway and you'll see a visitor's center, where you pay the entry fee. Be sure to pick up a map at the center, because the park's features – a series of nature walks, a diving platform and a couple of small caves – are not clearly marked. The park is about 6 miles (9.66km) from the visitor's center down a rough road – it's difficult to reach without your own transportation.

DANGRIGA
pop 8814

Once called Stann Creek Town, Dangriga is the largest town in southern Belize. It's much smaller than Belize City and, consequently, a friendlier and quieter place. Most travelers coming through Dangriga spend one night and move on, catching the bus to Placencia or a launch out to the popular diving and fishing spots off Glover's Reef

The Garifunas

Southern Belize is the home of the Garifunas (or Garinagus, also called Black Caribs), people of mixed South American Indian and African heritage, who inhabited the island of St Vincent in the 17th century. By the end of the 18th century, British colonizers had brought the independent-minded Garifunas under their control and transported them from one island to another in an effort to subdue them.

In the early 19th century, oppression and wandering finally brought many of the Garifunas to southern Belize. The most memorable migration took place late in 1832, when on November 19, a large number of Garifunas reached Belize from Honduras in dugout canoes. The event is celebrated annually in Belize as Garifuna Settlement Day.

The Garifunas, who account for less than 7% of Belize's population, look more African than Indian, but they speak a language that's much more Indian than African, and their unique culture combines aspects of both peoples.

Many of the citizens of Dangriga, chief town of the Stann Creek District, are Garifunas. Dangriga is the place to be on Garifuna Settlement Day, as the town explodes in a frenzy of dancing, drinking and celebration of the Garifuna/Garinagu heritage.

and Tobacco Caye, and most come away not thinking much of the place. Indeed, to the naked eye there's not much to see. Looking, listening and talking is the way you get to know Dangriga. Wander the streets in the early morning or late afternoon, hang out in the restaurants and talk to people. You'll walk with the blue sea always out of the corner of your eye, the ocean breeze on your skin, and Garifuna drumming and the unfamiliar cadence of Garifuna language in your ears. Early evening or mid-morning are the best times for exploring; that's when you'll meet the fisherfolk in from their early hours work or catch the townspeople as they relax and visit along the streets in the evening.

Dangriga comes alive on November 19th, Garifuna Settlement Day, which commemorates the Garifuna people's arrival in Belize.

Orientation

North Stann Creek empties into the Gulf of Honduras at the center of town. Dangriga's main street is called St Vincent St south of the creek and Commerce St to the north (the name changes to Havana St south of the Havana Creek Bridge). The main streets tend to be congested all day long. There's not much by way of sidewalks – vehicles share the road with pedestrians intent on walking three and four abreast through town. The bus station is on Havana St just north of the Shell fuel station. The airstrip is a mile (1.6km) north of the center, near the Pelican Beach Resort.

Information

The Riverside Café serves as the unofficial information center and water-taxi terminal, where you can arrange trips out to the southern cayes with local fisherfolk or tradespeople. It's best to stop in by 10am to find out when boats will be leaving.

Barclay's Bank, on Commerce St, north of the Stann Creek Bridge, is open 8am to 2:30pm Monday to Thursday, 8am to 4:30pm Friday; there is no charge for cash advances. Scotiabank, on St Vincent St south of the Stann Creek Bridge, is open 8am to 1pm Monday to Thursday, 8am to 4:30pm Friday, and charges US$8 for cash advances. Belize

Bank has the same hours as Scotiabank and charges US$5 for cash advances.

The post office, on Mahogany Rd just up from the sea, is open 8am to 5pm Monday to Thursday, 8am to 4:30pm Friday (closed during the noon hour).

You can get your clothes washed and check your email at Val's Laundry (☎ 5-23324), 1 Sharp St at Mahogany. A load costs US$5, as does a half hour on the Internet.

For police, fire and medical emergencies dial ☎ 90, or for police ☎ 5-22022, fire ☎ 5-22091, and sea or river emergencies ☎ 25-2174 ext 156.

The Dangriga Hospital (☎ 5-22078) is west of town on Stann Creek Valley Rd.

Things to See & Do

Eight miles (13km) northwest of town on Melinda Rd is **Marie Sharp's Factory** (☎ 5-22370), the source of Belize's beloved hot sauce. The primary ingredients are habanero peppers and carrots, purchased from local farmers. Casual tours, often led by Marie herself, are offered during business hours, and the shop sells hot sauce and jams at outlet prices. Marie Sharp's has an office (☎ 5-23559) in town on Pier Rd as well, if you can't make it to the factory but would still like to see the full line of sauces and jams. See the boxed text for more information on Marie Sharp.

There's an **open-air market** northeast of North Stann Creek, where merchants sell everything from fresh fish and vegetables to shoes and dishware; it's best to go early in the morning. North of the market a road trails up the coastline past a large sports field; near the end of the field is a monument to Thomas Vincent Ramos, known as the father of the Garifuna for his efforts to promote the culture and for founding Garifuna Settlement Day.

Creativities/GB Novelties (☎ 5-23649, St Vincent St & Yemeri) is a good place to pick up Garifuna art and drums. It's also an information center for those looking to delve deeper into Garifuna culture. Hours vary, but there's usually someone around the shop or at the house in back who can help you out.

SOUTHERN BELIZE

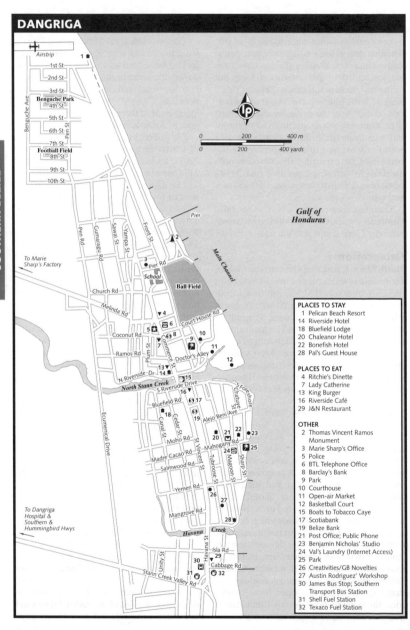

DANGRIGA

Airstrip
1st St
2nd St
3rd St
Benguche Park
4th St
5th St
6th St
7th St
Football Field
8th St
9th St
10th St

Benguche Ave
Pen St

Gulf of
Honduras

0   200   400 m
0   200   400 yards

Pier

To Marie
Sharp's Factory

Pen Rd
Gumaragu Rd
Sawai St
Vampa St
Front St

Main Channel

Pier Rd
School
Ball Field

Church Rd
Melinda Rd
Coconut Rd
Ramos Rd

Court House Rd

Commerce St
Plum St

Doctor's Alley
N Riverside Dr

North Stann Creek
S Riverside Drive

Bluefield Rd
Canal St
Cedar St
Moho St

Alejo Beni Ave
S Foreshore
Chatuye St

St Vincent St
Tubroose St
Mahogany St
Mapom St
Sharp St

Madre Cacao Rd
Salmwood Rd
Yemeri Rd

Ecumenical Drive

To Dangriga
Hospital &
Southern &
Hummingbird Hwys

Mangrove Rd

Havana St

Havana Creek

Isla Rd
Cabbage Rd

Unity St
Stann Creek Valley Rd

PLACES TO STAY
1 Pelican Beach Resort
14 Riverside Hotel
18 Bluefield Lodge
20 Chaleanor Hotel
22 Bonefish Hotel
28 Pal's Guest House

PLACES TO EAT
4 Ritchie's Dinette
7 Lady Catherine
13 King Burger
16 Riverside Café
29 J&N Restaurant

OTHER
2 Thomas Vincent Ramos
   Monument
3 Marie Sharp's Office
5 Police
6 BTL Telephone Office
8 Barclay's Bank
9 Park
10 Courthouse
11 Open-air Market
12 Basketball Court
15 Boats to Tobacco Caye
17 Scotiabank
19 Belize Bank
21 Post Office; Public Phone
23 Benjamin Nicholas' Studio
24 Val's Laundry (Internet Access)
25 Park
26 Creativities/GB Novelties
27 Austin Rodriguez' Workshop
30 James Bus Stop; Southern
   Transport Bus Station
31 Shell Fuel Station
32 Texaco Fuel Station

SOUTHERN BELIZE

Austin Rodriguez' Workshop (☎ 5-23752, 32 Tubroose St) sells drums and can also arrange performances and instruction. The Garifuna drums are made from mahogany, cedar or mayflower; the surface is stretched deer leather. They sell for US$100 to US$150.

Stop by **Benjamin Nicholas' Studio** (Mahogany Rd & Southern Foreshore) to have a look at his work in progress. Nicholas is often available to talk about his work and that of other artists in Belize. Nicholas, Belize's most famous painter, lives and works in Dangriga near the Bonefish Hotel. His paintings are displayed in banks, hotel lobbies and public buildings throughout the country.

Near Nicholas' place is a nice waterfront park with a bandstand and a large playing field.

Places to Stay

Bluefield Lodge (☎ 5-22742, 6 Bluefield Rd) Room with one double bed and shared bath US$15, room with two double beds and shared bath US$20, singles/doubles with private bath US$20/30; all have fans, some have cable TV. Book in advance, as this well-run lodge fills up fast. With six rooms in a pristine colonial-style building on a shady street, it's popular with aid organizations and gets plenty of return visitors. The proprietress has a wealth of information about Dangriga.

Chaleanor Hotel (☎ 5-22587, fax 5-23038, e chaleanor@btl.net, 35 Magoon St) Singles/doubles/triples with shared bath & fan US$8.50/14/16, with private bath and cable TV US$25/35/45; air-con is available for US$12 more a night. Named for Chad and Eleanor, the husband and wife who own it, this popular family-run hotel caters to a range of budgets. Located on a residential street, the main building (which houses the rooms with private bath) towers over its neighbors and offers a 360-degree view of Dangriga from its rooftop terrace. Reservations are advised, and the hotel often fills up with businesspeople spending a few days in Dangriga. Request an upper level room, since the ground floor rooms don't catch much breeze.

Pal's Guest House (☎/fax 5-22095, e palbze@btl.net, 868-A Magoon St) Doubles with shared bath US$10-16, seafront doubles with private bath US$32. The rooms are cell-like, and it's somewhat of a haul from the center of town, but this guest house's proximity to water is a draw. All rooms have cable TV.

Riverside Hotel (☎ 5-22168, Commerce St at N Riverside Dr) Rooms with shared bath US$10 per person. On the second floor of a wooden commercial building, this hotel's 15 small rooms are built around a cavernous parlor area. The interior is cool and dark in contrast to the riverside hustle and bustle from the streets below.

Bonefish Hotel (☎ 5-22165, fax 5-22296, e bonefish@btl.net, 15 Mahogany Rd) Doubles with private bath US$50-75. This hotel rents 10 charmless rooms with fan, air-con and TV. Rooms on the upper level are at the higher price. The hotel caters to divers and also operates the Blue Marlin Lodge on South Water Caye. There is a pleasant bar on the second floor, with a nice view of the sea to the east and a soccer field to the north. Dinner can be prepared here on request.

Pelican Beach Resort (☎ 5-22044, fax 5-22570, w www.pelicanbeachbelize.com) Rooms with fan US$73, with fan and seaview porch US$90, with air-con & cable TV US$100. On the north end of town just beyond the airstrip, Dangriga's upmarket hotel is on the waterfront, with two colonial-style buildings, spacious grounds, a sand beach and a full program of tours to area sites. It's about a 20-minute walk into town. The Pelican also runs the Pelican's Pouch on South Water Caye.

Places to Eat

Riverside Café (☎ 5-23449) Prices US$2-7. Open 6:30am-9pm Mon-Sat, closed Sun. Just southeast of the Stann Creek Bridge, this café is the town's unofficial tourist center – you can ask about boat charters and inland tours here, and goings-on about town are posted on the walls. The café boasts a large menu, but it's best to stick to the basics. Low-cost items off the lunch menu are available all day. It's a good people-watching spot – you'll meet other travelers and hobnob with the fisherfolk who come in for their meals. Coffee lovers will be pleased to taste real brewed coffee, rare for Dangriga. There are a couple of old guys who hang out in the front giving directions and washing cars – they do a nice job at both tasks, but can seem overly forward when you first meet them.

Ritchie's Dinette *(☎ 5-22112, 84 Commerce St)* Prices US$3-5. This is a local favorite for traditional Belizean food. While there is a small dining room, it's more of a takeout place. Meals are served in Styrofoam containers, and you must supply your own beer.

Lady Catherine *(☎ 5-20167, Coconut Rd at Commerce St)* Breakfast & lunch US$3-5, dinner US$6-10. Open for breakfast 7am-10:30am, lunch 11am-2pm, dinner 5pm-9pm. This is a new place, owned by a Canadian whose mission is to supply variety to the lives of Dangrigans. On the menu are pasta, pizza and Continental dishes.

King Burger *(☎ 5-22476, 135 Commerce St)* Prices US$2-7. Open 7am-3pm & 7pm-11:30pm Mon-Sat, closed Sun. With an old-time soda fountain look to it, this place serves burgers, chicken and rice and beans.

J&N Restaurant *(☎ 5-22649, 18 Havana St)* Prices US$3-7. Open 7am-9pm daily.

Marie Sharp

While in Belize, you'll find that you never eat alone: Your table and your meal are always enlivened by the Marie Sharps' inimitable presence. We caught up with Marie Sharp at her home in Dangriga and found a person who is as passionate about her work and her country as her hot sauce is fiery.

Sharp got into the hot-sauce business in 1981, and it happened by chance, as kitchen-table operations often do. She worked as an executive secretary at a citrus plant and, with her husband, ran a family farm in her spare time. One season she found herself with a surplus of habanero peppers when a buyer backed out of purchasing them after harvest. Sharp hated to see them go to waste, so she decided to figure out something to do with the peppers.

Working in the evening in her kitchen, she blended the excess habaneros into a mash and began to experiment with various concoctions. She found that other bottled hot sauces were often watery, tasteless and sometimes too hot to be flavorful. She wanted a sauce that would specifically complement Belizean cuisine, and one that didn't contain artificial ingredients. She came up with some interesting blends and took them around to her friends and family for taste-testing. By far, the favorite was one that used carrots as a thickener and blended the peppers with onions and garlic.

Once she had her formula, she embarked on a guerilla marketing campaign. She carried samples of the sauce, along with corn chips and refried beans, door-to-door to shopkeepers all over Belize. When the proprietors liked what they tasted, Marie asked them to put the sauce on the their shelves

On Sunday barbecue is served, and there are daily specials prepared for lunch, and often still available by dinner. Specials include Garifuna dishes like cowfoot soup, hudut, boil-up and pork chops. Located across from the bus station, its air-conditioned interior is popular with stop-over travelers.

Entertainment

Travelers tend to gather at the Riverside Café or J&N Restaurant. There are a few bars on the upper floors of buildings on Commerce St, although they may feel a bit rough and tumble if you're a tenderfoot.

Neighborhood kids often offer to perform for travelers, and an audience of one will draw peewee drummers and punta dancers out of the woodwork. They're an entrepreneurial bunch; a cup will be passed around between numbers. This is not the most equitable way to reward performers or encourage the arts, since the big kids usually keep the till. If you prefer a more structured performance, your hotelier will be able to arrange a performance for you and make sure payment is fairly distributed. Performances can also be arranged through Austin Rodriguez or Creativities (see Things to See & Do, earlier).

Marie Sharp

and agreed to take back the bottles that didn't sell. The sauce, then bottled under the brand name Melinda, which was the name of Sharp's ranch, caught on and was soon not only on store shelves but also on restaurant tables all over the country.

Marie worked at bottling the sauces from her kitchen for three years, finally bringing in a couple of workers to help her mix up the zealously guarded formula. She continued to work on modifications for her sauce, eventually hybridizing her own red habanero pepper – a mix of scotch bonnet and Jamaican red peppers – which contributes to the distinctive color of the sauce. Seeds were distributed to her producers with strict instructions on how to grow and maintain the hybrid. She opened her own factory in 1986 with two three-burner stoves and six women to look after her pots, and moved to her current factory in 1998 (see the Things to See & Do section for details on tours).

Her business suffered a setback in 1991, when she was forced to break ties with her US distributor for allegedly bottling other, lesser-quality products under the Melinda name. Rather than commit to a protracted court battle, Sharp signed off the Melinda name to the distributor and began bottling her top-secret formula under her own name.

Today, one half of all Marie Sharp's hot sauce is distributed to stores and restaurants in Belize, while the other half is exported to the US and Japan. She employs a workforce of 20, mostly women, who can package 1000 cases (12,000 bottles) of hot sauce in eight hours and are able to produce one shipping container full of sauce in a month.

In addition to hot sauces – which come in regular, mild, hot and XXX – Sharp also produces jams and chutneys made from mango and papaya, and a tamarind steak sauce that Sharp proudly claims is far superior to sauces made with raisins.

Along the way Sharp studied business management and marketing, and her company now serves as an example for small businesses in Belize and elsewhere. Sharp is committed to creating industry for Belizeans; her jams and fruit sauces are often created from locally grown fruit that is too small for export and would usually go to waste.

Sharp notes proudly that the folks running the X-ray machines at the airport have told her that bottles of her sauce are the most common item in the bags of departing vacationers. Those who can't carry enough can find the sauce in specialty shops in the US and Japan, or order online from w hotsaucecatalog.com.

Getting There & Away

Maya Island Air and Tropic Air serve Dangriga on flights heading from Belize City to Placencia and Punta Gorda.

Southern Transport buses head down the Hummingbird Hwy for Dangriga at 6am, 7am, 8am, 9am, 11am, noon, 1pm, 2pm, 2:30pm, 3pm, 4pm and 5:15pm. Buses make the return trip at 5am, 5:30am, 6:30am, 8:30am, 9am, 10am, noon, 3pm, 4pm and 5pm. There is one Belize City-Dangriga bus running down the Manatee Hwy at 5pm, and a Dangriga-Belize City bus at 5:15am. (The route takes four hours via Hummingbird Hwy, three hours via the Coastal Hwy). For details, see the Getting Around chapter.

TOBACCO CAYE, SOUTH WATER CAYE & GLOVER'S REEF

Tobacco Caye, South Water Caye and the resorts of Glover's Reef are accessed by boat from Dangriga. Their distance from Belize City has kept casual visitors away, protecting the reef from much human impact. Dolphins, manta rays and manatees are commonly sighted, and the quantity and variety of coral on display is incredible.

Tobacco Caye

Tiny Tobacco Caye is a 5-acre (2-hectare) island catering to travelers on a low-to-moderate budget, located off Dangriga at the northern tip of the South Water Caye Marine Reserve. Diving, fishing, snorkeling and hammocking are the favorite pastimes here. One of the best things about this little hideout is that there is good snorkeling to be done right off the shore. The island can be circumnavigated in less than 20 minutes, and while some of the islanders run fishing boats, tourism is the prime motivation. There is nothing here by way of shops or services, except what is offered through the handful of hotels. If you're expecting a full-service luxury-resort experience, look elsewhere. If you're looking for a secluded spot to get away from it all, this is the way to go. Here it's about old guest houses, run by families who have lived on the island for years.

Water Sports Diving can be arranged for around US$25 a dive, depending on the distance from the island. Dives to Glover's Reef and the Turneffe and Lighthouse Reef Atolls can also be arranged. Equipment rents for US$5. Fishing trips can also be arranged.

Places to Stay & Eat The island has no restaurants; meals are furnished by the island lodges, and prices are included in the cost of the rooms. Both Reef's End and Tobacco Caye Lodges have bars.

Gaviota's Reef Resort (☎ 5-12032) Doubles with shared bath US$25-30, meals included. This perennial budget favorite has a four-room building and six cabins on the south side of the island. Service is friendly and personal, and while the rooms are rustic, the owners strive to keep prices low for backpackers.

Paradise Resort (☎ 5-12101) Rooms US$25 per person, including all three meals. On the sandy northern tip of the island, this place has four rooms with private bath and two rooms that share a bath and a kitchen. The rooms are clean and airy, with homey touches that make it the best value on the island.

Lana's (☎ 5-12036, cell 14-7451) Rooms US$40 per person, including all three meals. On the west side of the island, Lana's has four rather cramped rooms, with private toilets and shared showers. The grounds are nicely landscaped with plenty of spots for lounging. The draw here is the meals, served in a rather formal but cozy dining room. The menu changes daily, and the evening meal is served by candlelight.

Tobacco Caye Lodge (☎ 5-12033, ⓦ www .tclodgebelize.com) Singles/doubles/triples with private bath US$60/90/135, meals are included. This place has six rooms in three spacious double cabins arranged in a row on the east side of the island. The west-facing, open-air bar is a great spot to watch the sunset. It's a good value for travelers on a larger budget.

Reef's End Lodge (☎ 5-12037, 5-22419, ⓦ www.reefsendlodge.com) Singles/doubles in a two-story hotel-style building US$60/ 100, cabanas US$125; all have private bath.

Cruiser off Southwest Caye, Glover's Reef

What passes for activity on Caye Caulker

Here's one for the brochures.

Caribbean-style wooden buildings on stilts are common accommodations in the northern cayes.

Funk is alive and well on Caulker.

Peace to you, too, man.

Although packed with high-end resorts, camping on the southern cayes is also possible.

On the southwest side of the island, Tobacco Caye's priciest accommodations feature a bar and cabanas built out over the water. Its popularity proves that people are willing to pay more for an over-the-waves experience. The bar stays jolly all day and serves as nighttime activity for the entire island.

Getting There & Away Passage to Tobacco Caye can be arranged along the river near the Riverside Café in Dangriga; show up around 9:30am to organize your trip. It's likely that your boat won't leave until later, however. Cost will be approximately US$15 each way. Your accommodations can also help with your transfer to the island, or contact Captain Boxter (☎ 5-23318).

South Water Caye

Five miles (8km) south of Tobacco Caye, South Water Caye is a much more exclusive island, with resorts offering combination diving-accommodation packages. The 15-acre (6-hectare) moon-shaped island, often referred to as Water Caye by the locals, is home to three resorts. The island's flora is an interesting combination of palm and pine trees. South Water Caye Marine Reserve protects the waters and reef surrounding the island.

Blue Marlin Lodge (☎ 5-22243, fax 5-22296, ☎ 800-798-1558 in the USA, W www.bluemarlinlodge.com) Diving package around US$1450 per person, per week. On the northern end of the island, this lodge has a cozy bar that gets business from the island's other resorts. Guests can choose to stay in new wooden cabanas or some older, funkier plaster cabins, all dispersed among the manicured grounds. The Blue Marlin is affiliated with the Bonefish Hotel in Dangriga. Weeklong fishing and diving packages include double occupancy, meals and transfers.

International Zoological Expeditions Leslie Cabins (☎ 5-22119, fax 5-23152, ☎ 800-548-5843 in the USA, W www.ize2belize.com) Nestled in the middle of the island, IZE's Leslie Cabins cater mainly to student groups doing a combined study trip at South Water Caye and Blue Creek in Toledo. However,

they do rent their spacious wooden cottages to non-student groups, individuals or couples for US$951 per week, or with a diving package for US$1266 per week.

Pelican's Pouch (☎ 5-22044, fax 5-22570, W www.pelicanbeachbelize.com) Doubles US$183, double cottages US$207, meals included. The cabins here run on solar power and have composting toilets. The five lodge rooms are located in a building that once served as a convent for Belize's Sisters of Mercy. The dorm building can sleep up to 26 people in five bunk rooms.

Passage to South Water Caye is usually arranged through the resorts, although it's possible, but pricey (over US$50 one way), to pick up a boat at the Riverside Café in Dangriga.

Glover's Reef

Named for the pirate John Glover, Glover's Reef holds a handful of secluded lodges, each on its own atoll.

Manta Resort (☎ 2-32767, fax 2-32764, e info@mantaresort.com, W www.mantaresort.com) Four-night packages non-diving/diving US$835/1050, seven nights US$1495/1695. This well-run operation on the private 14-acre (5.6-hectare) Southwest Caye offers diving packages including meals and transportation. Its elegant, elevated cabins, each with dark-wood interior, fan and air-con (though you're not likely to need it), are spaced well for privacy, and the chef gets high marks. Fishing packages are also available at similar prices, and the place gets its share of anglers attracted by the ample bonefish flats.

Glover's Atoll Resort (☎ 5-12016, cell 14-8351, e glovers@btl.net) Camping US$80 per week, dorm bunk US$99, double cabins US$149. You'll see signs all over Belize touting the praises of this ramshackle backpackers' resort on 9 acres (3.6 hectares) of Northeast Caye about 20 miles (32km) from the mainland. The prices look right, but extras – water, food, equipment – can add up. A sailboat departs for the island every Sunday at 8am from the Sittee River Guesthouse (see Places to Stay in the Hopkins section, later in this chapter). The trip takes three to four hours depending on the weather (US$30). It's not for everyone, and it can be quite costly getting back to the mainland if you find it's not for you. Ask around and check the travel message boards before you head out.

Slickrock Adventures and Island Expeditions also have camps on Glover's Reef for members of their countrywide expeditions (see the Organized Tours section in the Getting Around chapter).

HOPKINS AREA
pop 1100

The Garifuna farming and fishing village of Hopkins is 4 miles (7km) east of the Southern Hwy. The village was settled in 1942 by the inhabitants of Newtown, a nearby Garifuna settlement that was destroyed by a hurricane. It was eventually named for Frederick Charles Hopkins, a Catholic priest who drowned in the waters off the village site in 1923, but for a while the settlement was know as Yugada, which in Garifuna means 'village by the sea.' The town was leveled by Hurricane Hattie in 1961, but this time the villagers stuck around and rebuilt. The town stretches about 2 miles (3.2km) along a road that runs parallel to the sea.

Although there's a good travelers' scene here, it's fairly low-key. There are a number of bars and restaurants in the area, so while you can make your own party if you wish, it's probably not a good idea to come here looking for one. Instead you'll find friendly folks, quiet surroundings, sea views and easy access to inland tours. Not to mention quick access to some of the best diving in Belize: Glover's Reef is a mere half hour by boat. Lighthouse Reef and the Blue Hole are the same distance from here as they are from Ambergris. Dolphins and manatees are spotted regularly from the beach.

Travelers appreciate this as a place to retreat and be part of another world for a while. There are lots of young families around, and at dusk the main road becomes a promenade for school-age kids and adults out enjoying the breeze and saying hello.

This is a good base if you wish to do some independent explorations. You can

kayak offshore, on the Sittee River or to the freshwater lagoon just north of the village. The Sittee River is also a popular destination with anglers and those looking to live on the river for a few days. Because Hopkins is away from the highway, it's easy and relaxing to use bikes to explore the area. You're within a half hour's drive of Cockscomb Basin Wildlife Sanctuary, where you can hike on your own or sign on with a tour.

South of town is a cluster of resorts catering to higher-end active travelers. This group and the village seem to mix well, and travelers staying in Hopkins often head south to splurge on dinner or drinks.

Activities

From Hopkins you have quick and easy access to some of Belize's best dive sites. Glover's Reef is nearly at your fingertips (a 30-minute boat ride), and the Turneffe Atoll and Lighthouse Reef and the Blue Hole can be reached from here in the same amount of time it takes to reach them from San Pedro. Diving can be arranged from the **Hamanasi Dive Shop** (☎ 5-12073) or **Second Nature Divers** (☎ 5-37038, **w** *www .belizenet.com/divers.html)*. Local two-tank dives cost around US$70, three-tank dives to Glover's Reef or Turneffe cost around US$120 or US$130, respectively, and trips to Lighthouse Reef and the Blue Hole cost around US$170. Equipment can be rented for US$20.

Bicycles, kayaks and **sailboats** can be rented for around US$7 to US$20 for a full day.

Organized Tours

Cockscomb Basin tours are the most popular of all the inland day trips from Hopkins. Tours usually include early morning walks to see birds and nature, combined with a waterfall hike and a tube float (US$50).

On trips offered by **Sittee River Canoeing & Kayaking**, boaters start on the Sittee and float down to the sea, spotting iguanas and crocodiles along the way. Thickly vegetated tributaries at the mouth of the river are ideal for bird-watching – living in the area are egrets, herons, parrots, toucans and

HOPKINS AREA

PLACES TO STAY
5 Ransom's Cabana
7 Jungle Jeanie's
8 Hopkins Inn
10 Yugada Inn
13 Tipple Tree Beya
15 Sandy Beach Lodge
16 Hamanasi Dive &
   Adventure Resort
17 Jaguar Reef Lodge
18 Pleasure Cove
19 Beaches and Dreams

PLACES TO EAT
3 Iris' Restaurant
11 Innie's Restarant

OTHER
1 Newtown Tavern
2 Laru Beya Bar
4 C&O
6 Ventura's Store
9 Francis Zuniga Tours
12 Kulcha Gift Shop
14 Watering Hole

Hopkins Rd

To Jabiru Bar,
Southern Hwy
& Dangriga

**HOPKINS
VILLAGE**

Old School
House

Catholic
Church

Basketball
Courts

0   5   1 km
0   .25   .5 mile

Approximate Scale

**CARIBBEAN
SEA**

Hopkins/Sittee River Rd

To Sittee River
Village, Southern
Hwy & Dangriga

Sittee Rd

False
Sittee
Point

SOUTHERN BELIZE

motmots. Many may enjoy this trip just for the experience of tunneling through the jungle canopy (US$50).

Mayflower is a small partially excavated ruin near Cockscomb Basin. The ruin is not much to see; it's more interesting in the summer when archaeologists are at work. The draws here are two waterfall hikes: Antelope Falls is a 100-foot (30m) waterfall, and a bracing two- to three-hour walk. The hike to Three Sisters Falls is less strenuous; it takes less than an hour to reach. There are plenty of waterholes along the way. It's

buggy out here, so be sure to bring repellent and/or long pants and closed-toed shoes (US$50).

Even more elaborate trips – as far west as San Ignacio and Xunantunich (US$100) – can be arranged.

Hotels usually make arrangements for their guests, relying on a handful of tour operators including Francis Zuniga (☎ 5-37043), who offers village walking tours along with other inland trips, and Noel Nunez (☎ 14-8686), who also conducts fishing and snorkeling trips.

Places to Stay

Hopkins Village *Sandy Beach Lodge* (☎ 5-37006, ⓔ t-travels@btl.net) Dorm bunks US$10, single/double cabins with private bath US$13/18. Owned and operated by the Sandy Beach Women's Cooperative, this place is right on the sea and serves wholesome, delicious meals. It's popular with visiting archaeologists.

Yugada Inn (☎ 5-37089) Singles US$10, doubles US$15-25, meals served on request. Rooms are on the top floor of a large, friendly family home.

Jungle Jeanie's (☎ 5-37047) Cabanas from US$20. Jeanie's has a handful of rough-hewn cabanas built on stilts and joined by elevated walkways.

Tipple Tree Beya (☎ 5-12006, ⓦ www .tippletree.net) Doubles/triples US$40/47. This place, sturdily built with natural, unpainted planks on a beautiful stretch of beach, rents three rooms with private bath, coffeemakers and refrigerators, and one beach cabin with a kitchen. The owners have a wealth of knowledge about the region and are willing to help you make the most of your stay.

Hopkins Inn (☎ 5-37013, ⓦ www.hopkins inn.com, just south of the old schoolyard) Single/double/triple cabins with private bath US$40/50/60. Near the center of town, this place has three tiled cabanas with full bath, refrigerator, coffeemaker and fan. Breakfast is served in your cabana. A catamaran is available for guests' use. One cabin has a private bedroom and a sitting area with a foldout couch; it's ideal for families.

Ransom's Cabana (ⓔ cabanabelize@hot mail.com – the only method of contact) A two-room cabana with private bath & kitchen US$15 per person, long-term deals negotiated. This is the oldest travelers' establishment in Hopkins. Cozily furnished with worn antiques and rugs – even a rusty chandelier – it has the feel of a Jazz Age writer's grotto set within a luscious tropical garden. The owner lives on the premises and prefers to rent to couples or families rather than single travelers.

South of Hopkins

One mile south of Hopkins is a cluster of high-end resorts catering to divers with an interest in inland tours. Water buffs are finding that this is a good alternative to the resort atmosphere of San Pedro. You'll still get comfort and all the luxury you're willing to pay for, but in addition you'll have quick access to inland sites and culture. The resorts are arranged around False Sittee Point and well-planned for seclusion.

Hamanasi Dive & Adventure Resort (☎ 5-12073, 877-552-3483 in the USA, ⓦ www .hamanasi.com) Beachfront or tree-house doubles US$175, suites US$230, US$15 for each extra person; packages are available. This resort is a mile south of Hopkins on the Hopkins/Sittee River Rd (continue straight where the road veers). Hamanasi, its name derived from the Garifuna name for almond tree, is a gorgeous luxury property on 400 feet (120m) of beachfront. There are eight rooms in two buildings in addition to four secluded tree-house style honeymoon cabanas. Some rooms have two bedrooms. Details include colorful Mexican-tiled bathrooms (the showers in the honeymoon cabanas are screened in), heavy wooden furniture, air-con and ceiling fans. The hacienda-style rooms have sitting rooms and private verandahs. Hamanasi bills itself as an adventure hotel, although it primarily serves divers with an interest in land-based activities. There's a large pool, and bicycles are available to guests at no charge.

Jaguar Reef Lodge (☎/fax 2-12041 in Belize City, ⓔ jaguarreef@btl.net) Double garden-view cabanas US$195, beachfront cabanas US$220, quad garden suites US$370; quad sea-view suites US$410; quad suites have two bathrooms, extra people US$20. This place consistently gets good reviews from the travel press, though it's not as exotic as its neighbors. The cabanas are arranged on spacious grounds and solidly built, with a conservative, familiar design that you would find in Hawaiian or Mexican resorts. It's good for families or wary adventurers.

Beaches and Dreams (☎ 5-37078, ⓦ www .beachesanddreams.com) Single/doubles US$105/130, including breakfast. This smaller-scale resort offers casual, down-to-earth elegance and personal service. There are four rooms in two octagonal cabanas, arranged along a private beach with a view of False Sittee Point. Kayaks and bikes are offered free of charge.

Pleasure Cove *(☎ 5-12089, ⓦ www.pleasure covelodge.com)* Doubles US$110, packages available. Somewhat tamer than its tagline 'an adults only resort' implies, this resort's five rooms are arranged motel-style around a back courtyard – the seafront is reserved for the popular restaurant. Rooms are comfortable, but the earth-toned design isn't terribly inspired.

Toucan Sittee *(☎ 5-37039)* Rooms with shared bath US$8-12 per person, double apartments US$40-55. This is a good-value budget haven located on the Sittee River, southwest of Hopkins. It's a good choice if you prefer rivers to oceans, but still want access to all the activities offered around Hopkins.

Sittee River Guesthouse *(bookings: Glover's Atoll Resort ☎ 5-12016, cell 14-8351, ⓔ glovers @btl.net)* Bunks US$5. The boat that goes to Glover's Atoll Resort picks up passengers at this guest house, and some choose to overnight here before heading for the island. The rates may seem cheap, but the accommodations are not worth a penny more.

Places to Eat

Not to be missed is a Garifuna meal prepared in a private home. A couple of families in town offer this; inquire at your hotel or at Tipple Tree Beya.

A couple of small places south of the main road include ***Innie's Restaurant*** *(☎ 5-37026)* and ***Iris' Restaurant*** *(☎ 5-37019)*. They have menus, but your best bet is to simply ask what's cooking that day; this way you'll get the best and the freshest.

The higher-priced resorts south of Hopkins all have good restaurants with meals ranging from around US$15 to US$25. Hamanasi specializes in light seafood and pasta dishes; Beaches and Dreams gets rave reviews for its fusion of European, Caribbean and Latin cuisines; Pleasure Cove and Jaguar Reef offer excellent settings and service, with conventional resort-style menus.

Entertainment

There's a high ratio of bars to people in Hopkins, so you won't go away thirsty. ***Laru Beya Bar*** (Garifuna for 'on the beach') has the only draft beer in the area and often features live entertainment; travelers can find information on the area here. The cheery ***Jabiru Bar*** is set in a large palapa off the main road into town. The ***Newtown Tavern*** and the ***Watering Hole*** are local fisherfolks' bars, but they're not averse to welcoming strangers.

Shopping

There are a number of small grocery stores in the area with a limited selection of fresh fruit and vegetables; try ***Ventura's Store*** and ***C&O***.

Drop by the ***Kulcha Gift Shop*** to browse Garifuna handicrafts. In Sittee River, check out ***Sew Much Hemp***, specializing in woven hemp clothing and handbags, and soaps and creams made with hempseed oil – very soothing after exposure to sun or bugs.

Getting There & Away

The Hopkins turnoff is at Mile 15 of the Southern Hwy; the town is another 4 miles east. Buses that travel the Hopkins and Sittee River roads leave Placencia at 5:30am and 7am and Dangriga at noon and 5:30pm. Any bus traveling the Southern Hwy will stop at the Hopkins or Sittee River junctions; you'll need to walk or hitch your way into the village.

COCKSCOMB BASIN WILDLIFE SANCTUARY

The Cockscomb Basin Wildlife Sanctuary *(Jaguar Reserve; information Belize Audubon Society ☎ 2-35004, ⓔ base@btl.net, ⓦ www .belizeaudubon.org, admission US$5)* is a prime place for watching wildlife. The varied topography and lush tropical forest within the 98,000-acre (39,000-hectare) sanctuary make it an ideal habitat for a wide variety of native Belizean fauna. Several species of wildcats – including jaguarundis, jaguars, pumas, ocelots and margays – inhabit the reserve. Among the other resident animals, many the prey of these fierce cats, are agoutis, anteaters, armadillos, Baird's tapirs, brocket deer, coatis, kinkajous, otters, pacas, peccaries and the weasel-like tayras. Snakes here include boa constrictors and the deadly poisonous fer-de-lance. There are birds galore – over 290 species have been spotted here – including toucans, parrots and, if the time is right, the rare scarlet macaw. The best wildlife spotting can be done early in the morning.

Recently, eight jaguars have been tracked in the park, evidence that the population is healthy and growing enough to coax the animal closer to human population centers. Chances are slim to none that you'll see one of these stealthy creatures, but you will see evidence of their presence – perhaps a track or two, or remains from their evening meal.

You are quite likely to meet up with a community of howler monkeys, relocated from Burrell Boom and thriving in the basin.

Cockscomb first became a protected area in 1984, and the jaguar sanctuary was created in 1986 by American Alan Rabinowitz. Controversial was the relocation of a village of Maya who were living off the land in the basin. Many of the Maya relocated from the park now live in Maya Centre and work in the park as tour guides, attendants or maintenance workers.

In the early days of the camp, jaguars were captured and tagged (Rabinowitz' original traps are displayed on the premises). Nowadays jaguars are tracked by infrared cameras placed throughout the basin – a much less intrusive way to keep track. On the drive into the park you can stop and see the remains of a plane crash that Rabinowitz survived while he was working in the area.

Loggers also lived in this area way back when, pulling mahogany, cedar and other trees from the basin. The logging camps have long since been reclaimed by the jungle, but they still appear on some maps. Their names – Go to Hell, Leave If You Can – reflect the difficulty of the work and the terrain. Artifacts left by the loggers are on display near the visitor's center.

Orientation & Information

About halfway between Dangriga and Independence is the village of Maya Centre, where a track goes 6 miles (10km) west to the sanctuary.

Paying your way into Cockscomb is a somewhat convoluted process. First, you must check in at the Craft Shop at Maya Centre to pay your entrance fee (US$5) then proceed to the park's visitor's center, where you will be required to present your receipt. Here you can also purchase a map of the park for US$1, and there are some interesting displays on the animals to be seen in the park and the history of the area.

Trails

Cockscomb has a nicely maintained 12-mile (20km) network of trails, varying in length, terrain and degree of difficulty. Most of the walks are flat along the bottom of the basin. The longest is about 2½ miles (4km), but many of the trails intertwine to form longer walks.

TOM BOYDEN

You're still most likely to see jaguars at the Belize Zoo, but in protected habitats, their numbers have grown.

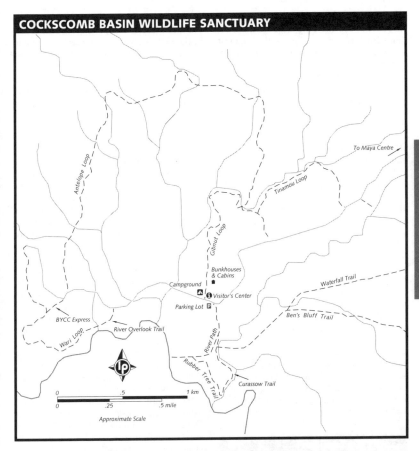

COCKSCOMB BASIN WILDLIFE SANCTUARY

To Maya Centre

SOUTHERN BELIZE

Antelope Loop

Tinamou Loop

Gibnut Loop

Waterfall Trail

Bunkhouses & Cabins

Campground

Visitor's Center

Parking Lot

BYCC Express

Ben's Bluff Trail

Wari Loop

River Overlook Trail

River Path

Rubber Tree Trail

Curassow Trail

0   .5   1 km
0   .25   .5 mile
Approximate Scale

There is a **self-guided trail** that loops together the Curassow Trail and the Rubber Tree Tail and returns along the River Path. Along the way you'll see evidence of the Mayan settlement that was abandoned in 1983. The Mayas, who practiced slash-and-burn farming, once grew plantains, sugarcane, cassava and cocoa here. Along the path is a sacred ceiba tree as well as epiphytes, bromeliads, ironwood (ziracote), strangler figs, cohune palms and rubber trees.

The River Path (0.3 miles/0.5km) and the Wari Loop (0.9 miles/1.5km) are good early-morning bets for seeing a wide variety of birds. Jaguar tracks are often spotted on the Gibnut Loop (0.9 miles/1.5km) and the short BYCC Express, which breaks from the Wari Loop to the road. The Antelope Loop (2.2 miles/3.5km) rises and falls through a variety of terrain and vegetation and offers a good sample of the geological features within the basin.

The Waterfall Trail (1.9 miles/3km) is one of the most popular trails. (Inner tubes can be rented for US$2.50 a day at the visitor's center.) Hikers are willing to endure some steep bits to be rewarded with a lovely waterfall and swimming hole at the end. Ben's Bluff (2.5 miles/4km) is the steepest and most strenuous trail, but will afford you a view of the entire basin. It's named for one of the original members of the Cockscomb Jaguar Sanctuary Project, who would make this climb daily to listen for signals from the radio transmitters that had been attached to the jaguars.

Organized Tours

Miles of the park are off-limits to visitors, including an area where there are unexcavated Mayan ruins. Tours can be arranged in Maya Centre, and are usually conducted by Mayas who lived in Cockscomb Basin and were relocated to Maya Centre when the Jaguar Reserve was created. This is an interesting dynamic; not only do they show you the animals and the history of the park, they'll also show you where they used to live, just 15 years ago. Some of the best include **Gregorio Chun** (e *tutzilnah@btl .net*, w *www.mayacenter.com*), **Julio A Saqui** (☎ 5-12042) and **Ernesto Saqui** (☎ 5-12021). Guided tours of the park average about US$25 per person, but tours, duration and rates can be customized. Night walks, early morning nature watches and tube floats on South Stann Creek can all be arranged. Chun also arranges trips to the unexcavated Mayflower ruins and waterfalls for US$135 for two to four people.

Don't Be Fooled

Victoria Peak has an imposter! There is another peak that is closer and appears to be larger than Victoria Peak, especially when looking at the mountain range from the sea. The real Victoria Peak is distinctive for its four peaks at the top. The imposter, called the Out-liar for its crime, has a rounded top. Of course, some say that Victoria Peak is itself an imposter, masquerading as Belize's highest mountain, when Doyle's Delight in Chiquibul National Park may actually be 13 feet (4m) higher.

A couple of groups, including Island Expeditions (see the Organized Tours section in the Getting Around chapter), run jungle expeditions into the basin; you take a day or two to walk in, carrying inflatable kayaks, then float down South Stann Creek. Island Expeditions also runs tours up Victoria Peak, widely considered to be Belize's highest peak at 3675 feet (1103m). The trip takes about four days and covers some serious jungle terrain.

Places to Stay & Eat

In the Park Visitor facilities at the reserve include three **campsites** (US$2.50-5 per person), a newish **dorm** area with 12 bunks in four rooms, male and female toilet facilities, solar electricity and cold-water showers (US$17 per person), and an older, more rustic **cabin** with no electricity and shared bath (bunks for US$7.50). There are also two basic **private cabins** with no electricity and shared bath (US$15 for one room with one double bed and two bunks, US$30 for two rooms with one double bed and one single bed). Moving up the budget scale there is a cushier private cabin offering a private bath with a composting toilet and solar electricity (US$45 one single bed, one double in the same room). There's a larger cabin called the White House, with eight beds, flush toilets and a private kitchen (US$50).

There are no restaurants in the park. Your cheapest option is to buy supplies in Dangriga or Hopkins and bring them with you. There is a communal kitchen on the grounds that is available for US$2.50 a day for one person, US$5 for groups of two to five, US$10 for groups of six or more. In a pinch, arrangements can be made to have food brought in from the restaurants in Maya Centre; you'll have to pay for the cost of a taxi, around US$12.

In Maya Centre *Tutzil Nah Cabins* (☎ 5-12044, w *www.mayacenter.com, Mile 13.5 Southern Hwy*) Double cabins with shared bath US$14 per night. Breakfast US$4, lunch US$6, dinner US$8. Half a mile north of the Maya Centre junction on the road's east side and run by tour guide Gregorio Chun, these new cabins are dispersed around a stretch of green grass at the edge of a citrus grove.

Nu'uk Che'il Cottages (☎ *5-12021,* e *Nuukcheil@btl.net, Mile 14 (Km 23) Southern Hwy)* Camping US$3.50, dorm bunk US$7.50, singles/doubles/triples US$18/20/27, all with shared bath. Aurora Saqui, a relative and apprentice of the legendary Don Elijio Panti of the Rainforest Medicine Trail at Ix Chel Farms – see the Cayo District (Western Belize) chapter – manages these accommodations with her husband Ernesto, who also operates tours to the park. They're located in Maya Centre off the road that leads into Cockscomb. Saqui also maintains the ***Hmen Herbal Center Medicinal Trail*** (*entrance fee US$2);* it's worth a look if you're not going to be able to make it to the Rainforest Medicine Trail in Cayo.

Mejen Tz'il's Lodge (☎ 5-12020, e *lsaqui @btl.net)* Singles/doubles with shared bath US$7.50/17.50. This lodge has basic rooms and a small dining area.

Getting There & Away
The turnoff to the park is at Mile 14 Southern Hwy. From there a dirt road leads 6 miles (10km) into the park. Any Southern Hwy bus will drop you at the entrance, but there is no public transportation into the park. Taxis can be arranged in Maya Centre (US$12.50 one way for one or two people, US$15 for three or more). A walk in will take about two hours through relatively flat terrain.

PLACENCIA
pop 501

Placencia is perched at the southern tip of a long, narrow peninsula. Long considered a backpacker's hideout, lately it's becoming one of Belize's worst-kept secrets: The location is stunning, but the village is getting a bit crowded. Getting in and out via the long, bumpy road can be trying; if you're a traveler who likes to cover a lot of territory, you may feel marooned here.

But it's a nice space to be stuck: It's home to some of the nicest beaches in Belize and has a really fun, party atmosphere. The beaches attract an international crowd looking for sun and sand, and low-key pastimes, such as swimming, sunbathing and lazing about, are the preferred 'activities' for many visitors. The food is great, and the people are friendly; you'll get to know everyone pretty quickly here as you walk up and down the narrow sidewalk. You'll feel like a local in no time.

The extra crowds in Placencia have pushed travel traffic up the peninsula, mainly to a number of high-end resorts in communities like Seine Bight and Maya Beach.

There is a well-worn track of tour options in the area, out to Laughing Bird Caye and down to the Monkey River. Travelers also make the long day trip down to Lubaantun and Nim Li Punit, near Punta Gorda.

Orientation
The town owes its layout to years gone by, when all commerce and activity was carried out by boat, so streets were of little use. The village's main north-south 'street' is actually a narrow concrete footpath about 3 feet (1m) wide that threads its way among simple wood-frame houses (some on stilts) and beachfront lodges. An unpaved road skirts the town to the west, ending at the peninsula's southern tip.

An easy walk takes you anywhere in town. From the airstrip, it's about a half mile (0.8km) south to the village and a mile (1.6km) farther to the peninsula's southern tip. North of the airstrip, past various resorts scattered along the coast, lie the villages of Seine Bight and Maya Beach, both of which are struggling to develop their own tourism infrastructures. You'll find the key directional indicators are 'on the road' and 'off the sidewalk.'

Information
The Placencia Tourist Center is staffed by friendly and helpful villagers and located right at the bus stop to catch bewildered travelers and set them off on the right foot. Good Web sites to help with planning include w www.placenciabreeze.com (the town newsletter) and w www.placencia.com.

The village has no central landmark or town square. At its south end you'll find the wharf, fuel station, bus stop and icehouse.

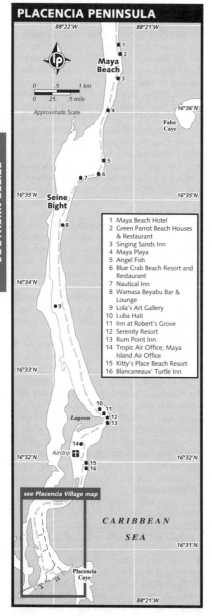

PLACENCIA PENINSULA

1 Maya Beach Hotel
2 Green Parrot Beach Houses
   & Restaurant
3 Singing Sands Inn
4 Maya Playa
5 Angel Fish
6 Blue Crab Beach Resort and
   Restaurant
7 Nautical Inn
8 Wamasa Beyabu Bar &
   Lounge
9 Lola's Art Gallery
10 Luba Hati
11 Inn at Robert's Grove
12 Serenity Resort
13 Rum Point Inn
14 Tropic Air Office; Maya
   Island Air Office
15 Kitty's Place Beach Resort
16 Blancaneaux' Turtle Inn

Atlantic Bank Limited, also on the south end of town, is open 8am to 2pm Monday to Friday. You can check your email at Jake's Purple Space Monkey Internet Café (☎ 6-24094) for US$2.50/15 minutes, US$6/hour. It's open 7am to midnight and has an espresso machine – a rare and welcome sight in southern Belize.

The police can be reached at ☎ 6-23129.

Laundry service is available from most of the hotels and guest houses on the peninsula for US$5 a load.

The village hospital (☎ 6-23326) is in the center of town behind the school.

There's yoga at the Dockside Bar from 8am to 9am Monday, Wednesday and Friday; it's led by Bianca Barkan (☎ 6-23172), who also does massage.

Diving

The barrier reef is 20 miles (32km) offshore from Placencia, and there's little boat traffic beyond the tour boats beating a wake between the village and the reef (45 minutes from dock to plunge). The reef is wider here than in points north, with plenty of dramatic walls, canyons and swim-throughs. In addition to the fanciful coral formations is the myriad of sealife living here relatively undisturbed. For those craving charismatic macro-fauna, there is the **Shark Hole** about 38 miles (61km) from Placencia. This formation was an underwater cave many moons ago, but part of the ceiling collapsed, forming an entrance for fish, sharks and, now, interested divers. The entrance is at a depth of 42 feet (12.6m).

Glover's Reef is a popular site for divers and takes about 2½ hours to reach from Placencia (see that section, earlier in this chapter, for a description).

Whale sharks can be seen at **Gladden Spit & Silk Cayes Marine Reserve**, north of Placencia, up to 10 days after the full moon, April through June. What attracts the whale sharks is the same thing that attracts divers and snorkelers – lots of species of fish. Only, the whale sharks aren't interested in seeing the fish, they're interested in the eggs of the fish, which spawn in great quantity after the full moon.

Inner-reef dives are better for beginning divers, since the water is calmer; there's plenty of marine life to see. Outer-reef dives present a more dramatic landscape of walls and canyons.

Dive Operators Seahorse Diving (☎ 6-23166), Natural Mystic Dive Shop (☎ 6-23182) and Advance Diving Services (☎ 6-24037) offer dive trips to the local reef, usually around Laughing Bird Caye. North of the village, Rum Point Inn, Robert's Grove and the Nautical Inn also have highly professional dive shops (see Places to Stay).

Two-tank dives cost around US$75, trips to the Shark Hole US$100, and whale-shark expeditions US$150. Certification is offered for US$350, including four open-water dives. Intervals on these dives are usually off one of the cayes. Inner-reef stops include Laughing Bird or Moho Cayes; outer-reef stops include Ranguana Caye and the Silk Cayes. Trips to Glover's Reef cost around US$100. Plan on an additional US$25 for gear.

Organized Tours

Vying to sign up customers for tours of the sort listed below are **Ocean Motion Guide Service** (☎ 6-23363, 6-23162) and **Nite Wind Guide Service** (☎ 6-23487, 6-23176), both operating out of small offices near the boat dock.

For inland tours, check with **Toadal Adventure** (☎ 6-23207, fax 6-23334), operating out of Deb & Dave's Last Resort, or with **Kitty's Place** (☎ 6-23227, e kittys@btl.net). Kevin Modera Guide Services (☎ 6-23243, w www.kevinmodera.com) offers fishing tours as well as inland adventures; check out the Web site, which gives a great overview of what's going on about town. **Clive Garbutt** (☎ 16-6715, 16-3323) offers the best Monkey River tour; the trips are usually consolidated to him from the tour operators in town. His family owns the restaurant where most tours stop for lunch.

Places to Stay

Budget and mid-range accommodations are in the village (you're likely to get a beachside cabana, but your neighbor will be just a

Placencia Tours: A Rundown

The following are some of the tours available from Placencia, along with ballpark prices.

Snorkeling or sea kayaking around **Laughing Bird Caye**, **Ranguana Caye** or the **Silk Cayes** usually includes a beach barbecue and some on-land explorations. There are a number of sites visited by boats in the area; the inner-reef sites are better for you if you're not a strong swimmer, the outer-reef sites offer more variety and drama – deeper water, bigger fish (US$45).

You could go bird-watching or try a tube float in the **Cockscomb Basin Wildlife Sanctuary** (US$55).

A trip up the **Monkey River** includes a short sea cruise south to the river's mouth, a trip upriver to see howler monkeys and crocodiles, then nature-viewing and a walk through Monkey River Village and a spin back out to sea to look for manatees (US$45).

A long day trip to the Mayan ruins of **Nim Li Punit** or **Lubaantun** will sometimes include a stop at Blue Creek Cave (US$70).

On a trip to the forests surrounding the village of **Red Bank** you'll see a seasonal population of scarlet macaws, an increasingly rare sight in Central America. For more information, contact the Programme for Belize office (☎ 2-75616, fax 2-75635 in Belize City) or inquire at hotels or guide services in Placencia (US$60).

A kayak tour through the **lagoon side of Placencia** features an educational talk on the ecosystem of the mangroves, plenty of birds on display and, if you're lucky, manatees and dolphins (US$20).

Custom overnight and multi-day trips can be a arranged. Gaining in popularity is a castaway tour, where you can be dropped off on a caye to spend the night in solitude. For more information on these tours contact Kitty's Resort.

couple of feet away); top-end places are north along the beach. Most hotels in the village are small and family-run, reflecting the interests and personality of the owners.

SOUTHERN BELIZE

PLACENCIA VILLAGE

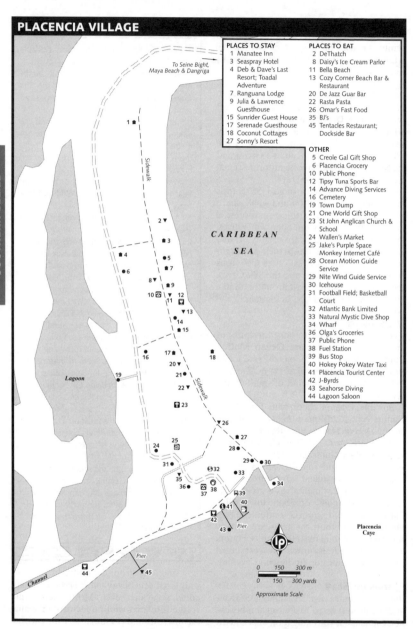

To Seine Bight,
Maya Beach & Dangriga

Sidewalk

CARIBBEAN
SEA

Lagoon

Sidewalk

Pier

Placencia
Caye

Pier

Channel

0   150   300 m
0   150   300 yards

Approximate Scale

PLACES TO STAY
1 Manatee Inn
3 Seaspray Hotel
4 Deb & Dave's Last
   Resort; Toadal
   Adventure
7 Ranguana Lodge
9 Julia & Lawrence
   Guesthouse
15 Sunrider Guest House
17 Serenade Guesthouse
18 Coconut Cottages
27 Sonny's Resort

PLACES TO EAT
2 DeThatch
8 Daisy's Ice Cream Parlor
11 Bella Beach
13 Cozy Corner Beach Bar &
   Restaurant
20 De Jazz Guar Bar
22 Rasta Pasta
26 Omar's Fast Food
35 BJ's
45 Tentacles Restaurant;
   Dockside Bar

OTHER
5 Creole Gal Gift Shop
6 Placencia Grocery
10 Public Phone
12 Tipsy Tuna Sports Bar
14 Advance Diving Services
16 Cemetery
19 Town Dump
21 One World Gift Shop
23 St John Anglican Church &
   School
24 Wallen's Market
25 Jake's Purple Space
   Monkey Internet Café
28 Ocean Motion Guide
   Service
29 Nite Wind Guide Service
30 Icehouse
31 Football Field; Basketball
   Court
32 Atlantic Bank Limited
33 Natural Mystic Dive Shop
34 Wharf
36 Olga's Groceries
37 Public Phone
38 Fuel Station
39 Bus Stop
40 Hokey Pokey Water Taxi
41 Placencia Tourist Center
42 J-Byrds
43 Seahorse Diving
44 Lagoon Saloon

SOUTHERN BELIZE

Placencia Village *Seaspray Hotel (☎/fax 6-23148, ⓦ www.belizenet.com/seaspray)* Double rooms & one cabana US$25-55. Right in the village center on the beach, this is the backpacker favorite. Seaspray has accommodations with shared or private bath (and hot water). The more expensive rooms are larger and have porches and sea views, and there's one deluxe cabana on the beach. The variety of rooms offered assures that you'll meet travelers from all over and all budgets.

Julia & Lawrence Guesthouse (☎ 6-23185) Singles/doubles with shared bath US$13/18, with private bath US$35/40. This guest house is central and clean. It's in a congested part of the village; rooms with shared bath are in an older back building, and newer higher-end rooms have sea views.

Sunrider Guest House (☎ 6-23486) Singles/doubles/triples with private bath US$18/23/28, one room with kitchenette US$30. One of the oldest hotels on the strip, Sunrider has a good location, although the rooms in this green two-level building facing the beach are worse for wear.

Deb & Dave's Last Resort (☎ 6-23297, fax 6-23334, ⓔ debanddave@btl.net) Singles/doubles with shared bath US$16/22. This resort, on the lagoon side of the peninsula, stays quieter than the beach places. The award-winning Toadal Adventures is run from here, so it's a good place to be if you want excellent information on what's going on in the area. Rooms are plain and snug.

Sonny's Resort (☎ 6-23103) Double cabins from US$22. Cabins here are made from a variety of materials and arranged around a courtyard perpendicular to the beach. It's expensive for what you get.

Cozy Corner (☎ 6-23280) This friendly place has modern, spacious rooms arranged motel-style around a sociable wraparound porch. The bar-restaurant is one of Placencia's primary social centers, so there's a lot of foot traffic during the day and evening, although the 10pm closing time is strict.

Manatee Inn (☎ 6-24083, ⓦ www.manatee inn.com) Singles/doubles/triples US$35/40/45. The newest hotel in Placencia, this is a charming and roomy two-level hotel on the west side of the sidewalk. There's a wide verandah good for catching breezes. The rooms have ceiling fans, and there's unfinished wood inside and out.

Serenade Guesthouse (☎ 6-23163, fax 6-23164, ⓔ serenade@btl.net) Rooms on the ground floor US$35, upper level rooms US$40, all with air-con. This is a big, new, white building on the west side of the sidewalk. The location is good, though the atmosphere is rather bland and the staff disorganized.

Ranguana Lodge (☎/fax 6-23112, ⓦ www .ranguanabelize.com) Doubles with shower US$50-60. This lodge has five attractive, good-sized mahogany cabins, but they're packed tightly together. Each room has a fan, refrigerator, coffeemaker and balcony. The more expensive rooms have sea views. Registration is in the Creole Gal gift shop next door, which is not staffed at night. The sea views from the porch are inspiring, but the noise from the wind here can be disruptive if you're a light sleeper.

Coconut Cottages (☎/fax 6-23234, ⓔ kw placencia@yahoo.com) Two simple, solid beachside cottages, doubles US$55. Management is not on the premises, so this is more a rental than a guest-house arrangement.

North of the Village Most of the lodging north of the village tends to be expensive destination-style resorts, but they're very satisfying, with tropical-isle ambience. All offer various water sports, activities and local excursions.

Blancaneaux' Turtle Inn (☎ 6-23244, fax 6-23245, ⓦ www.turtleinn.com) Single/double/triple cabanas set back from the sea US$110/150/175; beachfront cabanas US$175/210/235; single/double/triple/quad two-bedroom villa US$225/250/275/300. Francis Ford Coppola purchased this long-time favorite resort to offer his luxury-loving followers a beachside alternative to Blancaneaux in Cayo. It's a good choice: It has spacious grounds, rustic luxury and only a handful of cabanas, allowing for personal service by the attentive and well-trained staff. Spacious beachfront cabanas have a sitting area; lower-priced cabanas are set back from the sea and elevated to help air-circulation – they're slightly smaller and more rustic-looking. While Blancaneaux has more of an Italian feel to it, Turtle Inn has a meld of Mayan and Indonesian furnishings. There are future plans to add a pool to the grounds and Bali-style bathrooms where toilet, sink and showers are arranged in a private garden attached to the cabana.

Kitty's Place Beach Resort (☎ 6-23227, fax 6-23226, e *kittys@btl.net*, w *www.kittysplace.com*) Rooms with shared bath US$35/45 single/double, rooms with private bath US$75/100, deluxe beachfront cabins US$100/140. This Caribbean Victorian beachfront lodge, north of the village, is the longtime favorite for high-end travelers. Guests return year after year, and you'll find lots of personal recommendations and superlatives for this place. There are a variety of rooms to choose from, the best being the beachfront cabana suites with separate sleeping areas, tiled floors and gracious verandahs. In the standard category the garden rooms are the way to go. 'Garden' here isn't a euphemism for no view – the landscaping is lush, lovely and private, and there's a nice deck for bird-watching.

Rum Point Inn (☎ 6-23239, fax 6-23240, e *rupel@btl.net*) Singles/doubles/triples US$123/144/173. Meal packages US$30 per person. Open since 1974, this is Placencia's oldest resort. Guests can stay in mushroom-shaped stucco cabanas, designed with numerous small screened windows for optimum ventilation, but sometimes criticized for lack of privacy as there are no shutters. For the more modest, there are more conventional cabanas, winding through thick gardens and sandy walkways. Amenities include a library and pool.

Serenity Resort (☎ 6-23232, fax 6-23231) Doubles US$80. Conventional hotel and cabin rooms are offered here, all slightly worn around the edges, but still comfortable and spacious.

Inn at Robert's Grove (☎ 6-23565, fax 6-23567, w *www.robertsgrove.com*) Doubles US$150, suites US$175. This inn has modern and spacious rooms, beautiful grounds, a swimming pool, rooftop hot tubs and a tennis court. A dive shop is on site, and tours to all local attractions can be arranged. Shiny and new, this innovative place has shaken up the establishment by offering world-class service, but still staying in touch with the culture and feel of Belize. It's popular with Belize's elite.

Luba Hati (☎ 6-23402, fax 6-23403, e *lubahati@btl.net*, w *www.lubahati.com*) Singles US$120-150, doubles US$150-180. Meal packages US$40 per person. This place was designed as an Italian villa and built with Caribbean hardwoods, stucco and ceramic tile. Rooms in the main building have their own terrace and sea view. Cabanas offer more privacy and have open-air showers. Franco's restaurant has quite a following for successfully combining Italian and Caribbean cuisines.

Seine Bight *Nautical Inn* (☎ 6-23595, fax 6-23594, e *nautical@btl.net*, w *www.nautical innbelize.com*) Singles/doubles US$105/125. Proprietors Ben and Janie Ruoti are equipped for all adventures at this small, modern resort in Seine Bight. They provide independent-minded guests free use of bikes, snorkels, sailboats and kayaks and run daily diving expeditions and coastal tours. There are 12 comfortable rooms, and meal packages are available, offering guests a varied menu ranging from Southwestern US to Continental cuisine. If the buildings seem out of place, it's because the entire hotel was shipped down from Florida and assembled here back when building materials were harder to come by. There's a swimming pool and a pleasant deck and beach area.

Blue Crab Beach Resort (☎ 6-23544, e *kerry@btl.net*) Single/double cabanas US$60/85, rooms with air-con US$70/95. Meal plans US$35 per person. This tranquil, family-run place offers a couple levels of accommodations – rustic thatched-roof cabanas or modern cabins for those who prefer more hermetic lodging. Be sure to stop in to say hi to Bubbles the coatimundi. There's an excellent, though expensive, small restaurant here.

Angel Fish (☎ 16-7079) Doubles US$60. A new set of six cabanas on the beach, this is a good, simple, family-run place with ample grounds. Meal plans are available.

Maya Beach *Maya Playa* (☎ 6-37020, e *mayaplaya@btl.net*) Doubles US$60. Three thatched-roof cabanas – drafty and slightly worse for wear, but imaginatively built – have a loft bedroom accessed by a ladder and open-air bathrooms, Bali style. Barbecues, a kitchen, kayaks and bicycles are free to guests. It has a rough, hippie charm.

Singing Sands Inn (☎/fax 6-22243, w *www .singingsands.com*) Singles/doubles US$80/ 115. Six thatched-roof cabanas with rough mahogany interiors run perpendicular to the beach in an overgrown-garden setting. Some may be put off by the 'beware of dogs' signs, but they accompany fairly harmless canines.

Green Parrot Beach Houses (☎/fax 6-22488, w *www.greenparrot-belize.com*) Cabanas US$125, including breakfast & airport transfers. This place has six split-level, mahogany cabanas with loft bedrooms, kitchenettes and living rooms with foldout couches. Two honeymoon cabanas are set off from the rest of the resort so you'll have your own stretch of beach and an open-air shower.

Maya Beach Hotel (☎ 6-12040, w *www .mayabeach.com*) Under new ownership, this retreat is cheerful and comfortable. Each room is uniquely and colorfully decorated and furnished with good mattresses and thick cotton sheets.

Places to Eat

Omar's Fast Food (☎ 6-23236) Prices US$3-7. Open 7am-10pm Sun-Fri, closed Sat. Omar's offers homemade food. Try the cheap, good burritos or higher-priced menu items like conch steak (US$9).

Cozy Corner Beach Bar & Restaurant (☎ 6-23315) Prices US$3-8. Open 11am-10pm Mon-Sat, closed Sun. This place is popular all day long, and it's a good bet for an off-hour meal. It stays open for drinks until around 10pm; you can usually count on a crowd here.

Rasta Pasta (☎ 6-23479) Breakfast from US$4, dinner US$7-12. Open for breakfast 6:30am-noon, for dinner 5pm-9pm Wed-Mon.

(Closed for lunch, but pack lunches can be arranged.) Recently relocated after many years on Ambergris Caye, the folks at Rasta Pasta know what travelers want and don't mind giving it to them. The brewed coffee is the best you'll find in town. The menu changes daily, but, as the name suggests, there is always a selection of pasta on the menu, usually prepared with fresh vegetables. No beef or pork is served. Devotees return night after night.

BJ's (☎ 6-23202) Dishes US$5. Open 7am-10pm Mon-Sat, 7am-3pm Sun. Just south of the football field off the road into town, this is a good stop for low-priced Belizean food and friendly service.

Daisy's Ice Cream Parlor (☎ 6-21134) Meals US$7-10. Open 7am-10:30pm daily. Daisy's, in the center of town, west off the central pathway, serves meals (like burgers, US$2) as well as ice cream and other desserts. There's a pleasant patio area.

De Jazz Guar Bar (☎ 6-23163) Meals US$5-10. Open 7am-9pm daily. A juice bar, regular bar and restaurant just west of the sidewalk, this place is often full.

DeThatch (☎ 6-24011) Dishes US$2-4. DeThatch is small bar on the beach serving drinks and some meals, including delicious fish burritos (US$3.50).

Tentacles Restaurant (☎ 6-23333) Dinners US$7-15. Open 6pm-10pm Mon-Sat. This breezy, atmospheric place with its popular **Dockside Bar** built on a wharf out over the water is a favorite for the evening meal, although the traditional Belizean meals and seafood aren't very innovative.

Bella Beach (☎ 14-7013) Meals US$15-20. Open 4pm-10pm Wed-Mon. The sidewalk strip's most upmarket eatery, this place serves excellent seafood pastas and other Italian specialties, prepared almost traditionally, with lots of peppers and onions. Food is served in an open-air palapa. You'll pay US prices, but don't expect quick service. There's a good selection of Italian wines, and the bar serves up tropical drinks as well.

Blancaneaux' Turtle Inn (☎ 6-23244, north of the village) Mains US$12-25. Open for dinner 6pm-10pm daily. A touch of Italy, via northern California, this is your best bet for upscale pastas, seafood and wood-fired-oven pizzas. Dining is at a large beachside palapa, and there's a distinctive excavated bar where you'll sit in low beach chairs, face to face with the bartender. Reservations are suggested.

Blue Crab *(☎ 6-23544, Seine Bight)* Prices US$17-20. This place has unusual hand-crafted, Asian-inspired dishes served in a tiny, charming dining room. Reservations are required.

Entertainment
The bulletin board at the Placencia Tourist Center is a good spot to find information about special events happening on the peninsula.

Tipsy Tuna's Sports Bar Open 6pm-midnight Mon-Fri, 2pm-midnight Sat-Sun. In an imposing concrete building on the ocean side of the sidewalk, this is the newest game in town – and it's not limited to sports-watching. Special events, theme nights and live entertainment are often on the roster. There is a cluster of beach chairs in the front where you're welcome to sit, even if you're not imbibing.

Sunrise Bar is the local Rasta hangout. Un-escorted women have complained that the male clientele is often too forward for comfort; indeed female travelers will be put through a verbal gauntlet just by walking past.

J-Byrds *(☎ 6-23412),* open 9am to 10pm daily, is a lively fishermen's bar, right on the water at the tip of the peninsula.

Dockside Bar *(☎ 6-23333)* Open 11am-11pm daily. Over the water at the end of the Tentacles Restaurant, it's a pleasant spot that gets lively during NFL football and Club League soccer games and serene during morning yoga (9am Monday, Wednesday and Friday). There's a barbecue here on Sunday afternoon.

Kitty's *(☎ 6-23237)* has a high-end Mayan barbecue on Sunday night and a chicken drop on Friday night at 9pm. (You can buy your tickets in advance at the Placencia Tourist Center).

Nautical Inn *(☎ 6-23595)* serves a Garifuna meal with punta lessons, Garifuna

drumming and coconut bowling on Wednesday. Reservations by Wednesday noon required.

The ***Lagoon Saloon*** *(☎ 6-23289)* Open noonish-8pm Wed-Mon, closed Tues. This is a lively place on the lagoon side of town and a good spot for watching the sunset. Kayaks and canoes are available for rent.

Bands often play at ***Wamasa Beyabu Bar and Lounge*** *(☎ 6-24096, Seine Bight).* Thursday is Ladies Night.

Shopping
There are a handful of grocery stores off the Placencia Village road: ***Olga's Groceries*** *(☎ 6-23335),* open 7am-7:30pm daily, closed noon-1:30pm; ***Placencia Grocery*** *(☎ 6-23423),* and ***Wallen's Market*** *(☎ 6-23128).*

There are a number of gift shops up and down the sidewalk with the usual Belizeana. Notable for good selection and variety are ***One World Gift Shop*** *(☎ 6-23113)* and ***Creole Gal Gift Shop*** *(☎ 6-23451).* In Seine Bight, ***Lola's Art Gallery*** *(☎ 16-6391),* open 8am to 6pm, is worth a stop. You'll see Lola's colorful paintings in hotels and restaurants throughout the village. She's in great demand, and you can commission her to create a painting for you, but there may be a wait for it.

Getting There & Away
Air Maya Island Air and Tropic Air offer daily flights linking Placencia with Dangriga and Belize City to the north and Punta Gorda to the south. For details see the Getting Around chapter. The village begins a half mile (0.8km) south of the airstrip; taxis meet most flights (US$2.50 into town). If you're staying at one of the pricier resorts, ask to be picked up.

Bus Be aware that not all buses traveling the Southern Hwy make the Placencia Peninsula trip. From Dangriga buses go to Placencia at 12:15pm, 3:30pm and 5:15pm. The return trip is made at 5:30am, 6:30am and 1:30pm Monday to Saturday, 7am and 1:30pm Sunday. See the Getting Around chapter for details.

Boat There is a way to get to and from Placencia without grabbing a specific Placencia bus. Monday to Saturday, the *Hokey Pokey Water Taxi* (US$5) departs Placencia at 10am for Mango Creek, and makes the return trip at 2:30pm and 4pm. Many boats will do a charter run to or from Mango Creek for US$20 for up to six people. So, if you hop on any bus taking the Southern Hwy route that will reach Independence by 2:30pm, it's a short walk (less than 10 minutes) from the Independence bus stop to the Mango Creek water-taxi dock. This method can also, of course, be applied for passengers leaving Placencia as well, but it's more advisable if you're traveling south.

The *Gulf Cruza* (☎ 2-24506 or 6-23236) makes a Placencia-Big Creek-Puerto Cortés (Honduras) run on Friday. Call for details. The boat takes passengers only, no vehicles.

Getting Around

At press time the Placencia Shuttle Service had been discontinued. Visitors staying north of town must now rely on taxis or hotel transportation to get them to and from the village, although many of the northern resorts make bicycles available to guests. Taxi services include Papa's (☎ 6-23288, 14-7888), Brad's (☎ 16-4043) and Major Mac (☎ 6-23515). Taxis north to the airstrip will cost around US$5 per person, to Seine Bight US$10, to Maya Beach US$15. The price is negotiable for large groups.

You can rent bicycles for US$15 a day at Jake's Purple Space Monkey (☎ 6-24094) and at Deb & Dave's Last Resort. Placencia Auto Rental (☎ 14-7252, 14-9687) rents vehicles for US$85 for 24 hours.

PUNTA GORDA
pop 4329

The Southern Hwy ends at Punta Gorda, the southernmost town of size in Belize. Rainfall and humidity are at their highest and the jungle at its lushest here in the Toledo District. Prepare yourself for at least a short downpour almost daily and some sultry weather in between. This is the most remote, least explored part of the country, and getting around can be an expensive hassle, but it's a wonderland for the truly adventurous.

Known throughout Belize simply as 'PG,' this sleepy town was founded for the Garifunas who emigrated from Honduras in 1832. In 1866, after the US Civil War, some Confederate veterans received land grants from the British government and founded a settlement here, but it didn't endure.

Though still predominantly Garifuna, PG is also home to the typical bewildering variety of Belizean citizenry: Creoles, Kekchi Maya, Mopan Maya, Chinese and East Indians. There is also a healthy dose of expat Americans, Brits and Canadians in the area teaching and working with aid organizations. Fishing was the town's major livelihood for almost two centuries, but now farming is becoming equally important, as surrounding Mayan villages develop methods for sustainable agriculture.

This is an area where you can meet living Maya and witness firsthand how their ancient culture exists in modern times. Discussion is constant in the cafés and hotels about how to preserve the rich and treasured Mayan cultures in the region while protecting the rain forest from the deforestation of slash-and-burn farming.

One of the tactics has been to educate the Maya about modern ecological techniques and impress upon them the fragility of their environment. Rather than merely living off the land and consuming it in the process, the Maya are now learning methods for sustainable agriculture and working to create a system of tourism that keeps profits local. The concept is ambitious, but the level of dedication exhibited by the people of the area indicates that sustainability, growth and prosperity may all be possible.

There's not really much to do in town, but PG once served as an R&R center for the British Army, so there are plenty of hotels set up that once catered to the needs of soldiers. When the army left in 1992 the economy of the town changed dramatically, and tourism became less of a factor. The

SOUTHERN BELIZE

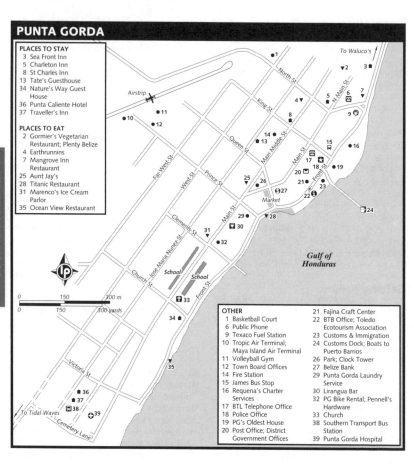

PUNTA GORDA

PLACES TO STAY
3 Sea Front Inn
5 Charleton Inn
8 St Charles Inn
13 Tate's Guesthouse
34 Nature's Way Guest House
36 Punta Caliente Hotel
37 Traveller's Inn

PLACES TO EAT
2 Gormier's Vegetarian Restaurant; Plenty Belize
4 Earthrunnins
7 Mangrove Inn Restaurant
25 Aunt Jay's
28 Titanic Restaurant
31 Marenco's Ice Cream Parlor
35 Ocean View Restaurant

OTHER
1 Basketball Court
6 Public Phone
9 Texaco Fuel Station
10 Tropic Air Terminal; Maya Island Air Terminal
11 Volleyball Gym
12 Town Board Offices
14 Fire Station
15 James Bus Stop
16 Requena's Charter Services
17 BTL Telephone Office
18 Police Office
19 PG's Oldest House
20 Post Office; District Government Offices
21 Fajina Craft Center
22 BTB Office; Toledo Ecotourism Association
23 Customs & Immigration
24 Customs Dock; Boats to Puerto Barrios
26 Park; Clock Tower
27 Belize Bank
29 Punta Gorda Laundry Service
30 Lirangua Bar
32 PG Bike Rental; Pennell's Hardware
33 Church
38 Southern Transport Bus Station
39 Punta Gorda Hospital

Gulf of Honduras

next incarnation of tourism for Punta Gorda – and indeed all of Toledo – appears to be aimed toward adventurous tourists interested in making PG the base for their excursions inland to the Mayan archaeological sites at Lubaantun and Nim Li Punit, and to the Mayan villages scattered throughout the area, and for active pursuits within the almost virgin rain forest that engulfs the region. Toledo has enormous potential in the ecotourism realm, and pundits predict that once the Southern Hwy is completed, tour operations will thrive to

rival their counterparts in Cayo. But you won't see masses of tourists here yet, which is a blessing and a curse, especially for budget travelers. The upside is, of course, that you get a less crowded, less packaged experience. The downside is that it's difficult and expensive to make arrangements, since the traffic isn't in place to support an organized tourist infrastructure. If you're coming here bring lots of patience, lots of money and/or lots of people so that you'll be able to afford the wealth of activities that are available. Planning ahead is key.

Orientation & Information

The town center is a triangular park with a bandstand and a distinctive blue-and-white clock tower. Saturday is market day, when area villagers come to town to buy, sell and barbecue. It's a fascinating and colorful mix. The town's oldest building is on Front St across from the police office. Erected in Punta Gorda in 1895, this dismantled English home made of cypress was brought over as ballast on a sugarcane trading ship. Notice the high-pitched roof, perfect to keep the snow off!

The Belize Tourism Board office (☎ 7-22531), on Front St, is open 8am to 5pm Tuesday to Sunday (closed for the noon hour). Staff are friendly and helpful, and there are numerous postings on the office walls to give you an idea of what's going on in Punta Gorda. Nature's Way Guest House (☎ 7-22119, 65 N Front St) serves as an unofficial information center for travelers.

Belize Bank, at Main and Queen Sts across from the town square, is open 8am to 1pm Monday to Thursday, 8am to 4:30pm Friday; cash advances are US$5.

The Punta Gorda post office, on Front St, is open 8am to 5pm Monday to Thursday, 8am to 4:30pm Friday (closed during the noon hour).

Earthrunnins (☎ 7-22007), 11 Main Middle St, is the town's Internet café and a meeting place for happening expats and sophisticated townspeople.

Punta Gorda Laundry Service is at 2 Prince St and charges US$1.50 per pound.

The Punta Gorda Hospital (☎ 7-22026) is on Main St between Victoria St and Cemetery Lane.

The Punta Gorda police can be reached at ☎ 7-22022.

Organized Tours

Unless you supply your own crowd, you're likely to be the only party interested in a tour that day, so essentially what you'll be doing is arranging a charter, not signing on for a group tour. And while there are numerous tour operators in town, most of them have other jobs as well, so arrangements must be made well in advance.

Expect to spend US$100 to US$150 a day for a tour for up to four people. Boats can be chartered for US$300 per day and usually accommodate six to eight people.

It is possible to explore the area on your own if you have your own transportation, but the sites around here, especially the Mayan villages, are going to be more interesting if you take a guide. Arrangements for this are best made in advance, although there is a chance that you can arrange a tour on the spot when you reach your destination.

Tours can be arranged through your hotel, or through the following tour operators. See the Around Punta Gorda section for descriptions of the sites covered in tours.

Desmond Pratt *(☎ 7-22833)* Pratt offers tours to Forest Home, former site of the Confederate army settlement, as well as nature walks.

Green Iguana Eco & Sea Adventures *(☎ 7-22475, 18-0431, **w** www.ecoiguana.com)* You can arrange both land and sea tours that are mostly activity-based adventures.

Plenty Belize *(☎ 7-22929, **w** www.plenty.org, Vernon St)* can arrange bird-watching tours in the Mayan villages, operated by locals – another effort to encourage villagers to develop income outside of slash-and-burn farming.

TIDE *(☎ 7-22129, **w** www.belizeecotours.org)* This is a new venture in southern Belize offering packaged tours and touting sustainable tourism. While they're not particularly accommodating for walk-ins, and not interested in cultivating a budget-traveler following, the packages they put together have received rave reviews.

Wild Encounters *(☎ 7-22300, at the Sea Front Inn)* This outfit specializes in nature-viewing and tours of the Mayan villages.

Places to Stay

Nature's Way Guest House (☎ 7-22119, 65 Front St) Singles/doubles/triples US$10/15/20, all with shared shower. This converted house is the intrepid travelers' gathering place. Trips by minibus and boat can be arranged to all points of interest around PG.

*Tate's Guesthouse (☎/fax 7-22186, **e** teach @btl.net, 34 Jose Maria Nunez St)* Rooms from US$12-37. Costlier rooms have air-con and kitchenettes. This is a shipshape establishment on a quiet street; the rooms are simple and comfortable.

St Charles Inn (☎/fax 7-22149, 23 King St), with singles/doubles with private bath and fan for US$15/20, and *Charleton Inn (☎ 7-22197, fax 7-22008, e charlein@btl.net, 9 Main St)*, with singles/doubles with fan for US$12/17, rooms on the top floor for US$20/25, with air-con US$25/30, are owned by the same family. Both offer good value for the money, and the rooms are clean and well kept. These places often fill up with tour or study groups.

Punta Caliente Hotel (☎ 7-22561, 108 Jose Maria Nunez St) Singles/doubles with bath & fan US$20/25. This hotel, near the Southern Transport bus station, has a good restaurant on the ground floor and well-priced rooms above. Each room has good ventilation.

Tidal Waves (☎ 7-22111, e bills_tidal waves@yahoo.com) Tent sites US$5 per person, rooms US$19-24, cabana with breakfast US$49. This retreat, on the sea at the south edge of town, has a range of accommodations. The two rooms include access to a kitchenette.

Sea Front Inn (☎ 7-22300, fax 7-22682, e seafront@btl.net, Front St) Doubles with private bath US$50-79. North of the town center, the newest hotel on offer is a ramshackle arrangement of wood and stone that towers above the rest of the town's buildings. It's the first choice for travelers willing to pay for a little more comfort. The rooms have cable TV and air-con.

Traveller's Inn (☎ 7-22568, fax 7-22814, Jose Maria Nunez St) Singles/doubles with private bath US$50/60. This inn is at the southern end of the street, next to the Southern Transport bus station. You get a modern – if stodgy – air-conditioned room with cable TV; breakfast is included. There's secured parking as well.

Places to Eat

Earthrunnins (☎ 7-22007, 11 Main Middle St) Meals US$3.50-6. Open 7am-10pm Wed-Mon, closed Tues. This cheerful place, functioning as a bar, restaurant and Internet café, attracts locals, expats and travelers alike. The low-priced menu features Belizean dishes and simply prepared specials like hummus,

burritos, burgers and sandwiches. There's a small dining room and a nice patio with hammocks. It's the best place in PG for morning coffee. Internet access is US$2.50/half hour, US$4/hour.

Gormier's Vegetarian Restaurant (☎ 7-22929, Vernon St) Prices US$3-4. Open for lunch only. Gormier's serves simple and delicious vegetarian dishes, soy drinks and fruit juices. Tofu made on the premises!

Punta Caliente (☎ 7-22561, 108 Jose Maria Nunez) Prices US$3.50-5. The restaurant at this hotel serves stewed pork, fish fillet, beans and rice with chicken and similar dishes. The interior dining room has Garifuna photos and artifacts on display.

Aunt Jay's (☎ 7-22756) Prices US$5-7. Open 7am-3pm & 6pm-10pm Mon-Fri, 7am-10pm Sat, 7am-10:30am for breakfast only Sun. Opposite the clock tower, this dining spot is popular with locals.

Marenco's Ice Cream Parlor (☎ 7-22572) Cones US$1, Meals US$2.50-6. Open 9:30am-2pm & 5:30pm-10pm daily. A pleasant outdoor spot on Main St, Marenco's serves homemade ice cream and respectable rice-and-bean plates. The staff even wears cheery ice-cream-parlor outfits.

Titantic Restaurant This place is built upstairs over the market, and you'll pay a higher rate for the sea view here, but only slightly higher. The food is dependably Belizean – chicken, rice and beans is your best bet.

Mangrove Inn Restaurant (☎ 7-39910, Front St) Prices US$6-8. Mangrove serves up fresh fish specials daily, good Mexican food and quite possibly the best fried chicken in Belize.

Ocean View Restaurant Prices US$3-6. Open 9am-2pm & 5pm-10pm daily. On stilts out over the water south of the market, this restaurant has traditional Belizean food served with a can't-be-beat view.

Punta Gorda Pizza (☎ 7-22574) US$12 for a large. Open Thur-Sat. You can order OK pizza for takeout only here; there's no dining room.

Call *Mrs Oksana (☎ 7-22236)* and she'll fix you a home-cooked vegetarian meal, also on a take-out basis.

Entertainment

Waluco's (☎ 7-39905, Front St) has Garifuna drumming several nights a week and brings in a swinging expat crowd.

Lirangua Bar, on Main St, is the in-town nightclub. It gets going late on weekends.

Shopping

Each morning along Front and Queen Sts there's an open-air market with vendors selling everything from just-hooked fish to plastic buckets. Some stalls in the market are open all day, every day, but the fish and produce areas are active only early in the morning. This is especially true Monday, Wednesday, Friday and Saturday, when buses from the surrounding villages bring tradespeople in to buy and sell their wares. Saturday is the busiest day – not only is the trading heavy, but also numerous barbecue stands are set up in the square to accommodate townspeople and visiting villagers. It's a lively and festive mix.

Fajina Craft Center (no ☎, Front St) Open 8am-11am Mon, Wed, Fri. The hours here accommodate the market-bus schedules for the villagers who run the shop. Next door to the post office, it's a good place to pick up local Mayan handicrafts, such as *jippy jappa* baskets, slate carvings and embroidered shirts, dresses and wall hangings.

Getting There & Away

Air Punta Gorda is served daily by Maya Island Air and Tropic Air. For details see the Getting Around chapter. Ticket offices are at the airport. If you plan to fly out of PG, be at the airstrip at least 15 minutes before departure time, as the planes sometimes leave early.

Bus James Buses leave Belize City for PG via Belmopan and Dangriga at 5am, 9am, 10am and 3pm. Southbound connections leave Dangriga for Punta Gorda at 10:30am, noon, 3:30pm and 5:30pm. James Buses head north from Punta Gorda at 6am, 8am, 11am and noon. Southern Transport has buses from Belize City to Punta Gorda at 6am, 8am, noon and 3pm. Southern Transport buses leave PG for points north at 3am, 4am, 5am and 10am. See the Getting Around chapter for more information.

Boat Requena's Charter Services (☎ 7-22070), 12 Front St, operates the *Mariestela,* departing Punta Gorda at 9am daily for Puerto Barrios (Guatemala), returning at 2pm. Tickets cost US$12.50 one way. Based in Puerto Barrios, the Pichilingo (☎ 7-22870) runs boats from Puerto Barrios to Punta Gorda at 10am and returns at 4pm.

Getting Around

Four-wheel-drive Troopers are available for rent from Dwayne Wagner at the Charleton Inn for US$65 per day; gas is extra.

Most everything in Punta Gorda is walkable, but you may need a cab to and from the airport (US$2.50). Galvez Taxi (☎ 7-22402) is dependable. Trips to Blue Creek will cost US$100, to Lubaantun or Nim Li Punit US$125.

Bicycles can be rented at PG's Bike Rental (☎ 7-22014), which also happens to be Pennell's Hardware, for US$6 a day. The bikes aren't in top condition, but they'll get you around town.

AROUND PUNTA GORDA – OUT TO SEA

There are two marine reserves off the coast of Punta Gorda: the Port Honduras Marine Reserve and the Sapodilla Cayes Marine Reserve. Within these marine reserves are a number of cayes that people can enjoy, including the Sapodilla Cayes (six cayes arranged in a 'J' formation, 36 miles/58km from PG), neighboring Hunting Caye, and the Snake Cayes, 15 miles (24km) off the reef. Snorkeling trips and overnights can be arranged through the tour operators listed in the Punta Gorda section. Half-day tours to the closer cayes will cost around US$100 for four; plan on spending US$300 to reach the cayes farther out.

Half-day kayaking trips (US$12.50, minimum two people) on the Deep River or Joe Taylor Creek can be arranged through Green Iguana Eco & Sea Adventures (see Organized Tours in the Punta Gorda section).

Equipment is shared with other tour groups, so it's necessary to make arrangements more than 24 hours in advance.

AROUND PUNTA GORDA – ON LAND

Circling out from Punta Gorda are settlements from the area's ethnic groups. In the town's 'suburbs,' or outskirts, are East Indian settlements like Forest Home, Kiskadee and Deep River. Moving farther out but still in the flats and lowlands are the settlements of Kekchi Maya, who make their living by slash-and-burn farming, although they're learning new farming methods. Their primary crops are rice and corn, which they bring to market in Punta Gorda. The Mopan Maya live in the highlands – San Antonio is the largest village. They farm beans and coffee, which thrive in the higher elevations. These days the lines between the Kekchi and Mopan are blending. Tours to these villages can be arranged in Punta Gorda – see Organized Tours in that section, earlier.

Forest Home

There's an interesting slice of history here. In 1868, eight interrelated Confederate

AROUND PUNTA GORDA – ON LAND

families from Texas, Louisiana and Alabama created a settlement to grow and mill sugarcane. Most didn't last more than a generation: Life was hard, disease was rampant and as the children became school-aged, they left for the states and stayed. The most significant remains of the settlement can be found in an old cemetery off Forest Hill Rd. Look for a modern-day cemetery, follow the road past it and you'll come to what's known as the **Confederate Cemetery**.

Tranquility Lodge (*☎ 7-22415,* e *amiller @btl.net*) US$40 per person for beds in two rooms. This is a newish lodge that has opened in Jacintoville, 8 miles (13km) west of Punta Gorda on the San Felipe road. There's a swimming hole, and horseback riding is offered for US$20 for an hour and a half. A guided trail ride including lunch and a swim costs US$35.

Lubaantun

The Mayan ruins at Lubaantun *(admission US$5; open 8am-5pm),* a mile (1.6km) northwest of the village of San Pedro Columbia, have been excavated to some extent but not restored. The many temples are still mostly covered with jungle, so you will have to use your imagination to envisage the great city that once stood here. In its heyday, the merchants of Lubaantun traded with people on the cayes, and in Mexico and Guatemala and perhaps beyond.

Archaeologists have found evidence that Lubaantun flourished until the late 8th century AD, after which little was built. The site covers 1 sq mile (3 sq km) and holds one of the only ruins in Belize with curved stone corners. Of its 18 plazas, only the three most important (Plazas III through V) have been cleared. Plaza IV, the most important of all, is built along a ridge of hills and surrounded by the site's most impressive buildings: Structures 10, 12 and 33. A visitor's center on the site exhibits Mayan pottery and other artifacts.

Fallen Stones Butterfly Ranch and Jungle Lodge *(☎/fax 7-22167)* Double cabins US$105. Breakfast US$8, lunch US$13, dinner US$23. Down the road from the ruins is this lodge, offering eight cabins looking out across 60 miles (96km) of virgin jungle, with views to the Maya Mountains. It's a splendid, if remote, setting. If you can't stay, consider visiting for a tour of the Butterfly Ranch (US$5) and lunch.

Toledo Botanical Arboretum & Dem Dats Doin Farm

This farm and arboretum *(☎ 7-22470,* e *demdatsdoin@hotmail.com, 1½ miles off the Lubaantun turnoff; tours by appointment only; suggested donation US$5)* are owned by Alfredo and Yvonne Villoria, who have devoted themselves to environmental education and offer tours primarily to Belize schools and educators. In the past, the farm itself, a model of sustainable agriculture, was the primary attraction here, but now an arboretum has been added, with over 1000 species of exotic plants and trees to be viewed, as well as examples of energy self-sufficient farming, such as methane gas from pigs for light and refrigeration, solar panels for electricity and natural insect repellents and fertilizers in place of chemicals.

Nim Li Punit

About 24 miles (38km) north of Punta Gorda, just west of the Southern Hwy, stand the ruins of Nim Li Punit *(Big Hat; admission US$5; open 8am-5pm).* Named for the headgear worn by the richly clad figure on Stela 14, Nim Li Punit may have been a tributary city to larger, more powerful Lubaantun.

The South Group of structures was the city's ceremonial center and is of the most interest. The plaza has been cleared, but the structures surrounding it are largely unrestored. Have a look at the stelae, especially Stela 14 – at 33 feet (10m) the longest Mayan stela yet discovered – and Stela 15, which dates from AD 721 and is the oldest work recovered here so far.

Mayan Villages of Toledo

Toledo's guest house stays are at the forefront of the world's sustainable tourism movement.

The most accessible Mayan village program for travelers is the **Toledo Ecotourism**

SOUTHERN BELIZE

Association's Village Guesthouse Program (☎ 7-22096 in Punta Gorda, e ttea@btl.net), which arranges stays in 13 traditional Mopan Maya, Kekchi Maya, Creole and Garifuna villages in the area. It's an admirable stab at sustainable tourism, a model in which the profits stay within the organization and the families in the village.

Their basic village guest house tour gives visitors overnight lodging in a guest house and three meals, each served in a village home. Village guest houses have been specifically designed for the program. They're rudimentary but comfortable. The cost of accommodations includes sheets, blankets and mosquito nets. There are separate, non-flushing toilets for males and females and a shower or spigot for washing. The buildings are constructed with local materials and have thatched roofs.

More than 80% of the tour fee stays in the village with the villagers, helping them to achieve a sustainable, eco-friendly economy as an alternative to slash-and-burn agriculture. Another goal is to sustain and preserve the culture and heritage of the villages by offering another form of income to the villagers.

Rooms in the guest houses cost US$9.25 a night, and meals cost US$3.25-4. A package is offered for US$42.50, which includes overnight lodging, three meals and a jungle and village tour. Guides can be hired for US$3.50/hour, usually at a four-hour minimum. The usual tours offered include a village tour (often by a woman in the village, a rare opportunity to get a female perspective on village life) and jungle tours to nearby caves, ruins, lakes or waterfalls (see the individual village descriptions, later). Craft lessons, evening performances or storytelling can also be arranged. Upon arrival in the village, guests are usually greeted immediately, and needs are sorted out easily.

Guests are invited into village homes for their meals. It's unlikely that the family will join you while you eat, instead they'll go about their family business while you're there. Some find this disconcerting, but if you're prepared, you'll find that it's a great opportunity to ask questions and learn more about Mayan village and home life. Meals usually consist of tortillas and *caldo* – a stew made of root vegetables and meat, usually chicken. Every effort is made to accommodate vegetarian and vegan guests.

As with everything in the Punta Gorda area, it helps to make arrangements in advance – at least a few days. If you miss your connection it can be quite expensive to get to the village on your own steam. Be aware that each village guest house is run independently, and your experience and service may differ. Let the organizers at TEA know if you have special interests or needs and they'll help you choose the village that will be the most satisfying for you.

Another village stay program, called the **Indigenous Experience Program**, is run by the folks at Dem Dats Doin (☎ 7-22470, e demdatsdoin@hotmail.com). This program puts travelers in villagers' homes, instead of in a guest house. It is recommended for cultural and anthropological academics interested in studying the Mayan culture, but travelers are cautioned that the level of immersion is intense. Guests stay with families in their huts, and privacy is scarce. Villagers have outhouses and bathing is by river, although, as with the TEA program, the families are trained to provide the level of food service and hygiene required to keep travelers hale and hearty.

The Villages Landscapes vary in the region, but there is usually a river or a stream at the heart of each village. Surrounding the villages are waterfalls, caves and Mayan ruins that can be best experienced with a local guide. Family homes in the villages are usually one- or two-room thatched-roof huts with wooden plank walls and dirt floors. Local government in the villages is a meld of the ancient *alcalde* system, where a leader is elected by majority and makes all the major decisions for the village, and a village-council system, where the decision-making is shared. The villages were established as early as the 1850s, mostly by Mayas fleeing oppression in Guatemala to settle in Belize.

San Antonio village is probably the best-known and most-visited Mayan village in

Southern Belize – Around Punta Gorda   217

Toledo, possibly the country. The population is 1000 to 3000, depending on who you talk to. The village is arranged on roads winding through foothills. It's picture-postcard imagery, complete with brightly dressed villagers, thatched-roof buildings, roaming livestock, a church built from stones taken from Mayan ruins and stained-glass windows from a church in St Louis, Missouri.

This is the most developed of the Mayan villages of Toledo, with electricity, a village telephone and running water. The Mopan Maya of San Antonio are descended from former inhabitants of the Guatemalan village of San Luis Peten, just across the border. Bells in the church are said to have been taken from the village of San Luis Peten when the settlers fled oppression there in the mid-1800s.

If you are here during a festival, your visit will be much more memorable. The Feast of St Luis, a harvest festival where the famous deer dance is performed, is celebrated here in late summer.

Santa Cruz and **Santa Elena** are Mopan Maya villages with a combined population of about 500. These are near Rio Blanco Falls and Uxbenka ruins. The ruins are not open to the public, but you can visit them with a guide from one of the villages. Three miles (5km) away is Pueblo Viejo ('old town' in Spanish), home to about 700 Mopan Mayas. It was the first settlement of the Mopan Mayas who fled Guatemala to settle in Toledo. There is a waterfall close to the village, and there is talk of building a road into Guatemala from here.

San Pedro Columbia is the largest Kekchi village in Toledo. It's home to about 700 villagers living on the banks of the Columbia River. There's plenty to do around this site: You can rent canoes for a trip on the Columbia River, and it's close to the neighboring village of San Migel and an hour's walk from the Lubaantun ruins.

San Miguel is a Kekchi village of 400 people, near the Southern Hwy close to the turnoff to the Lubaantun ruins.

San Jose is a Mopan village known for practicing organic farming methods. It's located in the foothills near the Guatemalan

border, and the rain forest surrounding it is said to be the most pristine in Toledo.

Blue Creek, formerly called Rio Blanco, is a village of 279. Approximately half are Kekchi, half Mopan. It gets plenty of traffic because it's the site of the Blue Creek Rainforest Preserve, which attracts visitors for its great swimming hole, canopy walk and cave.

Laguna, about 10 miles (16km) west of Punta Gorda, is just off the main road and quick and easy to get to. It has one of the best guest house facilities of all the villages: a two-story structure with outdoor showers. It's home to about 300 Kekchi Maya villagers. Its namesake lagoon is a two-hour walk through the wetlands of Aguas Calientes Wildlife Sanctuary, a great area for birdwatching. (Note that this area floods in the wet season and the trails can be impassable.)

Getting There & Away The trickiest part of the program is transportation. Most choose to catch a village bus that comes into Punta Gorda on market days, usually Saturday and Wednesday, although some villages make Punta Gorda runs on other days of the week as well. Village buses are brightly painted school buses (different colors for each village) that make regular runs into Punta Gorda to allow the villagers to visit the market to sell wares and buy supplies.

The buses drive in from the villages early in the morning and park at the town square or on surrounding streets until the afternoon, when villagers are ready to make their return trip. In the abstract, it sounds confusing, but when you get there it will become fairly straightforward – townspeople will help you find the bus and make sure you're in the right place at the right time to visit the village. Check with the TEA or with the BTB office in Punta Gorda for the most current bus schedules.

It is also possible to arrange for a taxi to take you to the villages; the price will be around US$50 to US$75 depending on the distance. Hitchhiking is a common way to get around. This should be done with extreme caution, and travelers, especially women, shouldn't hitch alone, but most feel comfortable hitching in groups around here.

On your return, you'll have to be prepared to get up early in the morning – the farther from PG the village is, the earlier you'll leave. Luckily everyone in your village will be aware of your presence, so you'll have plenty of help making your connection.

Blue Creek Rain Forest Preserve & Cave

About 12 miles (20km) south of San Antonio lies the village of Blue Creek, and beyond it the rain forest preserve *(open 8am-5pm)* and Blue Creek Cave. It's less than a mile (1.6km) hike into the site along a marked trail – you'll enjoy the rain forest around you and the pools, channels, caves and refreshingly cool waters of the creek system. There are guided nature walks, including a canopy walk and a climb to an observation deck accessed by rope ladder (you must wear helmet and harness) for US$15 per hour.

International Zoological Expeditions Guesthouse (☎ 14-3967, ⓔ bluecreek@btl.net)

Cabins with meals US$45 per person. This company operates seven cabins on the site, mostly for the use of student groups, although individual stays can be arranged.

Barranco

This is the only Garifuna village located south of Punta Gorda on the coast. It can be accessed by sea from PG in about 20 minutes; by dirt road the trip takes 45 minutes. The population of Barranco is about 150 and dwindling. You'll find lots of women, children and elderly folks staying put, while the men of working age head for the cities and better economic opportunity. Villagers here are proud of their home and recognize that their lifestyle is rare and disappearing. The village now supports itself by fishing, but in the past the area was heavily farmed; you'll see evidence of farming and plenty of fruit trees as you wander around. Barranco is a good starting point to tour the Sarstoon-Temash National Park.

Excursion to Tikal (Guatemala)

A favorite excursion for travelers in Belize is to hop the Guatemalan border and head to Tikal. And it's no wonder: The monumental ceremonial center at Tikal is among the most impressive of the Mayan archaeological sites. While many tourists come here on one-day or overnight package tours, travelers are strongly encouraged to stay over at least one night, whether in Flores/Santa Elena, El Remate or Tikal itself. In fact, Tikal is so big you'll need at least two days to see the major parts thoroughly.

Tikal is in the 2½-million-acre (1-million-hectare) Maya Biosphere Reserve, which includes most of northern El Petén and adjoins the vast Calakmul Biosphere Reserve, in Mexico, and the Río Bravo Conservation & Management Area, in Belize. From December to February, nights and mornings are cool, while March and April are the hottest and driest months, followed by rains – and mosquitoes – in May or June: Bring rain gear, repellent and, if you plan on slinging a hammock, a mosquito net. July to November is muggy and buggy, though by October the rains taper off and the temperature begins to cool down.

Warning In early to mid-2001, Tikal and the area around El Remate were the scene of an unfortunate slew of assaults and rapes. These crimes were most often perpetrated in the more isolated areas of the ruins, such as at Temple of the Inscriptions. At the time this book went to press, the criminals had been caught and tranquility had been restored to the area. However, caution is still recommended: Avoid going to remote ruins or towns alone, consider going on an organized

Guatemalan Phone Numbers

To call the telephone numbers listed in this chapter from Belize, dial Guatemala's country code – ☎ 502 – first. Guatemala has no area codes.

tour, inform someone at your hotel of your destination and talk to the guards about any new incidents.

TIKAL

Nestled in the jungle, Tikal offers an experience unlike other, more readily accessible Mayan sites. Towering pyramids jut through the rain forest canopy where howler monkeys swing noisily and brightly colored parrots and toucans dart, squawking, from perch to perch. But Tikal's most striking features are the steep-sided temples that rise to heights of more than 144 feet (44m). The ruins lie within the 222-sq-mile (576-sq-km) **Tikal National Park** *(US$6.50; open 6am-6pm daily),* of which the city's central area occupied about 6 sq miles (16 sq km) and contained more than 4000 structures.

For complete information on the monuments, pick up a copy of *Tikal – A Handbook of the Ancient Maya Ruins,* by William R Coe, available in Flores and at Tikal. *The Birds of Tikal,* by Frank B Smithe, available at the Tikal museums, is a good resource for birders.

For a day wandering around the monuments, wear shoes with good traction and take extra snacks and water. Expect to walk at least 6 miles (10km) to visit all of the major building complexes. Half-day tours with multilingual guides are arranged at the visitor's center for US$20. The hotels also arrange guided tours of the ruins. If you arrive after 3pm, your entrance ticket is valid for the following day.

History

On a small hill that elevated them above the low-lying swampy ground, the Maya began settling Tikal around 700 BC. Within 200 years, they began to build stone ceremonial structures, and by 200 BC a complex of buildings stood on the site of the North Acropolis. By about AD 250, Tikal had become an important religious, cultural and commercial city. The founder of this

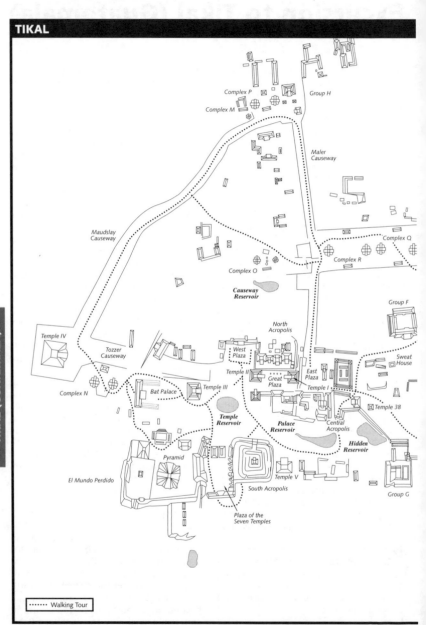

Complex P

Complex M

Group H

Maler
Causeway

Maudslay
Causeway

Complex Q

Complex O

Complex R

Causeway
Reservoir

Group F

Temple IV

North
Acropolis

Tozzer
Causeway

West
Plaza

East
Plaza

Sweat
House

Complex N

Temple II

Great
Plaza

Temple I

Bat Palace

Temple III

Temple
Reservoir

Palace
Reservoir

Temple 38

Central
Acropolis

Hidden
Reservoir

Pyramid

El Mundo Perdido

Temple V

South Acropolis

Group G

Plaza of the
Seven Temples

•••••• Walking Tour

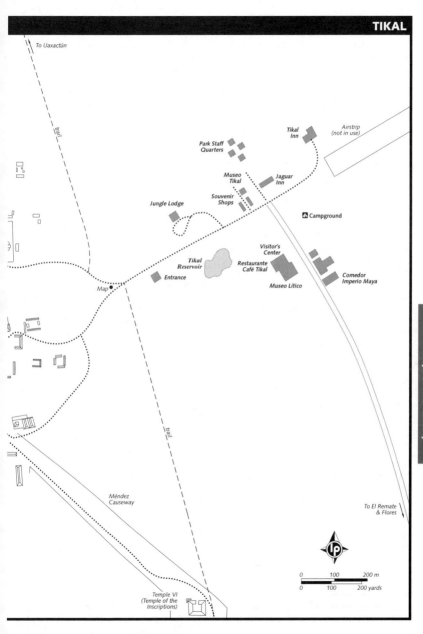

TIKAL

To Uaxactún

trail

Airstrip
(not in use)

Tikal
Inn

Park Staff
Quarters

Museo
Tikal

Jaguar
Inn

Jungle Lodge

Souvenir
Shops

△ Campground

Visitor's
Center

Tikal
Reservoir

Restaurante
Café Tikal

Entrance

Comedor
Imperio Maya

Museo Lítico

Map ●

trail

Méndez
Causeway

To El Remate
& Flores

TIKAL (GUATEMALA)

0   100   200 m
0   100   200 yards

Temple VI
(Temple of the
Inscriptions)

dynasty was King Yax Moch Xoc, whose reign began around AD 230.

Under King Great Jaguar Paw (who ruled in the mid-4th century), Tikal became the dominant kingdom in the region. By the middle of the 6th century, Tikal sprawled across 11½ sq miles (30 sq km) and had a population of perhaps 100,000. However, in 562, Lord Water, who had ascended to the throne of Caracol in southwestern Belize in 553, conquered and sacrificed Tikal's king. Tikal and other Petén kingdoms suffered under Caracol's rule until the late 7th century.

Around AD 700, Moon Double Comb (682–734), also called Ah Cacau (Lord Chocolate), ascended Tikal's throne, restoring the center's military strength and its primacy in the Mayan world. He and his successors were responsible for building most of the temples around the Great Plaza that survive today. The greatness of Tikal waned around 900, part of the mysterious general collapse of lowland Mayan civilization.

During the late 1800s and 1900s, archaeological and scientific interest in Tikal grew, starting with an 1848 Guatemalan-government-sponsored expedition, an account of which was published by the Berlin Academy of Science. Since 1956, the University of Pennsylvania and the Guatemalan Instituto de Antropología e Historia have conducted archaeological research and restoration of Tikal, which was declared a UNESCO World Heritage Site in 1979.

Great Plaza

The path leading into the plaza goes around Temple I, the Temple of the Grand Jaguar, built to honor – and bury – King Moon Double Comb. The king's rich burial goods included 180 jade objects, 90 pieces of bone carved with hieroglyphs, and pearls and stingray spines, which were used for ritual bloodletting.

At the top of the 144-foot (44m) temple is a small enclosure of three rooms covered by a corbeled arch. The lofty roofcomb that crowned the temple was originally adorned with reliefs and bright paint, and may have symbolized the 13 realms of the Mayan heaven.

The stairs up Temple I are closed, in reaction to the deaths of at least two people who fell while climbing to the top. The views from Temple II, once almost as high as Temple I, but now 124 feet (38m) tall without its roofcomb, are nearly as awe-inspiring.

The North Acropolis, while not as immediately impressive as the twin temples, is of great significance. Archaeologists have uncovered about 100 different structures, with evidence of occupation as far back as 400 BC. The Maya rebuilt on top of older structures, and the many layers, combined with the elaborate burials, added sanctity and power to their temples. Look for the two huge, powerful wall masks. The final version of the Acropolis, as it stood around AD 800, had more than 12 temples atop a vast platform.

Central Acropolis

On the south side of the Great Plaza, this maze of courtyards, little rooms and small temples is thought by many to have been a residential palace for Tikal's noble class. Others think the tiny rooms may have been used for sacred rites and ceremonies.

West Plaza

The West Plaza is north of Temple II. On its north side is a large Late Classic temple. To the south, across the Tozzer Causeway, is Temple III, 180 feet (55m) high, yet to be uncovered. The causeway leading to Temple IV was one of several sacred ways built among the temple complexes of Tikal for astronomical and aesthetic reasons.

South Acropolis & Temple V

Due south of the Great Plaza is the South Acropolis. Excavation has hardly even begun on this huge mass of masonry covering two hectares. The palaces on top are from Late Classic times (the time of King Moon Double Comb), but earlier constructions probably go back 1000 years.

Just east of the South Acropolis, Temple V is 190 feet (58m) high, was built around AD 700 and, unlike other great temples, has rounded corners and one room at the top, less than 3 feet (1m) deep, but with walls up to 15 feet (4.5m) thick. A team of Guatemalan and Spanish archaeologists and historians started restoration of this temple in 1991.

Plaza of the Seven Temples

On the other side of the South Acropolis is the Plaza of the Seven Temples. The little temples, clustered together, were built in Late Classic times. Note the skull and crossbones on the central temple (the one with the stela and altar in front). On the plaza's north side is an unusual triple ball court; another, larger version in the same design stands just south of Temple I.

El Mundo Perdido

About a quarter mile (400m) southwest of the Great Plaza, El Mundo Perdido (the Lost World) is a large complex of 38 structures and a huge pyramid. Unlike the rest of Tikal, where Late Classic construction overlays work of earlier periods, El Mundo Perdido has buildings of many different periods. The large pyramid is thought to be Preclassic (with some later repairs and renovations); the Talud-Tablero Temple (or Temple of the Three Rooms) is Early Classic; and the Temple of the Skulls is Late Classic.

The pyramid, 105 feet (32m) high and 262 feet (80m) along its base, has a stairway on each side. It had huge masks flanking each stairway but no temple structure at the top. Each side of the pyramid displays a slightly different architectural style. Tunnels dug into the pyramid by archaeologists reveal four similar pyramids beneath the outer face; the earliest (Structure 5C-54 Sub 2B) dates from 700 BC, making the pyramid the oldest Mayan structure at Tikal.

Temple IV & Complex N

Temple IV, at 210 feet (64m), is the highest building at Tikal. It was completed about AD 741, in the reign of King Moon Double Comb's son. From the base it looks like a precipitous little hill. A series of steep wooden steps and ladders takes you to the top for a panoramic view across the jungle

canopy. If you stay up here for the sunset, climb down immediately, as the path gets dark quickly.

Complex N, near Temple IV, is an example of the 'twin-temple' complexes popular among Tikal's rulers during the Late Classic period. These complexes are thought to have commemorated the completion of a *katun*, or 20-year cycle in the Mayan calendar. This one was built in AD 711 by King Moon Double Comb to mark the 14th katun of Baktun 9. The king himself is portrayed on Stela 16, one of the finest stelae at Tikal. More of the complexes can be found about 0.6 miles (1km) north of the Great Plaza.

Temple of the Inscriptions (Temple VI)

Compared to other Maya centers in the region, such as Copán or Quiriguá, the buildings at Tikal have relatively few inscriptions. The exception is this remote temple, ¾ miles (1.2km) southeast of the Great Plaza. On the rear of the roofcomb is a long inscription; the sides and cornice of the roofcomb bear glyphs as well. The inscriptions give the date AD 766. Stela 21 and Altar 9, standing before the temple, date from AD 736.

Museums

The larger of the two museums in the grounds, **Museo Lítico** *(visitor's center; admission free; open 9am-5pm Mon-Fri, 9am-4pm Sat & Sun)* houses a number of stelae and carved stones excavated from the ruins. Outside is a large relief map showing how Tikal would have looked during the Late Classic period, around AD 800.

The **Museo Tikal** *(near Jungle Lodge; admission US$1.50; open 9am-5pm Mon-Fri, 9am-4pm Sat & Sun)* has some fascinating exhibits, including the burial goods of King Moon Double Comb and other items recovered from the excavations.

Places to Stay & Eat

The three hotels at Tikal are often booked in advance by tour groups and are more expensive than those in Flores and Santa Elena; however, staying here allows you to savor the dawn and dusk, when most of the

TIKAL (GUATEMALA)

jungle fauna can be seen and heard. Perhaps the easiest way to get a room at Tikal is to sign up for an all-inclusive tour. Ask travel agents in Belize for one with lodging at the site. The hotels and campgrounds are all dependent on a generator for electricity and hot water, so they have set hours when both are available.

By the entrance road and airstrip, an **official campground** is set in a large, open lawn with some shade trees. Tent spaces (US$4.50 per person) are on the grass or on concrete platforms under palapas; you can hang your hammock here, too. The Restaurant Café Tikal, near the museum, rents camping equipment at reasonable rates.

Jungle Lodge (Guatemala City ☎ 476-8775, 477-0754, fax 476-0294, e reservaciones @junglelodge.guate.com, w www.junglelodge .guate.com) Singles/doubles US$26/31 with shared bath; US$54/72 with private bath. Built originally to house the archaeologists excavating and restoring Tikal, Jungle Lodge is the largest and most attractive of the hotels, and also the closest to the entrance. The 34 agreeable rooms in newer duplex bungalows come with two double beds, while the older section of the hotel has 12 much less attractive rooms. Amenities include a swimming pool, large gardens and a restaurant/bar with breakfast for US$6.60, lunch or dinner for US$10.50. Jungle Lodge is a good place to ask about organized tours around Tikal and other Mayan ruins in the area.

Tikal Inn (☎ 926-1917, ☎/fax 926-0065, e hoteltikalinn@itelgua.com) Singles/doubles with private bath & ceiling fan US$55/60; US$95/102 including breakfast & dinner; US$95/138 all-inclusive package. Past the Jaguar Inn as you walk toward the old airstrip, comfortable Tikal Inn is the next best choice, with plush gardens and a pool. The rooms are simple and clean, but the walls extend only partway up to the roof, affording little conversational privacy. The restaurant on the premises lacks any kind of atmosphere. The package includes airport pickup and transport to the hotel, park admission, bilingual tour, lunch and one night's stay.

Jaguar Inn (☎ 926-0002, fax 926-2413, e solis@quetzal.net, w www.jaguartikal.com) Camping/dorm bed US$3.25/10, singles/ doubles/triples US$32/50/68 with private bath & ceiling fan. To the right of the museum as you approach on the access road, Jaguar Inn has a small campground (hammocks can be rented for US$5) and nine bungalow rooms. The airy and spacious restaurant serves breakfast for US$4, lunch and dinner for around US$7.

Comedor Imperio Maya Meals US$4. Open 5am-9pm Mon-Sun. Of the many comedores serving huge plates of fairly tasty food at low prices along the road to the entrance to Tikal, this one seems to be a favorite. The meal of the day is usually roast chicken, rice, salad and fruit (enough to feed two people). You can buy cold drinks and snacks in the adjoining shop.

Restaurant Café Tikal (visitor's center) Mains US$10. Across the street from the comedores, this fancier restaurant serves lomito (beef tenderloin) and other meats. Plates of fruit cost less.

Getting There & Away

Coming from Belize, you can get off the bus at El Cruce/Puente Ixlú. Wait for a north-bound bus or minibus – or hitch a ride with an obliging tourist – to take you the remaining 22 miles (35km) to Tikal. Note that there is very little northbound traffic after lunch. If you arrive at Puente Ixlú in the afternoon, continue to Flores or El Remate for the night rather than risk being stranded at El Cruce.

If you're driving, continue to Flores/Santa Elena to fill your fuel tank.

From Flores/Santa Elena, shuttle mini-buses (US$5.25, one to 1½ hours) are the quickest and most convenient mode of transport, picking up passengers in front of their hotels (5am, 6am, 8am and 10am) and from the airport (meeting all flights). Any hotel can arrange a trip for you.

Return trips to Flores/Santa Elena generally depart from Tikal at 2pm, 4pm and 5pm. If planning to return to Tikal the following day, ask the driver to hold a seat for

The nocturnal, solitary kinkajou

Baird's tapirs: Belize's shyest creatures

Watch for crocs and other wildlife on the spectacular trip up the New River to Lamanai.

A sculptural frieze with astronomical symbols and hieroglyphics at Xunantunich in western Belize

'Temple of the Grand Jaguar,' Tikal, Guatemala

Fronting 'The Mask Temple,' Lamanai

Altun Ha, in northern Belize, is an easy day trip.

you on the same shuttle, or in a colleague's minibus. If staying overnight, it's a good idea to reserve a seat early the next morning for that afternoon's return trip. Don't wait until departure time and expect to find a seat. A slower option is Transportes Pinita buses, leaving San Juan Hotel daily at 1pm (US$1.50, two hours), and departing Tikal for the return trip at 6am.

A taxi from Flores/Santa Elena or the airport to Tikal costs US$40 roundtrip (for up to four people).

UAXACTÚN

Uaxactún (wah-shahk-**toon**), 14 miles (23km) north of Tikal along a poor, unpaved road that is often impassable in the rainy season, was Tikal's political and military rival in Late Preclassic times. It was conquered by Tikal's King Great Jaguar Paw in the mid-4th century, and was subservient to its big sister to the south for centuries thereafter. For those seeking out the more hidden gems of the area, this could be a good side trip; difficult to get to, it offers an added sense of serenity and authenticity.

The pyramids at Uaxactún were uncovered and stabilized but not restored. Repair crews used white mortar to patch cracks in the stone to prevent water and roots from entering. The ruins are always open and accessible, and admission is free. However, the turnoff onto the Uaxactún road is inside the gate to Tikal, so you must pay the US$6.50 admission fee there. Hotels in Tikal can arrange tours, which cost about US$60 for one to four people or US$15 per person for over four people. If you go, pack extra food and drink, though beverages and snacks are available in the village at Uaxactún.

Getting There & Away

A Transportes Pinita bus leaves Santa Elena daily at 1pm (US$2.50, three hours). You can catch the same bus at Tikal (US$1, one hour) on the way. The bus departs Uaxactún daily at 5am. If you're driving, fill your fuel tank in Santa Elena. You can hire a taxi from Flores to Uaxactún for about US$50; bargain hard.

FLORES & SANTA ELENA
pop 2000 & 17,000
Because it's the main transport and lodging center near Tikal, many travelers will end up passing through Flores, as this area is generally referred to, en route to the ruins. Some choose to stay: Lodging is cheaper than at Tikal, and many travelers have found that lazing about on a lakeside terrace is worth the extra day.

History
After their expulsion from Chichén Itzá, the Itzáes developed a new center, which they called Tayasal, on an island on Lago de Petén Itzá. Flores now stands at this site. In 1524, Hernán Cortés met peaceably with King Canek of Tayasal while en route to Honduras. The Maya of Tayasal eventually lost control to the Spaniards in March 1697, when the site was perhaps the last major functioning Mayan ceremonial center.

Orientation & Information
A 1600-foot (500m) causeway connects Flores to Santa Elena, a disorganized town of dusty unpaved streets on the lakeshore. Santa Elena's 'main drag' is 4a Calle.

INGUAT staffs tourist information desks at the airport (☎ 926-0533) and on the plaza in Flores (☎ 926-0669, e inguatflores@hotmail.com). The offices are open from 7:30am to 10am and 3pm to 6pm daily.

Santa Elena's 4a Calle has a number of banks, all of which have better exchange rates than what's on offer in Flores. Cash and traveler's check exchange and cash advances on credit cards are all possible, and there's an ATM. Exchange rates for US dollars are better than for Belizean dollars.

In Flores, Cahuí International Services (☎/fax 926-0494), next to the Hotel Santana, offers telephone, fax and travel agency services. EcoMaya (☎ 926-1363/3321, fax 926-3322, ☎ 800-429-5660 in the USA, e ecomaya@guate.net, w www.ecomaya.com), on Calle 30 de Junio, has similar services. Most of the travel agencies in Flores lead trips to Tikal and Uaxactún.

TIKAL (GUATEMALA)

FLORES & SANTA ELENA

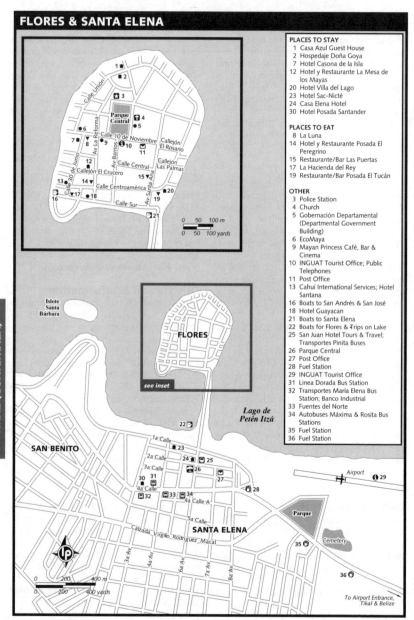

PLACES TO STAY
1   Casa Azul Guest House
2   Hospedaje Doña Goya
7   Hotel Casona de la Isla
12 Hotel y Restaurante La Mesa de los Mayas
20 Hotel Villa del Lago
23 Hotel Sac-Nicté
24 Casa Elena Hotel
30 Hotel Posada Santander

PLACES TO EAT
8   La Luna
14 Hotel y Restaurante Posada El Peregrino
15 Restaurante/Bar Las Puertas
17 La Hacienda del Rey
19 Restaurante/Bar Posada El Tucán

OTHER
3   Police Station
4   Church
5   Gobernación Departamental (Departmental Government Building)
6   EcoMaya
9   Mayan Princess Café, Bar & Cinema
10 INGUAT Tourist Office; Public Telephones
11 Post Office
13 Cahuí International Services; Hotel Santana
16 Boats to San Andrés & San José
18 Hotel Guayacan
21 Boats to Santa Elena
22 Boats for Flores & Trips on Lake
25 San Juan Hotel Tours & Travel; Transportes Pinita Buses
26 Parque Central
27 Post Office
28 Fuel Station
29 INGUAT Tourist Office
31 Linea Dorada Bus Station
32 Transportes María Elena Bus Station; Banco Industrial
33 Fuentes del Norte
34 Autobuses Máxima & Rosita Bus Stations
35 Fuel Station
36 Fuel Station

Places to Stay – Flores

Tiny Flores has a host of places to stay and all are easily found on the island. Just ask around for the one you plan to stay in.

Hospedaje Doña Goya (☎ 926-3538, Calle Unión) Singles with shared bath US$6, doubles with shared/private bath US$7.50/10. One of the town's best budget choices, with spotless rooms and comfortable beds, Doña Goya has a rooftop terrace with hammocks and lounge chairs from which you can enjoy lake views.

Hotel Villa del Lago (☎/fax 926-0629) Doubles with shared bath US$6.50, with air-con, TV & private bath US$19.50. Beside the lake, this cheerful, family-run spot is a good, clean place to stay. Rooms are simple, but the more expensive doubles are bigger and nicer.

Hotel y Restaurante La Mesa de los Mayas (☎/fax 926-1240, Callejón El Crucero) Singles/doubles/triples with private bath & fan US$15/20/25, with private bath & air-con US$20/25/30. Very clean and well kept, La Mesa de los Mayas accepts Visa and MasterCard, but tacks on a 10% fee.

Hotel Casona de la Isla (☎ 926-0523, fax 926-0593) Singles/doubles/triples with private bath, cable TV, phone & air-con US$35/41/48. With a lakeside Jacuzzi and pool plus an open-air bar/restaurant, Casona de la Isla is a romantic choice. All of the 27 rooms also have balconies with chairs.

Casa Azul Guest House (☎ 926-1138, fax 926-0593) Singles/doubles with private hot bath, cable TV, fridge, phone & air-con US$30/35. On the north shore, Casa Azul is a comfortable, quiet place. Each room is unique and spotless, and has a balcony.

Places to Stay – Santa Elena

Hotel Posada Santander (☎ 926-0574, 4a Calle) Singles/doubles with shared bath US$3.25/4, with private bath US$5.25/6.50. Santander is a simple but spotless hostelry in a convenient but loud location, with ample rooms; the ones with private bath have two good double beds. The owners also operate Transportes Inter Petén, a minibus service to Tikal and other places.

Hotel Sac-Nicté (☎ 926-0092, 1a Calle) Singles or doubles with private bath US$7.75-10.50. Closer to the lake, the more expensive and larger rooms at Sac-Nicté are upstairs with balconies and views across the lake to Flores. The hotel has a restaurant, parking and transportation service.

Casa Elena Hotel (☎ 926-2238/39, fax 926-0097, e casaelena@amigo.net.gt, in front of Parque Central) Singles/doubles with private hot bath, air-con, cable TV & phone US$35/45. Rooms at Casa Elena are clean and comfortable but a bit short on character. Some have park views, while others overlook the pool. Amenities include a bar, restaurant and roof terrace.

Places to Eat

All of the restaurants listed below are in Flores. Most of them are fairly simple and keep long hours. Local game animals, including *tepezcuintle* (a rabbit-sized jungle rodent known in English as the paca or cavy), *venado* (deer), armadillo and *pavo silvestre* (wild turkey) are common menu items, representing the people's dependence on the jungle, rather than ranchland, for their livelihood.

Restaurante/Bar Las Puertas (Ave Santa Ana) Decent but pricey food plus an interesting clientele make this a popular hangout. It's a good spot for friendly conversation, and serves real coffee. On weekends there's live music.

Restaurante/Bar Posada El Tucán (Calle Centroamérica) Breakfast US$2-3, lunch & dinner US$5-8. With a breezy lakeside terrace, El Tucán is a decent choice.

La Hacienda del Rey (Calles Sur & 30 de Junio) Mains US$11. All manner of steaks are on offer and served on a huge terrace, invitingly strung with lights. It opens at 4:30am for breakfast – perfect for a coffee before the early Tikal shuttle.

Hotel y Restaurante La Mesa de los Mayas Breakfast US$2, mains US$5-9. Popular La Mesa serves up good traditional foods, including some vegetarian options.

Hotel y Restaurante Posada El Peregrino (Avenida La Reforma) Meals US$3.25. The Posada El Peregino is highly recommended; dine here on succulent roasted chicken, french fries, salad and rice.

La Luna *(Calles 30 de Junio & 10 de Noviembre)* Meals US$8. Open for lunch & dinner Tues-Sun. Luna's menu tempts with innovative, delectable chicken, fish and beef dishes.

Entertainment
Mayan Princess Café, Bar & Cinema (Calle 10 de Noviembre & Avenida La Reforma) Free movies (some of dubious quality) are shown at 4pm and 9pm in the dining room at this Flores hangout. It has comfy chairs and imported beers.

Getting There & Away
Air The airport is on the eastern outskirts of Santa Elena, 1.2 miles (2km) from the causeway connecting Santa Elena and Flores. Upon arrival at the airport in Flores you may be subjected to a cursory customs and immigration check. Belize authorities collect BZ$30 (US$15) when departing for foreign destinations from Goldson International Airport. A US$30 departure tax is collected upon leaving Guatemala.

Tropic Air and Maya Island Air (see either the Getting There & Away or the Getting Around chapter for contact details) have flights from Belize City's Goldson International Airport to Flores daily at 8:30am and 2:30pm (leaving from San Pedro, Ambergris Caye, 1½ hours earlier), returning at 9:30am and 3:30pm. (US$88, 50 minutes one-way). The airlines offer one-day and overnight package tours, including airfare, ground transportation to Tikal, lunch and a guided tour of the archaeological site for US$285 from San Pedro or US$208 from Belize City; departure taxes and lodging are extra. Taking this kind of tour, even the overnight option, gives you very little time to explore the ruins. Indeed more time is spent in transit than at the site.

The other option is Grupo TACA (see the Getting There & Away chapter for contact details), which stops at Flores on its Belize City-Guatemala City route (US$85-94) on Monday, Wednesday and Friday.

Bus For details on bus service from Belize City and from the border crossing at Benque

Viejo del Carmen and Melchor de Mencos, see the Getting Around chapter.

To Belize City (US$20, five hours, 138 miles/222km), San Juan Hotel runs a daily shuttle that will pick you up from your hotel around 5am and arrive in Belize City around 10am (theoretically in time to connect with the boat to Caye Caulker and San Pedro, Ambergris Caye). Or take local buses from Santa Elena to Melchor de Mencos at the Belize border and change there.

To Melchor de Mencos (US$2, two hours, 62 miles/100km), 2nd-class Transportes Pinita buses leave at 5am, 8am and 10:30am. Rosita buses leave at 5am, 7:30am, 11am, 2pm, 4pm and 6pm. On the Belize side, buses (US$0.50) and share-taxis (US$2) leave for Benque Viejo and San Ignacio (30 minutes) every hour or so. At the border you must pay a small fee (around US$1.50) before proceeding to Benque Viejo.

For several destinations around Santa Elena, you'll have the choice of taking a tourist shuttle or a local 'chicken bus.' The latter will always be cheaper, but many find the slow pace and discomfort not worth the savings.

Getting Around
Boats *(lanchas;* US$0.15, five minutes) depart from both ends of the causeway connecting Santa Elena and the island. Rental car companies are in the arrivals hall at the airport and at many hotels.

A basic car with unlimited *kilometraje* (distance allowance) costs a minimum of around US$50 per day. If you're driving, fill your fuel tank in Flores/Santa Elena; no fuel is available at Tikal or Uaxactún. In Flores, you can rent bicycles from Cahuí International Services (☎/fax 926-0494) for US$0.85 per hour or US$6.75 per day; or from Hotel Guayacán (☎ 926-0351) for US$0.75 an hour.

EL REMATE & BIOTOPO CERRO CAHUÍ
A quiet alternative to Flores is the small lakeshore village of El Remate, 22 miles (35km) northeast of Santa Elena on the Tikal road. Nearby is the **Biotopo Cerro Cahuí** *(US$2.75; open 6am-4pm)*, which

protects 2.5 sq miles (651 hectares) of sub-tropical forest. Among the animals within the reserve are spider and howler monkeys, ocelots, white-tailed deer, raccoons, armadillos, turtles, snakes and Morelet's crocodile. Depending upon the season and migration patterns, birds spotted may include kingfishers, ducks, herons, hawks, parrots, toucans, woodpeckers and the ocellated (or Petén) turkey, resembling a peacock.

The reserve has a series of trails; a map is available at entrance. If the gate is closed, go to the administration center. You can camp at the reserve for an additional US$2.75; toilets and showers are available, but El Remate is the closest place to get food and other necessities.

Places to Stay & Eat
A couple of other good places are about 1.8 miles (3km) west of El Remate on the road around the lake's north side, near the Biotopo Cerro Cahuí.

Six beds in a thatch *rancho* are the basis for the communal **Casa de Doña Tonita** (US$3.25 per person). Conditions are simple (no fans or nets), but it could be a blast for a group, and it has a restaurant.

Parador Ecológico El Gringo Perdido (*☎/fax 334-2305 in Guatemala City*) Camping US$3-6 per person, dorm bed US$10, room with private bath US$14, bungalows US$25-50 per person, breakfast & dinner included. Right on the lakeshore, this is a bucolic parador of rustic hillside gardens. Each bungalow has its own patio with hammocks and a small private dock for swimming and sunning on the lake. The overall cost is cheaper if you get a room-and-meals package.

Getting There & Away
Any bus or minibus going north from Santa Elena to Tikal can drop you at El Remate. Buses to and from Melchor de Mencos can drop you at Puente Ixlú/El Cruce, fewer than 1.2 miles (2km) south of El Remate. Taxis from Santa Elena or the airport will cost US$20. Once you are in El Remate, you can hail any passing bus or minibus on the Flores-Tikal road to take you to Tikal or Flores, but traffic is light after midmorning.

TIKAL (GUATEMALA)

Lonely Planet Guides by Region

Lonely Planet is known worldwide for publishing practical, reliable and no-nonsense travel information in our guides and on our Web site. The Lonely Planet list covers just about every accessible part of the world. Currently there are 16 series: Travel guides, Shoestring guides, Condensed guides, Phrasebooks, Read This First, Healthy Travel, Walking guides, Cycling guides, Watching Wildlife guides, Pisces Diving & Snorkeling guides, City Maps, Road Atlases, Out to Eat, World Food, Journeys travel literature and Pictorials.

AFRICA Africa on a shoestring • Botswana • Cairo • Cairo City Map • Cape Town • Cape Town City Map • East Africa • Egypt • Egyptian Arabic phrasebook • Ethiopia, Eritrea & Djibouti • Ethiopian Amharic phrasebook • The Gambia & Senegal • Healthy Travel Africa • Kenya • Malawi • Morocco • Moroccan Arabic phrasebook • Mozambique • Namibia • Read This First: Africa • South Africa, Lesotho & Swaziland • Southern Africa • Southern Africa Road Atlas • Swahili phrasebook • Tanzania, Zanzibar & Pemba • Trekking in East Africa • Tunisia • Watching Wildlife East Africa • Watching Wildlife Southern Africa • West Africa • World Food Morocco • Zambia • Zimbabwe, Botswana & Namibia
Travel Literature: Mali Blues: Traveling to an African Beat • The Rainbird: A Central African Journey • Songs to an African Sunset: A Zimbabwean Story

AUSTRALIA & THE PACIFIC Aboriginal Australia & the Torres Strait Islands • Auckland • Australia • Australian phrasebook • Australia Road Atlas • Cycling Australia • Cycling New Zealand • Fiji • Fijian phrasebook • Healthy Travel Australia, NZ and the Pacific • Islands of Australia's Great Barrier Reef • Melbourne • Melbourne City Map • Micronesia • New Caledonia • New South Wales • New Zealand • Northern Territory • Outback Australia • Out to Eat – Melbourne • Out to Eat – Sydney • Papua New Guinea • Pidgin phrasebook • Queensland • Rarotonga & the Cook Islands • Samoa • Solomon Islands • South Australia • South Pacific • South Pacific phrasebook • Sydney • Sydney City Map • Sydney Condensed • Tahiti & French Polynesia • Tasmania • Tonga • Tramping in New Zealand • Vanuatu • Victoria • Walking in Australia • Watching Wildlife Australia • Western Australia
Travel Literature: Islands in the Clouds: Travel in the Highlands of New Guinea • Kiwi Tracks: A New Zealand Journey • Sean & David's Long Drive

CENTRAL AMERICA & THE CARIBBEAN Bahamas, Turks & Caicos • Baja California • Belize, Guatemala & Yucatán • Bermuda • Central America on a shoestring • Costa Rica • Costa Rica Spanish phrasebook • Cuba • Cycling Cuba • Dominican Republic & Haiti • Eastern Caribbean • Guatemala • Havana • Healthy Travel Central & South America • Jamaica • Mexico • Mexico City • Panama • Puerto Rico • Read This First: Central & South America • Virgin Islands • World Food Caribbean • World Food Mexico • Yucatán
Travel Literature: Green Dreams: Travels in Central America

EUROPE Amsterdam • Amsterdam City Map • Amsterdam Condensed • Andalucía • Athens • Austria • Baltic States phrasebook • Barcelona • Barcelona City Map • Belgium & Luxembourg • Berlin • Berlin City Map • Britain • British phrasebook • Brussels, Bruges & Antwerp • Brussels City Map • Budapest • Budapest City Map • Canary Islands • Catalunya & the Costa Brava • Central Europe • Central Europe phrasebook • Copenhagen • Corfu & the Ionians • Corsica • Crete • Crete Condensed • Croatia • Cycling Britain • Cycling France • Cyprus • Czech & Slovak Republics • Czech phrasebook • Denmark • Dublin • Dublin City Map • Dublin Condensed • Eastern Europe • Eastern Europe phrasebook • Edinburgh • Edinburgh City Map • England • Estonia, Latvia & Lithuania • Europe on a shoestring • Europe phrasebook • Finland • Florence • Florence City Map • France • Frankfurt City Map • Frankfurt Condensed • French phrasebook • Georgia, Armenia & Azerbaijan • Germany • German phrasebook • Greece • Greek Islands • Greek phrasebook • Hungary • Iceland, Greenland & the Faroe Islands • Ireland • Italian phrasebook • Italy • Kraków • Lisbon • The Loire • London • London City Map • London Condensed • Madrid • Madrid City Map • Malta • Mediterranean Europe • Milan, Turin & Genoa • Moscow • Munich • Netherlands • Normandy • Norway • Out to Eat – London • Out to Eat – Paris • Paris • Paris City Map • Paris Condensed • Poland • Polish phrasebook • Portugal • Portuguese phrasebook • Prague • Prague City Map • Provence & the Côte d'Azur • Read This First: Europe • Rhodes & the Dodecanese • Romania & Moldova • Rome • Rome City Map • Rome Condensed • Russia, Ukraine & Belarus • Russian phrasebook • Scandinavian & Baltic Europe • Scandinavian phrasebook • Scotland • Sicily • Slovenia • South-West France • Spain • Spanish phrasebook • Stockholm • St Petersburg • St Petersburg City Map • Sweden • Switzerland • Tuscany • Ukrainian phrasebook • Venice • Vienna • Wales • Walking in Britain • Walking in France • Walking in Ireland • Walking in Italy • Walking in Scotland • Walking in Spain • Walking in Switzerland • Western Europe • World Food France • World Food Greece • World Food Ireland • World Food Italy • World Food Spain **Travel Literature:** After Yugoslavia • Love and War in the Apennines • The Olive Grove: Travels in Greece • On the Shores of the Mediterranean • Round Ireland in Low Gear • A Small Place in Italy

Lonely Planet Mail Order

L onely Planet products are distributed worldwide. They are also available by mail order from Lonely Planet, so if you have difficulty finding a title, please write to us. North and South American residents should write to 150 Linden St, Oakland, CA 94607, USA; European and African residents should write to 10a Spring Place, London NW5 3BH, UK; and residents of other countries to Locked Bag 1, Footscray, Victoria 3011, Australia.

INDIAN SUBCONTINENT & THE INDIAN OCEAN Bangladesh • Bengali phrasebook • Bhutan • Delhi • Goa • Healthy Travel Asia & India • Hindi & Urdu phrasebook • India • India & Bangladesh City Map • Indian Himalaya • Karakoram Highway • Kathmandu City Map • Kerala • Madagascar • Maldives • Mauritius, Réunion & Seychelles • Mumbai (Bombay) • Nepal • Nepali phrasebook • North India • Pakistan • Rajasthan • Read This First: Asia & India • South India • Sri Lanka • Sri Lanka phrasebook • Tibet • Tibetan phrasebook • Trekking in the Indian Himalaya • Trekking in the Karakoram & Hindukush • Trekking in the Nepal Himalaya • World Food India **Travel Literature:** The Age of Kali: Indian Travels and Encounters • Hello Goodnight: A Life of Goa • In Rajasthan • Maverick in Madagascar • A Season in Heaven: True Tales from the Road to Kathmandu • Shopping for Buddhas • A Short Walk in the Hindu Kush • Slowly Down the Ganges

MIDDLE EAST & CENTRAL ASIA Bahrain, Kuwait & Qatar • Central Asia • Central Asia phrasebook • Dubai • Farsi (Persian) phrasebook • Hebrew phrasebook • Iran • Israel & the Palestinian Territories • Istanbul • Istanbul City Map • Istanbul to Cairo • Istanbul to Kathmandu • Jerusalem • Jerusalem City Map • Jordan • Lebanon • Middle East • Oman & the United Arab Emirates • Syria • Turkey • Turkish phrasebook • World Food Turkey • Yemen **Travel Literature**: Black on Black: Iran Revisited • Breaking Ranks: Turbulent Travels in the Promised Land • The Gates of Damascus • Kingdom of the Film Stars: Journey into Jordan

NORTH AMERICA Alaska • Boston • Boston City Map • Boston Condensed • British Columbia • California & Nevada • California Condensed • Canada • Chicago • Chicago City Map • Chicago Condensed • Florida • Georgia & the Carolinas • Great Lakes • Hawaii • Hiking in Alaska • Hiking in the USA • Honolulu & Oahu City Map • Las Vegas • Los Angeles • Los Angeles City Map • Louisiana & the Deep South • Miami • Miami City Map • Montréal • New England • New Orleans • New Orleans City Map • New York City • New York City City Map • New York City Condensed • New York, New Jersey & Pennsylvania • Oahu • Out to Eat – San Francisco • Pacific Northwest • Rocky Mountains • San Diego & Tijuana • San Francisco • San Francisco City Map • Seattle • Seattle City Map • Southwest • Texas • Toronto • USA • USA phrasebook • Vancouver • Vancouver City Map • Virginia & the Capital Region • Washington, DC • Washington, DC City Map • World Food New Orleans **Travel Literature:** Caught Inside: A Surfer's Year on the California Coast • Drive Thru America

NORTH-EAST ASIA Beijing • Beijing City Map • Cantonese phrasebook • China • Hiking in Japan • Hong Kong & Macau • Hong Kong City Map • Hong Kong Condensed • Japan • Japanese phrasebook • Korea • Korean phrasebook • Kyoto • Mandarin phrasebook • Mongolia • Mongolian phrasebook • Seoul • Shanghai • South-West China • Taiwan • Tokyo • World Food Hong Kong • World Food Japan **Travel Literature:** In Xanadu: A Quest • Lost Japan

SOUTH AMERICA Argentina, Uruguay & Paraguay • Bolivia • Brazil • Brazilian phrasebook • Buenos Aires • Buenos Aires City Map • Chile & Easter Island • Colombia • Ecuador & the Galápagos Islands • Healthy Travel Central & South America • Latin American Spanish phrasebook • Peru • Quechua phrasebook • Read This First: Central & South America • Rio de Janeiro • Rio de Janeiro City Map • Santiago de Chile • South America on a shoestring • Trekking in the Patagonian Andes • Venezuela **Travel Literature:** Full Circle: A South American Journey

SOUTH-EAST ASIA Bali & Lombok • Bangkok • Bangkok City Map • Burmese phrasebook • Cambodia • Cycling Vietnam, Laos & Cambodia • East Timor phrasebook • Hanoi • Healthy Travel Asia & India • Hill Tribes phrasebook • Ho Chi Minh City (Saigon) • Indonesia • Indonesian phrasebook • Indonesia's Eastern Islands • Java • Lao phrasebook • Laos • Malay phrasebook • Malaysia, Singapore & Brunei • Myanmar (Burma) • Philippines • Pilipino (Tagalog) phrasebook • Read This First: Asia & India • Singapore • Singapore City Map • South-East Asia on a shoestring • South-East Asia phrasebook • Thailand • Thailand's Islands & Beaches • Thailand, Vietnam, Laos & Cambodia Road Atlas • Thai phrasebook • Vietnam • Vietnamese phrasebook • World Food Indonesia • World Food Thailand • World Food Vietnam

ALSO AVAILABLE: Antarctica • The Arctic • The Blue Man: Tales of Travel, Love and Coffee • Brief Encounters: Stories of Love, Sex & Travel • Buddhist Stupas in Asia: The Shape of Perfection • Chasing Rickshaws • The Last Grain Race • Lonely Planet…On the Edge: Adventurous Escapades from Around the World • Lonely Planet Unpacked • Lonely Planet Unpacked Again • Not the Only Planet: Science Fiction Travel Stories • Ports of Call: A Journey by Sea • Sacred India • Travel Photography: A Guide to Taking Better Pictures • Travel with Children • Tuvalu: Portrait of an Island Nation

LONELY PLANET

You already know that Lonely Planet produces more than this one guidebook, but you might not be aware of the other products we have on this region. Here is a selection of titles which you may want to check out as well:

Mexico
ISBN 1 86450 089 1
US$24.99 • UK£14.99

Central America on a shoestring
ISBN 1 86450 186 3
US$21.99 • UK£13.99

Healthy Travel Central & South America
ISBN 1 86450 053 0
US$5.95 • UK£3.99

Guatemala
ISBN 0 86442 684 4
US$16.99 • UK£10.99

Yucatán
ISBN 1 86450 103 0
US$17.99 • UK£11.99

Latin American Spanish phrasebook
ISBN 0 86442 558 9
US$6.95 • UK£4.50

Available wherever books are sold.

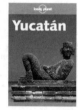

Index

Abbreviations

G – Guatemala

M – Mexico

Text

A

accommodations 55. *See also individual locations*
Actun Tunichil Muknal 166
AIDS 48
air travel 59–63, 64, **65**
alcoholic drinks 57
Altun Ha 90–1, 107, **91**
Ambergris Caye 34, 99–116
 accommodations 108–12
 activities 104–6
 entertainment 114–5
 history 100, 102
 restaurants 112–4
 shopping 115–6
 tours 106–8
 transportation 116
Amigos Wreck 105
archaeological sites 34, 153, 176–7
 Actun Tunichil Muknal 166
 Altun Ha 90–1, 107, **91**
 Baking Pot 156
 Barton Creek Cave 165–6
 Cahal Pech 163–4
 Caracol 174–9, **175**
 Cerros 144–5
 Che Chem Ha 166–7
 Cuello 132, 134
 El Pilar 164
 La Milpa 140–1
 Lamanai 107–8, 136–8
 Lubaantun 203, 215
 Mayflower 195
 Nim Li Punit 203, 215
 Nohmul 134–5
 Pacbitun 165
 Santa Rita 144
 Tikal (G) 219–25, **220–1**
 Uaxactún (G) 225
 Xunantunich 164–5, **165**

Arvigo, Rosita 44, 167, 168
ATMs 40

B

Bacalar Chico National Park & Marine Reserve 107, 145
Baird's tapirs 21
Baking Pot 156
bananas 27
bargaining 41
Barranco 218
barrier reef 17, 19, 54, 181, 202
Barrow, Dean 27, 29
Barrow, Jamal Shyne 29
Barton Creek Cave 165–6
Battle of St George's Caye 14, 15, 70, 127
Baymen 13, 14, 18, 70, 100, 141
beaches 99, 113
Belize Botanical Gardens 169
Belize City 35, 70–86, **73, 76–7**
 accommodations 79–82
 climate 17
 day trips 87–95, **88**
 entertainment 84
 highlights 70
 history 70–1
 restaurants 82–4
 shopping 84–5
 tours 74–5, 78–9
 transportation 85–6
Belize Valley Archeology Reconnaissance Project 176
Belize Zoo 93–4
Belmopan 152–5, **154**
Belmopan Vault 153, 154
Benque Viejo del Carmen 179–80

bicycling 54, 194. *See also* mountain biking
Biotopo Cerro Cahuí (G) 228–9
bird species 23–4
birding 23, 34, 92, 128, 142, 148, 156, 198
 field guides 43
 tours 121, 203, 211
bites 50–1
Black Rock River Lodge 170
black howler monkeys 20. *See also* Community Baboon Sanctuary
Blancaneaux Lodge 178
Bliss Institute 74–5
Blue Creek (village) 217
Blue Creek Rain Forest Preserve & Cave 218
Blue Hole National Park 185–6
Blue Hole Natural Monument 128
boats
 tours 106–7, 120–1, 137, 145
 transportation 63, 69
boobies 24, 128
books 43–4
border crossings 63, 147, 180
botflies 50
British colonization 14, 15, 16, 43
brukdown 28–9
buses 63, 64–7
business hours 53
butterflies 21, 167–9

C

Caana 175–6
Cahal Pech 163–4

camping 55
Cancún (M) 61
canoeing 165–6, 169, 194–5
Caracol 174–9, **175**
cars 63, 67–8
    driver's license 38
    insurance 68
    renting 68
    road rules 67–8
    safety 53
caves 34, 54, 108, 165–7, 173–4, 185, 186, 218
Caye Caulker 34, 116–27, **119**
    accommodations 121–4
    activities 118, 120
    entertainment 126
    history 117
    restaurants 124–6
    shopping 126
    tours 120–1
    transportation 126–7
Caye Chapel 127
Cayo. See San Ignacio
Cayo District (Western Belize) 150–80, **151**
Cerros 144–5
Chaa Creek Resort & Spa 171
Challilo Dam project 18–9
Chan Chich Lodge 141–2
Che Chem Ha 166–7
Chetumal (M) 147
chicle 132, 140, 141
children, traveling with 52–3, 61
Chiquibul National Park 172
climate 17–8
clothing
    laundry 45
    packing 36–7
Cockscomb Basin Wildlife Sanctuary 18, 43, 194, 197–201, **199**
coconut palms 19
Community Baboon Sanctuary 87, 89–90
Confederate Cemetery 215

Consejo Shores 147
consulates 38–9
cookbooks 44
coral 19, 23, 37, 105, 127, 128
Corozal 35, 142–7, **143**
costs 41
credit cards 40–1
Creoles 27, 28, 29
crime 41, 53
crocodiles 19, 22, 24
Crooked Tree 91–3
Cuello 132, 134
currency 40
customs 39–40
cuts 50

D

Dangriga 35, 186–92, **188**
Dem Dats Doin Farm 215
dengue fever 49
diarrhea 47–8
digital resources 42–3
disabled travelers 52, 61
diseases. See health issues
districts **16**
diving & snorkeling 34, 54
    Amigos Wreck 105
    Blue Hole 128
    book 43
    Gladden Spit & Silk Cayes Marine Reserve 202–3
    Glover's Reef 193–4, 202
    Hol Chan Marine Reserve 104
    Lighthouse Reef Atoll 128–9
    Shark Hole 202
    Shark Ray Alley 104
    shops & tours 79, 104–6, 118, 120, 183, 192–4, 203, 211
    tips 96–7, 99
    Turneffe Atoll 127–8
documents 37–8
dolphins 23
Douglas da Silva 174
Doyle's Delight 17, 200
drinks 57
driving. See cars
duPlooy's Jungle Lodge 171

E

economy 27
ecotourism 18, 215–6
education 28
El Pilar 164
El Remate (G) 228–9
electricity 45
email 42
embassies 38–9, 78
emergencies 53
employment 54–5
endangered species 24
entertainment 57. See also individual locations
environmental issues 18–9, 24, 173
Esquivel, Manuel 26, 27
etiquette 29
exchange rates 40

F

fauna. See wildlife
faxes 42
films 44
fishing 23, 54, 106, 127–8
Five Blues National Park 186
Five Sisters Lodge 178–9
flora. See plants
Flores (G) 225–8, **226**
food 55–7
    cookbooks 44
    safety 47
Forest Home 214–5
Fort George District 75, 78
frigate birds 23–4, 75

G

Gales Point 182–4
Gallon Jug 142
Garifunas 28, 29, 43, 55, 186, 187, 194, 209, 218
gay & lesbian travelers 52
geography 16–7
geology 17
Georgeville 156
Gladden Spit & Silk Cayes Marine Reserve 202–3
Glover's Reef 193–4, 202
golf 127
government 26–7

Bold indicates maps.

Guanacaste National Park 155–6
Guatemala
    border crossing 180
    claims of, to Belize 15, 16
    phone numbers 219
    Tikal area 219–29
    transportation to/from 61, 67

H

Half Moon Caye 128–9
health issues 45–51
    cuts, bites & stings 50–1
    diseases 47–9
    environmental hazards 47
    food & water 47
    immunizations 46
    insurance 38, 46
    medical kit 46
    women's 51
heat, effects of 47
hepatitis 48
highlights 34–5
hiking 54, 173, 198–200
history 13–6, 43–4
hitchhiking 68–9
HIV 48
Hol Chan Marine Reserve 104
holidays 53
Hopkins area 35, 194–7, **195**
horseback riding 169, 179
hotels 55
House of Culture 75
howler monkeys. See black howler monkeys
hurricanes 17–8, 182

I

Ian Anderson's Caves Branch Tours 108, 185
iguanas 22
Image Factory Art Foundation 78, 85
immunizations 46
independence 15–6
insects 21, 49, 50, 51
insurance
    car 68
    travel 38

international transfers 41
Internet
    access 42
    resources 42–3
Ix Chel Farm 167

J

jabiru storks 24
jaguars 18, 20, 43, 140, 198
jellyfish 51
jungle lodges 35
    Black Rock River Lodge 170
    Blancaneaux Lodge 178
    Chaa Creek Resort & Spa 171
    Chan Chich Lodge 141–2
    duPlooy's Jungle Lodge 171
    Five Sisters Lodge 178–9
    Lamanai Outpost Lodge 138
    Pine Ridge Lodge 178

K

kayaking 54, 106, 194–5, 203, 211
King, Emory 43, 44

L

La Milpa 140–1
Laguna 217
Lamanai 13, 107–8, 136–8
Lamanai Outpost Lodge 138
language 29, 32–3
Laughing Bird Caye 203
laundry 45
Lighthouse Reef Atoll 128–9
lobster 27, 100, 102
Lubaantun 203, 215

M

Macal River 169, 170–1
macaws 24, 34, 203
magazines 45
mahogany 14–5, 18, 27, 132, 133, 141
mail 41
malaria 49
manatees 19, 23, 24, 106, 120, 121, 182, 184

mangroves 19, 20
maps 36
marine life 22–3
marine reserves
    Bacalar Chico 107, 145
    Gladden Spit & Silk Cayes 202–3
    Glover's Reef 193–4
    Hol Chan 104
    Port Honduras 211
    Sapodilla Cayes 211
    South Water Caye 193
Maritime Museum 74
Maya. See also archaeological sites
    architecture 33
    calendar system 31–2
    contemporary 28, 35, 209, 214, 215–7
    counting system 32
    history 13, 15, 43–4, 100, 130, 132, 136, 142, 174, 219, 222
    language 28, 32–3
    meals 56
    medicines 167, 168
    music & dance 57
    religion 29, 30–1, 165
Maya Beach 207
Maya Mountains 16, 17, 150
Mayan villages of Toledo 17, 35, 182, 211, 215–8
Mayflower 195
measurements 45
medical kit 46
Mennonites 28, 139, 157
Mestizos 27–8, 100, 117
Mexico
    border crossing 147
    transportation to/from 61, 62
money 40–1
Monkey Bay National Park & Wildlife Sanctuary 94–5
Monkey River 203
monkeys 20–1, 87, 89
Mopan River 169
mosquitoes 49
motion sickness 47
motorcycles 63
mountain biking 54, 169

Mountain Pine Ridge Forest Reserve 19, 20, 171–4, **172**
Musa, Said 26, 27
museums 74, 223
music 28–9, 57

N

national parks. See parks & reserves
New River 137
newspapers 45
Nicholas, Benjamin 189
Nim Li Punit 203, 215
Nohmul 134–5
northern Belize 130–49, **131**
northern cayes 96–129, **98**

O

Orange Walk 131–6, **134**
Out-liar 200

P

Pacbitun 165
packing 36–7
Panti, Don Elijio 167, 168
parks & reserves 24–6, **25**
  Bacalar Chico National Park & Marine Reserve 107, 145
  Biotopo Cerro Cahuí (G) 228–9
  Blue Creek Rain Forest Preserve & Cave 218
  Blue Hole National Park 185–6
  Chiquibul National Park 172
  Cockscomb Basin Wildlife Sanctuary 197–201, **199**
  Community Baboon Sanctuary 87, 89–90
  Crooked Tree Wildlife Sanctuary 92
  Five Blues National Park 186
  Gladden Spit & Silk Cayes Marine Reserve 202–3

  Glover's Reef Marine Reserve 193–4
  Guanacaste National Park 155–6
  Half Moon Caye Natural Monument 128–9
  Hol Chan Marine Reserve 104
  Laughing Bird Caye National Park 203
  Monkey Bay National Park & Wildlife Sanctuary 94–5
  Mountain Pine Ridge Forest Reserve 19, 20, 171–4, **172**
  Port Honduras Marine Reserve 211
  Río Bravo Conservation & Management Area 139–41
  Sapodilla Cayes Marine Reserve 211
  Sarstoon-Temash National Park 218
  Shipstern Nature Reserve 148
  South Water Caye Marine Reserve 193
  Tapir Mountain Nature Reserve 156, 157, 166
  Tikal National Park (G) 219
passports 37
peccaries 21
phones 41–2, 219
photography 45
pine beetles, southern 19, 173
Pine Ridge Lodge 178
pirates. See Baymen
Placencia 35, 201–9, **202, 204**
planning 35–7
plants 19–20, 167, 168. See also individual species
politics 26–7, 43
population 11, 27–8
Port Honduras Marine Reserve 211
postal services 41
pregnancy 51
Price, George 26, 27
punta 28, 57

Punta Gorda 209–13, **210, 214**

R

radio 45
rafting 54, 169
Rainforest Medicine Trail 167
rays 23, 97, 104
Red Bank 203
red-footed boobies 24, 124
religion 29, 30–1
reserves. See parks & reserves
restaurants 55–6. See also individual locations
Río Bravo Conservation & Management Area 35, 139–41
ruins. See archaeological sites

S

safety 41, 53
sailing 54, 106, 120, 194
San Antonio 216–7
San Ignacio (Cayo) 35, 157–62, **158, 163**
San Jose 217
San Miguel 217
San Pedro 99–116, **101, 103**
  accommodations 108–10
  activities 104–6
  entertainment 114–5
  history 100, 102
  restaurants 112–3
  shopping 115–6
  tours 106–8
  transportation 116
San Pedro Columbia 217
sandflies 51
Santa Cruz 216–7
Santa Elena (G) 225–8, **226**
Santa Elena (Mayan village) 217
Santa Rita 144
Sapodilla Cayes Marine Reserve 211
Sarstoon-Temash National Park 218
Sarteneja 35, 147–9
scorpions 21, 51
Seine Bight 206–7
senior travelers 52

Bold indicates maps.

sexually transmitted diseases 48–9
Shark Hole 202
Shark Ray Alley 104
sharks 23, 97, 104, 128, 202
Sharp, Marie 55, 187, 190–1
Shipstern Nature Reserve 148
shopping 57–8. *See also individual locations*
slavery 13–4
snakes 21–2, 51
snorkeling. *See* diving & snorkeling
South Water Caye 34–5, 193
southern Belize 181–218, **183**
Spanish Lookout 157
special events 53
spiders 21, 50–1
sports 57
St George's Caye 127. *See also* Battle of St George's Caye
St Herman's Cave 185–6
St John's Cathedral 75
stingrays 23, 97, 104
stings 50–1
sugar 131–2, 133
sunburn 47
swimming 79, 99, 106, 120
Swing Bridge 74

T

Tapir Mountain Nature Reserve 156, 157, 166

tapirs 21
taxes 41
Teakettle Village 156
telephones 41–2, 219
television 45
Tikal (G) 61, 219–25, **220–1**
time zone 45
tipping 41
Tobacco Caye 34, 192–3
toilets 45
Toledo Botanical Arboretum 215
Toledo Ecotourism Association 215–6
toucans 24
tourism, responsible 37
tourist industry 12, 27
tourist offices 37
tourist seasons 35
tours 36, 69. *See also individual locations*
transportation
    air travel 59–63, 64, **65**
    boats 63, 69
    buses 63, 64–7
    cars 63, 67–8
    hitchhiking 68–9
    motorcycles 63
travel insurance 38
traveler's checks 40
Tropical Education Center 94
tubing 165–6, 169, 199
Turneffe Atoll 127–8
turtles 19, 22–3, 24, 105, 182–3
TV 45
typhoid 49

U

Uaxactún (G) 225

V

vaccinations 46
Victoria Peak 17, 200
visas 37–8
volunteer work 54–5

W

Walker, Jerry Jeff 29
Wallace, Peter 26
War of the Castes 15, 100, 117, 130, 132, 142
water 47, 122
waterfalls 167, 173–4, 195, 199–200
Web sites 42–3
western Belize. *See* Cayo District
wildlife. *See also individual species*
    books 43
    endangered 24
    species of 20–4
    watching 22, 34, 89, 92, 139–40, 197–8
windsurfing 54
women travelers 51–2
work 54–5
World Heritage Sites 19

X

Xunantunich 164–5, **165**

Z

zoo 93–4

Boxed Text

Air Travel Glossary 60
Archaeology: Not Just a
    Thing of the Past 176–7
The Battle of St George's Caye 14
Beach Barbecues 113
Beaches 99
Belmopan Vault 153
The Botfly - Myth or Mayhem? 50
Chicle & Chewing Gum 140
Diving & Snorkeling from
    Ambergris Caye 105
Don't Be Fooled 200
Emory King 44
The Garifunas 186
The Guatemala Claim 15
Guatemalan Phone Numbers 219
High-Velocity Winds 18
Hurricane Iris 182

Manatee Conservation 121
Marie Sharp 190–1
Medical Kit Checklist 46
The Mennonites 139
The Name Ambergris 100
The Name Caulker 118
Placencia Tours: A Rundown 203
Rice & Beans 56
Rosita Arvigo & Don Elijio Panti 168
The Southern Pine Beetles'
    Path of Destruction 173
Spotting Wildlife 22
Sweet & Sour Sugar Industry 133
Tips on Tours 36
Vital Statistics 97
Wallix, Ballix 26
What's That Smell? 122
World Heritage Sites 19

MAP LEGEND

ROUTES

City   Regional

Freeway
Tollway
Primary Road
Secondary Road
Tertiary Road
Dirt Road

Pedestrian Mall
Steps
Tunnel
Trail
Walking Tour
Path

ROUTE SHIELDS

(MEX 2) Mexico Highway
(5) District Highway
(9) National Highway
(34) Interamerican Highway

TRANSPORTATION

Train
Metro
Bus Route
Ferry

HYDROGRAPHY

River; Creek
Canal
Lake
Spring; Rapids
Waterfalls
Dry; Salt Lake

BOUNDARIES

International
District
County
Disputed

AREAS

Beach
Building
Campus
Cemetery
Forest
Garden; Zoo
Golf Course
Park
Plaza
Reservation
Sports Field
Swamp; Mangrove

POPULATION SYMBOLS

○ NATIONAL CAPITAL   National Capital
◉ DISTRICT CAPITAL   District Capital
● **Large City**   Large City
● **Medium City**   Medium City
● Small City   Small City
● Town; Village   Town; Village

MAP SYMBOLS

■   Place to Stay
▼   Place to Eat
●   Point of Interest

Airfield	Church	Museum	Skiing - Downhill
Airport	Cinema	Park-Jungle	Stately Home
Archaeological Site; Ruin	Dive Site	Park-Tropical	Surfing
Bank; ATM	Embassy; Consulate	Parking Area	Synagogue
Baseball Diamond	Footbridge	Pass	Tao Temple
Battlefield	Gas Station	Picnic Area	Taxi
Bike Trail	Hindu Temple	Police Station	Telephone
Border Crossing	Hospital	Pool	Theater
Buddhist Temple	Information	Post Office	Toilet - Public
Bus Station; Terminal	Internet Access	Pub; Bar	Tomb
Cable Car; Chairlift	Lighthouse	RV Park	Trailhead
Campground	Lookout	Shelter	Tram Stop
Castle	Mission	Shipwreck	Transportation
Cathedral	Monument	Shopping Mall	Volcano
Cave	Mountain	Skiing - Cross Country	Winery

Note: Not all symbols displayed above appear in this book.

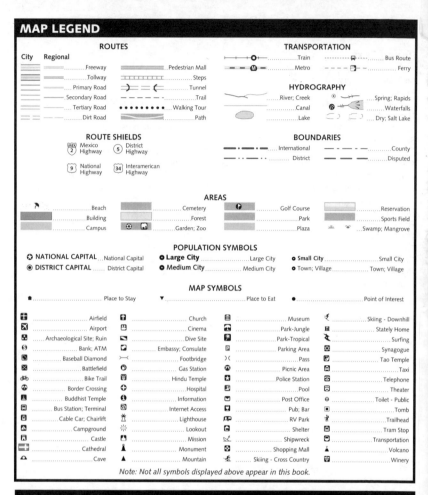

LONELY PLANET OFFICES

Australia
Locked Bag 1, Footscray, Victoria 3011
☎ 03 8379 8000 fax 03 8379 8111
email talk2us@lonelyplanet.com.au

USA
150 Linden Street, Oakland, California 94607
☎ 510 893 8555, TOLL FREE 800 275 8555
fax 510 893 8572
email info@lonelyplanet.com

UK
10a Spring Place, London NW5 3BH
☎ 020 7428 4800 fax 020 7428 4828
email go@lonelyplanet.co.uk

France
1 rue du Dahomey, 75011 Paris
☎ 01 55 25 33 00 fax 01 55 25 33 01
email bip@lonelyplanet.fr
www.lonelyplanet.fr

World Wide Web: www.lonelyplanet.com *or* AOL keyword: lp
Lonely Planet Images: lpi@lonelyplanet.com.au